# Business

## for Cambridge IGCSE™ and O Level

### COURSEBOOK

Medi Houghton, Leanne Burslem-Curl & Veenu Jain, with Mark Fisher

with Digital access

Shaftesbury Road, Cambridge CB2 8EA, United Kingdom

One Liberty Plaza, 20th Floor, New York, NY 10006, USA

477 Williamstown Road, Port Melbourne, VIC 3207, Australia

314–321, 3rd Floor, Plot 3, Splendor Forum, Jasola District Centre, New Delhi – 110025, India

103 Penang Road, #05–06/07, Visioncrest Commercial, Singapore 238467

Cambridge University Press & Assessment is a department of the University of Cambridge.

We share the University's mission to contribute to society through the pursuit of education, learning and research at the highest international levels of excellence.

www.cambridge.org
Information on this title: www.cambridge.org/9781009813501

© Cambridge University Press & Assessment 2025

This publication is in copyright. Subject to statutory exception and to the provisions of relevant collective licensing agreements, no reproduction of any part may take place without the written permission of Cambridge University Press & Assessment.

First published 2002
Second edition 2010
Third edition 2014
Revised third edition 2018
Fourth edition 2025

20 19 18 17 16 15 14 13 12 11 10 9 8 7 6 5 4

Printed in Poland by Opolgraf

*A catalogue record for this publication is available from the British Library*

ISBN 978-1-009-81350-1 Coursebook with Digital Access
ISBN 978-1-009-81348-8 Digital Coursebook (2 Years)
ISBN 978-1-009-81349-5 Coursebook – eBook

Additional resources for this publication at www.cambridge.org/9781009813501

Cambridge International Education material in this publication is reproduced under licence and remains the intellectual property of Cambridge University Press & Assessment.

Cambridge University Press & Assessment has no responsibility for the persistence or accuracy of URLs for external or third-party internet websites referred to in this publication and does not guarantee that any content on such websites is, or will remain, accurate or appropriate. Third-party websites and resources referred to in this publication are not endorsed.

For EU product safety concerns, contact us at Calle de José Abascal, 56, 1°, 28003 Madrid, Spain, or email eugpsr@cambridge.org.

# Contents

How to use this series — 5

How to use this book — 6

Introduction — 9

## 1 Understanding business activity
1. Business activity — 11
2. Economic sectors — 23
3. Enterprise, business growth and size — 35
4. Types of business organisations — 56
5. Business objectives and stakeholder objectives — 71

Section 1 case study — 87

## 2 People in business
6. Human resource management (HRM) — 92
7. Organisation and management — 114
8. Methods of communication — 134
9. Motivating employees — 149

Section 2 case study — 169

## 3 Marketing
10. Marketing and the market — 174
11. Market research — 193
12. Marketing mix: product — 212
13. Marketing mix: price — 224
14. Marketing mix: place — 235
15. Marketing mix: promotion — 244
16. Marketing strategy and legal controls — 256

Section 3 case study — 268

## 4 Operations management
17. Production of goods and services — 272
18. Costs, scale of production and break-even analysis — 292
19. Quality of goods and services — 312
20. Location decisions — 323

Section 4 case study — 334

## 5 Financial information and decisions
21. Business finance — 338
22. Cash flow forecasts — 359
23. Statement of profit or loss — 375
24. Statement of financial position — 389
25. Analysis of accounts — 401

Section 5 case study — 420

## 6 External influences on business activity
26. Economic issues — 424
27. Business and the international economy — 443
28. Environmental and ethical issues — 461

Section 6 case study — 479

29. Preparing for assessment — 482

Accounting formulae and ratios — 499

Glossary — 500

Index — 506

Acknowledgements — 517

Endorsement indicates that a resource has passed Cambridge International Education's rigorous quality-assurance process and is suitable to support the delivery of their syllabus. However, endorsed resources are not the only suitable materials available to support teaching and learning, and are not essential to achieve the qualification. For the full list of endorsed resources to support this syllabus, visit www.cambridgeinternational.org/endorsed-resources

Any example answers to questions taken from past question papers, practice questions, accompanying marks and mark schemes included in this resource have been written by the authors and are for guidance only. They do not replicate examination papers. In examinations the way marks are awarded may be different. Any references to assessment and/or assessment preparation are the publisher's interpretation of the syllabus requirements. Examiners will not use endorsed resources as a source of material for any assessment set by Cambridge International Education.

While the publishers have made every attempt to ensure that advice on the qualification and its assessment is accurate, the official syllabus, specimen assessment materials and any associated assessment guidance materials produced by the awarding body are the only authoritative source of information and should always be referred to for definitive guidance.

Our approach is to provide teachers with access to a wide range of high-quality resources that suit different styles and types of teaching and learning.

For more information about the endorsement process, please visit www.cambridgeinternational.org/endorsed-resources

# How to use this series

All the components in the series are designed to work together.

The coursebook is designed for students to use in class with guidance from the teacher. It supports the *Cambridge IGCSE™, IGCSE (9-1) and O Level Business* syllabuses (0264/0774/7081). The coursebook is split into six sections and contains in-depth explanations of business concepts, a variety of independent and group activities, as well as interesting case studies to engage students and help them make real-world connections.

A digital version of the coursebook is included with the print version and is also available separately. It includes access to video case studies as well as simple tools for students to use in class or for self-study.

The workbook provides further practice of all the skills presented in the coursebook and is ideal for use in class or as homework. It provides engaging activities, worked examples and opportunities for students to evaluate sample answers so they can put into practice what they have learnt.

A digital version of the workbook is included with the print version. It includes simple tools for students to use in class or for self-study.

The digital teacher's resource provides everything teachers need to deliver this course. It is packed full of useful teaching notes and lesson ideas, with suggestions for differentiation to support and challenge students, ideas for formative assessment, overcoming common misconceptions, and language support.

The digital teacher's resource contains downloadable worksheets.

All answers to coursebook and workbook activities are available to teachers via Cambridge GO.

# How to use this book

Throughout this coursebook, you will notice recurring features that are designed to help your learning. Here is a brief overview of what you will find.

### LEARNING INTENTIONS

Learning intentions open each chapter. These help you with navigation through the coursebook and indicate the important concepts in each topic.

### BUSINESS IN CONTEXT

Business in context introduces you to the content in a chapter. These place some of the key ideas contained in the chapter into a real-world business setting. Each one contains questions that allow you to discuss the topic.

### KEY TERM

Key vocabulary is highlighted in the text when it is first introduced. An accompanying definition tells you the meanings of these words and phrases. You will also find definitions of these words in the Glossary at the back of this book. In the digital edition of the coursebook, you will also find examples of the key term put into context.

### TIPS

Tips are provided throughout this coursebook to help with your learning. The tips might cover how to avoid common errors or misconceptions, advice on answering questions or key skills for your course.

### ACTIVITY

There are various activities throughout this coursebook. These give you opportunities to discuss topics or produce your own work either individually, in pairs or in groups.

### REFLECTION

Reflection activities enable you to look back on your work and encourage you to think about your learning. You will reflect on and assess the process that you used to arrive at your answers.

### LINK

These explain the links between topics in different sections of the coursebook.

### CASE STUDY

Case studies put the topics in each chapter into a recent, real-life context. The case study then includes questions or a task for you to apply your learning. In the digital version of the coursebook, you will also have access to a video case study in each chapter.

### BUSINESS IN ACTION

Business in action provides an insight into how real businesses around the world apply some of the key concepts of the subject. Designed to encourage group discussion, the short case studies and accompanying questions will help you to make connections between employment and studying business. The content here might sometimes go beyond the syllabus.

### DISCUSSION

Discussion questions are used throughout this coursebook to prompt thinking at key points within each chapter.

> ## SUMMARY
> At the end of each chapter, you will find a list that brings together the key information you have learnt. This list can also be used as a useful revision aid.

> ## CHECK YOUR PROGRESS
> Each chapter ends with a grid showing the Learning intentions from the start of the chapter. When you are revising, you might find it helpful to rate how confident you are for each of these statements. You should also provide an example to support your score.

## End-of-chapter practice questions

Each chapter contains a set of practice questions that are similar to questions you might find in your assessments. The questions focus on the syllabus assessment objectives that you will need for your course – knowledge and understanding, application, analysis and evaluation.

> ### END-OF-SECTION PRACTICE QUESTIONS
> These practice questions provide examples of case studies. The questions focus on the syllabus assessment objectives that you will need for your course - knowledge and understanding, application, analysis and evaluation.

# 2024 Cambridge Dedicated Teacher Awards

Our **Cambridge Dedicated Teacher Awards** are an opportunity to show appreciation for the incredible work teachers do every day.

Thank you to everyone who nominated this year; we have been inspired and moved by all of your stories. Well done to all of our nominees for your dedication to learning and for inspiring the next generation of thinkers, leaders and innovators.

## Congratulations to our winners!

**Global Winner**
Southeast Asia & Pacific
**Sydney Engelbert**
Keningau Vocational College, Malaysia

East Asia
**Pengfei Jiang**
Zhuji Ronghuai Foreign Language School, China

Pakistan
**Saeeda Salim**
SISA - School of International Studies in Sciences & Arts, Pakistan

South Asia
**Meena Mishra**
Dr Sarvepalli Radhakrishnan International School, India

Middle East and North Africa
**Gina Justus**
Our Own English High school Sharjah-Girls, United Arab Emirates

Sub-Saharan Africa
**Tajudeen Odufeso**
Isara Secondary School, Nigeria

Europe
**Aynur Bayazit**
Menekşe Ahmet Yalçınkaya Kindergarten, Türkiye

Latin America & the Caribbean
**Ramon Majé Floriano**
Montessori sede San Francisco, Colombia

North America
**Maria Medvetz Santos**
Seminole Ridge Community High School, United States

For more information about our dedicated teachers and their stories, go to dedicatedteacher.cambridge.org

# > Introduction

This new and updated fourth edition of the coursebook will help you with studying the Cambridge IGCSE™, IGCSE (9-1) or O Level Business syllabuses (0264/0774/7081) for examination from 2027.

You might be using this coursebook and studying business to provide a basis for you to understand business in the real world. Some of you may even be thinking about a career in business or setting up your own business in the future. There may be parts of the course that you find particularly interesting, such as Marketing or Finance, which you may wish to continue studying beyond Cambridge IGCSE level.

The book is divided into six themed sections: Understanding business activity, People in business, Marketing, Operations management, Financial information and decisions and External influences on business activity. Each section is sub-divided into chapters based on specific topics from the syllabus. In each chapter you will find case studies (some of which are in a video format) based on real-life businesses from around the world, activities and practice questions that will help you to develop your understanding of assessment objectives, suggested discussion questions and activities for reflection, and key terms that you will need to learn.

The book is designed to help you build your confidence and understanding of business concepts. As you progress through your course and this coursebook, you will start to see links between the topics and chapters. For example, you will be introduced to the concept of added value in Section 1 and then later in Section 3 you could think about how added value may influence the pricing method used by a business.

We hope that you enjoy using this coursebook and wish you every success in your course!

Medi Houghton, Leanne Burslem-Curl and Veenu Jain

# Section 1
# Understanding business activity

This section focuses on understanding the nature of business activity and the concepts of factors of production, how a business can increase added value and opportunity cost. You will learn about the different economic sectors, the role of entrepreneurs and how businesses are set up. Businesses can be small or large, so we will explore the different ways to measure size and why some businesses grow whilst others remain small. There are many types of business organisations and each type has its advantages and disadvantages. You will also learn about the objectives of each type of business and the relationship between a business and its many different stakeholder groups.

# Chapter 1
# Business activity

**LEARNING INTENTIONS**

By the end of this chapter, you will be able to:

- define and provide examples of the four factors of production
- understand the importance of 'added value'
- explain ways a business can increase added value
- understand the concept of opportunity cost.

# Introduction

Business activity is everywhere – from the food you eat, the clothes you wear and the bus or bicycle you use to get to places to the phone you use to keep in touch with friends. Nearly everything is likely to have been made by a business or involved some form of business activity.

Business provides us – consumers – with the goods and services that we need or would like to have. In this chapter, you will learn about the basics of business activity starting with the four factors of production that are used to help businesses turn resources into goods and services to meet people's needs and wants. You will learn about added value and how different businesses could increase added value. The chapter finishes with the concept of opportunity cost.

## BUSINESS IN CONTEXT

### Power Up! Here we go

Over 70% of the surface of the world is water, but according to the World Health Organization, 26% of the world's population does not have access to safe drinking water. One of the problems is that seawater is not safe for people to drink because it contains high levels of salts and other minerals. Water desalination is a process that can turn seawater into water that people can drink. However, traditional water desalination plants are very expensive to build and operate. Most desalination plants also rely on fossil fuels, such as oil, to provide a constant supply of electricity; although this fuel is not always available or can be expensive to use.

Hydro Wind Energy (HWE) is a business based in Dubai, London and San Francisco. HWE uses new technology to find practical solutions to help with these problems. One way is by using renewable energy to provide low-cost electricity. For example, using wind power, HWE has developed a system called SubSea RO. Wind power is used to replace non-renewable resources (fossil fuels) to desalinate water. By replacing fossil fuels, the costs of water desalination are reduced by over 90%. This makes safe drinking water more accessible and cheaper and at the same time causes less damage to the environment. Another product HWE is developing is QuenchSea. This is a handheld device that can be easily carried anywhere so that people can use it to turn seawater into drinking water.

**Figure 1.1:** Dubai is finding ways to manage the amount of water it has to meet the needs of different users

### Discuss in pairs or groups:

1. Which type of business activity is Hydro Wind Energy involved in?
2. What might be the possible advantages of using Hydro Wind Energy's technology?

# 1 Business activity

## 1.1 Understanding business activity

A business is an organisation set up by a person or people to satisfy the needs and wants of consumers or customers. Business activity is about providing products (goods and services) that meet these needs and wants.

A need is any good or service that people must have to be able to live, whereas wants are any goods or services that people would like to have to make their lives more enjoyable. Wants are not essential for living. Figure 1.2 includes examples of needs and wants.

**Figure 1.2:** Do these images show needs or wants?

> **TIP**
>
> Customers or consumers? Technically, these are different concepts – customers buy the goods or services while consumers are the people who use them. They may be different people. Generally, it is fine to use either term.

### ACTIVITY 1.1

1. Make a list of five 'needs' that you have.
2. Make a list of five 'wants' that you would like to have.
3. In pairs, compare your two sets of lists – what do you notice? Are any items the same? Which items are different? Can you think of reasons for these differences?
4. In pairs, produce a simple image or diagram that show the difference between needs and wants.

## Factors of production

Resources are needed to make goods and services. A business will use a combination of resources to produce these goods and services.

The resources are known as **factors of production**:

- **Land** – all the natural resources, including renewable and non-renewable, that can be obtained from the land or sea.
- **Labour** – the skills and number of people who help provide goods and services.
- **Capital** – the human-made resources and finances that are used to produce goods and services.
- **Enterprise** – the ability and willingness to take risks to bring together and organise the other three factors of production to produce goods and services.

Figure 1.4 has a summary of the four factors of production.

> **KEY TERM**
>
> **factors of production:** the resources needed by a business to produce goods and services – land, labour, capital and enterprise.

> **LINK**
>
> You can find more information about enterprise in Chapter 3.

### ACTIVITY 1.2

land    labour    capital    enterprise

Match the pictures in Figure 1.3 to the correct factor of production in the word box above.

**Figure 1.3:** A different combination of factors of production is used to make different products

The mind map in Figure 1.4 shows the factors of production that a business will use.

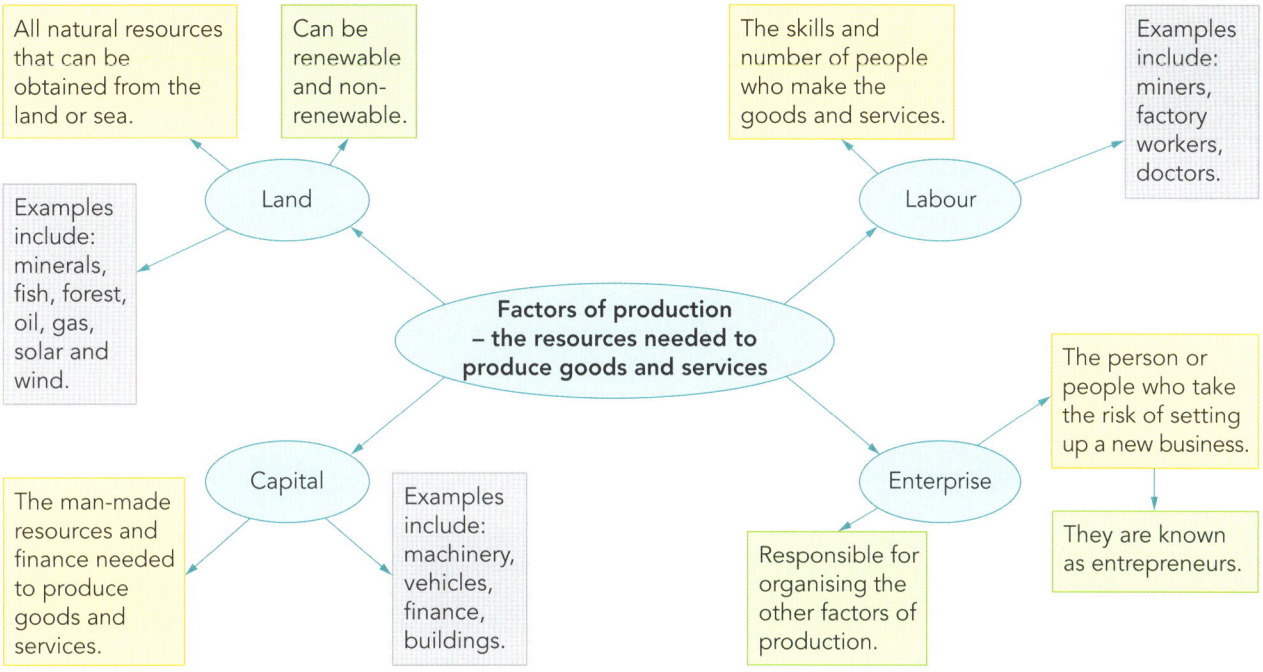

Figure 1.4: Factors of production mind map

## CASE STUDY 1.1

**Smart Logistics Solutions, Kenya**

Figure 1.5: SLS produces pre-cooked beans for people who do not have the time or fuel to cook the beans themselves

Kenya's economy, like those of many African countries, is largely based on agriculture and small-scale farmers. The farmers grow grains and vegetables on tiny plots of land to provide food for themselves and other families in large towns and local villages.

Rose Mutuku is the Managing Director of Smart Logistics Solutions (SLS), a manufacturing business based in Kenya. SLS's 66 employees operate the machinery that allows them to turn sorghum, a type of grain, into flour which can then be used to make food. Sorghum is an important crop in Kenya and other parts of the world where there are droughts or water is scarce. This is because sorghum does not need much water to grow and is not affected much by pests or disease. SLS buys the sorghum grains from more than 4 000 farmers around Kenya.

# BUSINESS FOR CAMBRIDGE IGCSE™ AND O LEVEL: COURSEBOOK

> **CONTINUED**
>
> SLS's factory also produces pre-cooked beans (see Figure 1.5); these are beans customers can eat straightaway. Like the sorghum, the beans are bought from small-scale farmers. Large industrial-sized ovens are used to cook the beans. The beans are then dried and packed, ready for sale. SLS produces between 200 and 300 kilos of beans each week. These ready-to-eat beans are sold in small packets to people living in Kenyan cities who do not have the time or fuel to cook the beans themselves.
>
> **Discuss in small groups or as a class:**
>
> 1 What is the purpose of Rose's business?
> 2 Using examples from the case study, which factors of production does Rose's business use?

Every business is likely to use different amounts of each factor of production based on what is being produced or sold. For example, one business may use high levels of machinery and need a large space to operate, whereas another business may use many employees.

> **ACTIVITY 1.3**
>
> In pairs or small groups:
>
> 1 Research a local business that interests you. Each group should research a different business.
> 2 Produce a poster showing images of the four factors of production they use. Share your poster with the class.
>   a What similarities do you notice between the factors shown in other posters?
>   b Which resources do most businesses use? Why?

**TIP**

Starting a blog or news diary is a great way to help find out what is happening in business and the economy around you.

All four factors of production are needed to make products. Some businesses will find it easier to find the resources than other businesses.

> **ACTIVITY 1.4**
>
> Fatima currently works in a bakery but is unhappy working there. Fatima's grandfather has given her $5 000 and she is going to use this money to start her own business. She plans to make cakes for special occasions such as birthdays and weddings. Fatima plans to use her kitchen at home to make the cakes as she has plenty of equipment such as bowls and a large oven. She will employ two friends to help decorate the cakes.
>
> 1 Individually, name the four factors of production Fatima will need to use to start up her new business.
> 2 Using the information in the case study, provide one example for each of the factors of production Fatima could use in her new business.
> 3 In pairs, discuss your answers with a partner. Did you find different or similar examples?

**TIP**

Use the information from the scenario, such as in Activity 1.4, to help you answer the questions. This is a good way to show application. Application does not have to be complex – just select words or suitable references to the business that make sense in relation to the point being made. Mentioning the name of the business is not application.

# Adding value

There are two elements to **added value** – selling price and cost of bought-in materials.

A business will try to sell its products at a price greater than the cost of the bought-in materials used to make the good or service. The difference between these two elements is known as added value. This is shown in Figure 1.6.

> **KEY TERM**
>
> **added value:** the difference between the selling price and the cost of bought-in materials.

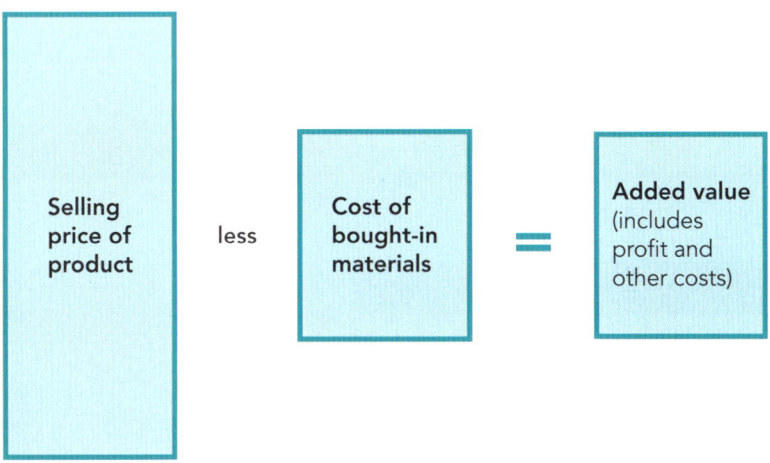

**Figure 1.6:** The concept of added value

> **TIP**
>
> Added value is different to profit. Other costs including labour and electricity must be deducted from added value to calculate profit. Only what is left after all costs have been paid is classed as profit.

## How added value can be increased

A business could increase added value by increasing the selling price or lower the cost of bought-in materials. However, simply increasing the selling price without a good reason could lower demand. Using cheaper or lower-quality materials could lower costs, but it could damage the business' reputation. See Table 1.1 for ways a business could increase added value.

> **LINK**
>
> You can find more information about profit in Chapter 17.

**Table 1.1:** Ways for a business to increase added value

| Ways | How it could help increase added value |
|---|---|
| Branding | Developing a logo, name and other promotional activities can help make the product appear to be worth more or more trusted, so customers are willing to pay a higher price. |
| Improve quality | Providing a high standard of service to customers may make them feel/think that they are getting more value for their money and are willing to pay more. |
| Design | Adding extra features or improving the design can make their product more desirable than similar products on the market and allow the business to charge a higher price. |
| Add convenience | Customers may pay a higher price for goods and services that they can have straightaway or that save them time. |

Some ways could increase costs, and if this increases the cost of bought-in materials it could affect the amount of added value created.

For example:

A flower shop – instead of selling single flowers, they can add value by:

- producing bunches of flowers to order
- having bouquets already made up for customers who are passing by and need a gift quickly (convenience)
- using packaging to make the flowers look more appealing (design)
- providing a high-quality service for customers.

Therefore, creating the opportunity to increase added value could allow the business to set higher prices.

### ACTIVITY 1.5

Find an object that you have at school or home. Think about the ways a business might have increased the added value of this object. For example, as shown in Figure 1.7, a mobile phone.

**Figure 1.7:** A business could increase the added value of a mobile phone

1 Choose one possible way the business might have added value to this product.

2 Write a sentence about how this way might help increase added value? Include a comment about why this way might be suitable for a mobile phone.

3 Share your work with a partner. For example, which ideas are the same and which ideas are different?

4 Repeat the activity with another object. Use the feedback from your partner to help you complete the activity.

## CASE STUDY 1.2

**Neemans: Best foot forward!**

**Figure 1.8:** Finding ways to increase added value in the shoe business is important

Footwear is a big business in India. In 2022, the International Market Analysis Research and Consulting (IMARC) group valued the size of the Indian shoe market at $15.1 billion. There is plenty of competition with popular international brands, including Bata and Puma, operating in the market. Finding ways to increase added value is therefore important (see Figure 1.8).

Neemans is one of these Indian shoe businesses. Based in Hyderabad, Neemans makes shoes using only natural or renewable materials. For example, the top part of the shoe is made from Merino wool. Sheep grow wool naturally as it protects them against the weather. When the weather is warmer, farmers must cut the wool off the sheep to keep the animals cool. The wool must be kept short to protect the sheep against infection. The bottoms of Neemans' shoes are made from recycled plastic bottles. Each pair of shoes comes in a box made from recycled cardboard with Neemans' unique logo on it.

**Discuss in pairs or groups:**

1  Explain how having a unique design might help Neemans increase added value.

2  What other ways might Neemans use to increase added value to its shoes?

## DISCUSSION

Hold a whole class or small group discussion about which two ways Neemans could use to increase added value. Write a one-minute summary, explaining which way you would choose and why you rejected the other option.

## REFLECTION

Individually, how did you decide which was the best way for Neemans to use? For example, did you consider the advantages and disadvantages of each way? Or were you persuaded by the points made by someone else in the class or group? If so, what was said that made you change your mind?

Make notes on how you made your decision. Is this an approach you could use for similar questions in the future?

# Opportunity cost

The basic economic problem is that there are not enough resources to make all the goods and services necessary to meet the needs and unlimited wants of everyone. This scarcity of resources means choices must be made because resources used for one purpose cannot be used for another purpose. When an option is chosen, something will have to be given up doing it.

Every decision involves making choices. Consider the example in Figure 1.9. If you buy the latest computer game, then you must think about what else you could have used the money for.

**Figure 1.9:** Every decision involves making choices, whether it is buying the latest computer game or buying a ticket to a music festival or saving up the money so that it could be put towards something else in the future

Business persons are similar – they just make different types of decisions and use different terms when explaining what they do; for example, what resources to use, what product to produce, whether to stop or continue production, whether to expand, and so on.

When making decisions, the business person will consider what else they could do with the same resources – or factors of production – and the value of the option they do not choose is known as the **opportunity cost**.

Like most decisions, there is no 'right answer' – it is just about making the best decision you can with the information to which you have access.

For example, a farmer may decide to grow onions in one field. This land cannot then be used to grow other vegetables. The potential benefit or value that could be gained from growing other vegetables here is the opportunity cost (see Figure 1.10).

> **KEY TERM**
>
> **opportunity cost:** the next best alternative given up by choosing a different option.

**Figure 1.10:** A field to grow onions cannot be used to grow other crops such as turmeric

## BUSINESS IN ACTION

### High Speed 2 (HS2)

**Figure 1.11:** A high-speed rail line could help to lower traffic congestion

HS2 was a UK Government project designed to provide a high-speed rail line connecting Manchester and Birmingham to London. The new rail line could reduce the number of car journeys between these three cities which could help lower traffic congestion. However, in 2023, the government announced that the Manchester part of the line would not go ahead. From the original cost of £42.6 billion (approximately $54.2 billion) in 2013, an independent review in 2022 estimated the cost could rise to £107 billion (approximately $136.1 billion). As the UK Government only has a certain amount of finances available, it decided that the funds could be better spent on other projects, including small-scale transport improvements in local communities.

Discuss in small groups or as a class:

1. What is likely to be the opportunity cost of the government's decision to stop the HS2 link to Manchester?
2. If you were part of the government, would you make the same decision? Give reasons for your answer.

## SUMMARY

You should now know:

- Business activity is about providing goods and services that meet needs and wants.
- A business will use a combination of resources – the factors of production – to produce goods and services.
- A business will try to sell its good at a higher price than the cost of the materials used to make it. By widening the gap between selling price and cost of bought-in materials added value will increase.
- There are limited resources available to make goods and services, so choices must be made. The value of the option given up doing something else is known as the opportunity cost.

# Chapter 1 practice questions

1. Maria is currently employed as a carpenter by a construction company. In her spare time, Maria makes wooden toys that her brother sells at the local market. Maria buys the wood and other resources from a local supplier. She plans to leave her job to start up a toy-making business using all her savings. Her business will make use of the four factors of production. Maria understands there will be an opportunity cost to her decision and finding ways to increase added value will be important.

    a   Define 'opportunity cost'. [2]

    b   State the **four** factors of production. [4]

    c   Explain **two** factors of production Maria might use in her business. [6]

    d   Explain **two** ways Maria could add value. Which is likely to be the best way for Maria to use? Justify your answer. [8]

2. CPX manufactures pottery products, such as plates and bowls. The business makes use of all four factors of production. CPX employs 50 skilled production workers at its factory to operate the machinery including the kiln. All the products are sold to hotels and restaurants. CPX's marketing manager has been asked by the directors to consider ways the company could increase the added value of its products.

    a   Define 'factors of production'. [2]

    b   Outline **two** ways CPX could increase 'added value'. [4]

    c   Explain **two** ways CPX could increase the added value of its products. [6]

    d   Explain **two** factors of production CPX might use. Which factor is likely to be the most important for CPX? Justify your answer. [8]

    **Total available marks: 40**

## CHECK YOUR PROGRESS

How well do you think you have achieved the learning intentions for this chapter? Give yourself a score from 1 (still need a lot of practice) to 5 (feeling very confident) for each learning intention. Provide an example to support your score.

| Now I can ... | Score | Example |
| --- | --- | --- |
| define and provide examples of the four factors of production | | |
| explain the importance of different factors of production | | |
| state what 'added value' means | | |
| explain the different ways to increase added value | | |
| understand the concept of opportunity cost. | | |

# Chapter 2
# Economic sectors

**LEARNING INTENTIONS**

By the end of this chapter, you will be able to:
- understand the purpose of the primary, secondary and tertiary sectors
- explain the difference between the primary, secondary and tertiary sectors
- understand the meaning and purpose of the private and public sectors
- explain the difference between the private and public sectors.

# Introduction

Every country has an economy – it is a measure of all the activities that take place within the country involving the production, buying and selling of goods and services (products). Many different businesses are involved in this, but the activities of some of these businesses are similar. It is helpful to group (classify) different types of businesses in an economy together based on common features. These groups are called economic sectors. In this chapter, you will learn about different ways businesses are grouped together and why it is important to group them together.

## BUSINESS IN CONTEXT

### The seeds of sustainability

Sustenir is a business based in Singapore. It grows a range of vegetables, including spinach and kale, in the city centre. While traditional farms grow vegetables outside in fields, often in the countryside, Sustenir grows its products inside specially built facilities called vertical farms (see Figure 2.1). Technology is used to control the growing conditions allowing Sustenir to grow vegetables all year round, whatever the weather and without needing to use any chemicals. Sustenir does not have to worry about heavy rains or extreme heat as computers control the amount of water the plants receive. This reduces the amount of water used, but still ensures plants have enough water to grow.

As Sustenir is based in the city centre, this reduces the distance the vegetables must travel from the farm to the customer, which lowers the transport costs. Sustenir's employees are also able to harvest and deliver the products to customers daily, which helps reduce the amount of food waste.

### Discuss in pairs or groups:

1. What does this business do differently from similar businesses in its industry?
2. What might be the advantages of Sustenir's approach to farming?

**Figure 2.1:** Vegetables can be grown inside specially built facilities called vertical farms

While every business is different, some businesses will share similar characteristics based on what they do.

## ACTIVITY 2.1

1. In small groups, use the internet, newspapers and library resources to make a list of the different types of business activity or jobs that you can find; for example, making clothes, restaurants and gold mining.
2. Do you notice any similarities between the different activities? For example, which jobs involve making or selling something? Use the similarities to sort the activities into groups (try to limit these to three or four groups).
3. As a group, give each of your business groups a simple title that describes the business activity they do.

## 2.1 Primary, secondary and tertiary sectors

Businesses can be grouped together into sectors based on the types of products or activities they are involved in. There are three main sectors.

### Primary sector

Businesses involved in the extraction or harvesting of natural resources from the land or sea are classed as **primary sector** businesses (see Figure 2.2). These businesses will extract or capture products that naturally exist (e.g., oil or wind) or might be involved in growing the resources (e.g., businesses that grow trees to obtain wood).

### Secondary sector

Any business that takes the raw materials provided by the primary sector and turns these materials into goods is classed as a **secondary sector** business. Examples include food canning, furniture making, car manufacturing and house building.

> **KEY TERMS**
>
> **primary sector:** business activity that involves the extraction or harvesting of natural resources.
>
> **secondary sector:** businesses that turn raw materials into manufactured goods.

**Figure 2.2:** Oil fields in the Middle East are an example of a primary sector business

---

**CASE STUDY 2.1**

**Malón Bambú Bikes, Argentina**

**Figure 2.3:** Malón Bambú Bikes produces bicycles made from bamboo harvested in Argentina

Malón Bambú Bikes (MB) produces bicycles (see Figure 2.3). Every bicycle is made from bamboo, which is harvested from farms in Argentina. Using materials produced locally helps reduce MB's impact on the environment. But why bamboo?

Bamboo is a natural material which is quick and easy for farmers to grow. According to the Guinness World Records, some types of bamboo can grow at nearly 4 cm an hour. This means when farmers harvest the bamboo, it does not take long for new bamboo shoots to appear. The speed of growth means bamboo is a renewable resource which is quick and easy to obtain.

> **CONTINUED**
>
> Bamboo is a great material when making bicycles because it is flexible, so it is easy to bend and shape into the bicycle frame. Bamboo is strong, so the bicycle frames do not break easily and therefore can last for a long time. Bamboo is also lightweight which is helpful for customers when they are trying to ride the bike up and down hills!
>
> **Using an example from the case:**
>
> 1 Outline one reason why Malón Bambú Bikes is classed as a manufacturing business.
>
> 2 Explain the difference between a primary sector and secondary sector business.

> **TIP**
>
> When asked to apply knowledge (as in Case study 2.1 where it says 'Using an example from the case'), chose suitable words from the case study that make sense in relation to the point being made.

## Tertiary sector

The **tertiary sector** involves providing services to consumers or other businesses. These activities include a wide range of services including banking, insurance, tourism, computer services, healthcare and education. For example, many manufacturing businesses will use the services of transport businesses and retailers to get their products from the factory to the customer. Figure 2.4 shows an example of a tertiary sector business.

> **KEY TERM**
>
> **tertiary sector:** involves providing services to consumers or other businesses.

**Figure 2.4:** A transport driver delivering parcels to customers and other businesses

## ACTIVITY 2.2

1. Classify the following as either primary, secondary or tertiary sector activities.

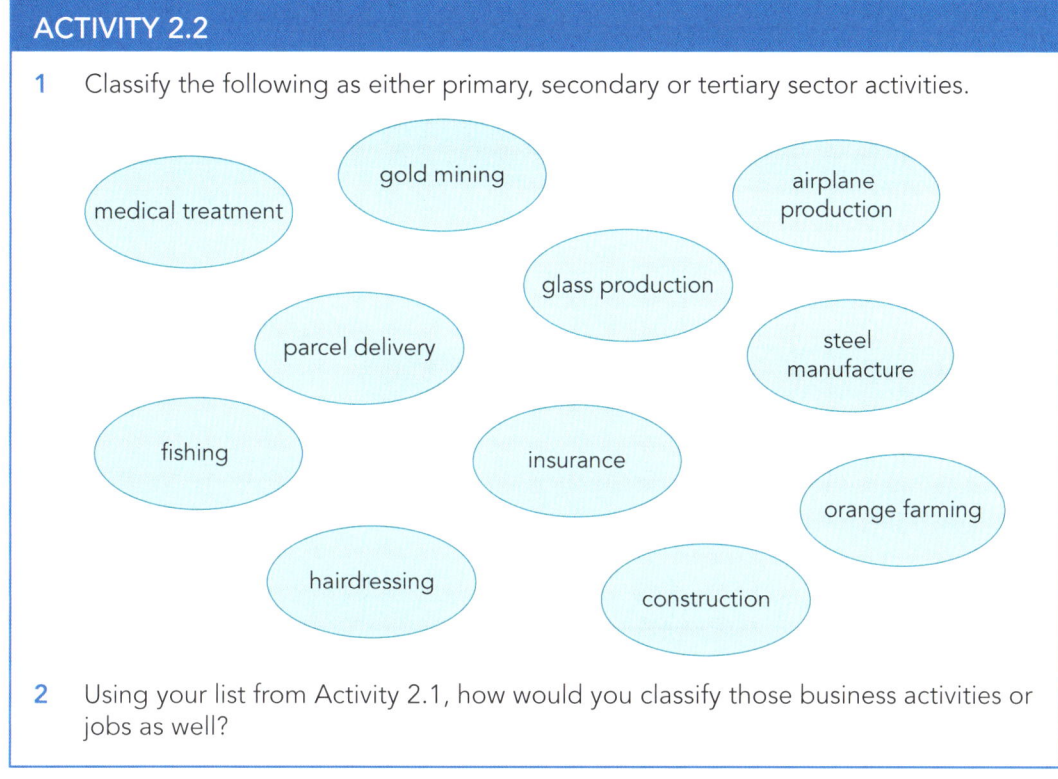

2. Using your list from Activity 2.1, how would you classify those business activities or jobs as well?

Businesses operate in different sectors, depending on what they do. Figure 2.5 shows a summary of the type of business activity likely to be found in each economic sector.

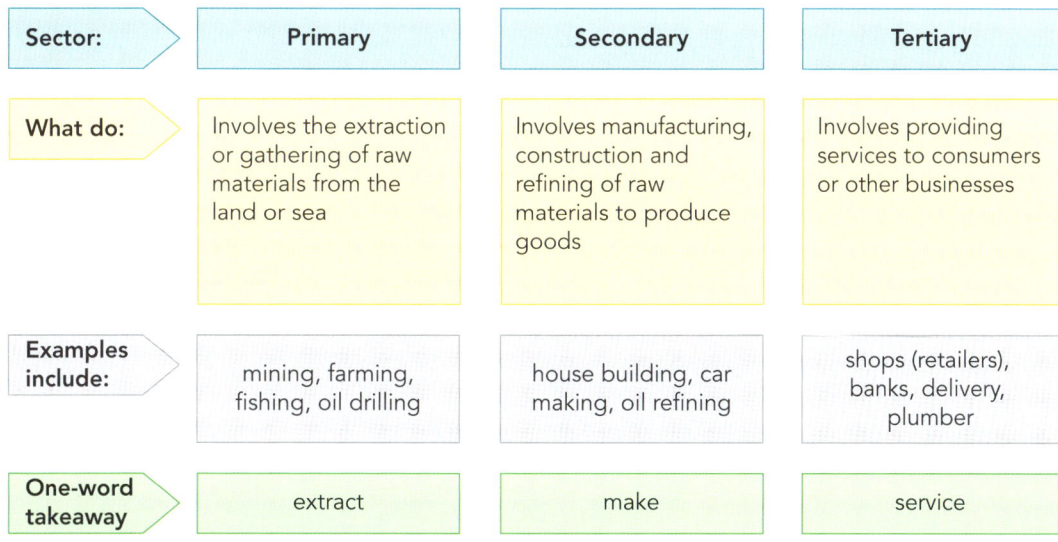

Figure 2.5: Types of business activity by economic sector

### ACTIVITY 2.3

In small groups, make a list of either the primary, secondary or tertiary sector businesses in one region/area of your country. You should include what the business extracts, grows or manufactures or which service they provide. Each group should make a list for a different region/area of the country.

Share the information with the other groups in a creative way. This could be in the form of a presentation, poster or video montage – you choose.

### DISCUSSION

As a small group or class:

- Which type of business activity is the most common in your country? Can you think of any reasons for this?
- Which type of business activity is the least common in your country? Can you think of any reasons for this?

### REFLECTION

As a small group, choose another country. What types of business activity are found there? How do these activities compare to your country? Is your list of reasons relevant for this other country? What other reasons might there be?

Discuss your findings with another student in your group. Did you both have the same reasons? Did their approach to this task differ from yours? Can you learn any new ideas from how they approached this task?

## Sectors can work together

Obtaining goods and services can often involve businesses from primary, secondary and tertiary sectors.

For example, a T-shirt. Where do the materials for T-shirts come from? Who makes the T-shirts? Where do you buy T-shirts? How does the T-shirt get there? There is a lot of business activity involved in getting the T-shirt to you. Figure 2.6 shows the production of a T-shirt and the sectors involved in the process.

## 2 Economic sectors

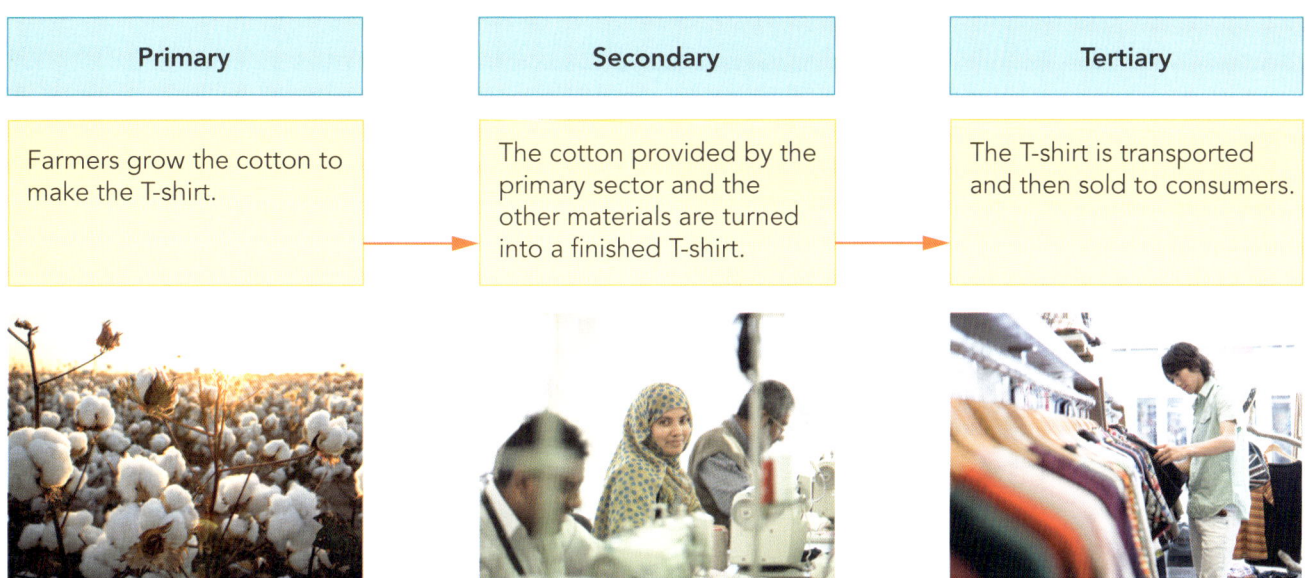

**Figure 2.6:** The production of a T-shirt and the three economic sectors

### ACTIVITY 2.4

Using Figure 2.6 as an example, choose an item in your classroom or home, such as a table or food product, and produce an image or diagram showing how the primary, secondary and tertiary sector businesses work together to get the product to the customer.

### DISCUSSION

In pairs:

- Which economic sector do you think is the most important for your country? Why?
- Do you think this sector is the most important for all countries? Why/why not?

## CASE STUDY 2.2

**BRAC Bank**

**Figure 2.7:** Banking in Bangladesh

BRAC Bank Limited is one of Bangladesh's most sustainable banks. BRAC Bank is different to many other banks. It was started in 2001 because many small- and medium-sized businesses struggled to obtain bank loans or bank accounts from other banks in Bangladesh. Most of the financial services offered by BRAC Bank are given to support environmentally friendly or socially responsible projects in Bangladesh and other countries across Asia and Africa.

Without access to finance, these businesses cannot operate properly and have limited opportunity to grow. One way in which BRAC Bank tries to help is by employing local people to provide banking services to others in rural communities. Local people are then able to pay in or withdraw money easily without having to travel miles to the nearest town where a traditional bank might be located. Many of the people employed by BRAC Bank are women. Not only do the women earn money but this also helps improve the level of financial understanding in each community.

**Discuss in pairs or groups:**

1. Which economic sector does BRAC Bank belong to?
2. Using examples from the case, explain the type of service BRAC Bank provides to its customers.

## 2.2 Private and public sectors

Most countries have both a **private sector** and **public sector**; this is called a mixed economy.

- **Private sector** – organisations owned and controlled by individuals or groups of individuals. Making a profit is important for these businesses and this influences the decisions made by the owners or managers. Examples include sole traders, partnerships, private limited and public limited companies.

- **Public sector** – organisations owned by the country as a whole and controlled by the government on behalf of the people. Decisions about what, how and for whom to produce are made by the government. These businesses are likely to be funded through taxation. Examples of public sector activities include education, healthcare and power such as electricity.

### KEY TERMS

**private sector:** the part of the economy that is owned and controlled by individuals and companies for profit.

**public sector:** the part of the economy that is owned and controlled by the state or central government.

### LINK

You can find more information about the types of private sector businesses in Chapter 4.

## ACTIVITY 2.5

As a small group or as a class activity, use the internet, library resources or other sources to find examples of public sector businesses in your country:

- Make a list of the products provided. Why do you think the public sector provides these products?
- Are there any products that are provided by both the private sector and the public sector? Why do you think both sectors provide these products?

## TIP

All private and public sector organisations are involved in some form of business activity – it is only what, for whom and why they produce goods and services that is different.

## CASE STUDY 2.3

### Indian Railways

India is one of the largest countries in the world covering over 3.2 million kilometres. The country also has the highest population of people in the world with over 1 billion people. Being able to move people and goods around a large country quickly and at relatively low cost is important. Train travel is a popular mode of transport because it is both affordable and safe. According to Statista, approximately 22 million people used trains every day in 2022.

Indian Railways is the largest public sector organisation in India. It also has one of the largest railway networks in the world with over 13 000 trains operating every day between 7 300 stations.

Indian Railways is the eighth largest employer in the world with nearly 1.1 million employees. It is easy to see why Indian Railways might be important to the Indian economy.

**Figure 2.8:** Indian Railways has one of the largest railway networks in the world

**Discuss in small groups or as a class:**

1. Why Indian Railways might be important for the Indian economy.
2. Write a short newspaper article (maximum 100 words) explaining the main points discussed.

> **BUSINESS IN ACTION**
>
> **Ørsted**
>
> Ørsted used to be one of the largest coal-based energy companies in Denmark. Today, all that has changed. The business has stopped using fossil fuels, such as coal, and only uses renewable energy to produce the electricity it provides to its customers. Ørsted has done this by building offshore wind farms around the coastline of Denmark (see Figure 2.9). Huge wind turbines capture the wind and help convert the wind into energy that can be used to produce electricity for businesses and people's homes. Ørsted also builds and operates solar farms across Denmark to capture power from sunlight.
>
> The change took Ørsted ten years to complete. An important part of the process involved introducing new technology, which was expensive to do. Ørsted's directors knew it would not be a simple change to make and it would involve many difficult decisions. The directors hoped it would be a good decision for both Ørsted and the environment. Ørsted has not stopped there. The business is also trying to help other companies change from using fossil fuels and move towards using renewable energy sources.
>
>
>
> **Figure 2.9:** Ørsted has built offshore wind farms around the coastline of Denmark
>
> **Discuss as a class the following statement:**
>
> All businesses should make the change Ørsted did.
>
> 1 Split into groups. Some groups could prepare a list of advantages of making this change and other groups could prepare a list of disadvantages of making this change. Have a class discussion about the advantages and disadvantages.
>
> 2 Then, individually, write a sentence explaining whether you agree or disagree with the statement, giving a reason for your answer.

## SUMMARY

You should now know:

- Businesses can be classified, according to what they do, into primary, secondary and tertiary sectors.

- The private sector consists of businesses that are owned and controlled by individuals or groups of individuals.

- The public sector consists of organisations that are owned and controlled by the government on behalf of the people.

- Most countries will have both a private and a public sector. Unlike organisations in the private sector, public sector organisations are more concerned with social objectives than profit objectives.

# Chapter 2 practice questions

1. PTD is a business in the private sector. It manufactures jewellery including rings and necklaces. All the jewellery is handmade in its factory by PTD's 40 skilled employees. PTD buys most of its raw materials from local gold and diamond mines. The jewellery is then sold to retailers in 30 countries. PTD makes use of the services of many tertiary sector businesses. The Managing Director thinks retailers are likely to be the most important tertiary sector business that PTD uses.

   a  Define 'private sector'. [2]

   b  State **four** examples of business activity in the primary sector. [4]

   c  Explain **two** tertiary sector businesses (other than retailers) that PTD might use. [6]

   d  Do you think retailers are the most important tertiary sector business that PTD might use? Justify your answer. [8]

2. ZXG is a large bank in the public sector. It employs 5000 workers and has bank branches in 50 towns across Country X. The bank offers a range of financial services including loans to businesses and individuals. Many of ZXG's competitors are in the private sector. The Managing Director knows being in the public sector has advantages and disadvantages.

   a  Define 'public sector'. [2]

   b  Identify **four** types of business organisations found in the private sector. [4]

   c  Explain **two** ways ZXG, a public sector business, might be different to a private sector business. [6]

   d  Do you think the advantages of ZXG of being a public sector business are greater than the disadvantages? Justify your answer. [8]

   Total available marks: 40

> BUSINESS FOR CAMBRIDGE IGCSE™ AND O LEVEL: COURSEBOOK

## CHECK YOUR PROGRESS

How well do you think you have achieved the learning intentions for this chapter? Give yourself a score from 1 (still need a lot of practice) to 5 (feeling very confident) for each learning intention. Provide an example to support your score.

| Now I can … | Score | Example |
|---|---|---|
| explain the difference between the primary, secondary and tertiary sectors | | |
| classify examples of the primary, secondary and tertiary sector activities | | |
| define what is meant by the private sector and public sector | | |
| identify examples of private sector and public sector organisations. | | |

# Chapter 3
# Enterprise, business growth and size

## LEARNING INTENTIONS

By the end of this chapter, you will be able to:

- explain the characteristics of successful entrepreneurs
- understand the key elements and importance of a business plan
- explain why and how governments support business start-ups
- know the methods and problems of measuring business size
- understand the reasons why some businesses grow and others remain small
- describe the different ways a business can grow both internally and externally
- explain the advantages and disadvantages of different methods of growth
- understand the reasons why some businesses succeed and others fail.

# Introduction

Behind every successful business is a person or group of people. Who are these people and which characteristics do they share? An important document used by business people is a **business plan** – so what is it and why is it useful? Many governments will offer support to business start-ups – so how and why do governments help them? You will learn about the people behind these successful businesses, the role of business plans and how governments might support new businesses.

Businesses can be large or small, so how can business size be measured, and what are the problems of using different methods? Some businesses may decide to remain small while other businesses will want to grow. You will learn about the different ways a business might grow and the advantages and disadvantages of growth. You will also learn about the possible reasons why some businesses are successful and others fail.

> **KEY TERM**
>
> **business plan:** a detailed written document outlining the aims and objectives of a business and what it intends to do to achieve them.

## BUSINESS IN CONTEXT

### Aha!

Have you ever had an aha moment? That very brief period when you have a great idea or inspiration that helps you solve a problem, or you are planning something and everything just falls into place, and you go, "Yes, that's it!"? Well, that is what happened to Aadit Palicha.

Aadit was born in Mumbai, India, before moving with his family to Dubai. A keen computer programmer, he used these skills to help him start his first business at the age of 17. Getting to and from school in a busy city was not easy. Parents had jobs to get to and other children to take to school and other activities. Aadit had the idea of a car sharing app – GoPool – to provide a simple way for parents to organise lifts to and from school. Then, while studying computer engineering at Stanford University in the US, Aadit and his friend, Kaivalya, came up with another business idea for a quick-commerce grocery app called Zepto. The app would allow people to order food from a local supermarket and have it delivered to them within ten minutes. So excited about the idea, they left university halfway through the course to focus on being **entrepreneurs** and start up their new business. When Aadit went to see investors to ask for finance, they laughed at his idea and said it would never work. Aadit and Kaivalya did not give up. Customers liked the idea, and within six months of starting the business it was valued at over $570 million.

**Discuss in pairs or groups:**

1. What information from the above text supports the idea that Aadit might be an entrepreneur?
2. Create a simple definition of what you think an entrepreneur is.

**Figure 3.1:** Apps allow people to order food and have it delivered to their home

> **KEY TERM**
>
> **entrepreneur:** an individual who has an idea for a new business and takes the financial risk of starting it.

> **TIP**
>
> Try to avoid using examples when asked to define terms as this does not necessarily explain the term.

# 3 Enterprise, business growth and size

## 3.1 Enterprise and entrepreneurship

Enterprise is about seeing an opportunity to provide products – a good or service – that people might be willing to buy. The idea for an enterprise may be:

- something completely new because a person has spotted a gap in the market
- a solution to an existing problem
- someone wants to make a difference in their local community.

Others may simply want to make money doing something somebody else is doing successfully. The person (or people) who takes the risk of turning the idea into a business is called an entrepreneur.

There are many famous entrepreneurs around the world including Elon Musk, the South African-born founder of Space X and Tesla; Cher Wang, the founder of HTC, a smart phone manufacturer; Mark Zuckerberg who started Meta (Facebook); and Huda Kattan of Huda Beauty, a business based in Dubai. But what makes these people successful?

> ### DISCUSSION
>
> Truckistan is based in Lahore, Pakistan. The business was started in 2022 by Abid Butt and Zafar Khan. Truckistan uses a unique computer software program to help small businesses transport goods between towns and cities across Pakistan. Many small businesses in Pakistan do not have enough goods to transport between destinations to fill the space available in a big truck (lorry). Businesses used to have two choices – wait and risk losing sales or pay the transport cost of using a big lorry. Truckistan's computer software allows businesses to share space in lorries going to the same destination.
>
> It is a good solution – the trucks are full, individual customers pay lower transport costs and there are fewer lorries on the roads which reduces pollution.
>
> #### Discuss in pairs or groups:
> - What are the possible advantages of businesses using Truckistan's software program?
> - Is there an environmental problem or other issue affecting your local area or country? Can you think of simple ways to help solve it?

## Characteristics of successful entrepreneurs

Every entrepreneur is different, but they often share similar features or qualities known as characteristics. These are shown in Figure 3.2.

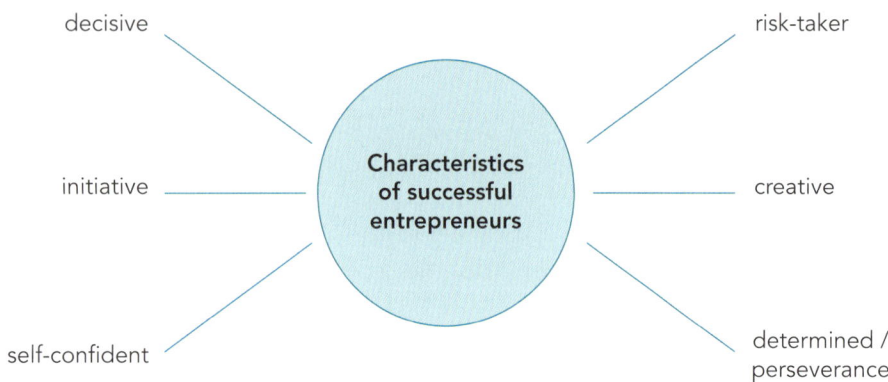

**Figure 3.2:** Characteristics of successful entrepreneurs

You can find examples on why each of these characteristics may be helpful in Table 3.1.

**Table 3.1** Examples of why each characteristic of successful entrepreneurs may be helpful

| Characteristic | What it is | Example of why it may be helpful |
|---|---|---|
| Risk-taker | Willing to take chance or risks knowing that it may not work | The idea may not work, so you need to be prepared to lose everything you have put into an idea |
| Creative | The ability to think up new ideas or different ways of doing things | New ideas could provide the opportunity to fill a gap in the market or gain a competitive advantage |
| Determination/ perseverance | Will keep working on an idea and not give up when things do not go as expected | It may take time to turn the idea into a suitable product. Lenders may refuse to lend the finance so you need to find other sources of funds |
| Self-confident | Having trust in your own ability and ideas to carry them out successfully | May have to convince people to provide money or resources or buy your product |
| Initiative | Being willing to take on new ideas or projects to make things happen | Allows you to take advantage of opportunities that others may miss or be afraid to take |
| Decisive | Ability to make decisions, even if it involves making difficult choices | This can save time or resources, so that unnecessary work is not done |

# 3 Enterprise, business growth and size

### CASE STUDY 3.1

**Eco Hustle: No such thing as rubbish**

**Figure 3.3:** Many new products can be made from waste materials

Eco Hustle is a business based in Mauritius. The business has two brands – Sakili and Recycle Moi. The business was started by Lalita Purbhoo-Junggee and her husband. Sakili is a range of products including sport bags, backpacks, purses, laptop case, key chains and pencil cases. All the products are made from waste materials produced by advertising companies. Lalita found out that many of the materials businesses used to produce banners and billboards could not easily be recycled or reused, so it ended up as litter in the streets or ocean causing pollution for her local community in Mauritius.

Lalita wanted to help solve this problem, so she left her job as a journalist to start up her business. Her husband created the designs for the products, but Lalita had other skills that she thought could be useful. When she started the business, she had no business experience and limited funds, but she would not give up. It took over three years before the first of Sakili's upcycled products were sold.

**Discuss in pairs or groups:**

1 Using examples from the case study, describe two characteristics of an entrepreneur that Lalita has shown.

2 Individually, choose one of these characteristics. Write a sentence explaining why you think this characteristic is more important than the other. Share your answer with each other. Can you understand the reason for each other's choices? Explain this to your partner.

It is important to understand that entrepreneurs may not have all the characteristics listed in Table 3.1, but this does not mean they will be unsuccessful. Sometimes it is about having the right balance of skills (and luck) to get the business started. Even if the entrepreneur has the 'right' characteristics, it does not mean the business will be successful.

You will learn more about why some businesses are successful and others fail later in this chapter.

### ACTIVITY 3.1

1 Working in small groups, use newspapers, magazines, library resources or the internet to research an entrepreneur from your country, or one who your group thinks has had a big influence on business activity in your country. Each group should research a different entrepreneur.

2 Prepare a poster to share with the class about your chosen entrepreneur. Things to include could be their name, their idea, the business that they started, the characteristics they have shown or any other relevant information.

> **TIP**
>
> Do not confuse an entrepreneur and a manager. A successful entrepreneur is not the same as a good manager, and the manager may not be the person who started the business.

## 3.2 The purpose and key elements of a business plan

Every business plan is unique to each business and will change depending on what the business is trying to achieve. However, most business plans are likely to include the same key elements, as shown in Table 3.2.

**Table 3.2:** The key elements of business plans

| Element | Likely to include information about |
|---|---|
| Overview or summary | Basic information about the entrepreneur and the business including what is the idea and who you plan to sell the product to. |
| Objectives | Explains the business goals, i.e., what the business hopes to achieve. For example, to provide a service or to make a profit. |
| Market research | The market, including the current size of the market and the product's main competitors – helps to show the level of demand. |
| Marketing | Information about what the product is, the name, potential price, where it could be sold and how the business intends to attract people to buy the product. |
| Finance | Data about the costs involved and the amount of money that could be gained from sales can allow businesses to work out the amount of funding needed. |
| Resources | The place from where the business will operate; machinery and any other equipment and materials needed to provide the good or service. |
| People | The number, skills and expertise of managers and/or employees to be recruited. |
| Operations | How the product will be made, how long it may take to make, and who and where the resources can be obtained from. |

> **LINKS**
>
> You can find more information in about market research in Chapter 11, business objectives in Chapter 5 and marketing in Chapter 10.

## The importance of a business plan for entrepreneurs

A business plan is important for both new and existing businesses because it can help:

- Raise finance, including bank loans, as the lender can see the business is able to repay.
- Set goals or targets, so the entrepreneur can clearly see what they need to do to achieve their goals. This can provide a sense of purpose and direction.

- Understand potential risks the business might face, so there is time to plan for possible solutions that can help reduce the risk of failure.
- Act as a checklist – this can be used to monitor business progress towards its targets.
- Inform decision-making (see Figure 3.4), so the business does not waste resources, time or money on making and selling the wrong products.

Figure 3.4: A business plan can help inform decision-making

### ACTIVITY 3.2

In pairs or small groups, imagine you are going to start up your own business at school. This might be selling food or stationery or organising an end-of-term event for the class.

1. Create a simple outline of business plan for your idea. You could include information such as:
   - the name of your business (try to have a name that is interesting but relevant to your product)
   - what the product is (what it will look like and do)
   - who you plan to sell the product to
   - how many people are interested in buying your product
   - the price you intend to sell the product or service for
   - what might you do to make customers aware of your product and encourage them to buy it
   - where will you sell it and why would it be a good place to choose
   - how might you attract customers to buy your product

### TIP

Do not just learn the main element of a business plan. It is also important to understand why each of these elements are helpful to a business.

> **CONTINUED**
>
> - what the product will cost to make/buy
> - what resources you will need to make/provide the good or service
> - who will work in the business and what they will need to do, including any skills they will need
> - where the product will be made (or bought from).
>
> 2 Present your business plan to another group, or the class, for them to offer feedback.

> **REFLECTION**
>
> Review the feedback others have given you. How can you use this to improve how you approach similar tasks in the future? For example: Did you approach this task in a logical way, working through the points one by one or randomly writing down ideas? Which part of the task did you find easier or harder to complete – was it thinking about the points to make or the presentation?
>
> Did others have any ideas or suggestions that you could use when attempting other research tasks in the future?

## 3.3 Why governments support business start-ups

Governments want to encourage business start-ups because they can provide many advantages to the economy. These advantages include:

- **Job creation** – although each small business may not employ many workers, together they can employ a large percentage of the working population, helping to lower the level of unemployment.
- **Increased competition** – this can lead to more customer choice and having more businesses offering similar products may lead to lower prices.
- **May provide specialist goods and services** to consumers which larger businesses may not be willing to provide.
- **Increase output** – each business will add to the total number of goods and services produced, which can help increase the size of the economy.
- **May grow into larger businesses (if successful)** – which may provide additional jobs and contribute more tax revenue to the government.

## 3.4 How governments support business start-ups

Many governments provide financial and other support to new businesses. However, the type of support is likely to vary from country to country.

The most common types of government support include:

- grant (amount of money that may not need to be repaid) and low-interest loans
- low tax rates on profits in the early years
- low-cost or rent-free premises for a certain period
- free or low-cost training schemes for employees
- information, advice and support from specialist agencies
- arranging business fairs for entrepreneurs to attend (see Figure 3.5).

Figure 3.5: Entrepreneurs at a business fair exchanging ideas

## CASE STUDY 3.2

### Glass2Sand

Figure 3.6: Udit's machine ensures fewer used glass bottles are left lying around on the streets or end up in landfills

It all started when the waste collectors stopped visiting his neighbourhood. Udit Singhal, a 16 year old child from New Delhi, asked his parents why. They explained that the amount of money the collectors received for gathering the empty bottles did not cover their costs. With no collections, this meant all the empty glass bottles would go to landfills. Udit learnt in school that a single glass bottle can take over 4 000 years to break down naturally, which is not good for the environment.

Udit decided he wanted to do something about this. He discovered a business in New Zealand that had created an environmentally friendly machine to crush the glass. However, Udit lived in India and he was worried about the environmental cost of transporting the machine to India.

> **CONTINUED**
>
> Udit decided to create his own simple machine to crush the glass bottles into sand. The first version was basic, but the idea impressed the New Zealand High Commission in India, who provided Udit with a financial grant to develop his idea. Udit's machine ensures fewer glass bottles end up in landfills, thereby reducing pollution. Even better, the sand produced can be used by construction businesses to build roads or buildings.
>
> **Discuss in pairs or groups:**
>
> 1 How could the grant help Udit's business?
>
> 2 Describe two other ways a government could support Udit's business.

## 3.5 Ways to measure business size

Some businesses are small and others are classed as large. What is the difference? To help understand this, we need to measure the size of a business.

There are many ways that business size can be measured.

### Number of employees

Counting the number of employees is a quick and simple way to measure business size. You would think a large business is likely to have more employees (see Figure 3.7).

However, two businesses can produce a similar level of output, but one business may use more machinery and fewer employees. Alternatively, the business may have part-time employees who share the work among them. This would add to the total number of employees and make the business look larger than it is.

**Figure 3.7:** Do you think a large business is likely to have more employees?

## Capital employed

This is the total value of all long-term finance invested in a business. It is used to buy the things that a business needs to provide goods and services, for example, the factory/office buildings, machinery and inventory. A small business is likely to invest less capital than a large business in the same industry. For example, a small bakery may only have one shop, one food mixer, one oven and a few raw materials, whereas a large bread manufacturer is likely to have more equipment and a large inventory of raw materials to produce high volumes of output.

Some industries such as car manufacturing might need a large amount of capital investment, but others such as computer software design do not.

## Value of output or sales

The amount businesses earn from selling their products can be used to compare the size of businesses in the same industry. A small business is likely to have less revenue – earnings from sales – than a larger business. For example, a small general store is likely to have fewer customers than a large supermarket and, therefore, will earn less revenue.

However, it can be difficult to compare businesses that sell different products. For example, a designer clothing shop sells a high-value product compared to the low-value products sold by a street vendor. If the two businesses sold the same number of products, the revenues received would be very different (see Figure 3.8).

**Figure 3.8:** Different products can be high value or low value

## Volume of output or sales

Business size can be measured based on the number of units produced or sold. A large business is likely to produce or sell more units. Calculating these numbers should be relatively simple to do.

However, this method ignores the value of each product sold. For example, consider a soft drinks manufacturer and an airplane manufacturer. The airplane manufacturer is likely to build and sell only a small number of airplanes, but the price of each airplane will be significantly higher than the price of each soft drink.

> **TIP**
>
> Profit is not an acceptable measure of business size as there are many factors that influence the amount of profit made by the business.

## Problems of measuring business size

It can be difficult to compare the size of individual businesses. This is because different measures can produce different results. Comparisons between businesses in different industries is not easy to do for many reasons, including:

- Businesses might use different amounts and types of labour.
- The amount or type of machinery used will depend on what they make or sell.
- The value of the product will vary between businesses.

Figure 3.9 shows the advantages and disadvantages of the different ways to measure business size.

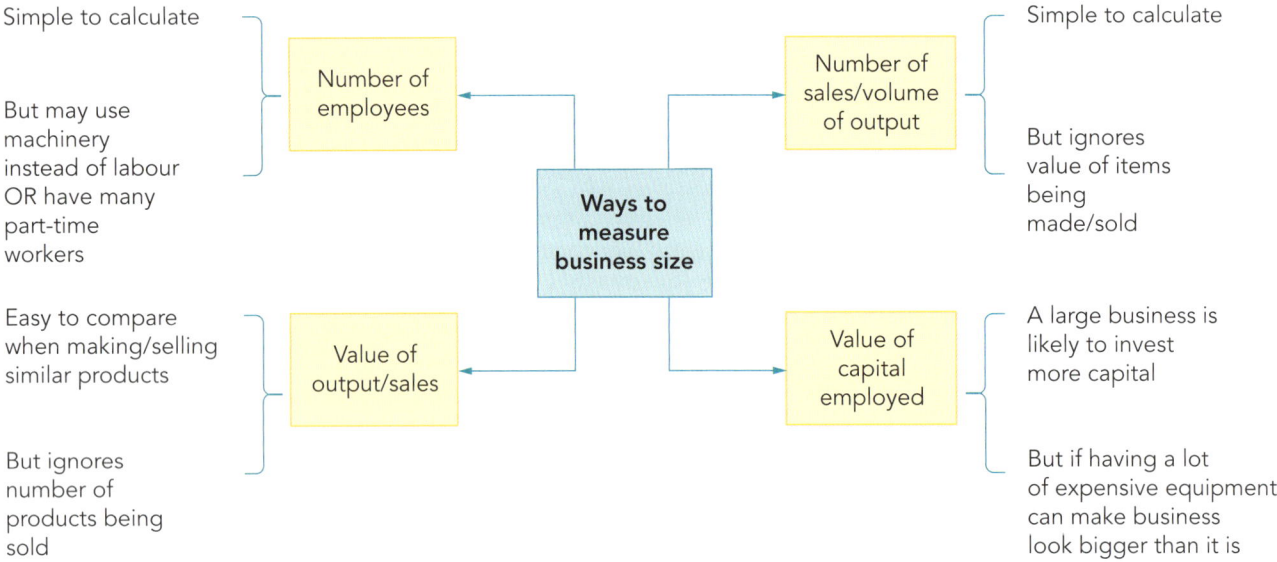

**Figure 3.9:** The different ways to measure business size and the problems of using these measures

### ACTIVITY 3.3

The table below shows data for three businesses that manufacture televisions and other electrical products.

| Business data | Business A | Business B | Business C |
| --- | --- | --- | --- |
| Revenue | $280 000 | $380 000 | $410 000 |
| Capital employed | $200 000 | $500 000 | $350 000 |
| Number of employees | 60 | 35 | 50 |

In pairs or small groups, use the data in the table to answer the following questions.

1. Each business thinks it is the largest in the industry. Why could this be true?
2. Why might the number of employees **not** be a good measure of size in this industry?
3. Which of the three companies do you think is the largest? Give reasons for your answer.

## 3.6 Why some businesses grow and others remain small

Many entrepreneurs may want to grow their businesses but this is not true for all businesses. We will explore the reasons for growth, the different ways a business can grow and the advantages and disadvantages of each way.

### Why business owners might grow a business

Growing a business can bring many advantages including increased profit, increase in market share, lower average costs and spread risk.

#### Increased profit

A larger business may be able to produce more goods or provide more services. If this output is sold then sales increase. Increased sales usually increase revenue and, if the business has kept control of its costs during its growth, it may increase profit.

#### Increase in market share

The larger the share of the market the business has, the more influence it may be able to have over the prices set in the market or its suppliers.

#### Lower average costs

Larger businesses can spread the costs over a larger number of output. Lower average costs may allow the business to lower its prices and become more competitive resulting in higher sales.

#### Spread risk

Growth can provide the opportunity to enter new markets or offer new products, so the business does not have to rely on one set of customers for its sales.

### Different ways businesses can grow

Businesses can grow in different ways, either through internal growth or external growth.

#### Internal growth

Internal growth can happen when a business:

- increases the number of goods it can produce, for example, by buying more or better machinery
- develops a new product
- finds new markets for its products.

Although internal growth is often slow, it can help reduce the risk of losing control which could happen if the business tries to grow too quickly.

## CASE STUDY 3.3

**Yao Secret**

**Figure 3.10:** Shampoo bars are an eco-friendly hair care product

Yao Secret was started in 2021 by Xim Jiao and Nadine Katherine. The business, based in Guangzhou, China, produces a range of beauty products including shampoo bars. Xim and Nadine spotted an opportunity to create a range of sustainable, eco-friendly hair care products using fermented rice water as its main ingredient. Rice water is simply the water used to cook rice, which is then left to turn sour or ferment.

Yao Secret use a unique type of fermented rice water which is obtained directly from the Red Yao tribe in Guangxi, China. Fermented rice water is a traditional method used by the women of this tribe to help maintain healthy hair.

Yao Secret began with just two products: one shampoo bar and one conditioner. Most of the products are sold online to customers in Australia and Europe. However, as sales have increased, the business looked to expand. It has already started selling its products to customers in Singapore and has plans to sell the products in shops in Europe.

**Discuss in pairs or groups:**

1. What type of growth are Yao Secret planning to use?
2. Explain one advantage and one disadvantage to Yao Secret of using this method of growth.
3. Explain another way Yao Secret could expand.

## External growth

External growth takes place when a business merges with or takes over another business in the same or a different industry. The process is known as integration. A **merger** happens when two businesses agree to merge or join whereas a **takeover** is when one business buys the other.

Types of integration include horizontal and vertical integration.

- **Horizontal integration** brings together two firms in the same industry that are also in the same sector of business activity; for example, two wheat farmers (primary sector), two computer manufacturers (secondary sector) or two banks (tertiary sector). The advantages and disadvantages of horizontal integration are shown in Table 3.3.

**Table 3.3:** Advantages and disadvantages of horizontal integration

| Advantages | Disadvantages |
| --- | --- |
| • Reduced competition leading to an increase in market share. | • Increased risk – as operating in same industry if demand falls. |
| • Possible cost savings including bulk discounts as able to order materials in large amounts. | • May be difficult to combine two sets of employees or business systems. |

> **KEY TERMS**
>
> **merger:** when two businesses agree to join to become a single, larger business.
>
> **takeover:** when one business buys a controlling interest in another.
>
> **horizontal integration:** when two businesses at the same stage of production join to become a single, larger business.

Figure 3.11 shows an example of horizontal integration.

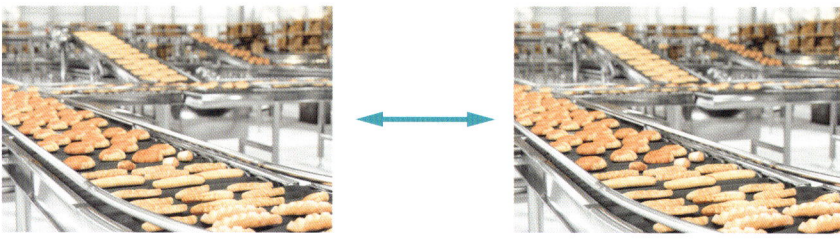

Bread manufacturer          Bread manufacturer

**Figure 3.11:** Example of horizontal integration

- **Vertical integration** brings together two businesses in the same industry, but each one is at a different stage of the production process. Thus, a business could buy another business which is a customer (forward vertical integration) or a supplier (backward vertical integration). For example, a shoe manufacturer and a shoe retailer. The advantages and disadvantages of vertical integration are shown in Table 3.4. An example of vertical integration is shown in Figure 3.12.

> **KEY TERM**
>
> **vertical integration:** when two businesses at different stages of production within the same industry join to become a single, larger business.

**Table 3.4:** Advantages and disadvantages of vertical integration

| Advantages | Disadvantages |
|---|---|
| • Better access to suppliers or customers, which may have a reliable source of materials/products or outlet to sell products. <br> • Helps spread risk as less reliant on one market. | • Few cost savings as both businesses are at different stages of production process. <br> • May be difficult to combine two different businesses leading to higher average costs. |

Forward vertical integration          Backward vertical integration

Bread manufacturer takes over or merges with a bakery shop | Bread manufacturer | Bread manufacturer takes over or merges with a farm growing wheat

**Figure 3.12:** An example of forward and backward vertical integration

## ACTIVITY 3.4

1 Copy and complete the table below.

| Form of integration | Business activity | Business activity |
|---|---|---|
| forward vertical | oil refining | |
| | large car manufacturer | small car manufacturer |
| backward vertical | | fruit canning |

2 Explain one possible advantage to the fruit canning business of backward vertical integration.

3 Discuss the possible advantages to the large and the small car manufacturers of their integration.

The advantages and disadvantages to a business of using internal and external growth are outlined in Table 3.5.

Table 3.5: Advantages and disadvantages to a business of using internal and external growth

| | Internal growth | External growth |
|---|---|---|
| Advantages | • Low cost (compared to external growth).<br>• Easier to manage changes – can reduce the risk.<br>• Owners able to retain control of the business. | • Quick way to grow.<br>• Gain customers of the other business.<br>• Gain assets, technology and skills of other business – leading to new ideas.<br>• Reduce competition – more power to influence prices or suppliers. |
| Disadvantages | • Slow – business may miss out on opportunities and competitors may increase their market share.<br>• Likely to be a limit to possible expansion due to factors such as finance and space. | • High cost of takeover/merger – possible financial problems.<br>• Control and/or communication problems as each business has different ways of working – could lower efficiency. |

> **TIP**
>
> Advantages of one method can sometimes be presented as a disadvantage of another method. For example, internal growth is slow and external growth is quick, but this is the same point. Always try to make clearly different points when answering questions.

## Problems linked to business growth

If the growth is not managed carefully, the expected advantages such as increased market share and spread risk may not happen. Instead, the business will have to manage problems including:

- lower employee motivation – increasing labour turnover
- poor communication – leading to possible errors
- difficult to coordinate operations – reducing efficiency
- difficult to control larger business – leading to mistakes being made
- difficult to raise enough finance to fund the growth
- access to suitable skilled employees
- access to the necessary equipment and resources.

If the business cannot solve these problems, it can lead to higher average costs.

Figure 3.13 provides a summary of the advantages and disadvantages of growth, and the different ways a business might grow.

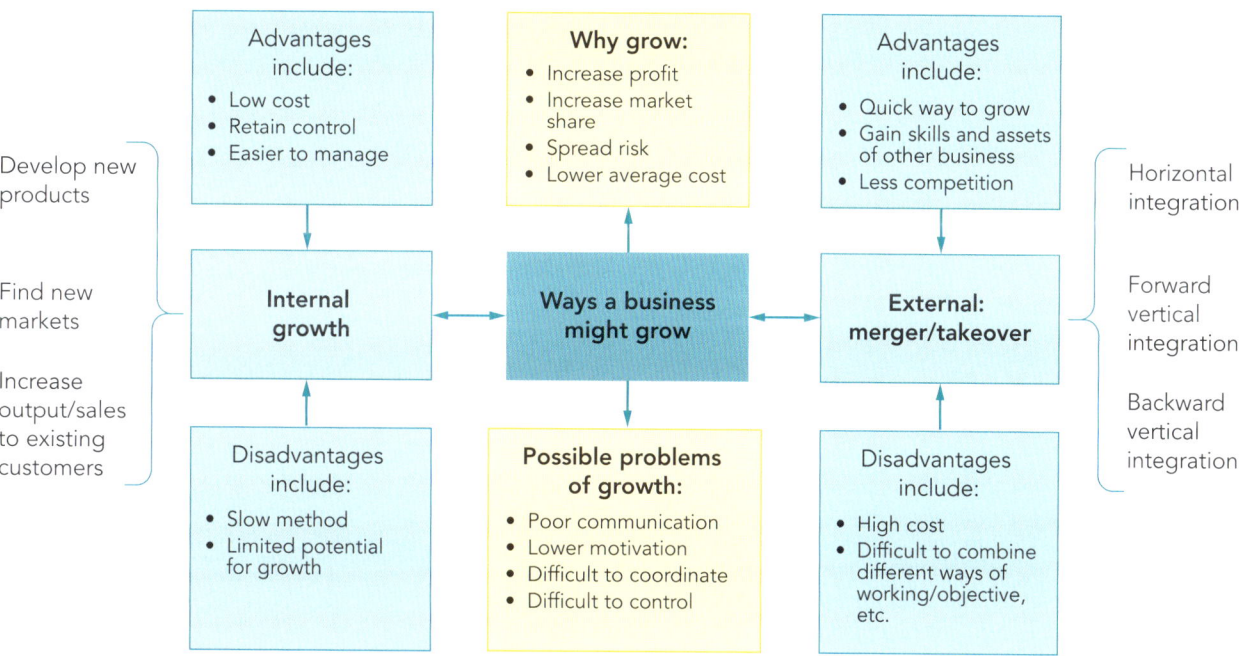

**Figure 3.13:** Advantages and disadvantages of growth

## Why some businesses remain small

Some businesses do not grow or choose to remain small. There are many possible reasons for this, as shown in Table 3.6.

Table 3.6: Reasons why businesses remain small

| Reasons | Why it may be important |
|---|---|
| Owners' choice | May not want the responsibility of managing a larger business<br>May want to keep control of the business |
| Access to and availability of capital | Banks may be less willing to lend to small businesses as they are perceived to have a higher risk of failure, so difficult to borrow the amount of funds needed to grow the business |
| Market size | If the market the business operates in is small, there may be limited potential for growth |
| Type of product/service offered | Some businesses only serve customers in the local area or offer specialist services, so have few customers to target |

# 3.7 Why some businesses are successful and others fail

Businesses are not always successful. Many new businesses fail within the first one or two years of trading. Even long-established businesses can fail. But why? Figure 3.14 highlights the main factors.

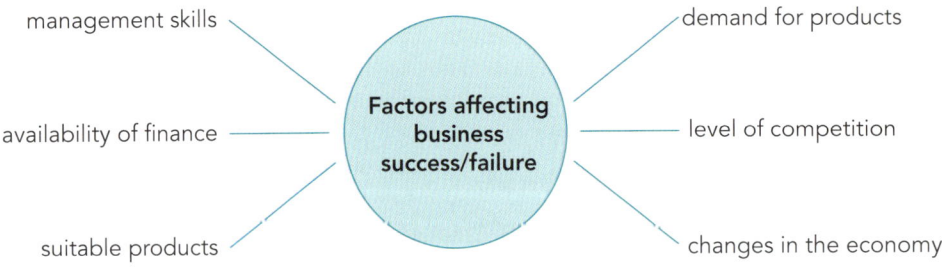

Figure 3.14: Factors affecting whether businesses are successful or fail

## Management skills
Business owners need to have the necessary management skills and experience to run their business efficiently. For example, having the ability to organise, control, coordinate, plan activities and command people within the business.

## Availability of finance
Finance is needed to buy new equipment or buildings and to pay the day-to-day expenses from operating the business. A business must have access to sufficient finance to take full advantage of the opportunities available to them.

## Suitable products
Businesses must produce and sell goods and services that customers need or want to buy. If not, the business will not be able to earn sufficient revenue to cover its costs.

> **LINKS**
>
> You can find more information about finance in Chapter 21, and market research in Chapter 11.

# 3 Enterprise, business growth and size

## Demand for products
Successful businesses are ones that can identify and meet the needs of its customers. Market research can help identify the potential size of the market, the level of competition and what consumers need or want. Businesses that do not carry out market research are more likely to fail.

## Level of competition
All businesses face competition. Other businesses are likely to be selling similar products and services. Businesses that are unable to compete on price and quality are unlikely to survive in the long run.

## Changes in the economy
Many factors such as unemployment, high interest rates and taxation may reduce the amount of money consumers have to spend on goods and services. This can reduce the number of sales for a business. Does the business have the finance available to continue if it is unable to cover its costs?

> **LINK**
>
> You can find more information about changes in the economy in Chapter 27.

### ACTIVITY 3.5

1. In pairs/small groups, research a successful business from your country. Each group should research a different business.

2. Prepare a short report (maximum 100 words) to the owners of the business explaining three reasons why the business is successful. Share your report with the class.

### BUSINESS IN ACTION

#### Starbucks

**Figure 3.15:** Starbucks sells a range of products in its shops

Even successful businesses do not get it right every time. Knowing when to stop or pull out when a project is not working is important. If not, the whole business might fail.

Starbucks started as a small coffee beans shop in Seattle in the 1970s. The business was then bought by Howard Schulz, who turned Starbucks into one of the largest chains of coffee shops in the world. Starbucks sells a wide range of products including different types of coffee, other drinks with different syrups or toppings and sweet treats such as doughnuts. Customers can drink or eat the products in the shop or take them away to consume elsewhere.

In 2000, Starbucks decided to open its first coffee shop in Australia. Market research showed that Australians love coffee – at least 75% of them drink at least one cup of coffee each day – but most tend

> **CONTINUED**
>
> to drink coffee at home or at a local independent coffee shop. The most popular drinks for Australians are instant coffee or espresso. Australian customers are less interested in the flavoured or sweet coffee-based drinks sold by Starbucks, which tend to be more expensive to buy.
>
> Starbucks struggled to gain the sales it needed to cover its costs. In 2008, Starbuck's directors took the decision to close two-thirds of its shops in Australia, after making a loss of $105 million.
>
> **Discuss in small groups or as a class:**
> 1. Why was Starbucks not successful in Australia?
> 2. When is the right time for a business to stop or pull out of an idea or project? Be ready to support your point of view.

> **SUMMARY**
>
> You should now know:
>
> - An entrepreneur is someone who has an idea for a new business and is prepared to take the financial risk to set it up.
> - A business plan provides purpose and direction for the business by clearly setting out details such as the objectives, financial information and the resources needed to achieve these objectives.
> - Capital employed, number of employees, value of output or sales, and volume of output or sales are the ways to measure business size.
> - Although some businesses might remain small, others will choose to grow using internal or external methods including developing new products and horizontal or vertical integration.
> - There are many reasons why some businesses are successful and others fail, including level of competition, demand for products, management skills and availability of finance.

# Chapter 3 practice questions

1. Grace wants to be a successful entrepreneur. She would like to start up a business making furniture out of sustainable wood, including mango wood. Grace is considering selling the furniture at local markets. She has found a factory where she can make the products, but the rent is $110 per week. Grace knows preparing a business plan is important, but she has no experience of preparing one. She has also been told government support is available to help start-up businesses.

    a. Define 'entrepreneur'. [2]

    b. Identify **four** characteristics of a successful entrepreneur. [4]

    c. Explain **two** advantages to Grace of preparing a business plan. [6]

    d. Explain **two** methods of government support that might be available to Grace. Which is likely to be the best method for Grace to use? Justify your answer. [8]

2. PTR is a large business with 5000 employees. It manufactures a range of low-cost jewellery including rings and necklaces. PTR has three factories across the country, with each specialising in making different products. PTR's Managing Director wants to grow the business. One option is to take over one of its competitors, MSL. MSL employs 3000 skilled workers to make its high-quality jewellery. Some of PTR's directors are worried about the possible problems linked to growth.

   a  State **two** ways (other than employees) of measuring the size of a business. [2]

   b  Outline **two** reasons why the Managing Director of PTR wants to grow the business. [4]

   c  Explain **two** problems for PTR linked to business growth. [6]

   d  Do you think the advantages to PTR of taking over one of its competitors are greater than the disadvantages? Justify your answer. [8]

   Total available marks: 40

## CHECK YOUR PROGRESS

How well do you think you have achieved the learning intentions for this chapter? Give yourself a score from 1 (still need a lot of practice) to 5 (feeling very confident) for each learning intention. Provide an example to support your score.

| Now I can … | Score | Example |
| --- | --- | --- |
| explain the characteristics of successful entrepreneurs | | |
| understand the key elements of a business plan and provide reasons why a business plan is important | | |
| explain why and how governments support business start-ups | | |
| identify the methods and problems of measuring business size | | |
| understand the reasons why some businesses grow and others remain small | | |
| describe the different ways a business can grow, both internally and externally | | |
| explain the advantages and disadvantages of different methods of growth | | |
| explain the reasons why some businesses succeed and others fail. | | |

# Chapter 4
# Types of business organisations

### LEARNING INTENTIONS

By the end of this chapter, you will be able to:

- identify the different types of business organisations – sole traders, partnerships, private and public limited companies
- explain the advantages and disadvantages of the different types of business organisations
- recommend the best type of business organisation to use in a given situation
- understand the different forms of business organisations – franchises, joint ventures and social enterprises
- explain the advantages and disadvantages of franchises to franchisors and franchisees
- explain the advantages and disadvantages of joint ventures.

4 Types of business organisations

# Introduction

In this chapter, you will learn about the different types of organisations found in the private sector. You will learn about the advantages and disadvantages of different forms of private sector organisations, and how entrepreneurs choose the best form of organisation for their business.

## BUSINESS IN CONTEXT

### Handmade Heroes

Singapore has a population of 5.4 million. In 2023, Singapore was ranked as one of the best places in Asia to start a business. In November 2023, ACRA data showed there were over 587 000 businesses operating in Singapore, as shown in Figure 4.1.

One of these businesses is Handmade Heroes, which produces a range of handmade skincare products. All products are made using natural ingredients without any chemicals or plastics, such as microbeads, which can pollute the sea.

Back in 2015, Lynsey Lin could not find any skincare products suitable for her sensitive skin, so she started making her own lip balms and face creams in her kitchen. Lynsey then started giving her balms and creams to family and friends as gifts. It was only when others asked if they could buy Lynsey's balms and creams that Handmade Heroes was started.

Starting from a two-person operation, the business has grown significantly. To help finance its growth, Handmade Heroes became a private limited company (a type of business with shareholders). Handmade Heroes' products are sold to customers around the world, often through online retailers including Amazon. To meet the high demand, Handmade Heroes has already built its first factory in Malaysia and a second factory is planned.

**Types of business in Singapore (%), Nov 2023**

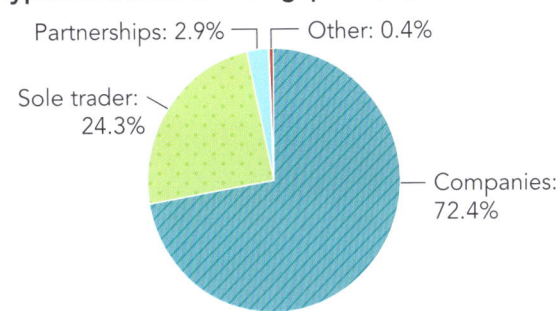

**Figure 4.1:** Types of businesses in Singapore as of November 2023

### Discuss in pairs or groups:

1. Using the data provided, which are the two most common types of business organisations in Singapore?

2. Why do you think there are different types of business organisations? Make a list of possible reasons.

57

# 4.1 Forms of business organisations

Business organisations in the private sector are defined by their legal structure. Figure 4.2 shows the types of business organisations you need to study as part of your Cambridge IGCSE/O Level Business course.

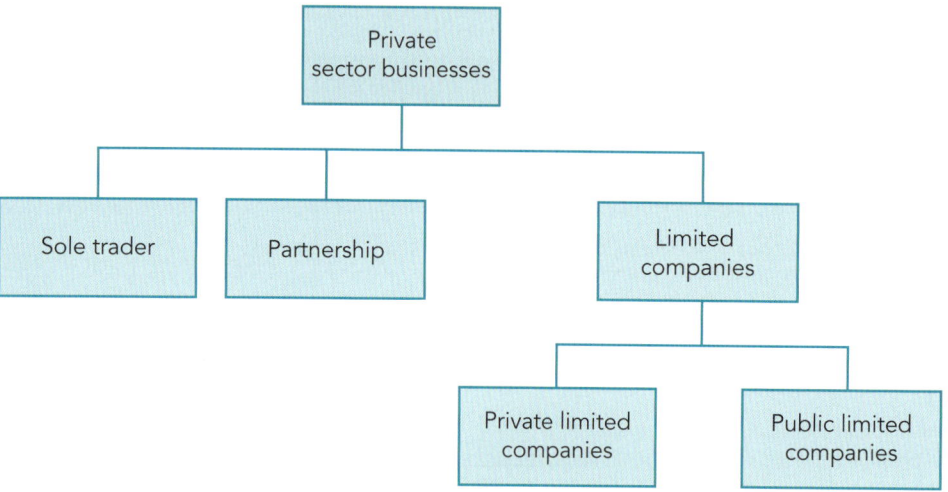

Figure 4.2: Main types of business organisations in the private sector

### TIP

Do not confuse sole traders and small businesses. They are different concepts. While most sole traders are small businesses not every small business is a sole trader.

## Sole traders

The most common type of private sector business is a **sole trader**. The business has one owner but can have employees to help with the work. Sole trader businesses are usually small in size and may remain small. Examples include hairdressers, plumbers and street vendors.

### KEY TERM

**sole trader:** a business that is owned and controlled by just one person.

### LINKS

You can find more information about reasons why businesses remain small in Chapter 3, and sources of business finance in Chapter 22.

Figure 4.3: A customer having their hair dried by a hairdresser

# 4 Types of business organisations

Being a sole trader allows the person to be their own boss; they can make all the decisions and keep all the profits. However, they have unlimited liability – this means the owner is fully responsible for the debts of the business and risks losing personal possessions, such as their house, to pay for any unpaid business debts. The advantages and disadvantages of sole traders are shown in Table 4.1.

Table 4.1: Advantages and disadvantages of being a sole trader

| Advantages | Disadvantages |
| --- | --- |
| • Quick and easy to set up, as there are few legal requirements to complete. | • Unlimited liability, which risk losing personal assets to pay business debts. |
| • Owner is their own boss/has complete control, so no need to consult with anyone before making a decision. | • Limited access to sources of finance – can be difficult to raise funds to expand the business. |
| • Keep all the profit, so owner has an incentive to keep working hard. | • No one to share decision-making with, which may lead to wrong decisions. |
| • Business/financial information is kept private (no one to share loss or risk with). | • No continuity – business will no longer exist if the owner is not able or does not want to operate the business. |
| • Can make all the decisions. | • No one to share loss or risks with. |
| • Able to choose when to work. | • May have to work long hours. |

## ACTIVITY 4.1

Aaron does not like working in an office and plans to leave to start up a window cleaning business. Aaron has identified he will need a ladder, buckets and sponges and a vehicle so that he can visit customer's houses. He likes the idea of being a sole trader because it is easy to set up, but does not know why this is important. He would like you to explain why this might be an advantage for his business.

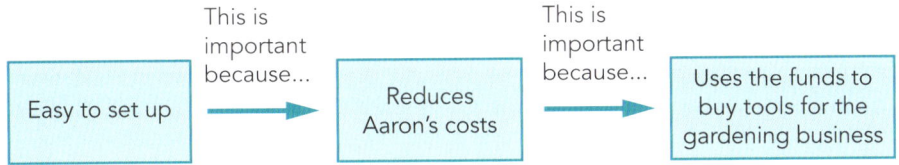

Figure 4.4: Advantage of sole trader for window cleaning business

1. Individually, copying the example in Figure 4.4, draw three boxes with arrows linking the boxes together. Write 'Own boss' in the first box. In the second box, provide one reason why this is important. In the third box, develop this reason.

2. Repeat the activity with each of the following starting words – 'unlimited liability' and 'limited access to finance'.

3. In pairs, compare your answers. Did you develop the points in the same way? Do you think each other's answers make sense? Give reasons.

## TIP

When asked to explain statements in an answer (like in Activity 4.1), think about why or how the point you have identified is likely to be important and how it might or might not help the business.

## Partnerships

A **partnership** is formed when at least two people agree to set up and run a business together. Partnerships are relatively easy to set up (but not as easy as sole trader). A legal agreement may be signed setting out the rights and obligations of each partner, but this is not essential. Examples of business partnerships include professional services such as accountancy and legal firms.

> **KEY TERM**
>
> **partnership:** a business owned and controlled by two or more people.

Figure 4.5: An accountant preparing financial data

Partnerships share some of the advantages of sole traders, but can help avoid some of the disadvantages. For example, a partnership is likely to have greater access to finance because there is more than one person investing funds. However, both are unincorporated businesses. This means the owners and the business are legally viewed as the same. Owners are responsible for the debts of the business, so have unlimited liability. Table 4.2 outlines some of the advantages and disadvantages of partnerships.

Table 4.2: Advantages and disadvantages of a business partnership

| Advantages | Disadvantages |
| --- | --- |
| • Additional finance can be raised (compared to a sole trader) as all partners contribute funds.<br>• Can share workload/responsibilities – allows time for each partner to focus/specialise on different activities.<br>• Greater range of skills/ideas – can help business be more competitive.<br>• Decision-making is shared – may lead to better decisions.<br>• Partners can share the costs – this can reduce the risk and potential losses. | • Unlimited liability – personal possessions of partners are at risk if the business cannot pay its debts.<br>• Risk of disagreements, which can slow down decision-making.<br>• Must share any profit made.<br>• If one of the partners leaves, the business will no longer exist (no continuity).<br>• All partners are bound by the decisions of other partners. |

## 4 Types of business organisations

### ACTIVITY 4.2

1. Individually, draw two overlapping circles. In one circle, write the advantages and disadvantages of being a sole trader. In the other circle, write the advantages and disadvantages of being in a partnership. In the overlapping section, write down the points that are true for both types of business organisations. A partially completed example is shown in Figure 4.6.

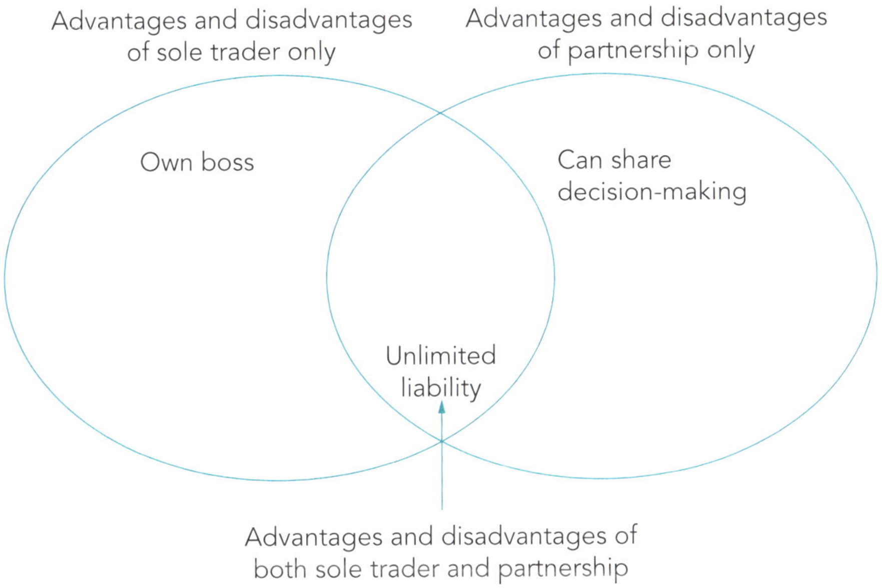

Advantages and disadvantages of sole trader only — Own boss

Advantages and disadvantages of partnership only — Can share decision-making

Advantages and disadvantages of both sole trader and partnership — Unlimited liability

**Figure 4.6:** Partially completed Venn diagram comparing sole traders with partnerships

2. In pairs or small groups compare your answers. Discuss any differences and update your diagram as necessary.

### TIP

It is important to understand the differences between sole trader and partnerships. While they both share some common advantages or disadvantages, there are not the same types of business.

### KEY TERMS

**shareholder:** a person or organisation who buys shares in a limited company, which means they own part of the business.

**limited liability:** owners of a company are only responsible for the debts of the business up to the amount they have invested in the company.

## Limited companies

A limited company is a business that is owned by its **shareholders**. These are investors who invest money in the company in exchange for shares – each share represents a unit of ownership. Limited companies are different to sole traders and partnerships because the business has a separate legal identity to the owners. This allows the owners to benefit from **limited liability** – this means the owners are not fully responsible for business debts. Unlike, sole traders and partnerships, the personal possessions of shareholders are not at risk if the business cannot pay its debts.

There are two types of limited companies:
- private limited companies
- public limited companies.

## Private limited companies

These businesses are owned by shareholders and usually only have a small number of shareholders. Most of the shareholders are likely to be family members or close friends. The word 'private' is important. This means shares cannot be freely sold to anyone who wants to buy them, and all the shareholders must agree to the sale or purchase of the shares.

The advantages of a **private limited company** include:

- **Can raise finance by selling shares** – these funds can be used to finance growth.
- **Limited liability for owners** – so personal possessions are protected, which helps reduce risk.
- **Continuity** – the business will still exist even if one or more shareholders leaves or sells their shares.
- **Can control who buys shares** – this can reduce the risk of takeover without agreement of owners.

However, the disadvantages include:

- **Cannot sell shares on the stock exchange** (a marketplace where shares are bought and sold) – this can restrict the amount of funds raised.
- **Some financial information must be made available for the public to look at** – competitors may find out information that could allow other business to gain a competitive advantage.
- **Large amount of paperwork to complete** – this can increase costs.
- **Owners may expect dividends** (a share of the profit that represents a return on the investment) – this can reduce the funds available for reinvestment.

> **KEY TERM**
>
> **private limited company:** business that is owned by shareholders that can only sell its shares to family and friends.

> **TIP**
>
> Make sure you understand the difference between unlimited and limited liability, and what this means for the owners of a business.

### CASE STUDY 4.1

**Karma Drinks**

Karma Drinks manufactures a range of soft drinks using ethically sourced ingredients. For example, the cola nuts for its Karma Cola are bought directly from small-scale farmers in Sierra Leone (see Figure 4.7). This ensures the farmers who grow the cola nuts receive a fair price for their products. The business also donates a share of the money made from sales of its products to the farming communities.

Karma Drinks was originally set up by three friends – Chris, Matt and Simon – in 2012 as a business partnership and became a private limited company two years later. As sales increased, the business was able to expand its product range. The directors know that trying to sell their products is difficult in a market where there are so many soft drinks available for customers to choose from. Today, Karma Drinks is still a small business with about 25 employees, but the owners have plans to grow the business.

**Discuss in pairs or groups:**

1. Why do you think Karma Drinks started as a business partnership?
2. Explain two possible advantages to Karma Drinks becoming a private limited company.

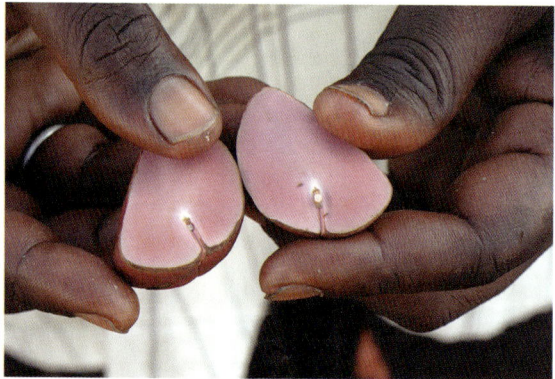

**Figure 4.7:** Karma Drinks manufactures a range of soft drinks using ethically sourced ingredients

## 4 Types of business organisations

## Public limited companies

A **public limited company** is owned by shareholders. This type of business tends to be larger than private limited companies. One reason for this is access to finance. While both public and private limited businesses can sell shares – the difference is who can buy these shares.

The word 'public' means anyone can buy or sell shares in a public limited company. This can provide both advantages and disadvantages to the business and its owners, as outlined in Figure 4.8.

> **KEY TERM**
>
> **public limited company:** business that is owned by shareholders that can sell its shares to the general public.

**Advantages**
- Limited liability
- Can sell shares on stock exchange
- Able to raise large amount of finance
- Shares do not need to be repaid

**Public limited company**

**Disadvantages**
- Must publish financial information
- Cannot control who buys shares
- Many legal requirements to complete
- Selling shares to public is expensive

**Figure 4.8:** Advantages and disadvantages of a public limited company

### CASE STUDY 4.2

**Tao Kae Noi**

**Figure 4.9:** Seaweed is a natural ingredient that can be used to make snacks

Tao Kae Noi is a well-known seaweed-based snack from Thailand. The business was started by Itthipat Peeradechapan when he was 19 years old. Itthipat developed a new way of cooking seaweed to produce his first crisps, which he sold to one local supermarket in Thailand. Seaweed is a healthy, natural ingredient that contains lots of vitamins and minerals. The crisps soon became popular with customers and the business grew quickly. Within five years, Tao Kae Noi had become a private limited company and was exporting the crisps to other countries. As demand increased, the business built a second factory in Thailand. The owners then took the decision to become a public limited company allowing its shares to be sold on the Thai Stock Exchange. Itthipat Peeradechapan was named as Chief Executive Officer (Managing Director). Horizontal integration has also been used to grow the business. For example, Tao Kae Noi bought a manufacturing business in the United States to further increase production of its seaweed crisps.

**Discuss in pairs or groups:**
1 What might be the possible reasons why Tao Kae Noi became a public limited company?
2 What might be the possible disadvantages of Tao Kae Noi being a public limited company?

While private and public limited companies share some common features, such as limited liability and the ability to raise funds by selling shares, it is important to understand there are differences too. For example, who can buy the shares, how easy is it to sell the shares and how much finance each type of business organisation can raise from selling shares.

> ### ACTIVITY 4.3
>
> 1. Individually, using information you have learnt, produce a summary explaining the main differences between a private limited company and a public limited company. This could be a simple mind map or poster.
>
>    Factors to consider include: how many shareholders does the business have, who can buy the shares, how easy is it to buy and sell shares and how much capital can be raised.
>
> 2. Use this information to confirm whether the following statements are true or false:
>
>    a  A public limited company can sell shares to the general public.
>
>    b  A private limited company has lots of shareholders.
>
>    c  A private limited company is likely to be able to raise more finance than a public limited company.

> ### TIP
>
> Do not confuse public limited companies with public sector organisations. Public limited companies are in the private sector. Public sector organisations are owned and controlled by the government on behalf of the people.

## Franchises

A **franchise** is not a legal type of business but a legal agreement between two businesses where one business which already has a successful product or service – called the franchisor – agrees to allow another business – the franchisee – to use the franchisor's trade name, logo and products in exchange for a license fee.

The franchisee makes the decision about whether to operate as a sole trader, a partnership or a limited company.

For the franchisor, it is a quicker and cheaper way to grow because the franchisee is responsible for the day-to-day running of the business, and they receive a share of the profits from the franchisee.

Entrepreneurs may decide to enter into a franchise agreement because this can reduce the risk of failure compared to setting up their own business.

Examples of franchises include Steers of South Africa and Tumbledry in India. Buying a franchise can also be a good way for a business to grow into other countries. For example, Marrybrown started in Malaysia but now has franchises in countries including the United Arab Emirates and Tanzania.

The advantages and disadvantages to both the franchisor and franchisee of entering a franchise agreement are outlined in Figure 4.10.

> ### KEY TERM
>
> **franchise:** a business agreement where one person or business buys the right to use the name, logo and product of an existing business.

# 4 Types of business organisations

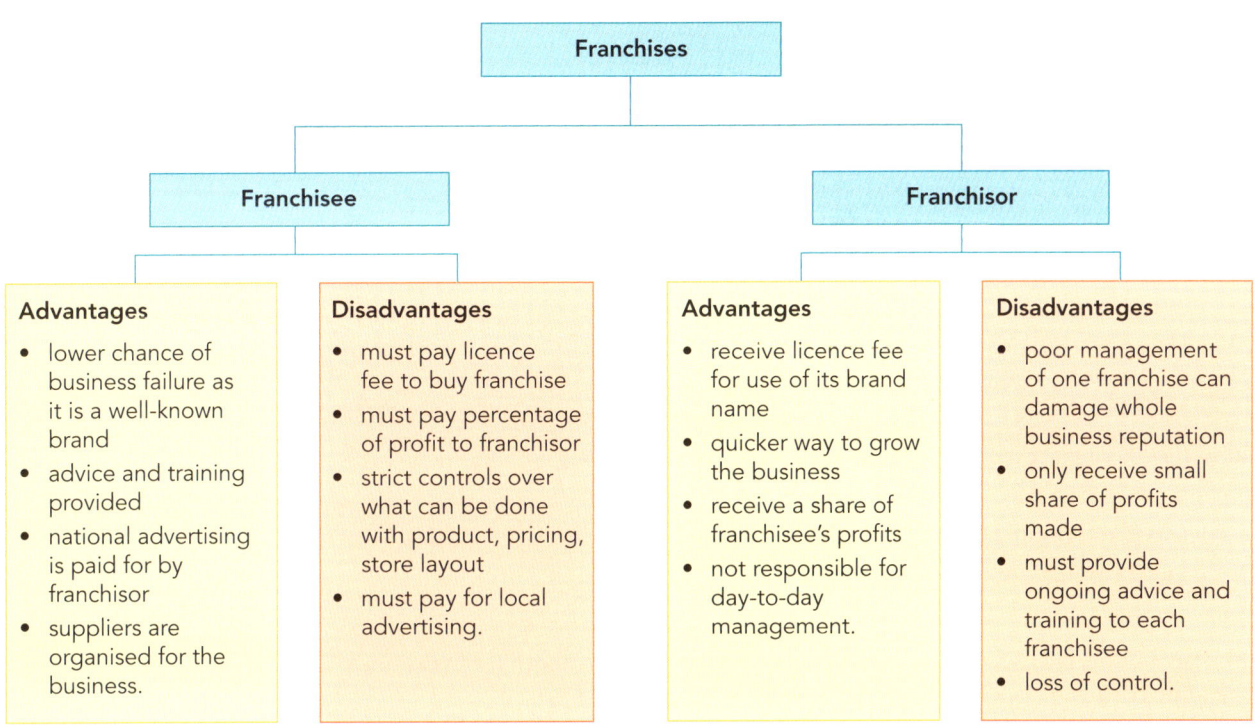

**Figure 4.10:** Advantages and disadvantages to both the franchisor and franchisee of entering a franchise agreement

## ACTIVITY 4.4

Read the following franchise opportunities.

### 100% Natural Frozen Yoghurt

This is a great opportunity to sell healthy, natural frozen yoghurt in your own store. Your customers will love serving themselves with treats from the delicious menu, which features a natural frozen yoghurt selection. It also includes fruit smoothies with a wide choice of fresh fruit toppings including strawberry, blueberry, kiwi, pineapple and mango.

### Affordable House Cleaning

The house cleaning industry is lifestyle friendly. Unlike restaurant or retail industries, cleaning can be completed within normal business hours. Customers want to come home from work to a clean living space, which in turn creates a flexible schedule for you.

### Fabulous Mobile Phone Accessories (FMPA)

Our products and services allow people to express themselves through their most visible accessory – their phone. FMPA offers a wide selection of fashionable accessories, as well as providing services like phone repair, at shopping mall-based kiosks.

## TIP

Do not confuse a franchisor with a franchisee. Franchisors sell the franchise and franchisees buy it.

> **CONTINUED**
>
> 1. In pairs, discuss whether you think each of the three franchise businesses might work in your local area.
>
> 2. Choose the one which you think has the best chance of success; it does not have to be the same one as the person you are working with.
>
> 3. Write a short report explaining **two** reasons for your choice.

## Joint ventures

A **joint venture** is when two or more businesses work closely together on a business opportunity or project. The main advantages for a joint venture are:

- Share costs and resources – this can reduce the financial risk for each business.

- Each business brings different expertise – which can help with new ideas and solutions.

- Market and product knowledge can be shared to the benefit of both businesses in the joint venture.

However, there are disadvantages, including:

- Any mistakes may damage the reputation of each business in the joint venture, even if they were not the cause of the mistake.

- The businesses may have different ways of working or leadership styles, so decision-making can be difficult.

- Each business will have to share any profit made.

> **KEY TERM**
>
> **joint venture:** two or more businesses agree to work together on a project and set up a separate business for this purpose.

> **TIP**
>
> A joint venture is not the same as a merger or takeover. In a joint venture the businesses remain as separate organisations.

### CASE STUDY 4.3

**Jardine Schindler**

Jardine Schindler Group (JSG) is a joint venture between Jardine Matheson of Hong Kong, China (SAR) and the Schindler Group of Switzerland. The Schindler Group was started in 1874 to design, manufacture and install specialist elevators and moving walkways. It has 69 000 employees across 100 countries, with factories in Brazil, China, India, the United States as well as in Europe. Jardine Matheson is one of the largest businesses in Hong Kong, China (SAR) with over $109 billion in revenue. It operates in many different industries, including transport, engineering and construction of shopping centres, hotels and offices. The business has over 425 000 employees, who each have a wide range of skills and experiences.

**Figure 4.11:** A moving walkway being used by customers in a Bangkok shopping mall

> **CONTINUED**
>
> JSG is based in Hong Kong, China (SAR). The joint venture means Schindler's high-quality products can be easily used in buildings and projects built and managed by Jardine Matheson. JSG elevators (lifts) and moving walkways can be found in hotels, airports and shopping centres across Asia, including in Brunei, Cambodia, Hong Kong, China (SAR), Macau, China (SAR), Malaysia, Myanmar, Indonesia, the Philippines, Singapore, Thailand and Vietnam. An example of a moving walkway is shown in Figure 4.11.
>
> **Discuss in pairs or groups:**
>
> 1 Discuss one way in which Jardine Matheson and Schindler benefit from being in a joint venture.
>
> 2 Discuss the possible disadvantages for Jardine Matheson and Schindler being in a joint venture.

# Choosing the type of business organisation

There are many types of business organisations, from sole traders to public limited companies. It is important to understand there is no perfect type of business organisation – each business must choose the best option based on its individual situation.

However, there are many common factors to consider. These include:

- **Whether it is a new or existing business** – Most businesses start as a sole trader or partnership because these are easier to set up. To become a limited company will involve completing many legal forms.
- **Business objectives** – Some businesses want to grow and others remain small. Limited companies are likely to provide access to more sources of finance to fund growth.
- **Control** – Sole traders have full control of the day-to-day business decisions whereas shareholders in public limited companies have little to no influence.
- **Attitude to risk** – The owners of sole trader businesses and partnerships have unlimited liability and owners in limited companies benefit from limited liability.
- **Potential size of the market** – Most businesses start small and many will remain small because of factors such as size of the market or the owners' choice. These businesses are more likely to be set up and remain as sole traders or partnerships.

> **TIP**
>
> It is highly unlikely a start-up business would choose to be a public limited company due to the costs and time involved.

> **LINKS**
>
> You can find more information about business objectives in Chapter 5, and sources of finance in Chapter 21.

> **ACTIVITY 4.5**
>
> Ousmane has worked in a bank for ten years but wants to leave because he does not like taking orders from his manager. Ousmane plans to set up a photography business and has identified he will need to buy equipment including cameras and lenses. Ousmane will also need a vehicle to transport his equipment around. The total cost to start his business is likely to be $3 000, which is the same amount Ousmane has in his savings account. His friend, Mariama, is also a keen photographer who has won awards in local competitions. Mariama has offered to start up the business with Ousmane if he wants a business partner.

> BUSINESS FOR CAMBRIDGE IGCSE™ AND O LEVEL: COURSEBOOK

### CONTINUED

Imagine you are a business advisor and you have been asked to recommend a suitable type of business organisation for Ousmane.

1. Discuss the advantages and disadvantages of two possible types of business organisations that Ousmane could choose.

2. Write a short email to Ousmane stating which type of business you would recommend. Give reasons for your choice, include why this option is better than the alternative.

### REFLECTION

How did you decide which option to recommend to Ousmane? Were any factors more important than others when making your decision?

Compare your answers with another student's. Did you choose the same option? If so, did you give the same reasons? If your answers were different, can you understand the reason for their choice? Could you explain your approach to the other student? Find out how they approached the task. Can you learn anything from their approach?

## Social enterprises

**Social enterprises** produce goods or services and sell them to customers just like other private sector businesses. However, social enterprises put social objectives before financial objectives such as profit. This means any profit made is likely to be reinvested into the business to expand their activities or used to benefit the local community or other groups.

This is a different approach to most other private sector businesses whose owners or shareholders may expect a share of profit as a reward for their risk or financial investment.

Social enterprises still need to choose a legal structure for their business, and many choose to operate as a limited company to take advantage of this type of business organisation.

### KEY TERM

**social enterprise:** a business with social objectives that reinvests most of its profits back into the business or into benefiting society at large.

### BUSINESS IN ACTION

**Tony's Chocolonely**

Chocolate is big business. Statista estimated the total value of chocolate sales around the world in 2023 to be $238.5 billion.

Tony's Chocolonely is a chocolate manufacturer based in the Netherlands. It is a social enterprise. When a Dutch journalist found out that many chocolate manufacturers used child labour or unpaid workers to grow the cocoa beans on farms, he decided to start up his own business.

The main objective of Tony's Chocolonely is to help cocoa growers in Africa receive fair payment for their products. The amount paid to each farmer for the cocoa beans is 25% higher than the standard price paid by most manufacturers. The growers can then use the money they receive to send their children to school or buy food in their local communities.

## 4 Types of business organisations

### CONTINUED

Figure 4.12: A cocoa farm with ripe pods growing on the cocoa trees

However, only using ethically sourced cocoa beans does increase the cost of ingredients. Higher costs mean the price of its chocolate bars is higher than many of its competitors. This could mean fewer sales. Higher costs and fewer sales can lead to low profit, which might mean less funds to finance growth. Unlike many of its competitors, none of the profit made by Tony's Chocolonely goes to shareholders.

Discuss in small groups or as a class:

1  Tony's Chocolonely is a social enterprise. What evidence in the case study supports this statement?
2  Do you think it is possible for all businesses to operate as social enterprises?

### SUMMARY

You should now know:

- The main forms of business organisations found in the private sector are sole trader, partnerships and limited companies – namely private limited companies and public limited companies.
- There are advantages and disadvantages to each type of business organisation.
- A franchise is an agreement between a franchisor (the owner of a well-known brand) and a franchisee (a business who pays to use the brand name of the other business).
- A joint venture is an agreement between two businesses to work together on a specific project.
- When choosing a suitable type of business organisation, a business will consider a number of factors including whether it is a new or existing business, its objectives and the owners' attitude to risk.
- A social enterprise is a private sector business that makes profit not for the owners or investors, but to benefit local communities and reinvest to grow the business.

## Chapter 4 practice questions

1  An and Bo are in partnership together. Their business, A&B, sells electric bicycles and e-scooters at their shop in the city centre. A&B has been operating for 2 years and is profitable. The owners want to grow the business and plan to offer a repair service for customers. However, the partners do not have the capital needed for this expansion. Bo's sister, Jiao, has offered to become a partner and invest $10 000. An and Bo are considering changing the legal structure to a private limited company.

| | | |
|---|---|---|
| a | Identify **two** features of private sector organisations. | [2] |
| b | Identify **two** advantages and **two** disadvantages to An and Bo being in a business partnership. | [4] |
| c | Explain **two** benefits to An and Bo expanding their business. | [6] |
| d | Do you think the advantages to An and Bo changing the business to a private limited company are greater than the disadvantages? Justify your answer. | [8] |

2  MTR is a public limited company based in Country X. It builds motorways and other types of road networks. KCD is a business in Country Y. It manufactures large earth-moving equipment for use in the construction industry. The government of Country Y has recently announced plans to build a new motorway that will run 120 km from the north to the south of the country. MTR has asked KCD to join it in a joint venture to build the new motorway.

| | | |
|---|---|---|
| a | Define 'private sector'. | [2] |
| b | Outline **two** advantages to MTR being a public limited company. | [4] |
| c | Explain **two** possible reasons why MTR might want to expand into Country Y. | [6] |
| d | Do you think MTR should enter into a joint venture with KCD? Justify your answer. | [8] |

**Total available marks: 40**

## CHECK YOUR PROGRESS

How well do you think you have achieved the learning intentions for this chapter? Give yourself a score from 1 (still need a lot of practice) to 5 (feeling very confident) for each learning intention. Provide an example to support your score.

| Now I can ... | Score | Example |
|---|---|---|
| identify the different types of business organisations – sole trader, partnerships, private and public limited companies | | |
| explain the advantages and disadvantages of the different types of business organisations | | |
| recommend the best type of business organisation to use in a given situation | | |
| understand the different forms of business organisations – franchises, joint ventures and social enterprises | | |
| explain the advantages and disadvantages of franchises to franchisors and franchisees | | |
| explain the advantages and disadvantages of joint ventures | | |
| understand the purpose of a social enterprise. | | |

# Chapter 5
# Business objectives and stakeholder objectives

### LEARNING INTENTIONS

By the end of this chapter, you will be able to:

- identify the different objectives a business can have
- understand why objectives are important for a business
- identify different stakeholder groups and their objectives
- explain the role of different stakeholder groups in a business
- understand how the objectives of different stakeholder groups can conflict.

# Introduction

The things you want to do and achieve are your personal objectives. How you achieve your personal objectives will not happen by accident. They require careful planning. Objectives help as they can provide you with a target – something to aim for.

Just as you have things that you want to do and achieve, so do businesses. Each business will have its own objectives – statements of what it wants to achieve through its activities. These activities are likely to affect individuals or groups inside and outside the business – stakeholders. However, not all these different groups will have the same objectives and this may lead to conflict.

## BUSINESS IN CONTEXT

### One brick at a time!

According to the Global Status Report for building and construction, the construction industry and the buildings and structures created by these businesses are responsible for about 37% of all carbon emissions. Reasons for this include the use of fossil fuels and the traditional process of making building materials such as cement and bricks. However, there is an increasing number of businesses that are trying to make construction more sustainable.

Ecotel is a start-up business in Pakistan. The business collects old vehicle tyres, which are difficult to recycle and often end up in landfill sites, and turns the tyres into bricks (see Figure 5.1). Ecotel's process involves washing the tyres before cutting them up into small pieces and mixing the rubber pieces with other waste materials to produce environmentally friendly bricks. These bricks are then used to make small eco huts, which operate as cafes to sell hot and cold drinks. The cafe is important because it allows Ecotel to earn revenue which the business can use to pay its costs.

MMA Architects is a business based in Johannesburg, South Africa. The business designs buildings for a range of purposes including office spaces, government buildings and other projects. MMA Architects has also designed a way to build houses using sandbags instead of bricks. This saves natural materials that would have been used to make bricks. Sand has other advantages as a building material because it is readily available and requires no expensive machinery to make, which helps lower the costs of building. Lower costs mean more affordable homes for local people.

### Discuss in small groups or as a class:

1. What is the purpose of each business?
2. Why might it be important for Ecotel to make a profit?
3. What are the possible advantages of using sand to build the houses designed by MMA Architects?

**Figure 5.1:** A mountain of old and disused vehicle tyres in a landfill site

# 5.1 Business objectives

**Objectives** act as a target for business. Most businesses are likely to have more than one objective, and these objectives will vary between each business. For example, new businesses are likely to have different objectives to established businesses. The most common business objectives are shown in Figure 5.2.

> **KEY TERM**
>
> **objective:** a statement of a specific target to be achieved by a business.

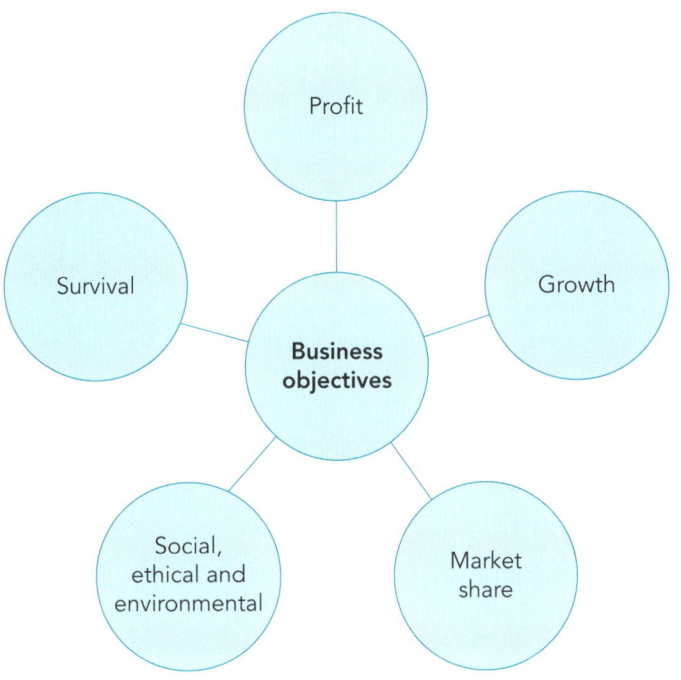

**Figure 5.2:** Business objectives

> **LINKS**
>
> You can find more information about business plans and entrepreneurs in Chapter 3 and changes in the economy in Chapter 27.

## Survival

A business needs to be able to keep operating to have any chance of being successful. This means being able to earn enough revenue to cover its costs. For example, many new businesses fail in their first year of trading, so survival is important. Even established businesses may have survival as an objective, especially when there are significant changes in the economy. For example, during an economic recession, demand could fall significantly.

## Profit

Profit is the difference between total revenue and total costs. Most private sector businesses will aim to make a profit. Profit is important as it acts as a reward to owners and as a source of finance to fund business growth.

## Growth

As discussed in Chapter 3.3, some owners will want to grow the business, but others will remain small. Growth can bring advantages including spreading risk and lowering average costs. Being able to increase output could help reduce the cost of producing each item, which could make the business more competitive leading to higher revenue.

## Market share

Market share refers to the value of sales a business has as a percentage of the total market. As a business grows it could make more sales, which may increase its market share. A larger market share could allow the business to have more influence over prices or increase the business reputation, which could lead to higher sales and/or revenue.

## Social, ethical and environmental issues

Many businesses take an interest in social, ethical and environmental issues by considering the effect that business decisions and activities might have on other stakeholder groups, such as employees, customers, the community and the environment. Businesses that ignore their social responsibility run the risk of bad publicity and possible legal action. This can damage the reputation, sales and revenue of a business.

> **LINKS**
>
> You can find more information about profit in Chapter 23, and market share in Chapter 10.

> **TIP**
>
> Do not just learn a list of business objectives. You must understand why each objective might be important to a business.

### ACTIVITY 5.1

1. Write down something you would like to achieve once you have left school. Think about what you might need to do to help achieve this. Share your idea with a partner. Do you have a similar goal? Do you have different ways you plan to achieve it?

2. Have a group/class discussion on possible reasons why having objectives might be important. Write a one-minute summary based on ideas discussed.

Objectives can be either short-term or long-term. Short-term objectives are objectives that can be usually achieved within months or less than a year while long-term objectives may take many years to achieve.

> **ACTIVITY 5.2**
>
> Read the following scenarios:
>
> | | |
> |---|---|
> | Yosef has just opened a new hairdressing business. There is a high level of competition in the local area. | XPG is a large manufacturing business that makes one type of steel. The directors are worried as all of its steel is sold to a single customer. |
> | A restaurant decides to reduce the amount of waste produced by the business. | A computer retailer wants its shop to be the one every customer wants to visit. |
>
> 1. In pairs or groups, identify the main objective each business is likely to have.
> 2. Describe what actions the business might take to help reach its objective. Present your ideas to another group in the form of a short report to the business owners. Ask for feedback from the other group on your ideas.

## The importance of business objectives

Setting objectives helps managers and owners in many ways. Objectives can:

- Provide a target or goal to work towards – this helps ensure everyone is working in the same direction. This can help the business to remain focused on what it wants to achieve.

- Help with decision-making – because the business knows what it wants to do, time and resources are not wasted on unnecessary things.

- Provide a way to measure success – as objectives can provide a point of reference to compare progress against.

- Can help motivate employees as employees also have a target to work towards.

> **CASE STUDY 5.1**
>
> **Ocean Bottle – Make a splash**
>
> Old single-use plastic is a huge global problem. The *National Geographic* magazine estimated that there are 5.25 trillion pieces of plastic waste floating around in the ocean.
>
> Ocean Bottle (OB) is a private limited company based in the UK. The business manufactures and sells reusable drinks bottles. Each reusable bottle is made from recycled plastic bottles. The business pays local people, who live in villages or towns by the oceans in a range of countries including Brazil, Ghana, Egypt and Indonesia, to pick up used plastic bottles lying on the shoreline or collected from the ocean. The waste plastic is then turned into reusable drinks bottles. The reusable bottles are then sold across the world to consumers, which in turn helps reduce the amount of single-use plastic bottles bought.

> **BUSINESS FOR CAMBRIDGE IGCSE™ AND O LEVEL: COURSEBOOK**

**CONTINUED**

**Figure 5.3:** Used or waste plastic can be turned into recycled bottles

In its first year, Ocean Bottle's revenue reached $1 million. Since then, the business has grown quickly from 2 to 18 employees and the Managing Director has plans to grow the business even further.

One of Ocean Bottle's targets is to collect and therefore stop seven billion empty plastic bottles from ending up in the ocean within its first six years of setting up the business.

**In pairs or groups:**

1. Describe the two stated objectives of Ocean Bottle.
2. How might having a clear objective help Ocean Bottle? Give reasons for your answer.

## 5.2 The role of stakeholder groups

A **stakeholder** is any individual or group who may be affected by the decisions and activities of a business. Figure 5.4 shows the main stakeholders of a business. For example, you are a stakeholder in all the businesses you buy goods and services from. Members of your family might be stakeholders in the business they work for or businesses they own.

> **KEY TERM**
>
> **stakeholder:** an individual or group that has an interest in a business because they are affected by its activities and decisions.

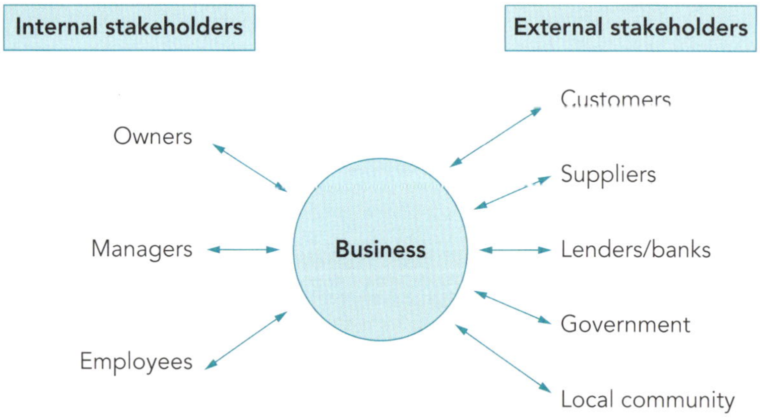

**Internal stakeholders**
- Owners
- Managers
- Employees

**External stakeholders**
- Customers
- Suppliers
- Lenders/banks
- Government
- Local community

(Business)

**Figure 5.4:** The main stakeholder groups of a business

A business cannot exist without stakeholders. For example, without stakeholders there is no one to start the business, no one to make the products and no one to buy them.

There are two types of stakeholder groups:

- internal stakeholders
- external stakeholders.

# 5 Business objectives and stakeholder objectives

## Internal stakeholders

Internal stakeholders are people inside the business who have an interest in the decisions and activities of a business. These people either own or work for the business including owners, managers and employees.

### Owners

In sole trader and partnerships, these are the people who decided to start the business and they make all the important decisions about what the business does.

In a limited company, the owners are known as shareholders. These people provide finance and can influence whether the business is able to expand or not. However, shareholders are not usually involved in the day-to-day operations of the business.

In simple terms, without owners there is no business. Owners are likely to set profit as an objective as this can provide a return on their investments.

### Managers

These are usually the people responsible for the day-to-day decisions in the business. In sole trader and partnerships, the owners and managers may be the same people. Without managers, who will plan, organise, command, coordinate and control operations? Managers want the business to be successful, so they may benefit from higher pay, bonuses and more status.

### Employees

These are the people who make the goods or provide the services for the business. Without employees, there may not be anything to sell. Employees are likely to want good working conditions, fair pay and job security. If the business is not successful, employees could lose their jobs.

> **TIP**
>
> Do not confuse stakeholders with shareholders. Shareholders are only one stakeholder group of a business.

> **LINK**
>
> You can find more information about managers in Chapter 7.

**Figure 5.5:** A group of employees listening to a business presentation

Each stakeholder group has its own objectives and can influence whether the business is successful or not.

Table 5.1 outlines possible objectives and ways each stakeholder group might influence a business.

Table 5.1: The objectives and influence of internal stakeholder groups

| Stakeholder | Objectives might include: | Possible ways can influence the business include: |
|---|---|---|
| Owner | • to receive high returns/profit as a reward for their investment<br>• increase in value of business. | • may decide to close the business<br>• may invest more funds into the business to fund its growth. |
| Managers | • more status and power<br>• benefit from financial and non-financial methods of motivation<br>• opportunities for promotion. | • make important decisions that can affect the level of output and/or sales<br>• how to organise, control and command other employees. |
| Employees | • good working conditions<br>• job security<br>• benefit from financial and non-financial methods of motivation<br>• payments on time<br>• opportunities for promotion. | • can affect the quality or number of goods/services provided<br>• may leave – business may not have sufficient employees to complete work. |

# External stakeholders

External stakeholders are people outside the business who have an interest in the decisions and activities of a business. These people do not work in the business, but the actions of the business can directly affect them.

## Customers

These are the people who buy the goods or services of the business. Without customers there are no sales, and therefore no revenue. Customers will want good quality products at low prices. The main way customers can influence businesses is by deciding whether to buy its goods or not.

> **LINK**
>
> You can find more about financial and non-financial methods of motivation in Chapter 9.

Figure 5.6: A customer choosing which product to buy in a local shop

## Suppliers

These are the individuals or organisations who provide materials and other resources to the business. Without suppliers, there are no materials for the business to make the products with or inventory to sell. Suppliers want the business to pay a fair price for the materials provided and for all payments to be made on time. They can influence a business in many ways. For example, deciding whether and when to supply products to the business.

**Figure 5.7:** A large warehouse storing goods to be sent out to businesses or customers

## Lenders/banks

Lenders and banks provide the business with finance and capital. Most businesses are likely to need finance to start up, operate or expand. Without sufficient funds, the business could be forced to close. Lenders will want to ensure that any funds provided to the business can be repaid along with any interest. If not, banks may not lend the business the amount of finance it needs to operate or grow.

## Government

The government runs the country on behalf of everyone in the country. The government will want businesses to provide jobs that can help lower unemployment and to pay taxes that it can use to fund public services. Governments can influence businesses in many ways. For example, they can pass legal controls that affect how or whether businesses can operate and by providing financial and other support to encourage business activity.

## Local community

Everyone who lives in the area where the business is located is part of the local community. They will want the business to provide jobs that can help increase peoples' standard of living. The local community will also want the business to reduce or minimise pollution which can harm the health of people in the local area.

> **LINKS**
>
> You can find more information about profit in Chapter 3, limited companies in Chapter 4 and pressure groups in Chapter 28.

Table 5.2 provides a summary of the main external stakeholder groups, their objectives and the way each group might try to influence business behaviour.

**Table 5.2:** The objectives and influence of different external stakeholder groups

| Stakeholder | Objectives might include: | Possible influence on business includes: |
|---|---|---|
| Customers | • receive a variety of and good quality products<br>• low or fair prices<br>• good customer service. | • stop buying its products<br>• write bad reviews about the business. |
| Suppliers | • regular/increased orders from the business<br>• to receive payment for goods on time<br>• to receive fair prices for goods provided. | • decide whether/when to supply goods<br>• can increase/decrease its prices<br>• decide whether/how long will give business to pay. |
| Lenders/banks | • to receive interest payments when due<br>• to have loans repaid when due. | • decide whether to offer loans to finance business growth<br>• can request existing finance to be repaid. |
| Government | • to be paid the correct amount of taxes on time<br>• for the business to provide jobs – can lower the amount of benefits government must pay. | • can introduce/remove legal controls<br>• provide financial and other support to the business<br>• can change tax rates which increase/decrease costs. |
| Local community | • jobs for local people<br>• support projects in local community, e.g., sponsor local events<br>• reduce pollution caused by business activity. | • arrange protests or other actions through pressure groups<br>• lobby government. |

> **TIP**
>
> The easiest way to decide if a stakeholder is internal or external is to ask whether they work in the business or not. For example, employees are internal because they make or provide the products, whereas suppliers are external because they simply provide the materials but do not work in the business.

# 5 Business objectives and stakeholder objectives

## CASE STUDY 5.2

**Hotel Properties Limited**

**Figure 5.8:** A luxury hotel located on one of the islands in the Maldives

Hotel Properties Limited (HPL) is a successful hotel business based in Singapore. The business has 4394 employees across its 38 luxury hotels and resorts located in 15 countries around the world. In 2022, HPL reported an increase in revenue to $525.5 million, and $38.3 million in profit. This allowed HPL to pay a 0.04 SGD dividend for each share held.

The growth of tourism has had significant effects on many countries including the Maldives. The island is built on a series of coral reefs in the Indian Ocean. Large numbers of tourists have led to the construction of hotels which has caused sand and other natural materials to be worn away. Most of the food served in the hotels needs to be imported and rubbish left behind by tourists causes pollution.

Nine of HPL's 38 hotels are in the Maldives. One of these hotels is Gili Lankanfushi. This hotel is located on a private island in the north of the country. The luxury hotel has won awards for its efforts to reduce environmental damage. For example, the hotel only uses sustainable wood and natural materials in its 45 rooms or huts. Customers are encouraged to eat plant-based foods grown on the island or by people on other nearby islands.

**Discuss in pairs or groups:**

1. Using examples from the case, outline the main stakeholder groups of HPL.
2. Which of these stakeholder groups is likely to have had the most influence on the actions of HPL? Rank the stakeholders in order of importance. Give reasons for your ranking.
3. Share your ranking with another group. Did you have the same order? Do you understand the reasons given for any differences? If not, ask them.

It is important to note that some people can belong to more than one stakeholder group. For example, people in the local community may also be employees and/or customers of the business. Some suppliers may buy the businesses' products and live in the local community. People are likely to have differing objectives depending on which viewpoint or stakeholder role they are representing.

## ACTIVITY 5.3

The following statements are based on the objectives of IKEA, a leading furniture manufacturer.

IKEA wants to:

- Help and inspire people to live more sustainably, by offering its customers money-saving, resource and energy-efficient products.
- Offer a fair and sustainable rate of pay to all its 230 000 employees.
- Work together with the communities where the business operates to help improve the lives of the people living there, the local economy and the environment.

> **CONTINUED**
>
> - Only using renewable or recycled materials to manufacture its products by 2030.
> - Cooperating with its 1 600 suppliers.
> - Becoming climate positive by 2030 (this means saving more carbon emissions than the business creates).
>
> 1 Identify the different stakeholder groups mentioned in the above statements.
>
> 2 Identify stakeholder group(s) not mentioned in any of the above statements.
>
> 3 For each of the stakeholder groups you have identified in Question 1, explain the importance of these stakeholders for IKEA. Which stakeholder group do you think might be more important? Note down reasons for your choice.
>
> 4 Then, in pairs, discuss your answer to Question 3. Did you identify the same stakeholder? Do you understand the reason for your partner's choice?

## How stakeholder objectives can conflict

Each stakeholder group is likely to have different objectives. It is possible that the objectives of one stakeholder group can clash or conflict with the objectives of another stakeholder group. This is because it is not always possible for a business decision or activity to satisfy the differing objectives of each stakeholder group.

The decisions and activities of a business may have positive or negative effects on different stakeholder groups.

For example:

- Shareholders might want the business to focus on ways to increase profits which could mean higher prices for customers.
- Suppliers may want regular large orders from a business, but managers may want a price discount for placing these large orders.

Sometimes, a single business decision or activity might have positive and negative effects for the same stakeholder. For example, customers may want more choices, but to develop these new products could mean higher rather than lower prices.

Any change in the business environment can affect business decisions. For example, machine learning (ML) or artificial intelligence (AI) is a disruptive technology where the computer 'learns' to think like humans. The computer programming allows the computer to learn to find patterns and trends for itself when handling, processing and analysing large volumes of data. AI can be used in a wide range of applications, from understanding consumer shopping habits in supermarkets to automating processes such as checking financial records. This could lead to some jobs being replaced by computers and new jobs being created. Figure 5.9 shows how one business decision to introduce AI might affect different stakeholder groups.

> **LINK**
>
> You can find more information about technology and production of goods and services in Chapter 17.

# 5 Business objectives and stakeholder objectives

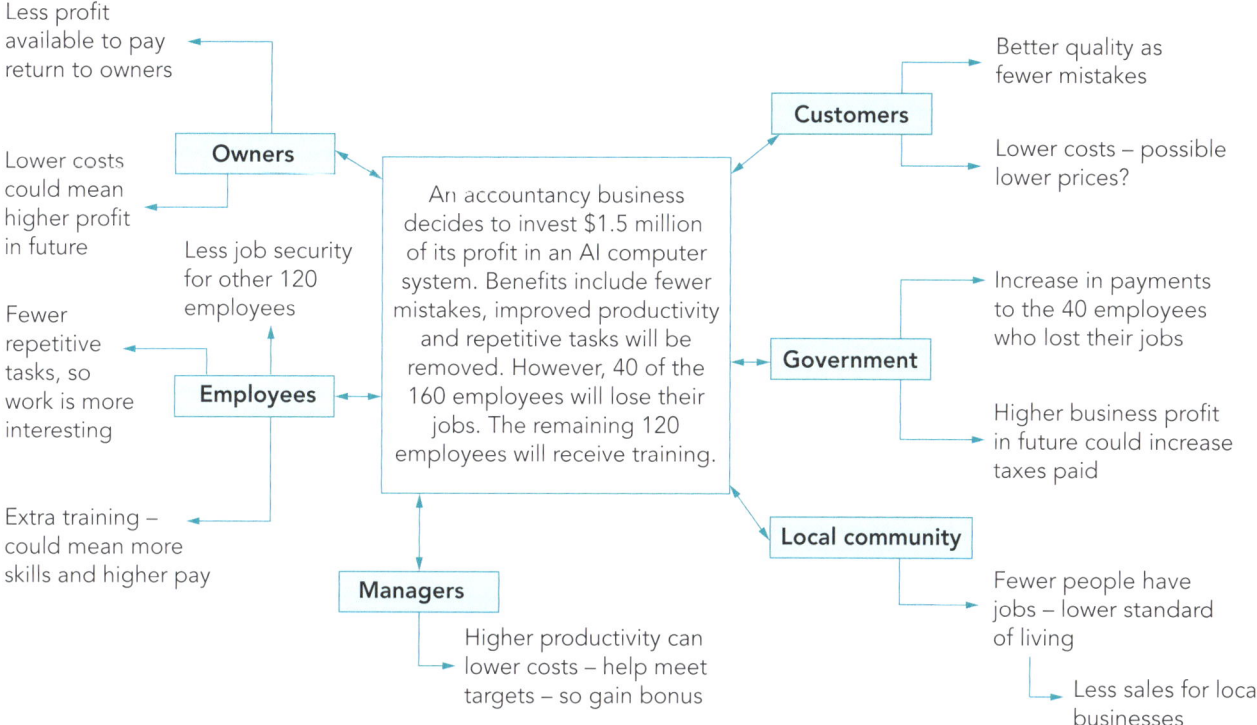

Figure 5.9: How one business decision to introduce AI might affect different stakeholder groups

### ACTIVITY 5.4

Look at each of the following statements about the decisions and activities of different businesses.

#### Statement A

A local supermarket has decided to expand the size of its store. It will now be able to add an in-store bakery. The expansion will be financed through a long-term bank loan.

#### Statement B

The owners of a mobile phone manufacturer have decided to produce some of the products in another country where labour costs are lower. This will increase the profit margins and help to keep the price of the business' mobile phones below that of its competitors.

1 For each of the above statements, identify two stakeholder groups who might be affected by the action taken by the business.

2 For each statement, identify the positive and/or negative effects of the business activity on each of the stakeholders you have identified in Question 1. Present your work as a chart, like the one in Figure 5.5.

3 For each statement, explain how there might be a conflict between any two groups of stakeholders.

> **DISCUSSION**
>
> In small groups, research one real-life example of a business decision from your local area or country. Each group should research a different example. Consider how different stakeholder groups might be affected by the business decision. Which stakeholder group do you think is likely to be most affected? Present your findings to the class in the form of a two-minute presentation. Ask for feedback from the class to see whether they agree with your decision.

> **REFLECTION**
>
> How did your group decide which stakeholder group was likely to be affected the most? Did you rank each point in order of importance or use some other method? Did the example itself influence your choice? Did the class understand your reasoning?

> **BUSINESS IN ACTION**
>
> **Patagonia**
>
>
>
> **Figure 5.10:** People wearing outdoor clothing when climbing a mountain
>
> Patagonia manufactures high-quality outdoor adventure clothing to wear when walking and climbing. The business has 3 000 employees and factories in 16 countries. Patagonia's products are sold in a range of retail shops across the world. The business was set up as a family-owned private limited company. According to Statista, the total value of Patagonia's sales in 2022 was estimated at $1 023 million.
>
> Patagonia is not afraid to do things differently. The business is known for its quality products and strong interest in environmentalism. For example, over 66% of its clothing is made using recycled materials. Patagonia has previously produced advertisements telling customers to only buy its products if it was necessary to reduce the effect on the environment. If the clothing is damaged, the business encourages customers to send the item back to Patagonia to be repaired.
>
> In September 2022, the Managing Director and founder, Yvon Chouinard, announced a change in Patagonia's ownership. In a press release on its website, he wrote an open letter explaining why the 'Earth is now Patagonia's only shareholder'. This means that the share of profit that would have gone to other shareholders will now be spent on projects designed to protect the environment.
>
> **Discuss in small groups or as a class:**
>
> 1. How might this decision affect other stakeholders? Give reasons for your answer.
> 2. Should a business put the interests of one stakeholder above all the others?

# 5 Business objectives and stakeholder objectives

> **SUMMARY**
>
> You should now know:
>
> - It is important for every business to set objectives.
>
> - The main objectives of private sector businesses are likely to focus on survival, profit, growth, market share and social, environmental or ethical issues.
>
> - All businesses have internal and external stakeholders. These are individuals or groups who have an interest in the activities of the business.
>
> - Each stakeholder group will have their own objectives, and these might conflict with the objectives of other stakeholder groups or with the objectives of the business.

## Chapter 5 practice questions

1   Aisha is a qualified hairdresser. She opened her own hair salon as a sole trader five years ago. At first, the business did not have many customers due to competition from other salons. The first six months for Aisha's business was difficult and she struggled to cover her costs. However, within a year, the business revenue was higher than costs and Aisha was able to recruit two employees. Aisha is now considering opening a second hair salon in the town and will need to recruit a manager to run the new salon. Aisha knows that this is a risk. She also knows setting business objectives is important.

   a   Define 'business objective'. [2]

   b   State **four** objectives a business might have. [4]

   c   Explain **two** advantages to Aisha setting business objectives. [6]

   d   Explain **two** objectives Aisha might have set for her business. Justify your answer. [8]

2   WCM is a mining business based in Country X. It is a private limited company. One of WCM's objectives is to increase profit. WCM has three mines and 1 000 employees. WCM's directors plan to grow the business by opening a new coal mine. The Managing Director knows many of its stakeholder groups will be affected by this decision. She said, 'It will create 500 jobs at the mine and 1 500 jobs within the local community. All the machinery and other resources will be obtained from local suppliers. The coal can be used by manufacturing businesses across Country X, which will reduce the number of imports.'

   a   Define 'stakeholder group.' [2]

   b   Outline **one** possible objective for each of the following stakeholder groups of WCM.

       Employees:
       Suppliers: [4]

**c** Explain **one** way each of the following stakeholder groups' objectives might conflict with WCM's objective to increase profit.

Customers:
Government: [6]

**d** Explain **two** ways the local community might be affected by WCM's decision to open the new mine. Which way is likely to be more important? Justify your answer. [8]

**Total available marks: 40**

## CHECK YOUR PROGRESS

How well do you think you have achieved the learning intentions for this chapter? Give yourself a score from 1 (still need a lot of practice) to 5 (feeling very confident) for each learning intention. Provide an example to support your score.

| Now I can … | Score | Example |
| --- | --- | --- |
| identify different business objectives | | |
| understand why objectives are important for a business | | |
| identify the different stakeholder groups and their objectives | | |
| explain the role of different stakeholder groups in a business | | |
| understand how the objectives of different stakeholder groups can conflict. | | |

# Section 1 case study

## CASE STUDY

### Tabansi's drinks and smoothies

From an early age Tabansi displayed many characteristics of a successful entrepreneur. At age 13, Tabansi made soft drinks which he sold by the glass to customers who visited the tourist sites near his home. Tabansi saved all the profit from this business and two years later he bought a bicycle and cooler bags (these are bags that help to keep drinks cool) so that he could take his drinks to a wider market. When he left school, Tabansi had enough money to pay for the rent of a stall at his local market. He expanded his product range to include freshly squeezed fruit juices and fruit smoothies. Although he was making a living as a market trader, Tabansi knew that to earn the money he wanted to provide for his future and to support his family, he had to be more ambitious and start up a business.

Tabansi recently met an old school friend, Uba. Uba's father has a small building for sale in the town where Tabansi lives. Tabansi arranged with Uba to visit the property. He saw the potential for adapting the building into a small factory for his drinks business. Tabansi agreed to buy the building. He has produced some financial data for the purchase of the building. This data is shown in Appendix 1.

Tabansi went to see a small business adviser. Following the meeting, the adviser has written to Tabansi (see Appendix 2) and told him that he should set clear objectives for his business. The bank will want to see a business plan before it will consider lending Tabansi the finance he needs as start-up capital. As part of his business plan, Tabansi has produced some financial information for the next three years. This can be found in Appendix 3.

# Appendix 1

**Financial data for Tabansi's new factory**

|  | $ |
|---|---|
| Cost of building | 10 000 |
| Cost of equipment | 4 000 |
| Personal savings | 6 000 |
| Amount of funds to be borrowed | 8 000 |

## Appendix 2

**Letter from the business adviser**

Dear Tabansi,

It was good to see you yesterday and I hope you found the meeting useful. I am writing to confirm the main points of our discussion. These are:

1. You need to set clear objectives for your business.
2. You should produce a business plan for the business.
3. You should consider changing your business into a private limited company.

If you need any further assistance from me or the team at the small business advisory service, please get in touch.

Yours sincerely,

S. P. Godwin

## Appendix 3

**Financial information for the next three years ($)**

|  | Revenue | Profit |
|---|---|---|
| Year 1 | 13 000 | 7 000 |
| Year 2 | 14 800 | 9 000 |
| Year 3 | 17 300 | 12 000 |

1. a. Explain **two** characteristics that might have made Tabansi a successful entrepreneur.

    Characteristic 1:

    Explanation:

    Characteristic 2:

    Explanation: [8]

    b. Explain the importance of each of the following objectives for Tabansi's business. Which objective do you think is the most important? Justify your answer.

    Profit:

    Growth:

    Survival:

    Recommendation: [12]

2  a  Explain **two** advantages to Tabansi of being a sole trader.

   Advantage 1:

   Explanation:

   Advantage 2:

   Explanation: [8]

   b  Explain how each of the following **three** factors might influence Tabansi's decision to change his business to a private limited company. Which factor is likely to be the most important for Tabansi? Justify your answer.

   Limited liability:

   Additional source of finance:

   More owners:

   Conclusion: [12]

3  a  Explain **two** possible reasons why Tabansi's business might fail.

   Reason 1:

   Explanation:

   Reason 2:

   Explanation: [8]

   b  Consider the importance of each of the following elements of a business plan for Tabansi. Which element is likely to the most important for Tabansi? Justify your answer.

   Market research:

   Finance:

   Conclusion: [12]

4  a  Explain **two** ways Tabansi might increase his business's added value.

   Way 1:

   Explanation:

   Way 2:

   Explanation: [8]

   b  Consider why each of the following stakeholders might be interested in Tabansi's business. Which stakeholder group is likely to be most interested in the success of Tabansi's business? Justify your answer.

   Lenders/banks:

   Suppliers:

   Government:

   Conclusion: [12]

   Total available marks: 80

# Section 2
# People in business

People are a valuable resource for any business and can influence the success or failure of the business. These people may be owners, managers or other employees; they can be full-time, part-time or may benefit from flexible working. The recruitment, selection and training of employees is an important part of human resource management. Every business must be aware of legal controls over employment including employment contracts and the legal minimum wage. Trade unions will try to protect the interests of employees as well.

As a business grows it will need to have a clear organisational structure, with different functional areas and managers who can lead and manage other employees. This chapter will explore the functions of management, different leadership styles, and the importance of business communication.

You will also learn about the importance of having a well-motivated workforce and how managers might use theories of motivation to ensure that employees are motivated.

> Chapter 6

# Human resource management (HRM)

**LEARNING INTENTIONS**

By the end of this chapter, you will be able to:

- describe the stages of the recruitment process and methods of selecting employees
- explain the advantages and disadvantages of internal and external recruitment
- recommend who to employ in a given situation
- explain employment contracts and the various legal controls over employment
- understand the importance of training
- explain the different types of training, and the advantages and disadvantages of each type.

# 6 Human resource management (HRM)

## Introduction

You may know people who are looking for a job or who have recently started a new job. You will have teachers who leave your school or college and need to be replaced so that subjects can continue to be taught. All these are examples of situations that involve recruitment of employees.

Whether employees are starting a new job or existing employees are being asked to do new jobs within the business, training is often needed so that the employee's work is up to the required standard.

In this chapter you will find out how organisations recruit employees, the legal controls that affect employment issues and why it is important that employees receive training.

### BUSINESS IN CONTEXT

#### BYD – Driving the business forward

**Figure 6.1:** An electric car being charged with power

Build Your Dreams (BYD) is an electric car manufacturer based in Guangdong Province, China. The business started by making batteries for mobile phones before taking the decision in 2003 to buy a car manufacturing business. Five years later, BYD made its first electric car, its objective being to help cool the Earth by 1°C (see Figure 6.1). Production has grown quickly since then. In fact, in 2023, BYD sold 1.6 million electric cars making the business one of the largest electric car manufacturers in the world along with Tesla. According to Trading Economics, BYD had 570 000 employees in 2022 compared to 170 000 employees in 2011, a significant increase of 400 000 employees. BYD has factories in many countries, including India, with plans to open a new factory in Hungary, creating thousands of jobs for local people including managers, engineers and production workers.

Discuss in pairs or groups:

1  Why does BYD need employees?

2  How could BYD recruit the employees for its new factory?

## 6.1 Recruiting and selecting employees

One of the key factors to business success is having the best possible workforce. One role of the human resources function is to help the business find and retain suitable employees with the right skills.

### Recruitment and selection methods

All businesses will, at some point, recruit new employees. These employees may be needed for many reasons, including when the business is growing, someone has gained a promotion or an employee has left the business.

Recruitment of new employees can be time-consuming and expensive. However, it is important that the business recruits the right people, because if it does not do so it may have to go through the whole process again.

### Main stages in recruitment and selection of employees

Finding new employees requires a business to go through a recruitment and selection process. There are several stages to this process, as shown in Figure 6.2.

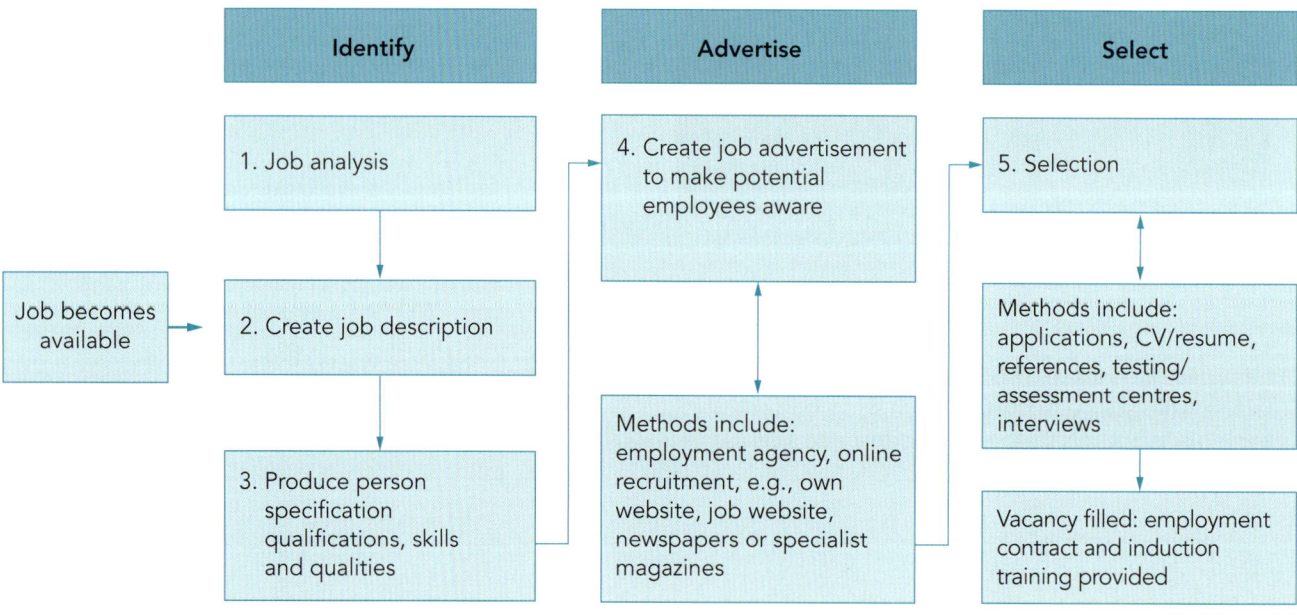

**Figure 6.2:** The recruitment process

## Job analysis

When a job vacancy becomes available, the business will collect information about the specific job position, including the activities, skills needed and where the work will be carried out. This information helps the business decide whether the vacancy needs to be filled. If there is a job vacancy, this information will form the basis of the **job description** and **person specification**.

## Job description

A job description is a written document that provides information about what a specific job involves. It will be sent to anyone interested in applying for the job.

A job description is helpful because it outlines the duties of the job. Interested people can then work out whether they are able to carry out the necessary tasks. This should help ensure that only suitable people apply for the position, saving the business time and cost when recruiting.

An example of a simple job description is shown in Figure 6.3.

> **KEY TERMS**
>
> **job description:** a document that includes the job title and a list of the key points about a job, key duties, responsibilities and accountability.
>
> **person specification:** a list of the qualifications, skills, experience and personal qualities looked for in a successful applicant.

> **TIP**
>
> Remember, a job description is mainly used to help managers decide what the job involves and select the applicant who best matches the requirements of the job.

| | |
|---|---|
| **Title:** | Sales and Marketing Executive |
| **Job purpose:** | To plan and carry out direct marketing and sales activities and to maintain and develop sales in accordance with agreed business plans. |
| **Key duties:** | 1  Maintain and develop a computerised customer database. |
| | 2  Plan and carry out direct marketing activities to agreed budgets and timescales. |
| | 3  Develop ideas and create offers for direct mail and marketing to major accounts. |
| | 4  Respond to and follow up sales enquiries by post, telephone and personal visits. |
| | 5  Monitor and report on activities and provide relevant management information. |
| | 6  Carry out market research, competitor and customer surveys. |
| **Responsible for:** | Sales and Marketing Assistant |
| **Accountable to:** | Sales and Marketing Director |

**Figure 6.3:** An example of a job description

## Person specification

A person specification is a written document providing details of the type of qualifications, skills, experience and personal qualities the business is looking for in applicants for the job.

This document is helpful because it clearly shows the qualifications, experience and skills expected for the job. This can help the business to decide between applicants when selecting who to employ based on how well each one matches the type of person they want.

An example of a person specification is shown in Figure 6.4.

> **Person specification – Sales and Marketing Executive**
>
> **Personality:** Self-driven, results-orientated with a clear focus on high quality and business profit. Reliable, tolerant, and determined. Able to get on with others and be a team player.
>
> **Specific job skills:** Excellent written communication skills. Understands the principles of marketing and advertising cost-effectiveness. Experience of managing marketing agency activities desirable but not essential. Must be an excellent face-to-face and telephone communicator.
>
> **Computer skills:** Must be adept in use of MS Office 365 or later, particularly Excel and Word, and ideally Access or similar database to basic level, internet and email.
>
> **Management ability:** Some people-management skills, experience and natural ability will be useful.
>
> **Qualifications:** Must be educated to A Level standard.

**Figure 6.4:** An example of a person specification

> ### ACTIVITY 6.1
>
> Think of a job you might like to do when you have finished your studies. Write the 'key duties' section of the job description for this job. Use the example of a person specification in Figure 6.4 to write the person specification.
>
> Once written, you should try to find real-life examples of a description for this job to see whether the job is the same as you expected.

> **TIP**
>
> Do not confuse a job description with a person specification. Learn the difference between the two documents and how each one is used in the recruitment process.
>
> Once the job description and person specification have been produced, the business needs to advertise the vacancy.

## Job advertisements

The job advertisement must be designed so that it attracts the right applicants and provides all the information people need to know about how to apply for the job being advertised. The business will also have to consider where the job is to be advertised so that suitable candidates can find out about the job. Otherwise, the business risks missing out on potential applicants.

Businesses are likely to use a range of methods to advertise a job vacancy depending on whether it is planning to use internal recruitment or external recruitment.

You will learn more about the difference between internal and external recruitment later in this chapter.

Methods to advertise jobs externally include employment agencies and online recruitment.

### Employment agencies

These are specialist agencies that help the business find suitable applicants for a job, which saves the business time that can be used to carry on with other activities. However, such agencies can be expensive to use.

## Online recruitment

Many businesses will use websites to help find and select applicants for jobs (see Figure 6.5). There are many websites available, some general and specialised ones for certain industries or professions. The software provided allows the business to design its own advertisement, and some platforms can also be used to carry out certain selection activities including interviews and testing.

There are other methods of advertising jobs, including:

- Many businesses include details of any job vacancies on their website. The advantages and disadvantages of this method are similar to those of recruitment websites.
- In some countries there are government-run job centres where vacancies can be advertised, usually for free.

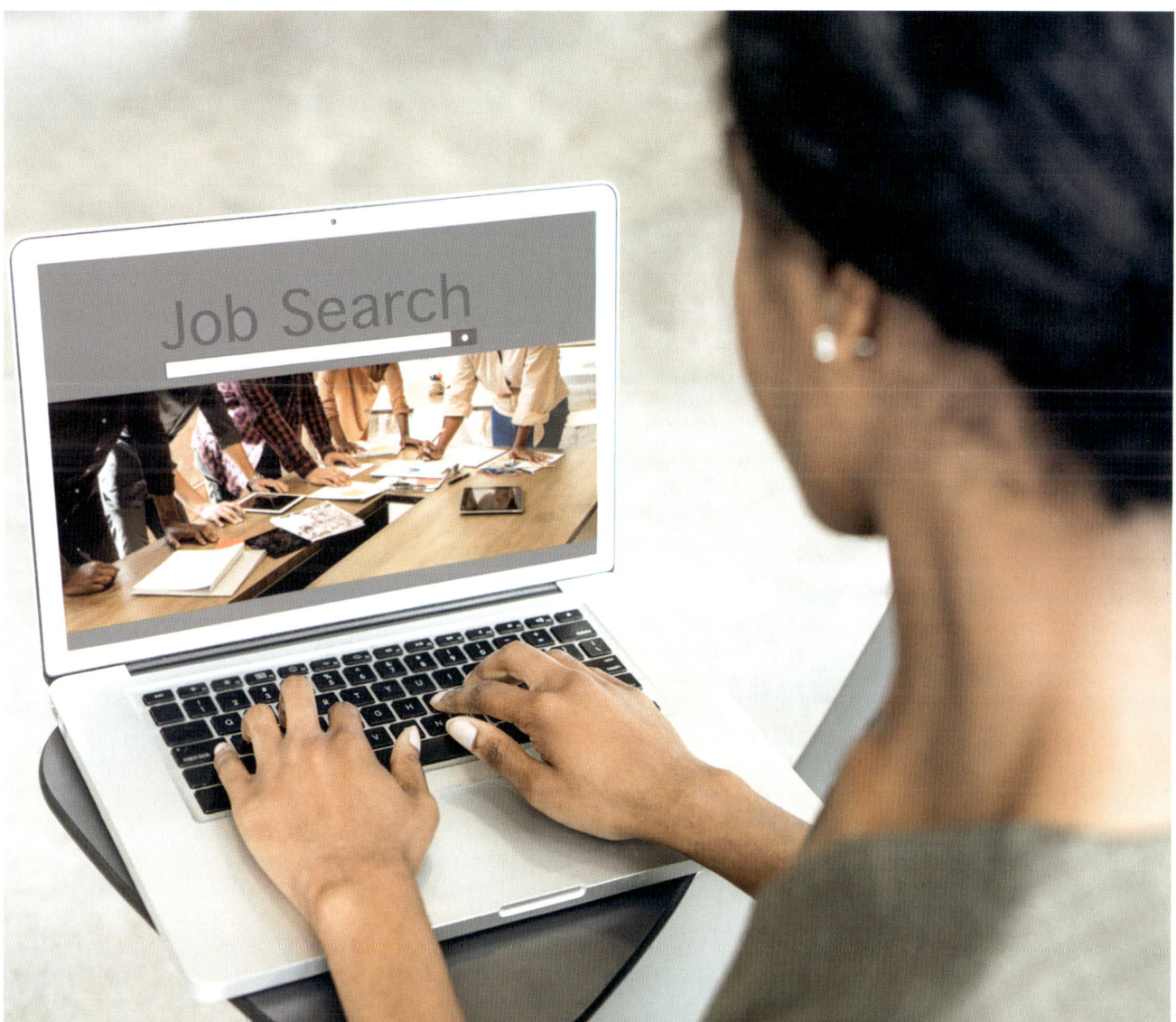

**Figure 6.5:** A person looking on a website for possible jobs

Table 6.1 shows the advantages and disadvantages of different methods of advertising jobs.

**Table 6.1:** Advantages and disadvantages of different methods of advertising jobs

| Method of advertising jobs | Advantages | Disadvantages |
|---|---|---|
| Employment agencies | • save time on advertising/shortlisting applicants that can be spent on other activities<br>• have expert knowledge, so only send suitable applicants to interview. | • high cost, which increases expenses<br>• may not fully understand your business so applicants might not fit culture of the business. |
| Online recruitment websites | • can reach a wider audience, which could mean more potential applicants<br>• easy/quick to post and update<br>• can add videos/images to advert – adding more detail. | • not everyone has access to or is able to use internet/online sites<br>• anyone can apply, so may get many unsuitable applicants. |
| Newspapers | • can target geographical locations<br>• advert can be maintained or referred to. | • cannot update easily<br>• only shown for a limited amount of time. |
| Specialist magazines | • targeted at people interested in industry. | • limits size of audience, so may miss out on potential applicants. |

The choice of method will often depend on factors such as type of job, how many jobs need to be filled, cost of advertisement and time available. For example, if it is a senior management job or the job requires specialist skills, using an employment agency may be suitable as there are likely to be fewer potential applicants for the job. Though it is expensive, the cost may be worthwhile.

### ACTIVITY 6.2

Read the following information:

Premium Floorcovering (PF) is growing and needs a new sales advisor. The duties include answering customer questions and selling its range of carpets and floor coverings. No qualifications are needed but the person will need good communication skills, good time management and ideally some experience of sales. Specific product training will be given.

The salary is $12 000 each year, plus commission. Other benefits include a 20% discount on PF's products.

Application forms should be requested directly from the HR team at PF.

1. Explain two possible methods PF could use to advertise the job. Write a sentence explaining your choice and include why the other method was not selected.
2. Use this information to create a job advertisement for your selected method.

## 6 Human resource management (HRM)

# Selecting the right candidate for the job

Once the job advertisements have been sent out, the business will use a range of methods to help select the best person for the job. Each business will use different methods or a different combination of methods depending on the job vacancy to be filled. For example, some businesses may use an application form instead of a curriculum vitae (CV), while others may use a CV, interview and testing.

The most common methods of selection include:

- application forms
- CVs
- references
- interviews
- testing or assessment centres.

## Application forms

Once the job has been advertised, the business may send out application forms to people who have shown an interest in applying (see Figure 6.6). This form is designed by the business and allows it to gather the exact information required. If everyone provides the same information, this can make it easier for the business to compare applicants.

**Figure 6.6:** A person completing an online application form for a job

## Curriculum vitae (CV) or resume

Those who decide to apply may be asked to send the business a **curriculum vitae (CV)** or resume. A CV provides a summary of the qualifications, skills and work experience that a person has. A sample CV is shown in Figure 6.7.

A business can use this document to check whether the applicant matches the requirements it is looking for in the person specification.

> **TIP**
>
> An application form is different to a CV. While both may include similar information, the application form is designed by the business, whereas the CV is produced by the applicant.

> **KEY TERM**
>
> **curriculum vitae (CV):** a document that outlines the details of the education, qualifications and work experience of a potential employee which can be sent to an employer when applying for a job.

99

| Curriculum Vitae | |
|---|---|
| **Name** | Address |
| | Home telephone number |
| | Mobile number |
| | Email address |

Education, including examinations and qualifications gained

Work experience (include dates from and to and reasons for leaving)

Other relevant qualifications and skills

Other interests and hobbies

Name and contact details of two references

**Figure 6.7:** CV template

### ACTIVITY 6.3

Use the CV template (see Figure 6.7) as a guide and write your own CV.

The business will look through all the applications to compare how well the information provided by the applicants compares with the job description and the person specification. This information can help produce a shortlist of possible applicants who are most likely to be suitable for the job. The business then must work out which of these candidates on the shortlist is the best person to select.

## References

A **reference** is a trusted person who knows the applicant and agrees to let the business ask them questions about the applicant's previous work, skills or abilities. References are likely to be previous employers or someone from the applicant's school or college. The business can check with the reference to confirm whether the information provided on the CV or application form is accurate. The reference can provide extra information that can help the business decide on the applicant's suitability for the job.

## Interviews

Potential employees could be invited to attend an interview (see Figure 6.8). The interview may be a question-and-answer session with one person interviewing the applicant, two or three interviewers or a group interview with many applicants being interviewed at the same time. The interviews could be conducted in person or virtually over the phone or internet. Whichever method is used, it allows the business the opportunity to ask in-depth questions to find out more about each applicant.

> **KEY TERM**
>
> **reference:** a trusted person who agrees to comment on an applicant's previous work, skills or abilities.

# 6 Human resource management (HRM)

**Figure 6.8:** Candidates waiting to be interviewed for a job

## Testing or assessment centres

Applicants could be asked to complete tests. The type of test will vary depending on the job role to be filled. These could include aptitude tests; for example, someone applying for a car mechanic's job may be asked to fix a problem on a car. Other tests may involve team activities or job-specific exercises, such as reading typical letters that the business is likely to receive and asking the applicant to decide on the best course of action to take in response.

### CASE STUDY 6.1

#### Egis

**Figure 6.9:** Tall buildings in the UAE

Egis is a design consultancy business based in the UAE (see Figure 6.9). The business has helped to design or manage sustainable construction projects across the Middle East and Asia including the Bangkok Metro line in Thailand and the Al Ain School in the UAE. For example, the school has been designed to include solar panels for heating and underground water tanks to capture rainwater, which can be used to water the school's playing fields.

Egis is recognised as one of the top employers in the UAE for its commitment to the practices it has introduced to ensure all employees are treated fairly. The Human Resources department is always looking for individuals with natural ability to join Egis to help work on new projects. Recruitment is done through a variety of methods including completing an online application form, sending in a CV or using an employment agency.

> **CONTINUED**
>
> An important part of the selection process is the interview, which is used in approximately 50% of Egis's job vacancies. This can be carried out either one-to-one or with two or three interviewers or an interview over the phone. Depending on the job, applicants may be involved in more than one interview. Other methods of selection used by Egis include case studies, presentations and skills tests.
>
> **Discuss in pairs or groups:**
> 1. Explain one advantage and one disadvantage of Egis using interviews as a method of selection.
> 2. Why do you think Egis uses a range of methods when recruiting employees?

## Selecting the right candidate

Based on the selection methods used, the business must then decide who it thinks is the best applicant for the job. Factors a business might consider include:

- experience
- qualifications
- skills, for example, are they good at communication
- whether they can carry out the duties of the task
- performance during the selection process
- how well they fit into the culture of the business
- references.

Once the successful applicant accepts the job and starts work, they will be given a contract of employment and induction training. If none of the applicants are suitable, the business may decide to advertise the job again.

## Difference between internal and external recruitment

When a business has a job vacancy to fill it can look for someone in its existing workforce – **internal recruitment** – or search outside the business – **external recruitment**.

### Internal recruitment

A business may decide there are already people within the business with the right skills to fill the job vacancy. When the business only looks for applicants from within its current employees it is known as internal recruitment.

The main advantages and disadvantages of internal recruitment are shown in Table 6.2.

> **KEY TERMS**
>
> **internal recruitment:** filling a vacant post with someone already employed in the business.
>
> **external recruitment:** filling a vacant post with somebody not already employed in the business.

Table 6.2: Main advantages and disadvantages of internal recruitment

| Advantages | Disadvantages |
| --- | --- |
| • Vacancy can be filled quickly.<br>• Lower cost than external recruitment.<br>• Applicants already know how the business works, so less likely to need induction training.<br>• The business already knows the strengths and weaknesses of applicants.<br>• Can motivate other employees as they can see that there are opportunities for promotion. | • It may not bring in any new ideas.<br>• More suitable candidates may be available outside the business.<br>• May cause conflict within the workplace if other internal candidates feel they should have got the job, which could lead to demotivation.<br>• May create another vacancy to fill, so business will need to spend time/money on a new recruitment process. |

## External recruitment

A business might decide that none of its current employees has the necessary skills or expertise to fill a vacancy, or it may want to increase the choice of candidates for a job. If so, the business can use external recruitment. This does not mean current employees cannot apply for and successfully get the job.

The main advantages and disadvantages of external recruitment to a business are shown in Table 6.3.

Table 6.3: Main advantages and disadvantages of external recruitment

| Advantages | Disadvantages |
| --- | --- |
| • Wider choice of applicants – could increase the chances of finding the best person for the job.<br>• May bring different skills, ideas and experience – could help improve efficiency.<br>• Avoids the risk of upsetting other employees when someone internal is promoted. | • It takes longer to fill the vacancy, which could delay operations.<br>• Expensive because of advertising costs and time spent interviewing candidates.<br>• Applicant may have no knowledge of how business works, so induction training will be needed, which increases expenses. |

### CASE STUDY 6.2

**Siemens**

Figure 6.10: An engineer at work

Siemens AG is an international electrical engineering and electronics business which has its headquarters in Germany. When the directors of Siemens needed to increase the number of employees working in its wind power business, they decided on using a different approach to recruitment. Instead of looking for engineers with a background in renewable energy, the Human Resources team set out to find engineers in different industries to join the team.

Dr Ronald Busch has been the President and Chief Executive Officer at Siemens AG since 2021.

> **BUSINESS FOR CAMBRIDGE IGCSE™ AND O LEVEL: COURSEBOOK**

### CONTINUED

He started at Siemens in 1994 as a project manager. Over the next 27 years he has worked in a wide range of divisions at Siemens and been promoted many times, including becoming Head of Mass Transit Division, Transportation Systems Group, in 2007; Chief Technology Officer and Chief Sustainability Officer in 2011. Dr Busch then joined the board of directors in 2019 as Labour Director.

**Discuss in pairs or groups:**

1. Explain the possible advantages to Siemens of using external recruitment for its engineers.
2. What might be the possible advantage to Siemens of recruiting its Chief Executive Officer from within the business?

Most businesses use a mixture of internal and external recruitment to fill job vacancies depending on factors such as skills and experience needed.

### ACTIVITY 6.4

CP is a large manufacturing business which produces sustainable packaging for food. Its products are sold to supermarkets and other food retailers across country X. Hardeep is CP's Human Resource Manager. The business has two vacancies:

- production supervisor
- factory manager.

Hardeep is considering whether to use internal or external recruitment to fill these posts.

1. Individually, think about the advantages of each method of recruitment for each post. Which method would you recommend for each post?
2. In pairs, share your ideas. Do you agree with your partner's recommendations? Did you have the same reasons? If not, can you understand the reason for their decision(s)? Produce a list of common points.
3. Share your ideas with another group. Do you agree? If so, did you have the same reasons? If you had different answers, can you understand the reasons for their choices?

# 6.2 Legal controls over employment issues

The governments of most countries have passed laws aimed at protecting employees from being exploited by employers. The main types of legal controls are discussed as follows.

## 6 Human resource management (HRM)

## Contract of employment

In most countries, it is a legal requirement that employees are given a written contract of employment. This is a legally binding agreement between the employer and the employee and may include details such as:

- the name of the employer and the employee
- the date when the job starts
- the amount the employee will be paid and when payments will be made; for example, weekly or monthly
- the number of hours or days the employee is expected to work
- the main duties and responsibilities of the employee
- the place of work
- the number of days holiday the employee will receive
- the amount of sick pay (money paid to employees when they are unable to work due to medical reasons).

A contract of employment has benefits to both the employer and the employee. Its main role is to help remove any misunderstanding that could arise over issues such as hours of work or rate of pay.

If an employer ignores the terms of the employment contract by, for example, paying the employee less than the amount agreed in the contract, the employee could take legal action against the employer.

Likewise, if an employee breaks the terms of the contract by, for example, refusing to work the agreed number of hours, the employee could be dismissed from the job.

## Unfair dismissal

In many countries, it is a legal requirement that employers treat employees fairly. For example, the employee cannot be dismissed from their job without good reason. If they are, this would be unfair dismissal.

An employee who thinks they have been unfairly dismissed can take legal action against the employer. If the employee is a member of a trade union, the union may fight the case on the employee's behalf.

If it is decided that an employee has been unfairly dismissed, the employer can be forced to give the employee their job back and/or compensate them for the loss of pay.

> **LINK**
>
> You can find more information about trade unions in Chapter 7.

## Discrimination

Discrimination is about avoiding treating employees unfairly (see Figure 6.11). The most common types of discrimination are on the grounds of gender, race, ethnicity, religion, disability or age. Any employee who feels they have been treated unfairly can take legal action against their employer.

**Figure 6.11:** A business cannot discriminate against people based on ethnicity or disability

## Health and safety

The workplace can be a dangerous environment for employees. Health and safety laws aim to protect employees from injury or physical discomfort; for example, being too hot or too cold.

Health and safety in the workplace can increase business costs as new equipment and training may be needed. However, if it reduces accidents then fewer days will be lost due to employee injury. This should help to keep output/service at high levels and the employer will not have to pay employees' health bills or compensation for any injuries that employees receive while at work.

## Legal minimum wage

This legal control sets out the minimum amount an employee must be paid for each hour they work. Minimum wage laws often increase business costs. However, if employees receive a reasonable amount of pay, this could motivate them to work harder and increase their productivity.

> **TIP**
>
> You do not need to know the names of specific legal controls. Simply make sure you understand the purpose of each legal control listed above and that these legal controls might affect what a business does.

# 6.3 The importance of training

## Why employees need training

Businesses offer training for many reasons, and both the business and employees can benefit from the training provided. The main advantages of training include:

- Employees are likely to be more efficient, which can help lower average costs.
- Improves employee skills and allows the business to benefit from a flexible workforce.
- Improves employee motivation. Employees are less likely to be absent from work or want to leave the business.
- Help to reduce mistakes, which reduces the cost of rework.

- Increased output, so business is better able to meet demand.
- Reduce the chance of accidents.

## Methods of training

There are three main methods of training:

- induction
- on-the-job
- off-the-job.

### Induction training

It is not enough for a business to recruit the right employees. Even the best qualified employees are likely to need some form of training when they start a new job. This training is known as **induction training**.

Induction training introduces the new employee to:

- other employees
- the organisation's structure and a clear outline of the employee's roles and responsibilities
- where they fit into the structure
- the health and safety procedures in the workplace.

The main advantage of induction training for the employee is that they quickly feel part of the business. Employees who are settled are likely to perform their tasks more effectively from the start of their employment.

One disadvantage of induction training is that it increases business costs. Also, during the period of induction training, employees are not contributing any work but are still being paid.

> **KEY TERM**
>
> **induction training:** a training programme to help new employees become familiar with their workplace, the people they work with and the procedures they need to follow.

### ACTIVITY 6.5

Working in pairs, imagine you have been given the responsibility for helping a new student to settle in quickly at your school.

Write an induction programme for this new student. Include all the things they will need to know, the people they will need to meet, the rules they must learn and the facilities they can use.

It is not only new employees who need training. Most businesses will provide employees with additional training for many reasons including to update their skills, reduce mistakes or learn how to use new technology. This could be on-the-job or off-the-job training.

### On-the-job training

**On-the-job training** involves the employee learning the skills they need to complete tasks in the workplace. They will often sit with an experienced employee and watch how they perform the task (see Figure 6.12). They will then complete the task under the guidance of the experienced employee.

> **KEY TERM**
>
> **on-the-job training:** training at the place of work; watching or following an experienced employee.

The main advantages and disadvantages of on-the-job training are shown in Table 6.4.

**Table 6.4:** Main advantages and disadvantages of on-the-job training

| Advantages | Disadvantages |
| --- | --- |
| • Low cost (compared to off-the-job training). | • Employees may pick up undesirable habits from person training them. |
| • Employees learn the way that the business wants the job done. | • Employees might not learn the most up-to-date methods. |
| • Employees carry on working, so some work is done. | • Employees may make mistakes when learning – this can increase waste/damage reputation. |
| • Business can control what is being learnt, so employee only learns necessary skills. | • Slows down or halts the work of the experienced employee who provides the training. |

**Figure 6.12:** A group of nurses being given on-the-job training

## Off-the-job training

**Off-the-job training** takes place away from the place of work, so the employee is not able to carry out their usual duties. The training is provided by specialist trainers and could take place in another location within the business or outside in places such as training centres, local colleges or universities. Training outside the business might involve travel costs.

Off-the-job training is often used where the job requires a high level of technical skill or there is no one in the business with the necessary skills to provide the training. Table 6.5 identifies the main advantages and disadvantages of off-the-job training.

> **KEY TERM**
>
> **off-the-job training:** training that takes place away from the workplace and the day-to-day duties of the job that the employee does.

Table 6.5: Main advantages and disadvantages of off-the-job training

| Advantages | Disadvantages |
|---|---|
| • Employees learn up-to-date/new skills and techniques.<br>• It does not disrupt the work of other employees.<br>• It allows for mistakes to be made while training without damaging business reputation.<br>• Skills gained could increase the opportunities for promotion. | • Using specialist trainers can be expensive.<br>• The employee does not produce any output during training.<br>• Skills may not be specific to business. |

> **TIP**
> Off-the-job training could take place in the same location where the employee works. It simply refers to the fact that employees are not carrying out their usual duties at the same time.

## CASE STUDY 6.3

**Marriott Hotels**

Figure 6.13: An employee helping a customer check in at a hotel

Marriott Hotels is the largest hotel group in the world with over 8 100 hotels and 377 000 employees. The business is well-known for the training and development provided to potential and existing employees. Programmes include:

- Ten week paid internship – for college or university students to experience what it is like working at one of its hotels.

- Induction training – all new employees are provided free stay at the hotel where they will work, including dinner and breakfast, before meeting up with other employees for a 3-day induction course. This helps introduce employees to the culture (the way the business works) at Marriott.

- Voyage Leadership Development Program – an internationally based 12–18-month course aimed at graduates, designed to fast track them into management roles at Marriott. Training includes direct experience working in hotels, and organised off-the-job training courses.

- 15-minute training – offered every day to all hourly paid employees to provide them with knowledge or practice skills needed to do their job effectively. Training could focus on issues including how to make beds, clean or serve food.

- InMotion! – a scheme aimed at providing supervisors with on-the-job experiences in other departments in the hotel to help prepare them for future management roles.

Maybe this helps to explain why in a survey of Marriott Hotel employees 40% said they would not leave the business for a similar job offering more pay and over 70% enjoyed going to work every day.

### CONTINUED

**Discuss in pairs or groups:**

1 What are the possible advantages to Marriott Hotels of training its employees?

2 Why might Marriott use different methods of training?

When deciding which method of training to use, a business might consider the following factors:

- cost of training
- skills needed to be taught
- number of employees to be trained
- whether anyone in the business has the necessary skills and time to train others.

The importance of each factor is likely to change depending on each individual situation.

### ACTIVITY 6.6

Ravinder is the owner of a small shop that sells printers, computers and other items of office equipment. He also offers his customers repair and maintenance services.

Ravinder is interviewing applicants for a new post of repair and maintenance engineer. He has decided to offer the job to Surjit. Surjit has limited experience of repairing and maintaining office equipment, but Ravinder thinks he will be a quick learner. However, Ravinder cannot decide on the best way to train Surjit. He asks himself: 'Should I use on-the-job training or off-the-job training?'

- Write a brief report explaining the advantages and disadvantages to Ravinder and his business of each method of training. You should finish your report by recommending which method Ravinder should use and why.

### REFLECTION

How did you decide which advantages or disadvantages were important? Did you organise the points in order of importance? Discuss your decision with another student. Did they decide on a different method? Can you understand the reason for their choice? Did they understand the reasons for your chosen method? Thinking about how you tried to solve this problem, what one thing would you do differently next time? For example, change the scenario to a factory setting. How might this change your answer?

A summary of the advantages and disadvantages of the different methods of training is shown in Figure 6.14.

# 6 Human resource management (HRM)

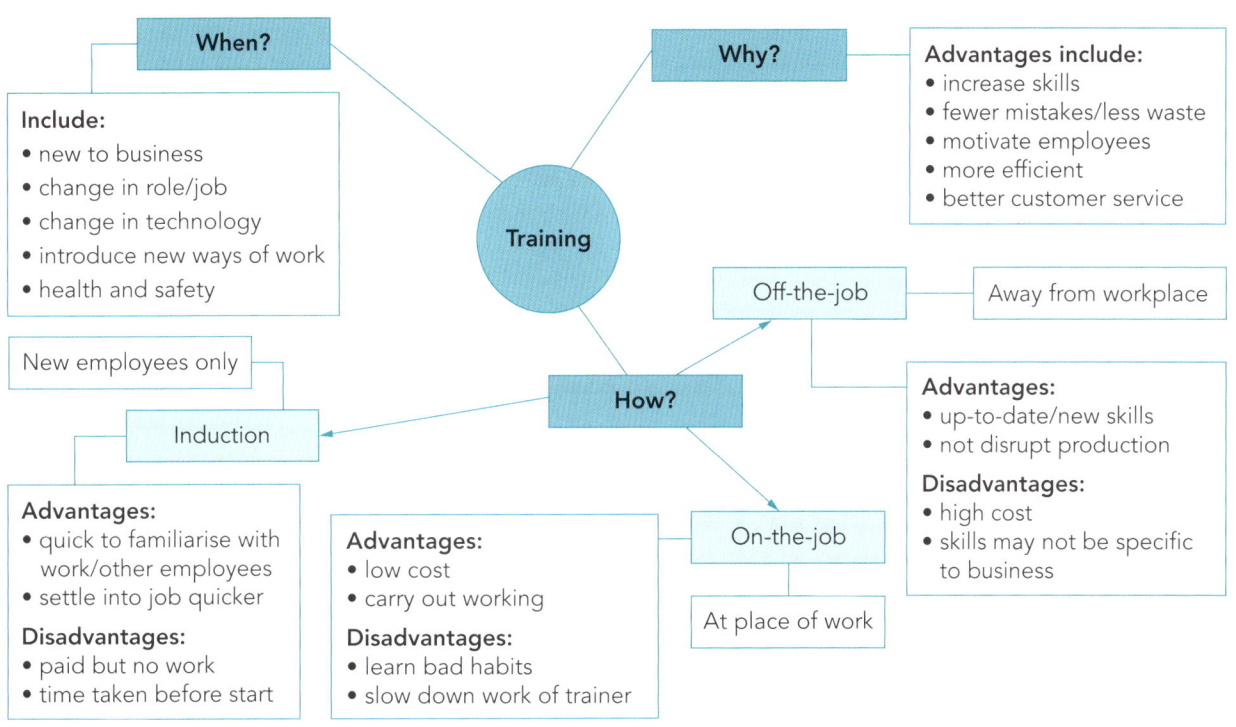

Figure 6.14: Advantages and disadvantages of the different methods of training

## BUSINESS IN ACTION

### Lojas Renner

Figure 6.15: A person buying jeans from a shop

Lojas Renner (LR) is a fashion retailer based in Brazil. The business sells its products across South America, including in its 600 shops, mobile and online. LR is known for its commitment to sustainable fashion. For example, 99.15% of the cotton used for its clothing is obtained from organic or recycled sources. The business now sells jeans that are 100% sustainable.

Respect, avoiding discrimination and inclusion is important to LR. Of its 21 000 employees, 64% are women and 61% of these are in leadership positions. In addition, 50% of employees identify themselves as black with 38% of those in leadership roles identifying themselves as black.

LR is committed to ensuring it has a diverse and inclusive workforce, using its PLURAL Program. As its website states, 'it makes communications, holds events and provides training to suppliers, teams and leaderships, in addition to having prepared our Diversity Guide.'

### Discuss in pairs or groups:

1. What actions could a business take to support diversity and non-discrimination?
2. What are the possible advantages to a business of having a diverse workforce?

> **BUSINESS FOR CAMBRIDGE IGCSE™ AND O LEVEL: COURSEBOOK**

> **SUMMARY**
>
> You should now know:
>
> - The main stages of recruitment include producing job descriptions and person specifications, advertising the vacancy and selecting suitable applicants.
>
> - Businesses can use internal and external methods of recruitment to fill a job vacancy.
>
> - There are legal controls over employment issues to protect employees in the workplace.
>
> - Induction, on-the-job and off-the-job training have advantages and disadvantages for both employees and businesses.

# Chapter 6 practice questions

1. GTH is a specialist lighting manufacturer. The business is expanding into new markets and needs to employ ten new production workers and a manager for its factory. All the new employees will receive induction training. The Human Resource Director is preparing job descriptions for the roles and has to decide whether to use internal recruitment for the new manager.

   a. State **two** advantages of a business producing a job description. [2]

   b. Outline **two** legal controls over employment that might affect GTH. [4]

   c. Explain **two** benefits of GTH using induction training. [6]

   d. Do you think internal recruitment is the best method for GTH to use for the new manager? Justify your answer. [8]

2. Aisha is the Human Resource Manager for BSK, an insurance business. BSK's directors have decided to introduce new technology. All BSK's 160 employees will need training. Aisha will have to decide on a suitable method of training for BSK to use. She has received a letter of resignation from the Marketing Manager. Aisha has now been asked to prepare a person specification for the new manager.

   a. Define 'person specification'. [2]

   b. Outline **two** ways a person specification could help BSK when recruiting the new manager. [4]

   c. Explain **two** benefits of BSK providing employees with a contract of employment. [6]

   d. Explain **two** methods of training BSK could use for its employees. Which is likely to be the best method for BSK to use? Justify your answer. [8]

   **Total available marks: 40**

## 6 Human resource management (HRM)

### CHECK YOUR PROGRESS

How well do you think you have achieved the learning intentions for this chapter? Give yourself a score from 1 (still need a lot of practice) to 5 (feeling very confident) for each learning intention. Provide an example to support your score.

| Now I can … | Score | Example |
|---|---|---|
| describe the stages of the recruitment process and methods of selecting employees | | |
| explain the advantages and disadvantages of internal and external recruitment | | |
| recommend who to employ in a given situation | | |
| explain the various legal controls over employment | | |
| understand the importance of training | | |
| explain the different methods of training, and the advantages and disadvantages of each type. | | |

# Chapter 7
# Organisation and management

## LEARNING INTENTIONS

By the end of this chapter, you will be able to:

- understand the main functional areas of a business
- interpret simple organisation charts
- understand the different methods of working, including the difference between full-time and part-time employees
- describe the functions of management
- understand the importance of delegation
- explain the advantages and disadvantages of the main leadership styles
- recommend a suitable leadership style in a given situation
- understand why reducing the size of the workforce is necessary
- recommend which workers should be made redundant in a given situation
- describe what a trade union is
- explain the benefits to employees of being members of a trade union.

# 7 Organisation and management

## Introduction

All businesses will need some form of organisational structure. Everyone in the business – even if it is just two partners – needs to know their roles and responsibilities and what the roles and responsibilities are of others in the business. This will help the business to operate efficiently.

In this chapter, you will learn the important features of organisational structure and how these can be represented in a chart.

You will also study the different styles of leadership and the importance of management functions. Managers must take many decisions and it may sometimes be necessary to reduce the size of the workforce. This chapter will explore the concept of downsizing and the role of trade unions in trying to protect the interests of employees.

### BUSINESS IN CONTEXT

#### A framework for success

**Figure 7.1:** Used and damaged metal ready to be recycled

SA Metal Group is the oldest and one of the largest metal recycling businesses in South Africa. The business was started in 1919 by Wolfe Barnett and it is still a family-owned business today.

SA Metals collects disused and damaged metals such as steel, iron, copper and tin from businesses across South Africa and from nearby countries including Botswana, Lesotho and Zimbabwe. These scrap materials are then sorted and cleaned before being turned into recycled steel or copper at its steel and copper processing factories. The rest of the recycled metals are sold to local businesses or exported all over the world for others to reuse.

SA Metals has over 500 employees and is divided into eight areas (functions) as shown in Figure 7.2. The management team includes Clifford Barnett, who is the owner of SA Metals, Daniel Barnett, one of the directors responsible for Sales and Clem Grunewald, who is responsible for purchasing materials and other services.

#### Discuss in pairs or groups:

1. What do you think is the role of the management team in a business?
2. What might be the advantage to SA Metals dividing the business into different areas?

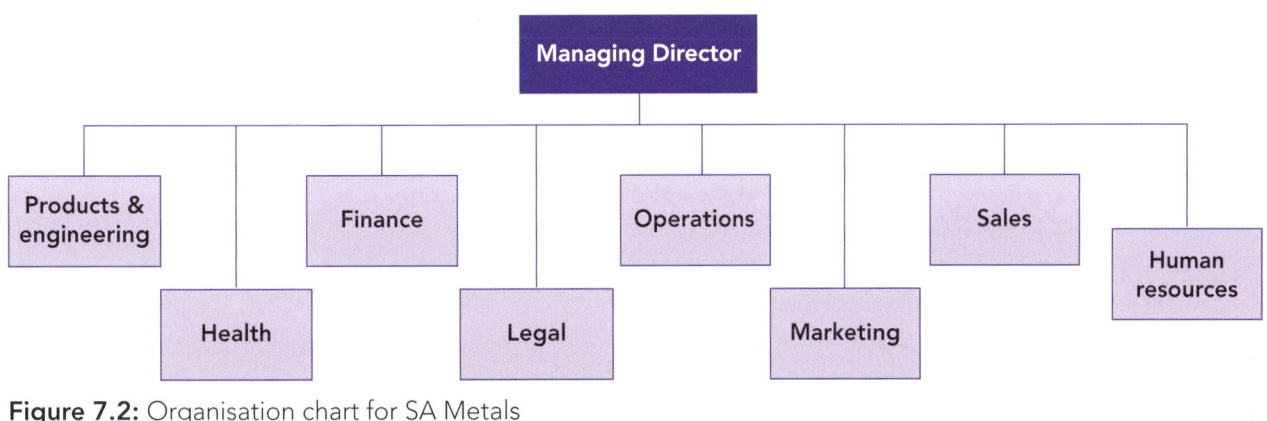

**Figure 7.2:** Organisation chart for SA Metals

## 7.1 Functional areas of a business

Whatever the size of the business, there are some activities, or functions, that all businesses need to carry out. In a small business, the owner or certain employees may carry out more than one function. As a business grows, it is likely to divide into separate departments to focus on one function.

The main functional areas of a business are likely to include:

- **Operations** – responsible for production of goods and services, from buying the necessary materials to turning them into finished products, as well as checking the quality of products. Without suitable products there is nothing to sell.

- **Marketing** – responsible for carrying out market research to find out what customers need or want, the marketing of the product, including setting prices and promotion of the product to gain sales for the business. Without marketing, the business may produce the wrong products or customers may not be aware of them, which could lead to fewer sales.

- **Finance** – responsible for all financial issues including obtaining sources of finance to fund the purchase of buildings, equipment and resources. It is also responsible for managing the day-to-day costs such as paying employees and suppliers. Without access to finance, the business may experience cash flow problems or may not be able to grow.

- **Human resources** – responsible for the employees of the business including recruiting, selecting and training them. This function is also involved in overseeing legal issues over employment, such as health and safety and discrimination. Without sufficient employees with the right skills, the business may not be able to provide the goods and services to meet customer needs.

For a business to be successful, each function must work together. For example, if the marketing function does not identify the right product to sell, operations may manufacture products that no one wants.

> **LINKS**
>
> You can find more information about human resources in Chapter 6; market research in Chapter 11; marketing in Chapter 10; operations in Chapter 17; finance in Chapter 21 and cash flow in Chapter 22.

## 7.2 Simple organisation charts

An organisation chart is a diagram denoting number of levels of responsibility in an organisation, visually displaying the **organisational structure** of a business. It identifies the different functional areas, job positions and roles of employees within the business and the relationship between the various employees in a business. This allows everyone to know who is responsible for what in the business and who to communicate with. It also shows employees where they fit into the business structure and who to report to.

The people with the most authority (power to make decisions and give orders) are shown at the top of the chart, with those having the least authority and decision-making power on the lowest level.

A business can be organised in many ways, such as by functional area, by product or by region, depending on the best fit for each business.

> **KEY TERM**
>
> **organisational structure:** an organisation chart denotes the number of levels of responsibility in an organisational structure.

## 7 Organisation and management

An organisational chart is important because:

- it shows how everyone is linked together in the business, and employees know who has authority over them and whom the individual has authority over. Also, it shows the formal lines of communication, so everyone knows who to speak to if there is a problem.

It can also be used to illustrate the **hierarchy**, span of control and chain of command in the business. Examples of simple organisational charts are shown in Figures 7.3 and 7.4.

> **KEY TERM**
>
> **hierarchy:** the number of levels of responsibility in an organisational structure.

# Simple hierarchical structures

The main features of an organisational structure are:

- levels of hierarchy
- chain of command
- span of control.

## Levels of hierarchy

This describes the different levels of responsibility or management in an organisational structure. In a small business there may be only two levels – the owner and any employees – whereas a large organisation will have many levels of hierarchy.

**Tall or flat?**

Organisational structures may be tall or flat, depending on the number of levels in the hierarchy.

Tall organisations have many levels of hierarchy and, therefore, more managers. This means the span of control is usually narrow and the chain of command is long. Communication and decision-making can be slower because messages must pass through several layers. An example of a tall organisational structure is shown in Figure 7.3.

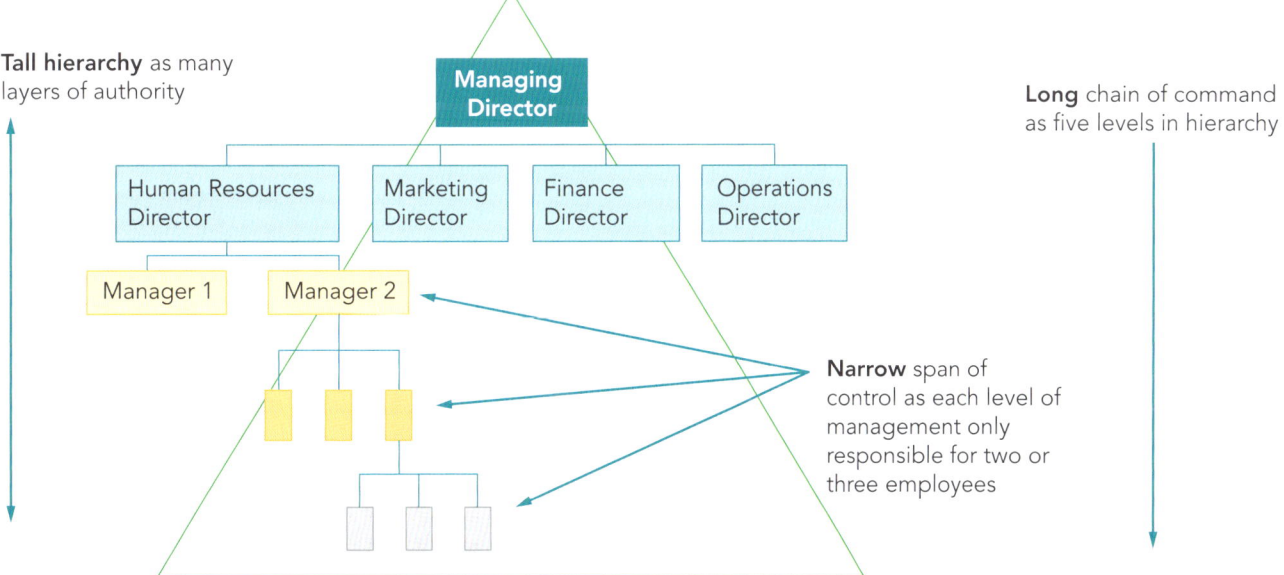

Figure 7.3: A tall hierarchical structure

Flat organisations have fewer levels of hierarchy, which means that the chain of command is very short. Communication and decision-making are likely to be quicker in a flat structure. As there are fewer managers in a flat structure, the span of control is usually wider. An example of a flat organisational structure is shown in Figure 7.4.

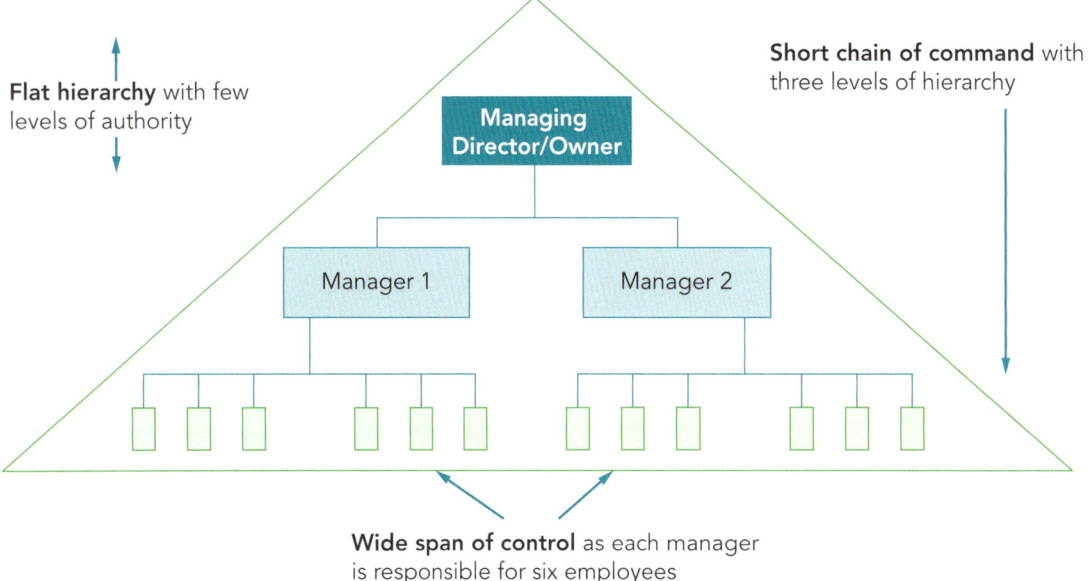

Figure 7.4: A flat organisational structure

> **TIP**
>
> The concepts of levels of hierarchy, span of control and chain of command are linked together. For example, a wide span of control implies a flat hierarchy and short chain of command. Why not create a simple memorable phrase to help you remember which three concepts connect? For example: *No Span Too high for a Long chain* (**N**arrow span of control, **T**all hierarchy, **L**ong chain of command).

## Chain of command

As a business grows it will recruit more employees. It is not possible for the person at the top to control all employees effectively. The day-to-day control of employees becomes the responsibility of managers lower down the hierarchy. The **chain of command** describes the way in which authority is passed down from managers at the top to those lower down the hierarchy.

In a typical business situation, instructions are passed down the chain of command, whereas information about performance, for example, monthly sales figures, is passed up the chain of command.

The chain of command can be short or long.

- A short chain of command – instructions pass through a few levels in the hierarchy. This helps instructions and decisions to pass through the organisation quickly. A flat organisational structure is likely to have a short chain of command.

**KEY TERM**

**chain of command:** the way in which authority and instructions are passed down through an organisation.

- A long chain of command – the instructions must pass through many levels of the hierarchy. This means communication is likely to be slower and this can lead to delays. There is a risk that the message gets distorted passing through the different levels which could lead to mistakes or wrong actions taken. Tall hierarchical structures have long chains of command.

## Span of control

Each manager is responsible for a certain number of employees or subordinates. The number of subordinates that report directly to each manager is called the span of control. A **span of control** can be described as 'wide' or 'narrow' depending on how many subordinates a manager is responsible for.

A wide span of control means that a manager is responsible for many employees. For example, in Figure 7.5 the manager is responsible for seven employees. Table 7.1 outlines the advantages and disadvantages of a manager having a wide span of control.

> **LINK**
>
> You can find more information about communication in Chapter 8.

> **KEY TERM**
>
> **span of control:** the number of subordinates that a manager is responsible for.

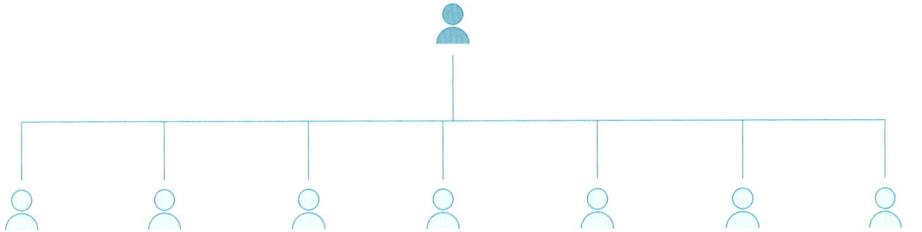

Figure 7.5: A manager with a wide span of control

Table 7.1: Advantages and disadvantages of a wide span of control

| Advantages | Disadvantages |
| --- | --- |
| - Fewer managers are needed – lower labour cost.<br>- Quicker communication is possible – could speed up decision-making.<br>- Encourages delegation – which could motivate employees. | - Less control over subordinates' work – less work might be done.<br>- Fewer managers/supervisor roles can reduce promotion opportunities.<br>- Possible communication problems as more employees to tell and/or ask.<br>- Managers may not have experience to manage large number of employees. |

A narrow span of control means that a manager is only responsible for a few employees. For example, in Figure 7.6, the manager is responsible for three employees. Table 7.2 outlines the advantages and disadvantages of a manager having a narrow span of control.

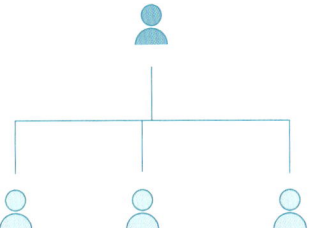

Figure 7.6: A manager with a narrow span of control

**Table 7.2:** Advantages and disadvantages of a narrow span of control

| Advantages | Disadvantages |
|---|---|
| • Easier to control a small number of employees.<br>• Manager may be able to maintain closer working relationship with employees.<br>• More opportunities for promotion, which can motivate employees. | • More managers needed which can increase labour costs.<br>• Slows down decision-making.<br>• Senior managers may be out of touch with what is happening lower down the organisation. |

### ACTIVITY 7.1

Produce an organisation chart for your school or college.

1 Use your diagram to provide examples of hierarchy, chain of command and span of control.
2 Would you describe your school's or college's organisational structure as tall or flat? Give reasons for your answer.

### TIP

There are a lot of technical terms in this chapter. You may find them easier to understand and explain if you construct a simple organisational chart.

There are many factors that can affect the size of the span of control including:

- **Type of work** – If the subordinates are doing simple and repetitive tasks, then a wide span of control can be used, whereas if the tasks are complex, a narrow span of control may be better.

- **Experience and skills of employees** – Highly skilled and experienced employees may require less supervision and therefore a wider span of control is possible.

- **Size of the business** – A small business with few employees might not need a wide span of control.

- **Skills and experience of the manager** – Experienced managers may be able to cope with a wider span of control whereas a new manager may prefer to have a narrow span of control.

- **Leadership style of the manager** – Some managers may want to have greater control over their subordinates, so will prefer to have a narrow span of control.

### ACTIVITY 7.2

Read the example and answer the questions that follow.

Mohinder is the owner of three restaurants. Each restaurant has a manager and employs one full-time chef and other full-time and part-time kitchen and front-of-house employees. Mohinder has produced an organisation chart for his business (see Figure 7.7).

The manager of each restaurant is responsible for recruiting their own employees, but all other decisions are made by Mohinder. He has an individual weekly meeting with each manager and a monthly meeting with all three managers together. These meetings are used to discuss the performance of the three restaurants.

# 7 Organisation and management

**CONTINUED**

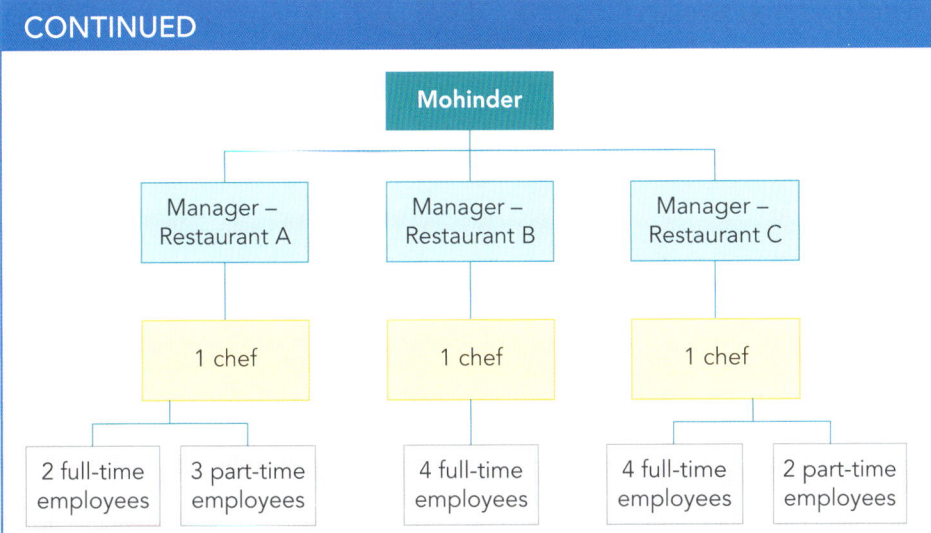

Figure 7.7: Organisation chart for Mohinder's business

1 Use the organisation chart produced by Mohinder to explain the meaning of the following terms:

   a hierarchy

   b span of control

   c chain of command.

2 Explain **one** advantage to Mohinder's employees of having an organisational chart.

## 7.3 Different ways of working

The traditional approach to work often requires workers to be in the office at 9 a.m. and leave at 5 p.m. or 6 p.m., five days a week. However, many businesses now offer employees more choice about how, when and where they work – this is known as **flexible working**. Providing choices can help attract and retain employees and increase motivation. Different ways of working include flexible hours and homeworking.

## Flexible hours

Working **flexible hours** allows employees to adjust when and for how long they work each day to suit their needs or personal situations. For example, an employee is contracted to work 18 hours a week over 4 days, but the employee might be allowed to work 6 hours for 3 days, so they do not have to work the fourth day.

## Homeworking

In most businesses, employees are expected to work at the business office, factory or shop. Due to changes in technology, it is now possible for some employees to be offered the option to work elsewhere, usually at home. This is known as **homeworking**.

> **LINK**
>
> You can find more information about motivation in Chapter 9.

> **KEY TERMS**
>
> **flexible working:** an agreement between employer and employee that allows the employee to change when, where and for how long they work to suit them.
>
> **flexible hours:** this allows employees to adjust when, where and for how long they work each day to suit their needs or personal situations.
>
> **homeworking:** the business allows employees to work from home instead of working at the business office.

# Advantages and disadvantages of part-time and full-time employees

Most employees are either full-time or part-time employees. The difference is simply that some employees are contracted to work more hours than others.

## Full-time employees

Full-time employees will often work for at least 35 hours a week, but this number will vary depending on the standard for the job, industry or country. The advantages and disadvantages of full-time employees are given in Table 7.3.

**Table 7.3:** Advantages and disadvantages of full-time employees

| Advantages | Disadvantages |
| --- | --- |
| • Consistent standard of work – improved reputation.<br>• Employees likely to be more loyal/committed to business.<br>• Easy to communicate with or update – could help improve efficiency.<br>• Fewer employees needed – lowers time and cost of recruitment. | • Need to pay whether there is work to do or not, which can increase costs.<br>• Fewer employees available to cover if someone is absent.<br>• Less flexible. |

## Part-time employees

Not all employees want, or are able to, work full-time. A part-time worker is simply someone who works fewer hours than a full-time worker. The advantages and disadvantages of part-time employees are shown in Table 7.4.

**Table 7.4:** Advantages and disadvantages of part-time employees

| Advantages | Disadvantages |
| --- | --- |
| • When not working, no need to pay wages – lower costs.<br>• Greater flexibility – as can work longer hours during busy periods and fewer hours when the business is less busy.<br>• Can provide cover when others are absent.<br>• Helps attract/retain well-qualified employees who only want to work for a few hours. | • Communication problems – as employees may not be at the workplace at certain times during the week.<br>• Lower quality of service might be offered to customers who may have to wait longer for a solution – damaging reputation.<br>• May need to recruit more employees. |

> **TIP**
>
> A part-time employee has the same legal rights as full-time workers; the only difference is the number of hours worked.

# 7 Organisation and management

## CASE STUDY 7.1

### Flexible working in Thailand

Figure 7.8: A business person working from home

In Thailand, 61% of businesses offer employees the opportunity for flexible working.

The Thai Union Group is a leading seafood manufacturing business in Thailand. In 2023, the business was listed in the Dow Jones sustainability indices for the 10th year in a row highlighting Thai Union's commitment to sustainable business practices. Employees are important to Thai Union. The business has over 44 000 employees and has won many awards for the way it helps support and develop its employees. To help employees achieve a good work-life balance, all employees are allowed to ask for flexible work hours or to work from home (such as the business person in Figure 7.8). However, which employees this option can be offered to will depend on the location or job role.

United Overseas Bank (UOB) is a large banking group in Thailand, with nearly 10 000 employees. UOB is committed to responsible financing, including offering low-cost loans to businesses and green home and car loans to individuals to help people move away from using fossil fuels. In 2022, the bank decided to offer more than 4 000 employees the opportunity to work from home two days a week. UOB already allowed all employees to take two hours off each month during working hours to attend to personal matters such as doctors' and dentists' appointments. In addition, all employees in non-customer-facing roles can select their start time each day between 0730 and 1000 hours to suit their individual needs.

**Discuss in pairs or groups:**

1. What might be the possible advantages to a business offering flexible working to employees?
2. What might be the possible disadvantages to a business offering flexible working?

## 7.4 The functions of management

Managers have many roles and responsibilities including decision-making and leadership. These are different to the functions of management that all managers are expected to perform.

The five functions of management are:

- **Planning** – setting clear objectives and deciding on the actions needed for these to be achieved.
- **Organising** – preparing and organising the resources needed to achieve the planned goals and objectives. Managers must decide the best way of completing important tasks at the lowest possible cost to the business.
- **Commanding** – giving instructions and supervising subordinates. Commanding should also help set standards and provide feedback to employees on how well they are performing.

- **Coordinating** – making sure that all the different parts of the business are working together towards achieving the business objectives.
- **Controlling** – checking to make sure that the business plan is working: will it be completed on time and to the required standard? If not, then action must be taken to correct it.

## 7.5 Delegation

It is not possible for managers to complete all business tasks by themselves. They do not have the time and/or may not have the necessary skills. Therefore, managers need to delegate (see Figure 7.9) some tasks to employees at a lower level of the business hierarchy – these employees are known as subordinates.

**Delegation** means giving the authority to subordinates to make decisions and complete tasks. Successful delegation requires the selected employee to be given not only the authority to complete the task but also the required resources and the cooperation of other employees.

> **TIP**
>
> It is important to understand what the five functions of management involve. These functions are different to the roles and responsibilities of managers so do not confuse them.

> **KEY TERM**
>
> **delegation:** when a manager gives authority to a subordinate to carry out specific tasks and make decisions.

**Figure 7.9:** Delegation means passing on a task to a subordinate to complete

Some of the advantages and disadvantages of delegation are shown in Table 7.5.

**Table 7.5:** Advantages and disadvantages of delegation

| Advantages | Disadvantages |
|---|---|
| • Managers have time to focus on more important tasks. | • Employees may not have the skills needed – leading to mistakes or increased cost of training. |
| • Can motivate employees – improving efficiency. | • Managers may fear they will lose control of decision-making. |
| • Developing the skills of employees can increase the flexibility of the workforce. | • Managers may feel threatened by subordinates who can complete a task to a better standard than the delegating managers. |

## ACTIVITY 7.3

Go-by-Car is a car rental company that operates through a large network of local offices across Country X. Each office has a manager who is responsible for planning, organising, controlling, coordinating and commanding the team at that office. Gautam is the manager for one office. He has identified five tasks that he must complete on Monday. He cannot decide which task is most important for him to do first.

- Organise resources such as fuel and cars and assign tasks to employees.
- Plan the weekly and monthly objectives for the office.
- Command employees so they know which tasks are to be assigned to them.
- Control by arranging a meeting to monitor progress against the previous set of objectives.
- Coordinate by communicating with everyone to check how well things are going this week.

1 Individually, think about how you would prioritise the tasks Gautam has to complete in order of importance.

2 In pairs, discuss your answers. Did you have the same order? Share your reasoning with your partner. Produce a combined list based on your discussions.

3 Share your list with another pair or group. How did your answers compare with the other pair/group? Discuss reasons for any differences.

## REFLECTION

How did you decide which tasks were more important than the others? What reasons did you give to support your choices? Did your partner understand them? Make notes on another way you might approach this task next time.

# 7.6 Leadership styles

Leadership is about being able to guide, inspire and influence others to help achieve business goals. Good managers may not always be good leaders, but it is helpful for a business if they are.

## Autocratic leadership style

An **autocratic leader** will make all the decisions without any discussion with others. The leader has total control and simply passes down instructions to employees to follow. One-way communication is used from the leader to the employees. The advantages and disadvantages of an autocratic leadership style are shown in Table 7.6.

This leadership style is often used when workers are unskilled or in situations that require an immediate response, for example, a crisis at work.

> **KEY TERM**
>
> **autocratic leadership:** a leadership style where the leader makes all the decisions without any input from employees.

**Table 7.6:** Advantages and disadvantages of an autocratic leadership style

| Advantages | Disadvantages |
|---|---|
| • Quick decision-making – able to respond to opportunities/situations sooner.<br>• Employees are clear about what they need to do.<br>• Decisions made by experienced people – so fewer mistakes. | • Low motivation as employees not able to share ideas.<br>• May miss out on good ideas of employees.<br>• No scope for employees to develop individual skills. |

## Democratic leadership style

A **democratic leader** will encourage employees to take part in decision-making by sharing ideas although the leader still makes the final decision. Employees are given information that allows them to fully participate in the business, which can motivate them. However, it can take time to listen to everyone's ideas. The advantages and disadvantages of a democratic leadership style are shown in Table 7.7.

This style of leadership is suited to a wide variety of business situations, but is useful where employees are skilled, experienced and keen to be involved in decision-making.

> **KEY TERM**
>
> **democratic leadership:** a leadership style where employees are involved in the decision-making process.

**Table 7.7:** Advantages and disadvantages of a democratic leadership style

| Advantages | Disadvantages |
|---|---|
| • Can motivate employees – improved efficiency.<br>• Employees may understand issues better – so provide better solutions.<br>• Improved communication between managers and employees. | • Time-consuming to listen to employees' ideas – could slow down decision making.<br>• May lead to conflict if individual ideas not accepted.<br>• Employees may not have the necessary experience to make suggestions. |

## Laissez-faire leadership style

Laissez-faire in French means 'let them do it'. A **laissez-faire leadership** style allows employees to make decisions and carry out tasks with limited or no input from the leader. The leader only provides a coordinating and supporting role for the employee if and when needed. The advantages and disadvantages of laissez-faire leadership style are shown in Table 7.8.

This leadership style can be effective for employees involved in creative tasks, for example, developing new products or designing a new advertisement.

> **KEY TERM**
>
> **laissez-faire leadership:** a leadership style where most of the decisions are left to the employees to make with limited or no input from managers.

Table 7.8: Advantages and disadvantages of a laissez-faire leadership style

| Advantages | Disadvantages |
|---|---|
| • Motivates employees. | • Poor coordination – can lead to inefficiency. |
| • Encourages employees to be creative or take responsibility. | • Inconsistent level of service – could damage reputation. |
| • Employees can use all their skills. | • Not clear who takes responsibility for actions. |

A mind map outlining the three main leadership styles is shown in Figure 7.10.

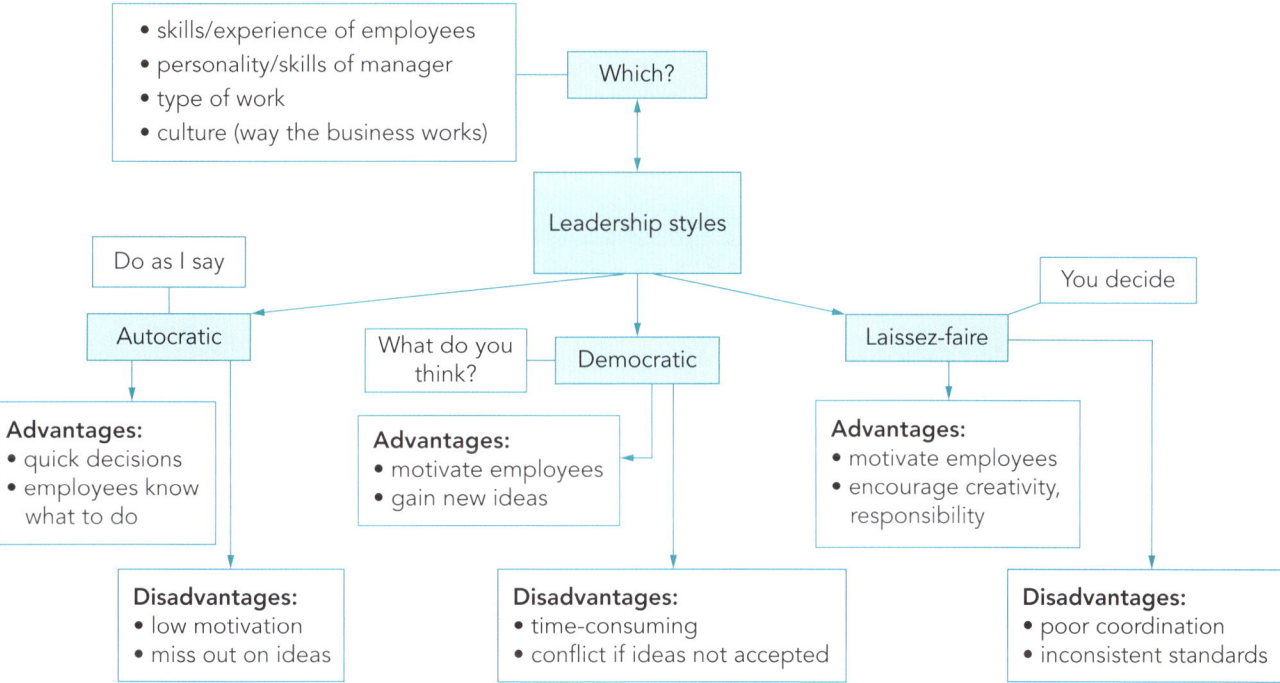

Figure 7.10: A mind map outlining the three main leadership styles

### ACTIVITY 7.4

In pairs, discuss which leadership styles might be the most appropriate in each of the following circumstances:

1  a business that designs and creates television advertisements
2  a business facing a potential financial crisis
3  a manufacturing business where employees are highly skilled
4  a business that operates in a market where competitors are constantly changing their marketing decisions
5  a large retailer with many departments selling different types of goods.

In each case, justify your choice, including why it is better than the other two methods.

### TIP

Do not simply describe leadership styles. Think about how they might link to the role of employees and how decisions are made in the business.

## Choosing a leadership style

There is no one 'best' leadership style. Different situations are likely to require a different type of leadership. The best one is likely to depend on many factors, including:

- **Skills and experience of the employees** – the more skilled and experienced employees are, the less important it is for the manager to make all the decisions and supervise employees.

- **Time available to make a decision** – if a decision needs to be taken quickly, there may be no time to discuss the situation with employees, so an autocratic style might be best.

- **Personality of the manager** – some managers are naturally autocratic or democratic. It can be difficult to use a leadership style that is opposite to their own personality.

- **Task to be completed** – depending on whether the task is complex, simple or creative, it may require different leadership styles.

### CASE STUDY 7.2

**Leadership styles**

Figure 7.11: People are likely to follow a good leader, such as Mary Barra

Elon Musk is the CEO (Managing Director) of Space X, X (formerly Twitter) and Tesla, the electric car manufacturer. He is known for his demanding leadership style. He likes to have close control over the business and to make quick decisions. He has admitted to making decisions at Tesla without the approval of the other board members.

Mary Barra (see Figure 7.11) is the CEO of General Motors, which manufactures cars including the Chevrolet Bolt EV. Barra is known for thinking that meetings should be used to discuss points and not simply pass on information. She prefers that everyone agrees with the decision but will make the final decision when necessary.

Warren Buffet is the CEO of Berkshire Hathaway, which owns or partly owns many businesses including the Chinese car manufacturer, BYD. Buffet is known for recruiting talented individuals and letting them have the freedom to make decisions. He trusts that managers and employees will do what is best for the business, based on his principles of behaviour.

**Discuss in pairs or groups:**

1. Using the information above, describe the leadership style of each of the three businesspeople.

2. Which type of leader would you prefer to work for? Give reasons for your answer.

# 7.7 Reasons for reducing the size of the workforce

There are many reasons why people may leave a business, including to start a job at another business, dismissal or redundancy. Dismissal happens when the employee breaks the rules set out in their contract of employment, for example, poor conduct or not performing tasks to the required standard. Here, we will focus on the concept of redundancy.

## Redundancy

**Redundancy** describes a situation where the job that an employee does is no longer needed (see Figure 7.12). The employee has done nothing wrong; there is simply no work role for them to do.

### The concept of downsizing

Downsizing is when a business reduces in size, and this leads to a permanent decrease in the number of workers that it employs.

### Reasons for downsizing the workforce

A business may need to reduce the size of its workforce for many reasons, including:

- reduction in demand for the product
- introduction of new technology that replaces tasks that employees currently do
- business moves to another site, perhaps to another country
- merger or takeover of the business
- closure of a factory, office or shop
- lower costs to help improve profitability.

**Figure 7.12:** A business that is closing down

> **KEY TERM**
>
> **redundancy:** ending of employment by the employer because the job is no longer needed.

> **LINKS**
>
> You can find more information about merger and takeover in Chapter 3, changes in demand in Chapter 10, costs in Chapter 18 and location decisions in Chapter 20.

### Deciding which employees to make redundant

Selecting employees to be made redundant must be done fairly, otherwise the employee could take legal action based on discrimination.

Factors a business might consider include:

- **Individuals who work in the affected part of the business, factory, office or shop** – technology or automation may replace some jobs so those employees may not be needed.

- **Skills, experience and qualifications of the employees** – someone who has other skills may be able to contribute to the business by doing other work. Some skills are hard to find, so it is important to retain these where possible.

- **Attitude, attendance or disciplinary record** – employees who are often late or absent may be less productive because they are not at work.

- **Performance** – a business may want to retain people who produce a high quantity of, or provide a high standard of work.

- **How long the employee has worked at the business** – it may cost the business less in redundancy payments to choose people who have only worked at the business for a short time.

- **Whether anyone volunteers to leave the job** – some employees may be close to retirement or want to do a different job at another business, so are willing to go.

## 7.8 Trade unions

A **trade union** is an organisation formed and financed by employees for the purpose of protecting the interests of its members, such as improving their pay and working conditions.

There are many different types of trade unions. Some of these represent specific types of employees, for example, the South African Democratic Teachers Union, whereas others have members from different industries, such as the General Workers Federation in Mauritius.

The main benefits of trade union membership for employees are:

- Negotiating with employers to improve pay and working conditions: The union will represent its members in talks with employers at national or local levels on issues such as pay, hours of work, holidays and health and safety.

- Collective bargaining or 'strength in numbers': The collective power of all the members of the trade union acting as one means they are likely to be more successful when negotiating with the business than if each employee were to do so on an individual basis (see Figure 7.13).

- Providing legal support and advice: For example, if an employee is treated unfairly by an employer, their trade union could help them take legal action against the employer.

- Protecting employees' job security: This could involve discussing with employers any major changes to the workplace that might involve job losses and/or redundancy. The trade union may encourage employers to look at options that might reduce the number of job losses.

> **KEY TERM**
>
> **trade union:** a group of employees who join together to protect the interests of its members.

# 7 Organisation and management

**Figure 7.13:** In a trade union, employees join together to protect the interests of its members

## ACTIVITY 7.5

In small groups, research a trade union in your own or a nearby country. Each group should research a different trade union. Use local newspapers, magazines, library resources or the internet for information.

1 What type of employees are the trade union's members? What services and benefits do they provide their members?

2 Make a short two-minute presentation to your class about your chosen trade union.

Where an employer is unwilling to negotiate with a trade union, it might recommend its members take industrial action such as work to rule, refuse to do overtime or, as a last resort, decide to go on strike and refuse to work.

## BUSINESS IN ACTION

### BYJU'S

**Figure 7.14:** A boy using a computer for online learning

BYJU'S is an Indian technology business started by Byju Raveendran and Divya Gokulnath that offers educational services for millions of students around the world. Students learn subjects such as maths and business using interactive games, quizzes and worksheets. BYJU'S was one of the most successful start-ups in India, with the business being valued at $22 billion at the end of 2022.

However, in 2022, the Managing Director announced that BYJU'S would be reducing its workforce by 2 000 employees. Then, in 2023, BYJU'S said it would be changing the organisational structure. A simpler structure may help everyone focus on their roles and lower business costs. This change would result in between 4 000 and 5 000 employees

131

> **CONTINUED**
>
> (5% of its workforce) being made redundant. Job roles to go would include senior managers, marketing personnel and software engineers.
>
> **Discuss in small groups or as a class:**
>
> 1 What reason was given by BYJU'S for reducing the size of the workforce?
>
> 2 What other actions might a business take instead of reducing the size of the workforce?

## SUMMARY

You should now know:

- The main functional areas of the business including operations, marketing, finance and human resources.

- The main features of an organisational structure, such as levels of hierarchy, chain of command and span of control, that can be explained with the use of simple organisation charts.

- The main functions of management are planning, organising, coordinating, commanding and controlling.

- There are advantages and disadvantages of delegation.

- The different styles of leadership are autocratic, democratic and laissez-faire.

- A business may have to reduce the size of its workforce for many reasons and will need to decide which employees to make redundant.

- Trade unions are organisations that aim to protect the interests of its members by improving pay and working conditions and providing other advice and support when needed.

# Chapter 7 practice questions

1 GLB is a large bank based in Country X. The bank has 630 branches and 58 000 employees. GLB has a tall hierarchical structure and each branch manager has a narrow span of control. Graeme is one of these branch managers. He knows there are many functions of management that he must successfully conduct as part of his job. Graeme is known for having an autocratic leadership style and he does not like to delegate. In the last year, 20 employees have left the branch where he is the manager. Graeme is wondering whether he should change his leadership style.

| | | |
|---|---|---|
| a | Define 'span of control'. | [2] |
| b | Identify **four** functions of management. | [4] |
| c | Explain **two** benefits to GLB of using delegation. | [6] |
| d | Do you think an autocratic leadership style is the best one for Graeme could use? Justify your answer. | [8] |

2   DLT is a large computer-manufacturing business. DLT has 130 000 employees, most of whom are members of a trade union. DLT's directors have announced plans to reduce the size of its workforce due to lower demand. This will lead to redundancy for 6 650 full-time employees from its 20 factories. The directors have asked the Human Resources Director to explain the possible factors DLT must consider when deciding which employees to make redundant.

   a   Identify **two** reasons (other than lower demand) that a business might have to reduce the size of its workforce. [2]

   b   Outline **two** benefits to DLT's employees of joining a trade union. [4]

   c   Explain **two** advantages to DLT of having full-time employees. [6]

   d   Explain **two** factors DLT should consider when deciding which employees to make redundant. Which factor is likely to be more important? Justify your answer. [8]

   Total available marks: 40

## CHECK YOUR PROGRESS

How well do you think you have achieved the learning intentions for this chapter? Give yourself a score from 1 (still need a lot of practice) to 5 (feeling very confident) for each learning intention. Provide an example to support your score.

| Now I can … | Score | Example |
| --- | --- | --- |
| understand the main functional areas of a business | | |
| interpret simple organisation charts | | |
| understand the different methods of working including the difference between full-time and part-time employees | | |
| describe the functions of management | | |
| understand the importance of delegation | | |
| explain the advantages and disadvantages of the main leadership styles | | |
| recommend a suitable leadership style in a given situation | | |
| identify reasons why reducing the size of the workforce is necessary | | |
| recommend which workers should be made redundant in a given situation | | |
| explain the benefits to employees of being members of a trade union. | | |

# Chapter 8
# Methods of communication

**LEARNING INTENTIONS**

By the end of this chapter, you will be able to:
- understand why communication is important for a business
- identify different communication methods, both internal and external
- explain the advantages and disadvantages of different methods of communication
- recommend and justify a suitable method of communication to use in a given situation
- identify examples of communication barriers
- understand the reasons for and problems caused by communication barriers
- explain how communication barriers can be reduced or removed.

# Introduction

Every day you are likely to communicate with many people using different communication methods. You speak to family members over breakfast, chat to your friends on the way to and from school, listen to and speak with teachers, message friends, read blogs and much more. Businesses also communicate with many individuals and groups and will use many different methods of communication.

In this chapter, you will study the importance of communication to businesses and the methods used to achieve this. You will also learn about barriers to communication, why there might be problems when trying to communicate information and how such problems might be reduced or avoided.

## BUSINESS IN CONTEXT

### Here is the news

Natura & Co is a personal care company based in Sao Paolo, Brazil. Natura & Co is a beauty brand that combines science and sustainably sourced ingredients mainly from the Amazon to develop a range of body, hair and skincare products that are ethically traded and are 100% cruelty-free. Natura & Co's products are sold door to door, online and in shops around the world.

In 2020, Natura & Co bought Avon Products, the international business owned by Avon. The takeover would increase the total number of countries in which Natura & Co operates to over 100 countries. As well as sharing the news in a press release on its website, Natura & Co produced a film to highlight what the takeover would mean for all its stakeholders. Recognised as one of the largest B Corp businesses in the world (an independent assessment showing the business meets high social and environmental standards), the film also reinforced Natura & Co's commitment to the environment.

Other methods of communication used by Natura & Co included posters and social media to welcome Avon, its customers and employees to its 'family' highlighting the company's objective of 'creating the best beauty company for the world'.

### Discuss in pairs or groups:

1. Why might Natura & Co have decided to produce a film to tell people about its takeover of Avon Products?

2. What are the possible reasons, other than to tell people about the takeover, why Natura & Co might want to communicate with its stakeholders?

**Figure 8.1:** Creating a film or video is one way that a business can share information with its stakeholders

## 8.1 Why communication is important

The process of communication involves a message, a medium or method, a sender and receiver(s). Good communication between two or more people or groups of people only works if:

- the message is sent using a suitable method of communication
- the message is sent to and received by the right person
- the receiver understands the message
- the receiver provides feedback to the sender to confirm that they have received and understood the message.

The purpose of communication is to give out information and collect information (see Figure 8.2). This can help a business avoid misunderstandings. For example, when a manager gives instructions to employees, it is important that the employees understand what they are being asked to do so that the work can be carried out efficiently.

Communication can be internal or external. Internal communication involves information being passed between people who are employed in the business, for example, in the same department or at another location where the organisation has offices or operations. External communication involves communicating with people and organisations outside the business, such as customers, suppliers, government agencies or lenders.

**Figure 8.2:** There are many ways to communicate the same information to people

Good communication is important for many reasons including:

- **Reduce mistakes** – if the person receiving the message does not understand it, the instructions or task may not be completed correctly which could waste time or resources.
- **Faster decision-making** – so the business can take advantage of business opportunities sooner or start related work as early as possible.

- **Improve coordination between functional areas** – for example, decisions taken by Marketing can affect other departments such as Operations. Each department needs to know what the other is doing to respond appropriately.

- **Improve employee motivation** – if the employees know what is going on in the workplace and can take part in discussions, it can make them feel part of the organisation, improving productivity.

- **Improve customer relationships** – keeping customers informed about the progress of their orders or any new products the business is selling can make them feel valued and incentivise them to continue buying from the business.

### ACTIVITY 8.1

In pairs or small groups, consider each of the following examples of business communication:

- an order to a supplier for raw materials
- a complaint from a customer about a product they have bought which is faulty
- a sales order from a customer
- new wage rates for all employees in three factories located in different parts of your country
- an advertisement for a new product the business is introducing to the market.

1 a  For each one, explain why it is important that these messages are sent and received by the right people.

  b  Select one situation and prepare a one-minute summary outlining why communication is important in this situation. Share this information with another pair or group.

## 8.2 Methods of communication

There are many methods of communication that a business might use. These include:

- **Meeting** – when a group of people gather to discuss issues directly. These meetings can be virtual or face-to-face. A meeting also allows the opportunity for asking questions to check understanding.

- **Phone call** – a telephone, whether it is a basic phone, a mobile phone or a smartphone, is a verbal method of communication, which allows messages to be sent or received immediately.

- **Email** – a written message sent electronically from one electronic device to another. It can be used to send additional information or documents in the form of attachments.

- **Text message (SMS)** – these are short electronic messages usually sent from one mobile phone to other mobile phones.

- **Social media** – an electronic form of communication that allows a business to communicate internally or externally, to give out and receive information.
- **Website** – many businesses now have websites. This could be anything from a simple page stating the business name, contact details and what it sells to a collection of linked electronic pages where a business can include information in different sections covering a range of issues for customers and other stakeholders to read.
- **Letter** – this is used for formal communication between the business and its stakeholders, such as employees and customers. For example, informing employees about a pay rise or replying to a customer complaint.
- **Poster** – contains written information or images that can be placed in various locations, inside or outside the business, for people to see as they pass by.
- **Noticeboard** – contains written information or images that can be placed in various locations, usually inside the business, for employees to see as they pass by (see Figure 8.3).

**Figure 8.3:** Employees checking a noticeboard at work

### ACTIVITY 8.2

In pairs or small groups, investigate all the different methods used in your school/college to communicate with pupils, parents, teachers and one other stakeholder group of your choice.

Each group should choose a different stakeholder group. Produce a poster or chart summarising the methods of communication used.

# 8.3 Advantages and disadvantages of communication methods

The advantages and disadvantages of the main methods of communication used by businesses are outlined in Table 8.1.

**Table 8.1:** Advantages and disadvantages of different methods of business communication

| Communication method | Advantages | Disadvantages |
|---|---|---|
| Meeting (face-to-face or virtual) | <ul><li>everyone gets the same message at the same time</li><li>allows for the possibility of discussion</li><li>can ask questions to check understanding</li><li>can see reactions/gestures of others.</li></ul> | <ul><li>time-consuming to organise/hold</li><li>cost of travel if meeting is face-to-face or equipment cost if virtual</li><li>may be difficult to find time that suits all meeting attendees.</li></ul> |
| Phone call (include mobile calls) | <ul><li>able to speak directly to people</li><li>can ask questions to make sure message is understood</li><li>easy to check if the message has been received.</li></ul> | <ul><li>no written record</li><li>receiver may not answer phone</li><li>receiver might not listen</li><li>receiver may not hear message correctly.</li></ul> |
| Email | <ul><li>can send to many receivers at the same time</li><li>written record to refer to</li><li>can send attachments with email</li><li>can send at time that suits sender</li><li>can be read at time that suits receiver.</li></ul> | <ul><li>sender may not know/have receiver's email address</li><li>equipment can be expensive</li><li>people may not see/open email in time</li><li>may go into junk mail.</li></ul> |
| Text messaging | <ul><li>can send to many receivers at the same time</li><li>receiver can read it when it suits them</li><li>written record to refer to.</li></ul> | <ul><li>not everyone has access to the equipment needed</li><li>equipment can be expensive</li><li>may not have a signal to send/receive message.</li></ul> |
| Social media | <ul><li>can send to many receivers at the same time</li><li>receiver can read it when suits them</li><li>written record to refer to.</li></ul> | <ul><li>not everyone has access to suitable device/internet/signal</li><li>cost of equipment can be expensive</li><li>cannot control what is written by others.</li></ul> |
| Website | <ul><li>can hold a large amount of information</li><li>accessible to large number of people</li><li>can be viewed at any time.</li></ul> | <ul><li>cost to set up website</li><li>danger that site may be hacked</li><li>need to update information regularly.</li></ul> |

(Continued)

**Table 8.1:** (Continued)

| Communication method | Advantages | Disadvantages |
|---|---|---|
| Letter | • written record<br>• can be confidential<br>• can contain detailed information. | • no personal contact<br>• no immediate feedback<br>• time taken to receive message<br>• cost of postage. |
| Poster | • can include colour and images to make message stand out<br>• can be seen by many people<br>• low cost to produce. | • easy to damage<br>• no guarantee it will be seen<br>• contain limited detail<br>• no opportunity for feedback. |
| Notice on a noticeboard | • can include colour and images to make message stand out<br>• can be seen by employees as they pass by<br>• low cost to produce. | • contain limited detail<br>• no opportunity for feedback<br>• easy for employee to miss message<br>• easy to damage. |

### CASE STUDY 8.1

**Methods of communication**

**Zappos**

Zappos is known for its good customer service, but employees matter too. Every three months, Zappos has an 'All-Hands Day'. This is an opportunity for all employees to get together to receive updates about what the business is doing, share ideas and stories about things that have happened at work or anything else that interests the employees.

**Stagecoach**

To engage its 24 000 employees, Stagecoach, a bus company, introduced a mobile phone app for them to use. Within the first week of its introduction over 80% of employees had used the app for a range of reasons including to keep in touch with people on different work shifts, finding out news about what was happening in the business and completing surveys and forms. Stagecoach noticed employee motivation increased and fewer employees wanted to leave the business.

**Figure 8.4:** Not all communication has to involve paper

### TIP

Advantages and disadvantages could apply to more than one method. Try to avoid repeating the advantages of one method as the disadvantages of another method because this could be seen as repetition. Try to focus on different points when discussing each method.

> **CONTINUED**
>
> **TED**
>
> TED is a communication business. It is known for organising talks by important individuals on topics including technology, entertainment and design. Research shows that most people can only focus on a speaker for 10–18 minutes, so all TED speakers are encouraged to keep their talks short. TED follows the same rules too – all its internal meetings are limited to a maximum of 18 minutes, and meetings are only organised if essential.
>
> **Discuss in pairs or groups:**
>
> 1. What are the possible advantages for each business of using these methods of communication?
>
> 2. What might be the disadvantages to each business of using these methods of communication?

# Choosing the best method of communication

There is no one single 'best' method of communication for a business to use. In most situations, there will be a range of possible methods that might work.

When choosing a suitable method of communication, businesses need to think about factors such as:

- **How important or urgent the message is** – for example, a telephone call may be suitable if the information is needed straightaway.
- **The amount and complexity of information to be sent** – if it is a long or complex message, methods such as emails or letters may be suitable so that the receiver has a written record to refer to.
- **How many people need to receive the message** – if the business needs to contact many people then letters, meetings or emails might be suitable.
- **Is a written record needed** – if yes, methods such as letters or emails should be considered.
- **Is feedback needed** – if yes, then a meeting or telephone calls may be suitable as these allow for two-way communication.
- **How sensitive or confidential the message is** – as letters can be sent to named individuals.
- **The cost of each method** – most methods will involve a cost. For example, email, text messaging and telephone calls require investment in equipment and ongoing payments to the phone service or internet provider.

> **TIP**
>
> A business can use many different methods of communication. Think about the answers to questions such as what, who, why and when to help decide on a suitable method to use in a given situation.

> **ACTIVITY 8.3**
>
> Work in pairs to discuss a suitable method of communication for each of the following situations:
>
> 1. a warning to an employee about the poor quality of their work
> 2. a complaint from a customer
> 3. late delivery of components from a supplier

> **TIP**
>
> There is usually no single correct answer to this type of question. What matters is that you can explain the reason for your choice(s).

## CONTINUED

4  a customer who has not yet paid for goods supplied two months ago

5  ten production employees who are to be made redundant

6  explaining future business plans to a workforce of 50 employees.

In each case, you must give a clear reason for your choice.

## REFLECTION

Share your answers with another pair – did you decide on the same method? If yes, did they have the same reason as you? If not, did they understand the reasons you had given? Discuss with your partner how your explanation could be improved.

Produce a simple short guide to help others understand the factors to consider when deciding on a suitable method of communication to use in a given situation.

## CASE STUDY 8.2

### Melia Hotels

**Figure 8.5:** People on holiday take pictures that they can share on social media

When there are over 1 200 major hotel brands in the world, it can be difficult to stand out from the competition. Finding ways to engage and communicate with its customers can help a business remain competitive.

Melia Hotels is a Spanish hotel group. It is well known for the creative ways in which it uses social media to communicate with potential and existing customers to provide news updates and encourage sales. These ways include:

- Using hashtags to help customers find interesting content on Instagram more quickly. One of its most successful campaigns is #SoulMatters, which highlights the Spanish origins of the business, its passion for offering good customer service and its commitment to sustainability. Customers are encouraged to share their experiences (see Figure 8.5) with others online on its website or Instagram. The #SoulMatters hashtag has over 32 000 followers.

- Having its own YouTube channel where it shares videos of what customers can expect when staying at a Melia hotel, and tips and advice for customers to know before they go.

- When Melia Hotels wanted to join TikTok, (a short-form video-sharing platform), it challenged groups of university students around the world to help create its strategy. This helped Melia understand what the next generation of hotel guests was interested in, which then helped Melia adapt its communications appropriately.

**Discuss in pairs or groups:**

1  What might be the advantages for Melia Hotels of using social media to communicate with its customers?

2  What other methods could Melia Hotels use to communicate with its customers?

## 8.4 Communication barriers

Anything that stops a message from being sent, received or understood clearly is known as a **communication barrier**. There are many reasons why communication barriers exist. Some of these are included in Table 8.2.

**Table 8.2:** Reasons why communication barriers exist

| Reason | Examples |
|---|---|
| Breakdown in communication process, whether with the sender, receiver, method of communication or feedback | - Wrong method of communication is used so the message may not be received.<br>- Wrong or unclear message sent so wrong action may be taken.<br>- The language used is too complex or includes technical terms that the receiver cannot understand.<br>- Too much information is being communicated in one message.<br>- Message is sent to the wrong person.<br>- Receiver may not hear the message properly.<br>- Lack of feedback so it is unknown whether the message has been received and/or understood. |
| Poor attitude of sender or receiver | - If an employee is demotivated, they may not send or may not listen carefully to the message.<br>- If a sender/receiver does not like each other, they may not make an effort to make message clear or check for understanding. |
| Physical | - Noise – meaning, the message is unclear or cannot be heard properly.<br>- Distractions – so sender/receiver cannot focus on message.<br>- Distance involved between the sender and receiver(s).<br>- Technical issues – such as the equipment/software does not work or there is no signal so message cannot be sent or received. |
| Organisational | - Message must pass through too many levels of the hierarchy, so it may get lost or distorted, or may take too long to be received. |
| Cultural | - Different cultural backgrounds and social norms can influence how or to whom messages are sent.<br>- Words and expressions can have different meanings in different cultures. |

> **KEY TERM**
>
> **communication barrier:** something that stops a message from being sent, received or understood clearly.

> **LINK**
>
> You can find more information about maintaining customer loyalty in Chapter 10.

**Figure 8.6:** Simply saying the words does not mean the other person can hear them

## Problems caused by communication barriers

Whatever the reason that a message is not sent, received or understood clearly (see Figure 8.6), it can cause problems for businesses including:

- Tasks are not completed or are completed incorrectly. This reduces efficiency and increases waste which could increase average cost.
- Mistakes made could damage the business reputation, leading to a loss of customers.
- Lower employee motivation – could lead to increased absenteeism and increased labour turnover.
- Fewer sales if advertising and other promotional messages are unclear.
- Recruitment and selection problems – if job descriptions, person specifications or job advertisements are poorly designed, the business may not attract the right candidates.

> **LINK**
>
> You can find more information about motivation in Chapter 9 (well-motivated workforce).

## 8.5 How communication barriers can be reduced or removed

The method used to reduce or remove communication barriers will depend on what is causing the problem. Ways of reducing and removing communication barriers include:

- using clear and simple language – avoid using complex or technical terms (jargon) that may not be understood by people without technical knowhow
- keeping the message short and only communicating one message at a time
- asking for feedback – to check the message has been received and understood

- choosing a suitable method of communication for the message to be sent
- communicating in places away from background noise or other distractions
- management must build a culture of trust and respect between all employees.

A summary of communication methods and barriers is shown in Figure 8.7.

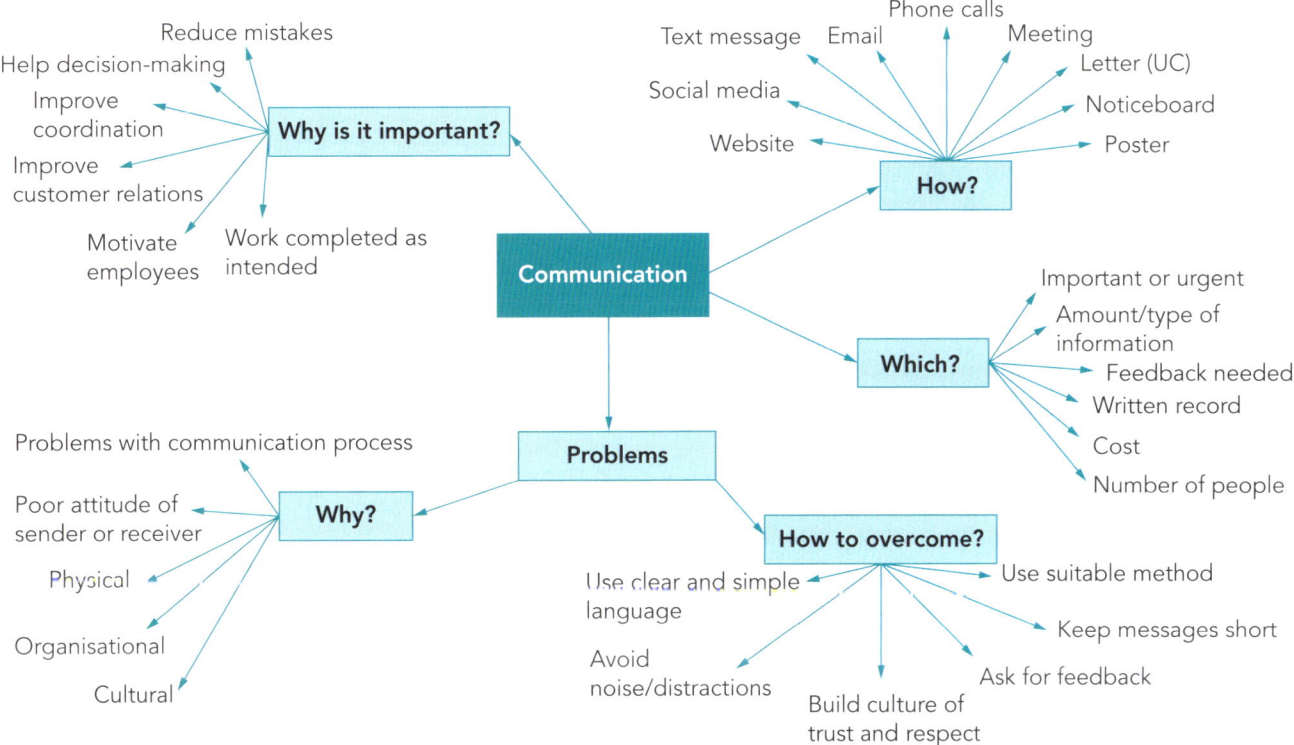

Figure 8.7: A summary of communication methods and barriers

### ACTIVITY 8.4

1  In pairs, for each of the following situations, identify the possible communication barrier(s) and discuss ways a business might overcome or reduce each barrier:

   a  sending an urgent text message

   b  discussing a problem with an employee in an engineering workshop

   c  sending a letter to a customer

   d  asking an employee to pass on an important message to other employees in their team

   e  making a telephone call to a supplier in another country.

### TIP

When you are thinking about communication and possible problems, think about the methods you use and the problems you sometimes have – they are likely to be similar problems for businesses. It is simply that business communication involves more people and the problems are likely to happen more often.

## BUSINESS IN ACTION

### Communication in the digital age

Figure 8.8: Technology has changed how people communicate at work

As every business is different, it is likely that the way it communicates with employees will differ too. Technology is also having a significant effect on the methods of communication being used (see Figure 8.8). For example: MTN is a telecommunications company based in South Africa. The business uses a chat bot (a computer program that tries to copy or replace a human conversation) to communicate with MTN's employees on a free popular instant messaging app. This allows the senior managers to send personalised messages, and share ideas and news with employees working throughout MTN. It also allows employees to send feedback and messages to senior managers directly, creating two-way communication. This helps managers know what their employees are thinking all the time.

HDFC is an Indian bank. The business uses a range of ways to strengthen relationships between managers and its employees, including offering listening courses for managers and 'circuit meets', a software tool designed for sharing ideas and feedback between groups in different areas of the business.

Astra Zeneca is a large pharmaceutical business with operations in 60 countries. To help keep everyone connected, it uses webinars that can be recorded and viewed based on the time zone in each respective country. Astra Zeneca also asks employees to record 20-minute videos showing what is happening at each location, so everyone feels like they are working together towards the same objectives.

Discuss in small groups or as a class:

1   Do you think non-digital methods such as letters, posters and noticeboards still have a role in business communication? Be ready to give reasons to support your answer.

## SUMMARY

You should now know:

- Good communication is when a message is sent using a suitable method and the receiver provides feedback to the sender to show that the message has been received and understood.

- Every method of communication has advantages and disadvantages. The most suitable method will depend on the specific situation.

- Communication might not be effective because of barriers such as problems with one element of the communication process, the attitudes of senders and receivers or physical problems.

- Businesses can use various methods to remove or reduce communication barriers including using clear and simple language and keeping messages short.

## Chapter 8 practice questions

1 GSD is an airline company. Due to technical problems, four of its planes will be unavailable for three months. GSD had already accepted bookings from customers for flights on these planes and the Operations Manager will need to inform customers that the bookings will be cancelled. The problem also means that GSD will not need as many employees. The Human Resource Manager has decided to reduce the hours of all 20 part-time employees for the next three months. She must choose a suitable method to communicate this information to employees.

   a  Identify **two** reasons why communication is important for a business. [2]

   b  Identify **four** factors a business should consider when deciding which method of communication to use. [4]

   c  Explain **two** communication methods the GSD might use to inform its customers about the cancelled bookings. [6]

   d  Explain **two** methods GSD's Human Resource Manager could use to communicate her decision to employees. Which is likely to be the best method to use? Justify your answer. [8]

2 CPA manufactures gardening products including gardening forks and spades. The business has 600 workers in two factories in different parts of Country Y. All important decisions are made by senior managers at the head office which are then communicated to the factory managers by email. The Managing Director knows there are many communication barriers for CPA to overcome. CPA directors plan to introduce new technology into its factories. The Operations Director cannot decide whether a meeting is the best method of communication to use to inform employees.

   a  Define 'communication barrier'. [2]

   b  Outline **one** advantage and **one** disadvantage of CPA using email to communicate with the managers. [4]

   c  Explain **two** communication barriers CPA might have to overcome. [6]

   d  Do you think the advantages of CPA using a meeting to inform the employees about the plan to introduce new technology are greater than the disadvantages? Justify your answer. [8]

Total available marks: 40

# BUSINESS FOR CAMBRIDGE IGCSE™ AND O LEVEL: COURSEBOOK

## CHECK YOUR PROGRESS

How well do you think you have achieved the learning intentions for this chapter? Give yourself a score from 1 (still need a lot of practice) to 5 (feeling very confident) for each learning intention. Provide an example to support your score.

| Now I can … | Score | Example |
|---|---|---|
| understand why communication is important for a business | | |
| identify different methods of communication, both internal and external | | |
| explain the advantages and disadvantages of different methods of communication | | |
| understand reasons for communication barriers | | |
| identify examples of communication barriers | | |
| understand the reasons for and problems caused by communication barriers | | |
| explain how communication barriers can be reduced or removed. | | |

> Chapter 9
# Motivating employees

**LEARNING INTENTIONS**

By the end of this chapter, you will be able to:
- identify the reasons why people work
- explain the importance of motivation in the workplace
- understand three main theories of motivation
- explain financial and non-financial methods of motivation
- recommend a suitable method of motivation for a business to use in a given situation.

# Introduction

In this chapter, you will learn about why people work and what motivates them to work. A well-motivated employee is likely to work more efficiently and enjoy what they do compared to an employee who has no interest in their job. You will also learn about three important theories about motivation at work and understand how these theories can help business managers achieve a well-motivated workforce. To help motivate employees, a business is likely to use different financial and non-financial methods of motivation.

## BUSINESS IN CONTEXT

### The only way is up

**Figure 9.1:** A pilot adjusting the switches during a flight

Working is a way to allow people to earn money to pay for basic things such as food or clothing. However, work can satisfy other needs as well.

Christina Ho started working at Cathay Pacific, the Hong Kong, China (SAR)-based airline business as a member of the cabin crew. She remembers clearly when she decided she wanted to become an airplane pilot. Taking advantage of one of the benefits of working for an airline, when she was going on holiday she was able to sit in the cockpit alongside the pilot. She was amazed not only by the view out of the window but by what the pilot did, the responsibility of having to do several tasks at once, including flying the plane and communicating with many different people at the same time. Becoming a pilot was not easy – it took over a year and a lot of studying, but Christina is happy she did it as she is now doing the job she loves.

Vidhya Rangaswamy is a Vice President in High Value Chemicals at Reliance Industries, the largest business in India. Vidhya and her team are responsible for developing biofuels (a type of fuel produced from renewable sources including plants and algae) and other high-value chemicals. Vidhya enjoys the freedom she and her team are given to experiment with new ideas that many similar businesses do not allow. Even at her level of the hierarchy, she has access to mentors who encourage her to challenge both herself and the business to help achieve her goals.

**Discuss in pairs or groups:**

1. Using the text, what needs might Christina and Vidhya satisfy by doing their jobs?
2. Do you think all people have the same reasons for working? Give reasons for your answer.

## 9.1 The importance of a well-motivated workforce

Everyone works for different reasons (see Figure 9.2). This may include to receive a paycheck, job security, interesting nature of the job and opportunities for promotion.

**Figure 9.2:** People working in a clothing factory

A business must understand the reasons why employees work because this can affect how they work. A business will want employees to be interested and committed to their job so that they work harder and more efficiently.

> ### ACTIVITY 9.1
> 1. Individually, ask five different working people you know why they work.
> 2. Working in groups, combine all the answers into similar groups, such as answers about pay, and then present the results in a table. (If you have access to computers, you could use a spreadsheet to record the answers.)
> 3. Which reasons were most common? Produce a diagram or short report summarising the main findings.

## 9.2 Benefits of a well-motivated workforce

Motivation is the reason or reasons that make people want to do something. Well-motivated employees are more likely to work efficiently and provide quality goods and services for customers. This could improve the reputation of the business, which can help attract customers; it can also help attract and retain employees. Figure 9.3 outlines the main benefits to a business of having well-motivated employees.

Motivated employees help a business to have improved labour productivity, reduce absenteeism, lower labour turnover, and instil greater willingness to accept change or new methods of working.

- **Improved labour productivity** (the output produced by each employee) – this can help reduce average costs which could allow the business to lower prices or increase its profit margin.
- **Reduced absenteeism** – employees who are motivated are less likely to take days off without a good reason. This could mean the work is completed on time and other employees do not need to cover the jobs of absentee employees.

- **Lower labour turnover** – (the number of employees leaving the business) if fewer employees leave, this can reduce recruitment and training costs.
- **Greater willingness to accept change or new methods of working** – this can help a business keep up to date with changes in the business environment and increase its competitiveness.

> **KEY TERM**
>
> **labour turnover:** the rate at which employees leave a business in a given period of time.

> **LINK**
>
> You can find more information about productivity in Chapter 17.

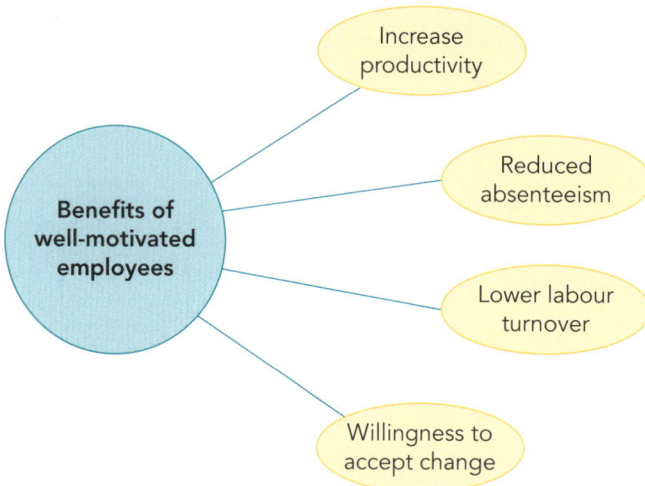

**Figure 9.3:** The benefits to a business of having a well-motivated workforce

### ACTIVITY 9.2

The senior managers of Farooq Fashions (FF), a clothing manufacturer, are concerned about the levels of employee motivation at one of its factories, Factory A. The FF's Human Resources Director has produced the data shown in Table 9.1 for last year.

**Table 9.1:** Employee data for Factory A

| Factory A | | Average productivity for FF's other factories |
|---|---|---|
| Average productivity per employee (each week) | 220 | 350 |
| Average number of days' absence per employee (for the year) | 19 | 8 |
| Number of employees who left in the year | 40 | 18 |
| Average wages per employee (each week) | $126 | $125 |

1. Using the information in Table 9.1, what evidence suggests that Factory A's employees may not be well-motivated.
2. Write a short report explaining to FF's senior managers why it is important to improve employee motivation at Factory A?

## 9.3 Main motivational theories

Motivation theory is the study of understanding what pushes a person to work towards a particular goal. It is relevant to everyone but is especially important to businesses. There are three main theories you need to know about for this course.

> **TIP**
>
> Using numbers or data provided in a question is a good way to show application skills. Always try to use the information provided to support the point being made.

### Maslow's theory

Maslow's theory is based on the idea that everyone is motivated by the same type of factors or needs. These are shown in Maslow's Hierarchy of Needs (see Figure 9.4).

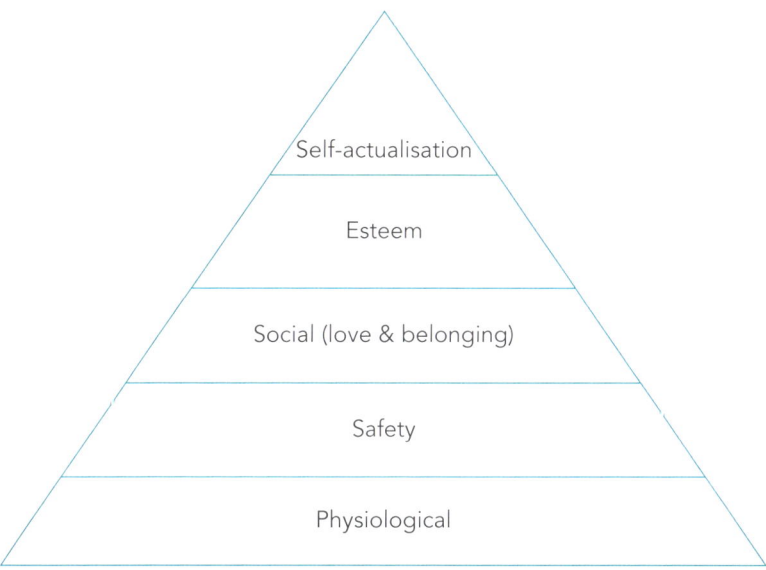

**Figure 9.4:** The five levels of Maslow's Hierarchy of Needs

A person will start at the lowest level of the hierarchy – physiological needs. Once they have satisfied their physiological needs, for example, hunger, thirst, sleep, being paid a good wage, then people are motivated to try to reach the next level – safety needs – and so on until they reach the top level of needs – self-actualisation. Once a need has been met, it no longer acts as a motivator.

Table 9.2 outlines the five levels of Maslow's Hierarchy of Needs and how businesses can use this to help motivate its employees.

**Table 9.2:** The levels of Maslow's hierarchy of needs and how this can help businesses motivate its employees

| Level | This means | Ways a business might use to help meet these needs include |
|---|---|---|
| Self-actualisation | • achieving their own goals or reaching their full potential. | • help employees set personal goals<br>• offer opportunities for training and promotion<br>• give employees challenging work. |
| Esteem | • being respected and having their achievements recognised by others. | • use praise or promotion to recognise good work. |

**Table 9.2:** (Continued)

| Level | This means | Ways a business might use to help meet these needs include |
|---|---|---|
| Social needs (love & belonging) | • being accepted by others and belonging to a group where social activities can be shared and enjoyed together. | • provide opportunities for team work<br>• clear communication so employees feel involved. |
| Safety needs | • idea of being safe from physical danger and having financial security. | • provide job security through an employment contract<br>• offer good working conditions. |
| Physiological needs | • basic needs to be able to survive, including water, food, shelter and clothing. | • pay reasonable wages/salaries for work done. |

## Taylor's scientific management theory

Taylor's theory is based on the idea that employees are motivated by money alone. Therefore, to get employees to increase their efforts they must be rewarded with more money. Paying employees a fixed amount for every unit they produce is known as **piece-rate**. This payment method should help increase efficiency, because the more units the employee produces the more the employee would be paid.

## Herzberg's two-factor theory

Herzberg identified that there were two groups of factors that influenced motivation. These are called **hygiene factors** and **motivators**. These factors are shown in Table 9.3.

**Table 9.3:** Herzberg's two-factor theory

| Hygiene factors | Motivators |
|---|---|
| • working conditions<br>• relationships with others<br>• salary or wage<br>• supervision<br>• business policies and rules | • the work itself<br>• responsibility<br>• growth/development<br>• advancement/promotion<br>• recognition<br>• achievement |

### Hygiene factors

These are factors necessary for people to work but do not motivate them to work harder or better.

- **Working conditions** – these include how clean and safe the workplace is and what facilities are provided for employees; for example, washrooms and drinks machines.
- **Relationships with others** – employees expect to have good working relationships with other employees – the need for friendship and to belong to a group. They may also want to have a good relationship with their manager, and to be treated fairly and with respect.

> **TIP**
>
> Do not assume that higher pay automatically motivates employees to increase output. There may be other factors that cause an increase in output.

> **LINK**
>
> You can find more information about piece-rate later in this chapter in Section 9.4.

> **KEY TERMS**
>
> **piece-rate:** a payment system where employees are paid based on the number of units they produce
>
> **hygiene factors:** one of the factors that must be present in the workplace to prevent job dissatisfaction.
>
> **motivators:** the factors that influence a person to increase their efforts at work.

- **Salary or wage** – people must be paid enough for them to carry out a job, but money is not enough for them to want to do the job well.
- **Supervision** – this factor considers the importance of leadership style and how closely employees are supervised by the person in charge of them.
- **Business policies and rules** – these are the rules and procedures that control and influence the way that employees work and their relationships with others in the workplace.

Employees are likely to expect basic, safety and social needs to be provided by their employer. Hygiene factors are important and must be present at a level acceptable to employees to prevent job dissatisfaction. Improving hygiene factors makes job dissatisfaction less likely but they will not motivate employees to work.

**Figure 9.5:** Employees expect to have good working relationships with other employees

## Motivators

Motivators allow employees to gain job satisfaction which encourages people to work harder. These are:

- **The work itself** – the work or tasks given need to be varied and challenging so the work is more interesting.
- **Possibility for growth** – giving employees the opportunity to learn new skills or develop as a person.
- **Advancement** – employees have opportunities for promotion.
- **Responsibility** – giving employees more responsibility for the tasks they perform, for example, allowing them to make decisions linked to their work. The manager is showing that they trust employees and value their contribution.
- **Recognition** – employees need to be praised or rewarded by management and the other people they work with for doing good work.
- **Achievement** – employees need to feel that they have reached challenging goals.

According to Herzberg, managers can use one or more motivators to increase employee motivation. However, these motivators will not work unless there is an acceptable level of hygiene factors to prevent job dissatisfaction.

> **TIP**
>
> Do not confuse hygiene factors and motivators. While both are necessary for people to work, only motivators will increase motivation – the clue is in the name!

### ACTIVITY 9.3

**Maslow**

Working in pairs:

1 Explain which need each of the following actions is designed to help meet.

   a  A business has a noticeboard in the entrance of the building that lists the names of employees who have provided exceptional service to customers each week.

   b  The business has a specially designed room where employees can play games or sing songs together or simply have somewhere to relax when not working.

   c  All employees are provided with protective clothing when working with machinery.

2 Identify **one** other example of how each need could be met by a business.

**Herzberg**

3 Working in pairs, rank the motivators in the order you think is likely to be the most effective (down to the least effective). Give reasons for your choices. Share your answers with another pair, explaining the reason for your ranking.

Figure 9.6 shows a summary of the three main theories of motivation and how businesses can use this information to help motivate employees.

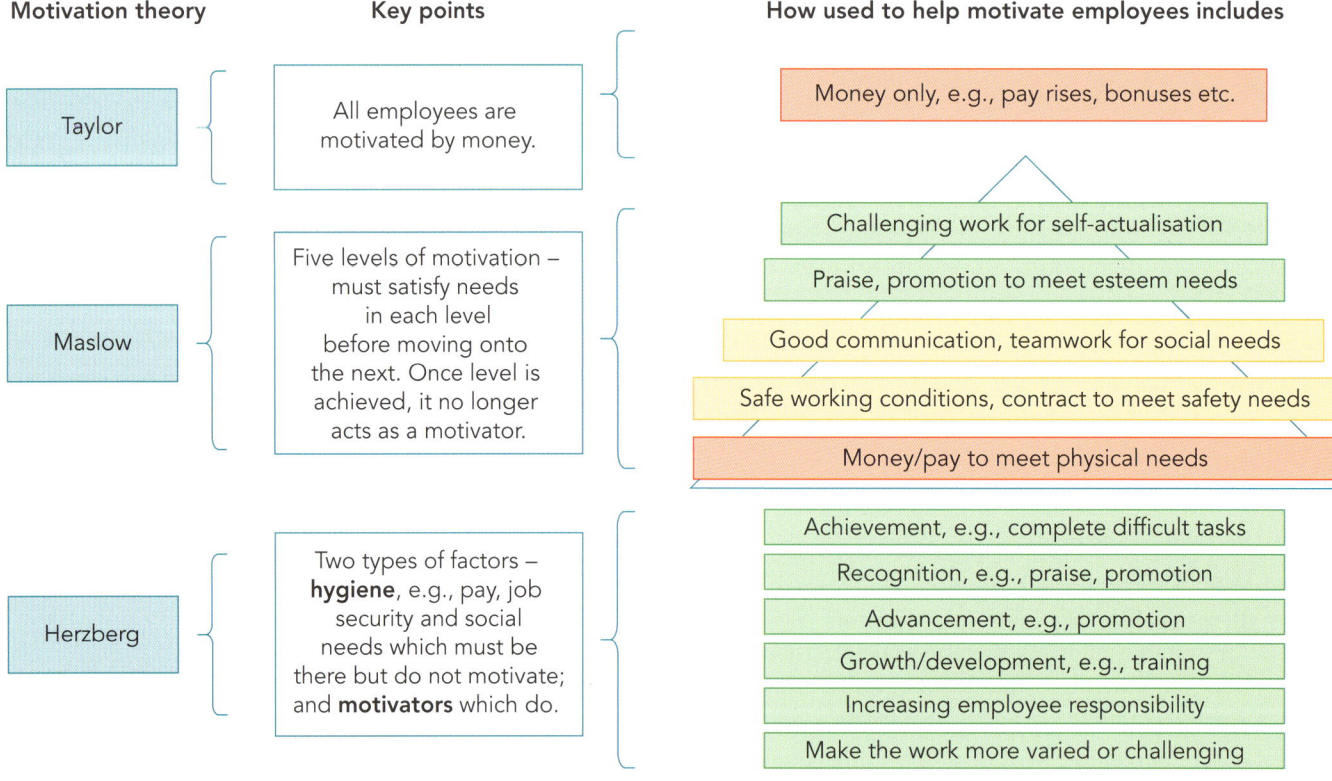

**Figure 9.6:** A summary of the three theories of motivation and how businesses can use this information to help motivate employees

## 9.4 Methods of motivation

There are many methods a manager can use to motivate employees. These can be divided into financial methods and non-financial methods.

## Financial methods of motivation

If money is an important motivator, then managers need to consider how best to use it to achieve a well-motivated workforce. The financial methods of motivation identified in Figure 9.7 are explained below.

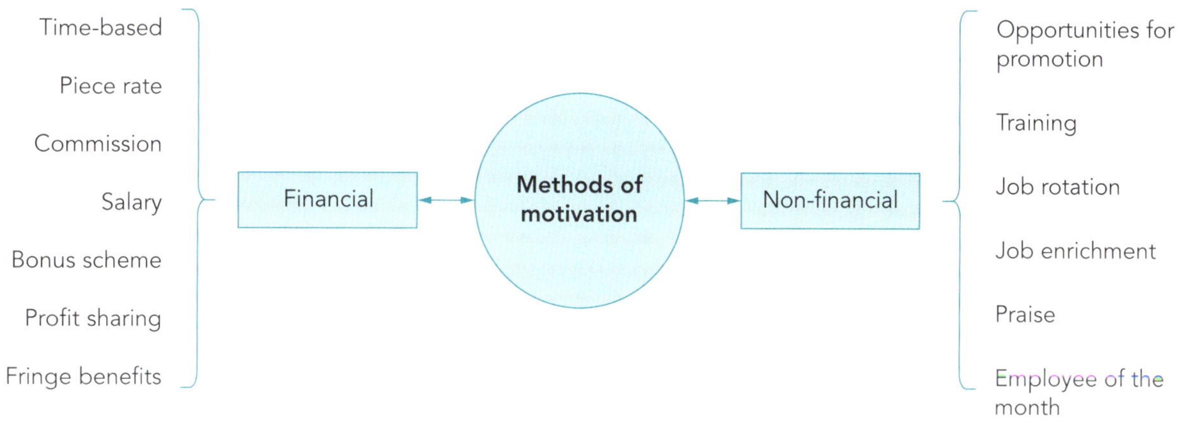

> **TIP**
>
> Do not simply learn the key points of the different motivation theories. You need to understand how the different theories can be used to help improve employee motivation.

Financial:
- Time-based
- Piece rate
- Commission
- Salary
- Bonus scheme
- Profit sharing
- Fringe benefits

Non-financial:
- Opportunities for promotion
- Training
- Job rotation
- Job enrichment
- Praise
- Employee of the month

**Figure 9.7:** Financial and non-financial methods of motivation

### Time-based

**Time-based** is a payment system where employees are paid a fixed amount for each hour worked (see Figure 9.8). The longer an employee is at work, the more they get paid. For example, if an employee is paid $5 per hour and works 40 hours in a week, then they will earn a wage of $5 × 40 = $200 for the week. This method is often used for employees such as shop workers where it is not easy to calculate output or productivity.

**Table 9.4:** Advantages and disadvantages of using time-based payment method

| Advantages | Disadvantages |
|---|---|
| • Only pay employees for the number of hours worked – can lower labour costs.<br>• Simple to calculate. | • Pay is not linked to how much the worker produces – so could lead to a slow rate of work.<br>• No incentive for employee to work harder or better. |

> **KEY TERM**
>
> **time-based:** a payment to employees based on a fixed amount for each hour worked.

Figure 9.8: An employee clocking in for work

> **TIP**
>
> Salary and wages are two different concepts. A salary is a fixed amount spread out in equal payments over the year whereas wages are usually based on the number of hours worked or the number of units made or sold.

## Salary

With a **salary**, employees are paid a fixed amount per year, which is usually paid as a regular amount each month. This method is best used for employees whose work effort is not directly linked to production; for example, managers.

Table 9.5: Advantages and disadvantages of using salary as a financial method of motivation

> **KEY TERM**
>
> **salary:** a fixed amount paid to employees each year, which is usually paid monthly.

| Advantages | Disadvantages |
|---|---|
| • Employees do not receive more pay even if they have work longer hours to complete a task.<br>• Easy to calculate. | • Pay is not linked to employee effort, or the amount produced.<br>• Less flexibility. |

## Piece-rate

Piece-rate is a payment system where pay is based on the number of units of output an employee produces. For example, if an employee is paid $0.25 for every unit they produce, and they produce 600 units in a week, then their wage will be $0.25 × 600 = $150. Piece-rate systems are only used for production employees.

Table 9.6: Advantages and disadvantages of using piece-rate as a financial method of motivation

| Advantages | Disadvantages |
|---|---|
| • Employees are paid only for the number of items they produce.<br>• Encourages employees to be efficient. | • Lower quality of goods because employees may work too quickly to increase their output and pay.<br>• Can be difficult to calculate pay in advance as it depends on numbers produced. |

## Commission

**Commission** is when pay is based on the value of sales made by employees. Sales employees are paid a percentage of each product or service they sell to customers (see Figure 9.9).

**Table 9.7:** Advantages and disadvantages of using commission as a financial method of motivation

| Advantages | Disadvantages |
|---|---|
| • Increased sales as amount of pay is linked to the value of goods sold.<br>• Only paid if products are sold. | • Can be difficult to plan costs as it is difficult to know how much to pay every employee each week.<br>• Employees may miss out important information or mislead customers to obtain sales, which could damage the business reputation. |

> **KEY TERM**
>
> **commission:** a payment to sales employees based on the value of the items they sell.

**Figure 9.9:** A car salesperson earns commission for each car they sell

## Bonus scheme

In a **bonus** scheme, employees receive an additional payment for achieving a performance target set by managers. If the targets set by managers are realistic then this can motivate employees to work harder because the employee knows they will receive a bonus.

> **KEY TERM**
>
> **bonus:** an additional reward paid to employees for achieving targets set by managers.

Table 9.8: Advantages and disadvantages of using bonus schemes as a financial method of motivation

| Advantages | Disadvantages |
|---|---|
| • Target can help employees remain focused on the work increasing output/productivity.<br>• Business only has to pay out if the target is reached. | • If the targets set are unrealistic, it could demotivate employees.<br>• May only provide a short-term boost to motivation. |

## Profit sharing

**Profit sharing** is an additional payment to employees based on the profit made by the business. It is usually paid once a year and is directly linked to the performance of the business. It may be in the form of a cash payment, calculated as a percentage of an employee's wage or salary, or employees may be given shares in the company.

> **KEY TERM**
>
> **profit sharing:** an additional payment to employees based on the profits of the business.

Table 9.9: Advantages and disadvantages of using profit sharing as a financial method of motivation

| Advantages | Disadvantages |
|---|---|
| • Can create team spirit/sense of belonging – which can lead to higher output/sales.<br>• Only payable if the business is successful. | • Might reduce the reward to owners.<br>• Might reduce the amount available to be reinvested into the business.<br>• If business makes little or no profit, there is nothing to share out. |

## Fringe benefits

**Fringe benefits** are an alternative to cash payments, which are paid in addition to a wage or salary. These could include discounts on the businesses' products, a company car, health insurance and/or pensions.

All employees could receive fringe benefits. However, the type of fringe benefits offered is likely to vary depending on the individual's status within the business. For example, all employees might receive a discount on the businesses' products, but only managers may be offered a company car.

> **KEY TERM**
>
> **fringe benefits:** non-monetary rewards that are offered to employees in addition to their wages or salary.

Table 9.10: An advantage and disadvantage for a business of using fringe benefits as a financial method of motivation

| Advantage | Disadvantage |
|---|---|
| • Help business recruit and retain employees as employee saves money that otherwise they would have to spend to obtain these benefits – reducing recruitment costs. | • Cost for the business to provide these benefits. |

## CASE STUDY 9.1

**Debswana**

**Figure 9.10:** A diamond mine in Botswana owned by Debswana

Debswana is a diamond-mining business with over 6 000 employees. It is the largest private sector business in Botswana and is responsible for 30% of the country's gross domestic product (GDP). Debswana's Jwaneng Mine is recognised as the largest mine in the world based on the value of diamonds extracted.

Debswana is recognised as one of the best companies to work for in Botswana. One reason for this is the competitive pay, which is higher than the 6 803 BWP ($495) average pay for most employees in Botswana. In addition to this, all employees can receive bonuses for meeting set targets, paid sick leave, life insurance, access to a company pension plan, paid holidays, a cell phone and paid overtime. All employees are also offered training and development opportunities.

**Discuss in pairs or groups:**

1. What fringe benefits does Debswana offer its employees?
2. What might be the possible advantages to Debswana of using a range of fringe benefits?

# Non-financial methods of motivation

Not all methods of motivation involve providing employees with money or other financial rewards. A business will often use non-financial methods to help increase employee motivation. The methods listed in Figure 9.7 are explained below.

## Job rotation

**Job rotation** involves employees switching from one job to another instead of always doing the same task. This can motivate employees as it makes the work more interesting and helps prevent boredom.

**Table 9.11:** Advantages and disadvantages of using job rotation as a non-financial method of motivation

| Advantages | Disadvantages |
|---|---|
| • Variety can make the work more interesting so fewer employees leave. | • Increased cost of training – increases cash outflows. |
| • Employees become multi-skilled, which helps create a more flexible workforce. | • Not all employees may be able to complete all tasks – could lower quality. |
| • Able to cover work of absent employees. | • Takes time to learn/switch between tasks. |
| • Increases employee skills. | |

### KEY TERM

**job rotation:** increasing variety in the workplace by allowing employees to switch from one task to another.

### TIP

Focus on understanding how the different methods may motivate employees, not just on learning what the different methods are.

## Job enrichment

**Job enrichment** is where work is organised so that employees are given more responsibility or more challenging tasks to do so they can use more of their skills and abilities. Employees feel more valued by their employer, and this can increase their motivation and efficiency.

**Table 9.12:** Advantages and disadvantages of using job enrichment as a non-financial method of motivation

| Advantages | Disadvantages |
|---|---|
| • Allows business to make full use of employee's skills – increasing the flexibility of the workforce.<br>• Less supervision is needed. | • May need training– which increases costs.<br>• Employees may ask for a pay increase for having more responsibility.<br>• May not be easy to add tasks to some jobs. |

> **KEY TERM**
>
> **job enrichment:** employees are given tasks that involve more responsibility or more challenging work.

The difference between job rotation and job enrichment is shown in Figure 9.11.

**Job rotation**

Employee moves from job to job for a limited time. Each job/task has a similar level of difficulty.

**Job enrichment**

Employee stays in the same job. Given tasks that are more challenging and involve more responsibility.

**Figure 9.11:** The difference between job rotation and job enrichment

### ACTIVITY 9.4

When TRK's directors introduced new technology into its carpet factory, production employees have not been happy. Many of TRK's 600 employees have left and those that remain are less productive and absenteeism has increased. Many of TRK's employees find the work boring and not challenging.

TRK's directors have appointed a new Operations Manager, Eduardo. He has been asked to improve employee motivation at the factory.

In pairs discuss the following:

1 Identify **two** factors that may have caused motivation problems at TRK.

2 Explain **two** advantages to TRK of improving employee motivation.

3 Prepare a poster explaining **two** possible methods TRK could use to improve employee motivation.

## Training

Training involves providing opportunities to employees to gain more knowledge and learn new skills. Training can increase motivation because by spending time and money on employees it shows the business values them. Training could be on-the-job or off-the-job training.

Table 9.13: Advantages and disadvantages of using training as a non-financial method of motivation

| Advantages | Disadvantages |
| --- | --- |
| • Increases employees' skills which may increase output and/or productivity.<br>• Trained employees can produce higher-quality work. | • Cost of training.<br>• Employees may explore opportunities at other businesses. |

> **LINK**
>
> You can find more information about training in Chapter 6.

## Opportunities for promotion

A job promotion is when a person moves from a job at a lower level of the hierarchy to one which is at a higher level. Usually, a promotion will involve the person having more responsibilities and authority. It shows the employee that the business values them.

Table 9.14: Advantages and disadvantages of using promotion as a non-financial method of motivation

| Advantages | Disadvantages |
| --- | --- |
| • Allows business to retain valued employees.<br>• Can increase motivation of others who see there are opportunities for promotion. | • Creates another job position that needs to be filled.<br>• Could create resentment if others are overlooked for the role. |

> **TIP**
>
> Promotion has many different meanings in business. Do not confuse promotion of people with promotion of products. Read questions carefully to ensure you understand which type of promotion is being referred to.

## Praise

Recognition does not have to cost money. Simply saying 'Well done!' can make an employee feel that their hard work has been recognised, which can help meet their esteem needs.

Table 9.15: Advantages and disadvantages of using praise as a non-financial method of motivation

| Advantages | Disadvantages |
| --- | --- |
| • No cost to the business.<br>• Can be offered to all employees. | • Can lose effectiveness if used too often.<br>• May be difficult to offer constructive feedback. |

## Employee of the month

An '**employee of the month**' is a scheme designed to recognise high-performing individuals within an organisation (see Figure 9.12). This could be due to high-quality work or exceptional service provided to customers. The successful employee may receive a prize, certificate or have their name added to a board for others to see.

**Table 9.16:** Advantages and disadvantages of using an 'employee of the month' scheme as a non-financial method of motivation

| Advantages | Disadvantages |
| --- | --- |
| • Can help build culture/team spirit.<br>• Quick to introduce.<br>• Highlights good practice/values the business wants to encourage. | • Can create disagreement/competition between employees.<br>• Need to set clear guidelines about what is being rewarded. |

> **KEY TERM**
>
> **employee of the month:** a scheme designed to recognise high-performing individuals within an organisation over a certain period of time.

**Figure 9.12:** An employee receiving an 'employee of the month' award

## CASE STUDY 9.2

**Shout out for success**

Figure 9.13: A Disney World theme park

The Walt Disney Company is an entertainment business that operates around the world. Employees at Disney shops and world theme parks including the United States (see Figure 9.13), Japan and China are all called cast members.

Disney uses many different methods to recognise the achievements of its cast members including:

**Disney Legacy Award** – this is given out once a year to cast members who have shown exceptional service to customers – based on Walt Disney's principles of 'dream, create and inspire'. Other employees are asked to put forward the names of cast members who have consistently tried to make customers' dreams come true, used creative ways to do this, and inspired other cast members to do the same. The winners are invited to a special awards dinner where the successful cast members are presented with a special blue name badge to wear at work for everyone to see. The award is special with only 1% of cast members around the world being selected to receive it.

**Recognise Now!** – this is an online app that allows cast members to send thank you notes and simple messages to other cast members to recognise good work or help offered to others.

**#CastCompliment** – Disney also encourages customers to recognise and thank cast members for excellent service or for helping others. Customers can post thank you messages on its My Disney Experience app or share a compliment on social media using the hashtag #castmember.

**Discuss in pairs or groups:**

1. Why might recognising cast members be important to Disney?
2. Do you think recognition is the best method of non-financial motivation for Disney to its employees? Give reasons for your answer.

# 9.5 Choosing a method of motivation

There is no 'best' method of motivation. Managers must choose the method that they think is best to motivate each employee. Managers may consider many factors, including:

- **Cost** – Most methods will increase costs. Can the business afford to offer pay raises or bonuses? Are the advantages to the business of using a given method greater than the extra cost of doing so?
- **Type of business** – Some methods of motivation can only be used for certain types of employees; for example, piece rate is only suitable for production employees and commission for salespeople.

- **Type of employee(s)** – Everyone is an individual. A method that works for one employee or group of employees may not work for others. For example, some employees might be motivated by higher pay, but others might accept lower pay for having a better work-life balance.
- **Type of manager** – The leadership style and personality of the manager can affect how successful different methods might be. For example, someone with an autocratic leadership style may not be willing or able to offer employees the freedom to make decisions.

### ACTIVITY 9.5

Working in pairs, write down on pieces of paper all the methods of motivation you have learnt about in this chapter. Put all the pieces of paper into a container, like a bag or something similar.

Starting with situation A, pick out two or three pieces of paper at random.

A   a shop assistant who works in a large fashion outlet

B   employees on a production line where the number of faulty products has increased over the past 3 months

C   a pizza delivery driver

D   someone who works as a bank cashier

E   a farm worker

1   a   Discuss the advantages and disadvantages of each method selected and then decide which might be the most appropriate method in situation A.

   b   Write a sentence explaining which is likely to be the best method and why the other method(s) was/were not chosen.

2   Repeat the activity with situations B – E.

### REFLECTION

How did you decide between the different methods? Did you identify any methods that were not appropriate for some situations (e.g., commission for a factory worker)? Did you consider the different factors? Are some factors more important for this job rather than others? Compare your answers with another pair – did you understand the reasons for their choices?

Repeat the activity for each situation picking different methods from the container to discuss.

# 9 Motivating employees

## BUSINESS IN ACTION

### Hello Chef – Valuing the culture

**Figure 9.14:** Ingredients for a pre-prepared meal ready for a customer to make at home

The idea of 'business culture' is that it represents the basic principles, values and attitudes of the business. This influences everything that a business does from how it treats employees, customers and other stakeholders.

Hello Chef is a food manufacturing business based in Dubai. The business is committed to helping reduce food waste. For example, as well as carefully planning out the ingredients for each recipe, Hello Chef gives away any unused ingredients at the end of the day to local charities to feed people in need. Business culture is just as important to Hello Chef as the pre-prepared meals it makes and sells to its customers across the UAE. The culture is based on four simple rules:

- Whatever it takes – do everything possible, with a positive attitude and passion to get the job done and to help provide the best possible service to customers

- Simplify – keep everything easy to understand

- Fun – enjoy what you do; work should not be boring or too serious

- Positive team and family spirit – be kind to everyone, from suppliers and customers to other employees, and appreciate their efforts.

Hello Chef is always looking for motivated individuals to join their 'family'. As well as offering a competitive salary and benefits, employees are invited to attend team and family events. The business also wants its employees to develop their own skills to help them grow as individuals as well as help the business.

### Discuss in small groups or as a class:

1. How might having motivated employees help Hello Chef?

2. Do you think business culture is something you would consider when deciding which business to work for? Give reasons for your answer.

## SUMMARY

You should now know:

- Having a well-motivated workforce can help a business reduce absenteeism, lower labour turnover and increase efficiency.

- Many factors that motivate people to work were identified by Taylor, Maslow and Herzberg's theories.

- Financial and non-financial methods of motivation, including bonuses, profit sharing, job rotation and job enrichment can be used to help a business have a well-motivated workforce.

- Each business will use different methods to motivate its employees.

# Chapter 9 practice questions

1. MFC manufactures pottery including plates and cups. The business has 200 skilled employees. All employees involved in the production of pottery at the factory are paid piece rate. Working conditions in the factory are poor and there are a high number of accidents. Many employees leave before completing 1 year of employment with the business. The Managing Director is considering financial and non-financial methods of motivation to help improve employee motivation as he knows having well-motivated employees is important.

   a  Define 'piece rate'. [2]

   b  Identify **four** non-financial methods of motivation the business might use. [4]

   c  Explain **two** financial methods MFC could use to improve the motivation of its employees. [6]

   d  Explain **two** reasons why having well-motivated employees might be important for MFC. Which reason is likely to be the most important? Justify your answer. [8]

2. ABC is a private limited company. The business sells furniture in its three shops across Country Y. ABC has 80 employees and five managers. All ABC's managers are part of a profit-sharing scheme. Each employee is paid using time rate, based on working 40 hours each week. The Human Resources Manager is concerned that many of its employees leave ABC within 16 months. She is considering ways to improve employee motivation, including offering bonuses.

   a  Define 'bonus'. [2]

   b  Outline **one** advantage and **one** disadvantage to ABC of using profit sharing. [4]

   c  Explain **two** non-financial methods ABC might use to improve employee motivation. [6]

   d  Do you think time rate is the best financial method of motivation for ABC to use for its employees? Justify your answer. [8]

   Total available marks: 40

## CHECK YOUR PROGRESS

How well do you think you have achieved the learning intentions for this chapter? Give yourself a score from 1 (still need a lot of practice) to 5 (feeling very confident) for each learning intention. Provide an example to support your score.

| Now I can ... | Score | Example |
| --- | --- | --- |
| identify the reasons why people work | | |
| explain the importance of motivation in the workplace | | |
| understand the three main theories of motivation | | |
| explain financial and non-financial methods of motivation | | |
| recommend a suitable method of motivation to use in a given situation. | | |

# Section 2 case study

## CASE STUDY

### Pottery Town (PT)

PT manufactures high-quality pottery including cups and plates, as shown in Appendix 1. The business has two factories and 120 employees. PT has a tall organisation structure and a narrow span of control. PT's Managing Director knows good communication is important. This helps ensure that the correct products are made and customer orders are completed on time. PT uses many methods of communication in its factories, including emails, noticeboards and letters to communicate important information to employees.

Most of the production workers are members of a trade union. Each skilled production worker is paid using the time-based method. A bonus is available if production workers can meet a production target of 2 500 units per month.

The Operations Director is concerned that output has reduced over the past three months, as shown in Appendix 2. She is considering different methods to improve the motivation of PT's production workers. She has sent an email to the Managing Director outlining possible methods (see Appendix 3).

One of the factory managers has announced that he is leaving PT at the end of the month. The Human Resource Director is considering whether to use internal or external recruitment to replace the factory manager. The Operations Director wants the new factory manager to have manufacturing experience and understand the importance of the functions of management.

## Appendix 1

> **Our handmade pottery is unique and cannot be bought anywhere else.**
>
> Made by our skilled employees – you will appreciate the quality.
>
> Buy from our shop today!

**Advert for PT's products**

## Appendix 2

**Extract of PT's output and employee data for the last three months**

|  | Month 1 | Month 2 | Month 3 |
|---|---|---|---|
| Average output per employee | 2 400 | 2 380 | 2 370 |
| Number of days employees have been absent | 232 | 240 | 230 |
| Number of employees leaving | 23 | 24 | 22 |

# Appendix 3

### Email from the Operations Director to the Managing Director

We need to improve employee motivation. Maybe we could introduce/change the payment method from time-rate to piece-rate, introduce job rotation or employee of the month. Let me know what you think.

1    a    Explain how a job description and person specification might help PT's Human Resources Manager when recruiting the new manager.

         Job description:

         Explanation:

         Person specification:

         Explanation:          **[8]**

   b    Explain the advantages and disadvantages to PT of using internal or external recruitment for the new manager. Which method should PT choose? Justify your answer.

         Internal recruitment:

         External recruitment:

         Recommendation:          **[12]**

2    a    Explain **two** benefits of PT's production workers being members of a trade union.

         Benefit 1:

         Explanation:

         Benefit 2:

         Explanation:          **[8]**

   b    Explain **three** functions of management carried out by PT's managers. Which function of management is the most important for PT's managers? Justify your answer.

         Planning:

         Organising:

         Coordinating:

         Conclusion:          **[12]**

3    a    Explain two advantages to PT of having well-motivated employees.

         Advantage 1:

         Explanation:

         Advantage 2:

         Explanation:          **[8]**

**b** Explain the advantages and disadvantages of each of the following methods of motivation PT could use to improve employee motivation. Which method should PT use? Justify your answer.

Piece-rate system:

Job rotation:

Employee of the month:

Recommendation: [12]

**4 a** Explain **two** advantages of PT's managers having a narrow span of control.

Advantage 1:

Explanation:

Advantage 2:

Explanation: [8]

**b** Explain the advantages and disadvantages of the following methods of communication PT might use when communicating important information to employees. Which method should PT use? Justify your answer.

Email:

Noticeboard:

Letter:

Conclusion: [12]

Total available marks: 80

# Section 3
# Marketing

In this section, you will learn about the role of marketing in business, including identifying and satisfying customer needs. You will also learn about the reasons why a market might change; perhaps consumer spending patterns have changed or markets have become more competitive. You will consider the advantages and disadvantages of both niche and mass markets, and the ways that a market can be segmented.

Methods of market research will be identified, alongside the advantages and disadvantages of both primary and secondary market research. The marketing mix is one of the biggest areas of this section. Each element of the marketing mix (price, product, promotion and place) will be explored, alongside how ecommerce provides advantages and disadvantages for both consumers and businesses. Finally, you will learn about the benefits of entering markets in other countries and the role that legal controls play in the marketing decisions of a business.

## Chapter 10
# Marketing and the market

### LEARNING INTENTIONS

By the end of this chapter, you will be able to:

- outline the role of marketing
- identify why markets change and how businesses respond
- calculate market share
- understand the difference between niche markets and mass markets
- explain how markets can be segmented and the advantages and disadvantages of doing so.

# 10 Marketing and the market

## Introduction

Think about something that you've bought recently. What persuaded you to buy it? An advert? A salesperson? Social media? Perhaps a friend? In this chapter you are going to begin your study of **marketing**. It is important to recognise that marketing is much more than just advertising and selling the goods and services of a business.

You will learn that the role of marketing includes identifying and satisfying consumer needs. You will look at how consumers and competitors influence markets. You will consider ways businesses might respond to changes in the market. You will also learn about the reasons why businesses might choose to operate in a niche or mass market. Finally, you will consider how and why businesses divide the whole market into smaller parts or segments.

> **KEY TERM**
>
> **marketing:** the process of identifying, anticipating and satisfying customer needs.

### BUSINESS IN CONTEXT

#### Bata Shoes

**Figure 10.1:** Ecommerce enables customers to buy shoes online

Ecommerce is the process of buying and selling goods via the internet. It has helped businesses increase their customer base as customers from all over the world are now able to purchase their products online as well. However, ecommerce means that businesses now have higher levels of competition. Ecommerce has also made it easier for customers to buy goods and services (see Figure 10.1). This is because consumers have more access to information than they did before ecommerce and it is easier to compare the products of different businesses.

Bata is a footwear manufacturer with its headquarters in Switzerland. They produce many different styles of footwear and sell them to customers around the world. In 2021, Bata launched a new and upgraded ecommerce website. This website aimed to improve convenience for customers to increase sales, including features such as exchange of footwear that are the wrong size. By using ecommerce, Bata sells footwear to customers worldwide. It provides products that meet customer needs by offering a variety of styles of high-quality footwear. In 2024, it had 27 production facilities in 20 countries around the world.

**Discuss in a pairs or groups:**

1. How has ecommerce made markets more competitive?
2. Should all businesses sell their products using ecommerce?

## 10.1 The role of marketing

Marketing is an essential part of a business's activities. There are five roles of marketing:

- identifying customer needs
- satisfying customer needs
- maintaining customer loyalty

- building customer relationships
- anticipating changes in customer needs.

## Identifying customer needs

Businesses identify the needs of customers by carrying out market research. Businesses will try to find out if there are any product features that would make customers more likely to buy their product.

## Satisfying customer needs

Once customer needs have been identified, a business must then decide if it is able to satisfy those needs. Businesses will consider whether they have the resources available to produce the product. They will also think about the cost of producing the product, at what price they could sell it and if this is a price that customers are likely to be willing to pay. Businesses will also use market research to check that the goods sold and services provided satisfy customer needs.

## Maintaining customer loyalty

Businesses will fall if they do not have any customers. Therefore, one of the most important roles of marketing is to create a group of customers that the business can sell its products to. This is known as a customer base. The business must then try to maintain the loyalty of its customers to it and its products.

Loyal customers will return to the business to buy their products again and again. This means the business has regular sales and can maintain revenue over a period of time. Businesses might use methods of promotion such as reward schemes to try to build and maintain customer loyalty (see Figure 10.2).

> **TIP**
>
> To be able to fully understand this topic, you must learn and understand the key terms of marketing, market segmentation, market share, niche marketing and mass marketing.

> **LINKS**
>
> You can find more information about market research in Chapter 10, different methods of market research in Chapter 11 and methods of promotion in Chapter 15.

**Figure 10.2:** Coffee shops and cafes often use loyalty cards to encourage customers to return

## Building customer relationships

Customer loyalty is most likely to be achieved if a business can build positive relationships with its customers. This can be achieved through successfully identifying and satisfying customer needs. Understanding the characteristics of customers is also important; for example, their income, lifestyle and buying habits. Customer relationships can also be achieved through using targeted emails (an email that is specifically designed so that it appears tailor-made to its recipient) to inform existing customers about products that they might be interested in.

## Anticipating changes in customer needs

It is important for businesses to recognise that customer needs might change over time. This could be due to factors such as:

- changes in tastes and preferences
- changes in customer income
- changes in technology.

A business should try to identify what changes might happen in the future. It should start planning for these changes in advance. This would help the business to maintain loyalty by continuing to meet customer needs. Market research can be used to try to anticipate changes in customer needs. If a business is to survive in the long run it must respond to these changes.

### DISCUSSION

In pairs, discuss the following:

- Which role of marketing do you think is the most important for a business? Why?
- Do you think this role is the most important for all businesses? Why/why not?

### CASE STUDY 10.1

**MTN invests in building customer relationships**

**Figure 10.3:** Technology in use in the classroom

MTN is a public limited company located in South Africa. It provides internet services to consumers around the country. Building customer relationships is very important to MTN. In 2023, it launched a campaign to raise awareness about the potential risks of using technology, particularly for young people. MTN also recognizes the importance of inclusivity. MTN provides IT facilities to schools to ensure both teachers and students have access to the right equipment (see Figure 10.3). It is aiming to develop customer loyalty through building positive relationships.

> **CONTINUED**
>
> **Discuss in pairs or groups:**
> 1. Define 'public limited company'.
> 2. Explain the importance of customer loyalty in the internet services market.
> 3. Do you think that the strategies mentioned in the case study will increase customer loyalty? Justify your answer.

## 10.2 Market changes

A market is a place where buyers and sellers come together to buy and sell goods and services (see Figure 10.4). Markets are not always physical places; they can also be online. An example of an online market is eBay. Changes in the market may be a result of:

- changes in consumer spending patterns (the buyers)
- changes in the level of competition (the sellers).

Figure 10.4: An open-air market

# 10 Marketing and the market

> **ACTIVITY 10.1**
>
> Use newspapers or the internet to research examples of businesses that have experienced a change in demand due to changing tastes and fashions.
>
> Working in small groups, choose one of these examples and create a pretend presentation to give to the company (which you will present in front of your class). Explain how you would recommend that the business responds to this change in the market.

## Why consumer spending patterns may change

The amount of money consumers are willing to spend on buying goods and services is affected by several factors:

- **Changes in the price of the product** – for most products, if a business increases the price of a product then it will lead to a decrease in the number of sales. Likewise, if a business reduces the price then there would be an increase in the number of sales made.

- **Changes in the price of competitors' products** – some businesses are in very competitive markets. If the products of two or more businesses are very similar, consumers are most likely to buy the product with the lowest price.

- **Changes in consumer income** – consumers might change the type of products they are buying if they have a change in their incomes. For example, if consumer income falls then consumers will buy things that they need for living; for example, water, food and shelter. They will buy fewer luxury items such as cars or holiday packages.

- **Changes in population size and structure** – an increase in a country's population leads to an increase in the size of the market. This could increase the potential number of sales of a business. The structure of the population might also change over time. For example, in some countries there are fewer children being born, but people are living longer. In such places, the sale of products for children will fall, but the sale of products for older people will rise.

- **Changes in tastes and fashion** – some products also become more, or less, popular with changes in consumer tastes and fashion. For example, in some countries consumers are more aware and concerned about healthy eating. This has increased the demand in these countries for healthier food and drinks. Businesses have responded by reducing the sugar or salt content of their products. For example, Bayn is a business that specialises in developing formulae to reduce the sugar content in its products.

- **Changes in spending on advertising and other promotional activities** – almost all businesses spend money promoting their goods or services. Advertising and promotion could persuade consumers to switch from buying from one business to another. It could also lead to an increase in sales for a business if consumers are more aware about its products.

> **BUSINESS FOR CAMBRIDGE IGCSE™ AND O LEVEL: COURSEBOOK**

### DISCUSSION

Changes in consumer income can occur due to changes in gross domestic product (GDP). GDP is the total value of goods and services produced by an economy over a period of time. Do you think that an increase in incomes is likely to increase demand for all businesses?

### ACTIVITY 10.2

Working in pairs and using your own country as a starting point, answer the following questions:

1. Can you think of any differences in consumer needs between the different regions of your country?

2. Are you able to identify how consumer needs in your country are different from consumer needs in other countries within the same part of the world?

3. Why might the needs of consumers in your country be different from the needs of consumers in a country on the opposite side of the world? Think of how things such as climate, tastes, wealth, and culture might create differences in needs.

You should be prepared to present your answers to your class.

## Why some markets become more competitive

Almost all markets have some level of competition within them. However, some markets have seen a much greater increase in the level of competition than others. There are several reasons for this.

### Government intervention in markets

In many countries, the government is an important influence on business activity. Governments can affect competition in markets through:

- Legal controls that prevent individual firms from dominating the market, for example, through charging a price that is too high. Many countries such as India have laws against anti-competitive behaviour. This makes it easier for businesses to compete in the market.

- Providing financial and other assistance to new and small- to medium-sized businesses. This will encourage business start-ups and increase the chances of new businesses surviving.

### Growth of free trade between countries

Regional free trade agreements remove or reduce barriers to trade between countries. This makes it easier to buy and sell products from one country to another. This means consumers have more choice about where to buy products, which makes markets more competitive.

## 10 Marketing and the market

### Improvements in infrastructure

Transports infrastructure relates to the availability of and the quality of roads, rail networks and flights. Improvements in this infrastructure makes it easier to transport products around a country or from one country to another. Markets are therefore more competitive as consumers can now purchase goods from all around the world.

### Development of ecommerce and social media networks

Many businesses have developed their own websites and use these to sell their products to customers in their own country and around the world. Some businesses only sell their products through ecommerce. The development of ecommerce has increased the size of a business's market and therefore increased the potential number of sales a business might make. It has also greatly increased the level of competition in that market.

Social media network sites such as Facebook and TikTok are also used by businesses to promote their products. Businesses can also use social media to target advertising to consumers. This means that consumers have much more information about the suppliers of products. While this has increased consumer choice, it has also increased competition within the marketplace.

> **ACTIVITY 10.3**
>
> A trade agreement could include not paying taxes on goods that are imported into your country. Use the internet, library and other printed material to research the different countries your country has trade agreements with. Create a poster of your findings.
>
> Can you think of any advantages and disadvantages to your country having these trade agreements? Include these in your poster, if so.
>
> You may find the World Trade Organisation website useful when completing this task.

## How businesses can respond to changing spending patterns and increased competition

Businesses are unlikely to survive if they do not respond to changing consumer spending patterns and more competitive markets.

Table 10.1 shows how businesses could respond to changes in spending patterns and an increase in the level of competition.

Table 10.1: How a business could respond to changes in competition

| Response | Explanation |
| --- | --- |
| Developing new products | Businesses could use market research to identify how the needs and wants of consumers are changing. It can use this information to develop new products. New products may be of higher quality than competitors or they could have a unique selling point (USP). This helps a business to remain competitive. |
| Increasing efficiency | Using resources more efficiently will help a business to reduce average costs. If average costs are reduced then a business might decide to reduce the prices of its products. You have already learnt that a decrease in price will increase sales. |
| Increasing promotion | Increasing advertising will help to persuade consumers to buy your product and not that of competitors. This is known as the product's USP. Promotion might also be informative and explain why your product is better than competitors'. Other promotional techniques such as buy-one-get-one-free and money-off coupons may also be used to persuade consumers to buy a firm's product instead of a competitor's product. |
| Looking for new markets | Sometimes consumer spending patterns change so much, or the level of competition in a market becomes so great, that the better option is for a business to look for new markets for its products. A business may look to enter markets where there is less competition and where consumers are more likely to buy the product. |

### DISCUSSION

Discuss in pairs:

Competition has increased in the market for mobile phones. In pairs, discuss what you think is the best way for a business to respond? Are there any disadvantages to responding in this way?

## 10.3 Market share

**Market share** calculates the value of one firm's sales as a percentage of total sales in the market. Figure 10.5 shows the market share of five firms in the supermarket industry. Increasing market share is a common business objective.

Market share is calculated by:

$$\frac{\text{Sales revenue of a business}}{\text{Total sales revenue for the whole market}} \times 100$$

For example, a business has a sales revenue of $1 000. The total sales revenue for the whole market is $10 000. The market share for the business is calculated by:

$$\frac{\$1\,000}{\$10\,000} \times 100 = 10\%$$

### KEY TERM

**market share:** the value of one firm's sales as a percentage of total sales in the market.

If a business's market share is increasing, this means that they are making a bigger percentage of sales in the market than they were previously.

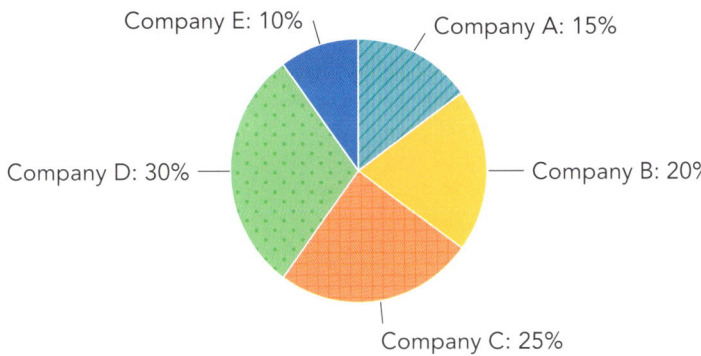

Figure 10.5: A pie chart to show the market share of five firms

### ACTIVITY 10.4

Hat sales in Country X were $500 000 last year.

| Business | Value of sales |
|---|---|
| Business A | $100 000 |
| Business B | $50 000 |
| Business C | $200 000 |
| Business D | $150 000 |

1. Calculate the market share for businesses A, B, C and D.
2. Draw a bar chart to show the market share for each of the four firms in the hat industry.
3. In pairs, discuss the following:
   a. What are the benefits to a business of having a high market share?
   b. How would you suggest that a business increase its market share?

### CASE STUDY 10.2

**Online streaming in the USA**

**Figure 10.6:** The market for online streaming has grown significantly in recent years

The market for online streaming (broadcasting/transmitting audio and video files over an internet connection) has grown significantly in the USA in recent years with many new competitors joining the market. Businesses such as Netflix, Disney, Paramount+ and Hulu all compete in this market. Netflix has the largest market share (44.21% in 2023). Paramount+ experienced a 53.9% growth in its market share in 2023, taking it to 4.34%.

**Discuss in pairs or groups:**
1 Define 'market share'.
2 How can Netflix respond to the increase in competition?

## 10.4 Niche markets and mass markets

Most markets can be divided into different sub-markets. These sub-markets can be either niche markets or mass markets.

### What is a niche market?

A **niche market** is a very small part of a larger market. Customers in a niche market usually have specific needs and wants. Niche marketing identifies the needs of this small part of the whole market and then develops products to satisfy those needs. For example, a business that specialises in supplying hand-tailored suits is part of the much larger market for men's clothing.

Niche marketing recognises that consumers do not all want the same product. For example, toothpaste can be manufactured for sensitive teeth, for children's teeth and in different flavours (see Figure 10.7). Dividing the market so that products better meet the needs of different types of consumers can help to increase sales and revenue.

> **KEY TERM**
>
> **niche market:** a small part of the total market where consumers have specific needs and wants.

**Figure 10.7:** Some toothpaste manufacturers develop toothpaste specifically for children

Products sold to a niche market are often seen as more desirable to consumers than products sold to a mass market. This is because they meet the specific needs of consumers. Examples of this include Rolex watches and Rolls-Royce cars.

## Advantages and disadvantages of niche markets

Table 10.2 outlines the advantages and disadvantages to businesses of operating in a niche market.

**Table 10.2:** Advantages and disadvantages of niche markets

| Advantages of niche markets | Disadvantages of niche markets |
|---|---|
| • Meet the specific needs of consumers. This can increase brand loyalty.<br>• Less competition in the market. This can make it easier to attract customers.<br>• Can charge higher prices. This can lead to an increase in profit margins. | • Higher profit margins could attract competitors into the market. This might result in a firm having to lower prices to become competitive.<br>• Unlikely to achieve economies of scale. This therefore increases average costs compared to operating in a mass market.<br>• Risk of over-reliance on one product or market. This could lead to business failure if the product is no longer in demand due to changing consumer preferences. |

# What is a mass market?

When businesses sell the same product to the whole market; for example oil (see Figure 10.8) or flour, this is known as a **mass market**. Mass markets have large groups of potential customers and these customers all have similar needs and wants. This means that advertising and promotions are designed so that they appeal to most customers. Products in a mass market are standardised and are therefore not specific to individual customer requirements. An example of this is oil – the same product is sold all around the world.

> **KEY TERM**
>
> **mass market:** selling the same product to the whole market.

**Figure 10.8:** Qatar Petroleum sells the same product (oil) to consumers all around the world

### Advantages and disadvantages of mass markets

Table 10.3 outlines the advantages and disadvantages to businesses of operating in a mass market.

**Table 10.3:** Advantages and disadvantages of mass markets

| Advantages of mass markets | Disadvantages of mass markets |
|---|---|
| • Produce higher levels of output than niche markets. This can lead to economies of scale.<br>• Higher level of sales. This can increase potential revenue.<br>• Higher brand awareness. This can increase sales and market share. | • High levels of competition. Therefore, prices may be reduced to attract customers. This can decrease profit margin.<br>• Products are standardised (and not specific to customer needs). This could limit potential sales.<br>• Likely to require high levels of promotion and advertising. This can increase costs and mean less funds are available to be invested into other areas of the business. |

> **LINK**
>
> More information about economies of scale can be found in Chapter 18.

## 10.5 Market segmentation

Different groups of consumers are likely to have different needs and wants. **Market segmentation** means that businesses can manufacture products that meet these differing needs. This is likely to lead to an increase in sales. It is also likely to create brand loyalty.

### What is market segmentation?

Consumers within a market can be divided into different 'groups'. Each group of consumers may want something slightly different to another group of consumers. Businesses can adapt existing products or create new products to meet these differences.

Each part of the whole market is known as a market segment. Dividing the whole market into different segments is called market segmentation. In Figure 10.9, the market has been divided into four segments. Each segment represents part of the whole market.

> **KEY TERM**
>
> **market segmentation:** dividing the whole market into segments based on consumer characteristics and targeting different products to each segment.

> **TIP**
>
> If you get asked to explain the advantages, disadvantages or impact of something, you will need to develop your points. This means that you should explain the effect of your initial point. Using connectives such as 'this means' and 'therefore' helps to develop a knowledge point into analysis.

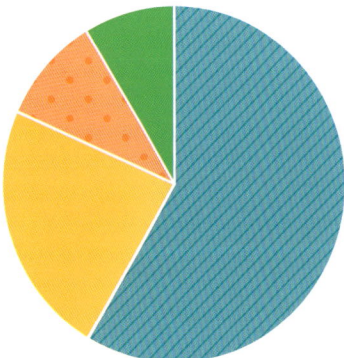

**Figure 10.9:** Market segmentation

## How markets can be segmented

Markets can be segmented in several ways. Figure 10.10 shows the main ways this can happen.

### Age

Businesses may segment the market by age. This means that some products might be targeted specifically towards a certain age group. Businesses that sell holidays might segment the market by age. They might sell some holidays to individual consumers aged 18–25, sell some holidays to families with young children and some to adults aged 60 and over.

### Income

Segmenting the market by income means that products are targeted towards consumers based on their disposable income. Some businesses may choose to target low-income consumers. However, businesses selling luxury cars may choose to target consumers with a high level of income.

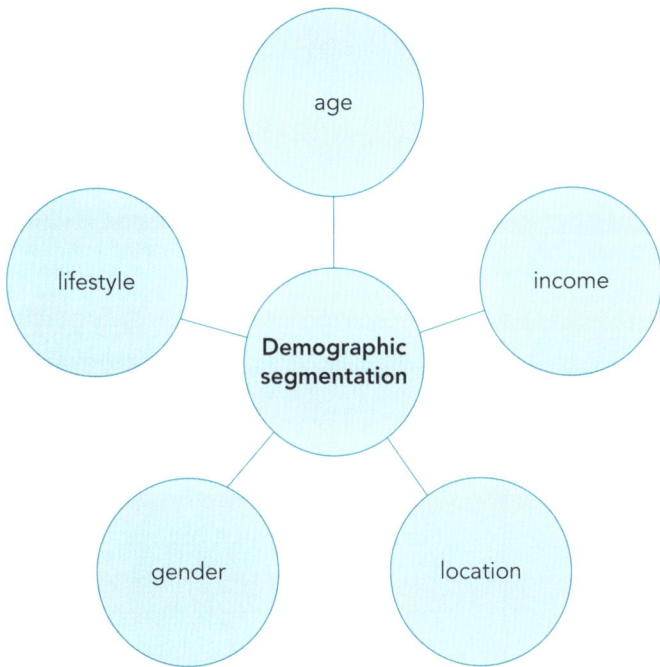

**Figure 10.10:** The ways a market can be segmented

### Location

By segmenting the market by location, businesses recognise that consumers in one location may have different needs to consumers in another location. The locations may be:

- different regions within the same country
- different regions of the world
- different countries in the world.

Location differences may be due to cultural reasons or even different climates. Multinational corporations, such as McDonald's, segment the market by location. Their menus are adapted to suit local markets. For example, they sell more ice cream products in countries with warmer climates.

### Gender

The market may also be segmented based on gender. This means products are produced and targeted towards either male or female consumer groups. Businesses selling clothes are a good example of this – they may have some products targeted towards male consumers and other products targeted towards female consumers.

### Lifestyle

This involves dividing the market according to the lifestyle, beliefs and attitudes of consumers. It is likely to be based on the interests of consumers. Sports clothing manufacturers are likely to segment the market by lifestyle. For example, they may target customers who have an interest in running or athletics.

> **TIP**
>
> If you need to recommend ways a business can segment the market, it is important to read the case study carefully to consider ways that would be appropriate for that business. For example, if a business sells in only one region then segmenting the market by region would not be relevant to that business.

## Advantages of segmentation to businesses

All these methods divide the whole market into smaller groups. Segmentation has many advantages and disadvantages as summarised in Table 10.4.

**Table 10.4:** Advantages and disadvantages of segmentation

| Advantages of segmentation | Disadvantages of segmentation |
|---|---|
| • Goods and services meet the specific needs of consumers in each segment. This is likely to increase sales. | • High promotional costs. Different promotions may be needed for different market segments. This is likely to result in a higher cost of promotion than if one method was used for the entire market. |
| • May identify a gap in the market. This can provide an opportunity to develop brand loyalty before other businesses enter the market. | • Risks are not spread. Businesses may be too reliant on sales from one or two market segments. If consumer preferences change in these segments, the business may experience a significant decrease in sales. |
| • Promotion can be better targeted. This avoids wasted investment as all promotional campaigns are relevant to the target market. | • High cost of market research. Market research is required to understand the specific needs and wants of each segment. This is expensive and means that less funds are available to be spent elsewhere in the business. |
| • It may be possible to charge higher prices for very similar products in one segment than in another. For example, airlines often use income segmentation to identify three groups of passengers – first class, business class and economy class. They all travel on the same aeroplane, but pay very different prices. This enables the airline to earn an increased profit margin from passengers prepared to buy first or business class tickets. | • Product development costs. Products may need to be adapted to suit different segments. This will make it harder for a business to benefit from economies of scale. |

## Choosing a method of segmentation

There is no one correct method of market segmentation. A business will consider a range of factors before deciding which method of segmentation should be used. These factors will include the product itself, the potential number of customers in each segment and the promotional budget available.

> **ACTIVITY 10.5**
>
> Consider the market for the following goods and services:
>
> - hotel accommodation
> - footwear
> - motor cars
> - rail travel
> - hairdressing.
>
> Working in pairs, discuss how you would segment the market for these goods and services. You must justify your choice.

**Figure 10.11:** Hotels use market segmentation

> **REFLECTION**
>
> When completing Activity 10.5, did you and your partner agree on the best way to segment the markets? If you disagreed, were you able to explain why you thought your method of segmentation was most appropriate?
>
> What factors did you consider when deciding on the best way to segment the market? Which factor do you think was the most important?

## BUSINESS IN ACTION

### The Hive

The Hive is a zero-waste store based in Malaysia. It sells products such as food, cleaning products and items for pets. It requires consumers to bring their own containers for products that they purchase. Its target market are consumers who are environmentally conscious or who have preferences such as vegetarian food.

### Discuss in pairs or groups:

1. What are the advantages of operating in a niche market?

2. Sometimes niche markets have the potential for less sales than mass markets. What could a business such as Hive's do to increase its sales?

3. Are there any disadvantages to a business of selling its products via a website? Explain your answer.

**Figure 10.12:** Zero-waste stores ask customers to bring their own containers for products

## 10 Marketing and the market

> **SUMMARY**
>
> You should now know:
>
> - Marketing is used to identify and satisfy consumer needs. This helps to build customer relationships and loyalty.
>
> - Businesses need to understand why and how consumer spending patterns change.
>
> - Businesses need to decide what they should do to respond to changing consumer spending patterns so that they are able to remain competitive.
>
> - Market share is a common business objective. It helps businesses to know how many sales they are making as a proportion of total sales in the market.
>
> - There are advantages to businesses of niche markets, such as the ability to charge higher prices, but also disadvantages, such as the unlikeliness to benefit from economies of scale.
>
> - There are advantages to businesses of mass markets, such as the likelihood of higher levels of sales, but also disadvantages such as higher levels of competition.
>
> - There are several methods of market segmentation. There are also advantages and disadvantages to a business of segmenting the market.

# Chapter 10 practice questions

1   Magda is an optician. Magda tests people's eyes and then sells them spectacles (eye glasses) if needed. However, customers do not have to buy their spectacles from Magda. Many customers have their eyes tested by Magda but then buy their spectacles from other spectacle suppliers. Many of these suppliers use ecommerce. These businesses have a good customer base because they are not only cheaper but also offer a wider choice of spectacles than Magda. Magda is thinking about using market segmentation to increase sales.

   a   Define 'market segmentation'. [2]

   b   Outline **two** factors that might influence consumer decisions when buying products from Magda. [4]

   c   Explain **two** effects of ecommerce on Magda's business. [6]

   d   Explain **two** ways Magda could respond to the competition from other suppliers of spectacles. Which one would you recommend? Justify your answer. [8]

**BUSINESS FOR CAMBRIDGE IGCSE™ AND O LEVEL: COURSEBOOK**

2. Gloria's Garments (GG) is a company that designs and manufactures fashion clothing. Most of its output is for the mass market. GG also provides a specialist service – the design and manufacture of bridal gowns. This is a niche market. Last year, GG's sales revenue from selling bridal gowns was $50 000. The total size of the bridal gown market was $1 000 000.

   a   Calculate GG's market share. [2]

   b   Outline **two** benefits to GG of mass marketing. [4]

   c   Explain **two** ways in which changing consumer needs might affect GG's sales. [6]

   d   Do you think the advantages to GG of operating in the mass market are greater than the advantages of operating in the niche market? Justify your answer. [8]

   Total available marks: 40

## CHECK YOUR PROGRESS

How well do you think you have achieved the learning intentions for this chapter? Give yourself a score from 1 (still need a lot of practice) to 5 (feeling very confident) for each learning intention. Provide an example to support your score.

| Now I can … | Score | Example |
| --- | --- | --- |
| explain the roles of marketing | | |
| identify why markets change and how businesses respond to these changes | | |
| calculate market share | | |
| explain the difference between niche markets and mass markets | | |
| explain how markets can be segmented. | | |

# > Chapter 11
# Market research

### LEARNING INTENTIONS

By the end of this chapter, you will be able to:

- understand and explain the role of market research
- identify primary and secondary methods of market research and explain the advantages and disadvantages of each
- explain the factors influencing the accuracy of market research
- analyse simple market research data.

## Introduction

Businesses carry out market research to find out what consumers want and what their competitors are doing (see Figure 11.1). The success of marketing activities and the effectiveness of marketing decisions depend on how well a business does this market research.

In this chapter, you will learn about the methods of market research a business may use and the benefits of doing so.

**Figure 11.1:** Market research findings need to be presented and analysed to be used in decision-making

### BUSINESS IN CONTEXT

#### Infosys

A business will conduct market research to find out information about its customers, the market and its competition. Primary or secondary market research may be used. Market reports are one example of secondary research that can be used. The research is often done by market research agencies that collect and analyse data which they then sell to other businesses. This type of research is conducted by specialists in this area and is relevant to a specific industry.

Infosys is a business based in Bangalore, India. One aspect of their business is to provide consultation services to other businesses in more than 56 countries around the world. Infosys helps businesses through 'digital transformation'; this means it helps businesses to increase their online presence and improve their use of ecommerce. Infosys has expertise in artificial intelligence and provides advice to businesses about this. As businesses have increased the use of technology as part of their product distribution, it has become increasingly important to ensure that there is consistency in the shopping experience whether in-store or online (see Figure 11.2).

**Figure 11.2:** Many businesses use technology to sell products to consumers

## CONTINUED

Infosys commissioned Vanson Bourne, a technology market research specialist, to undertake market research and over 1000 interviews took place. The purpose of the market research was to find out consumers' needs and wants when considering an 'integrated shopping experience'. It focused on what was important to consumers when thinking about the entire shopping experience, both online and in-store. Following the research, Vanson Bourne produced a report providing insights from consumers and retailers related to an integrated shopping experience. Some of the key findings were:

- 92% of respondents look to discover new products.
- 31% of respondents wish their shopping experience was more personalised than it currently was.
- Lack of technology is the most common factor preventing retailers from creating a more integrated customer experience within their organisation.

**Discuss in pairs or groups:**

1 Can you think of any potential advantages and disadvantages to a business of using secondary research?
2 What factors might influence the method of market research Vanson Bourne uses?

# 11.1 The role of market research and methods used

**Market research** provides businesses with important information about the markets in which they operate or are planning to operate. There are many methods of market research available for businesses to use including surveys (see Figure 11.3). Market research involves collecting, recording and analysing data about a business':

- customers
- competitors
- market.

> **KEY TERM**
>
> **market research:** the process of collecting, recording and analysing data about the customers, competitors or market for a product.

**Figure 11.3:** Some businesses use surveys as a method of market research

The information obtained from market research helps a business to:

- identify consumer tastes and preferences
- gain feedback about what consumers like and dislike about its products
- identify its main competitors and understand what is special about their products – this is known as the product's unique selling point (USP)
- know the size of the market
- predict how the demand for its products may change in the future.

It also helps businesses to make decisions such as:

- how to promote its products
- how to package its products
- how to distribute its products.

> **LINK**
>
> Promotion, packaging and distribution are all part of the marketing mix. You can find more information about the marketing mix in Chapters 12 and 13.

### ACTIVITY 11.1

Market research involves collecting, recording and analysing data about a business's customers, competitors and market.

1. Write a list of three things that a retail business might want to find out for each area of customers, competitors and market.

2. Compare your list with a partner's. Do you notice any similarities or differences?

## Uses of market research information

Market research information can be used by a business to:

- Identify consumer needs – this can help to reduce the risk when developing and launching new products because the products have been designed and produced based on market research findings.

- Discover the current and future market size for the product, perhaps due to changes in customer tastes and fashions – this can help to make decisions about how many products to produce. This means it is more likely that businesses will have enough products to meet demand or ensure that too many products are not produced which would increase waste.

- Identify the strengths and weaknesses of competitors' products – this information can be used to make sure that any new product development builds on the strengths of competitors' products while improving on the weaknesses. This can give the business a competitive advantage and make it more likely that customers would choose their product instead of a competitor's product.

- Take decisions about marketing – market research means businesses will be able to make more informed decisions on how to price and promote the product and how best to distribute the product to customers.

## Primary research and secondary research

The collection of market data can be divided into two main types:

- **Primary research** (sometimes called field research) involves collecting data first-hand; for example, interviewing people about their views on a product. This is data collected by a business for the first time and for its own specific needs.
- **Secondary research** (sometimes called desk research) uses data that already exists; for example, data that a business holds in its records about existing customers. Most secondary data have usually been collected by another organisation and for a different purpose.

> **KEY TERMS**
>
> **primary research:** the collection of first-hand data for the specific needs of the business.
>
> **secondary research:** the collection of data that already exists and that has been collected for another purpose.

### DISCUSSION

Which method of market research do you think is the most useful for a business? What do you think might affect which market research method a business chooses to use?

## Methods of primary research

Businesses can collect market research information in several different ways.

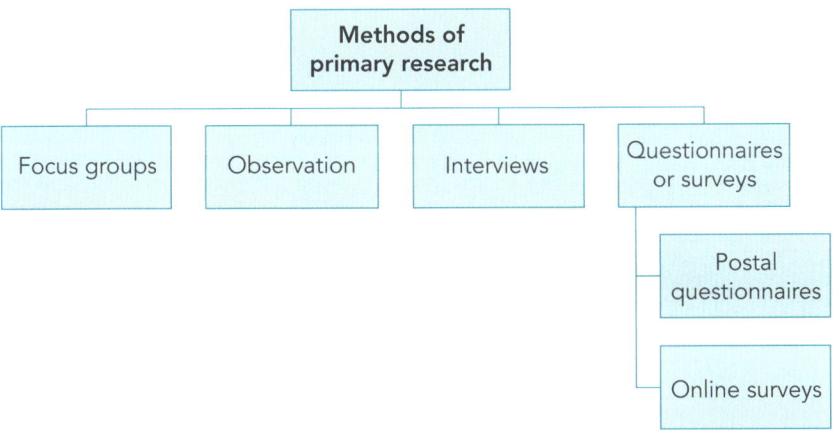

Figure 11.4: Methods of primary research

### Focus groups

A focus group involves inviting a group of consumers to discuss topics, such as new products, packaging, brand names and advertisements. The results of the focus group will be used to inform decision-making in the areas that have been discussed. It is common for focus groups to be recorded or filmed so that the decision-makers in the business can listen to consumers' responses after the focus group has finished.

Focus groups are advantageous because:

- in-depth responses are gained from consumers
- there is opportunity for follow-up questions to be asked.

However, the disadvantages of these focus groups are:

- they can be time-consuming to arrange
- the responses of one participant may influence other participants.

A focus group is used to gather information from current or potential customers (see Figure 11.5).

Focus groups are often used by Disney when new characters or concepts are being developed. The decision-makers at Disney meet with small groups of children to get their opinions on various aspects, such as episodes of a new series which is in development. This helps Disney to find out from its 'typical' consumers what they think about the product and its marketing.

**Figure 11.5:** Focus groups are one method of primary research

## Observation

An observation involves market researchers watching and recording the behaviours of consumers. For example, it could help a leisure centre to see how changing the positioning of equipment in its gyms affects how frequently it is used by gym-goers.

The advantages of observations are as follows.

- Findings are often more accurate as they are based on the actual actions of consumers (rather than the way a consumer says they will act).
- It is relatively simple to carry out as no interaction is required between the researcher and the participant.

However, the main problem with observations are:

- there is no opportunity to ask consumers why they behaved as they did
- it requires trained observers, which can be expensive.

This method of primary research is often used by large supermarkets who observe the behaviour of customers as they select their products from the many options available on the shelves (see Figure 11.6).

Some businesses also use observation to check the quality of service they are providing to customers. For example, a hotel might use a 'mystery guest' to visit and stay at the hotel and report back to management about their experience.

Figure 11.6: Supermarkets often use observation to see the behaviour of customers

### DISCUSSION

What do you think would make an observation 'successful'? Do you think observations should be carried out once or more than once? If more than once, do you think they should be carried out at the same time of the day or at different times of the day? Are there any other factors you think a business should consider when planning an observation?

## Questionnaires or surveys

Questionnaires or surveys can be used to ask questions of current or potential customers. They can be carried out in different ways, such as postal or online (see Figure 11.7).

The advantages of questionnaires or surveys are:

- the ability to ask questions to a large proportion of the market
- the researcher does not need to be present while the questionnaire or survey is being completed
- it is relatively simple to analyse the data.

The disadvantages of questionnaires or surveys are:

- it may be seen as 'junk mail' and therefore have a low response rate
- it may be subject to bias as only those with an interest in the subject of the survey may respond
- the questions may be worded badly or not fully understood
- it does not give the opportunity to ask follow-up questions.

### CASE STUDY 11.1

**4Sight**

4Sight is a market research company in the Middle East. They conduct market research specific to the needs of a business. One example of this was a bank that commissioned 4Sight to conduct market research on their behalf. 4Sight set up online surveys for customers of the bank. This helped the bank to gain as many responses as possible and enabled them to gather relevant feedback.

**Discuss in pairs or groups:**

1. What are the advantages to 4Sight of using online surveys?
2. Are there any potential disadvantages?

**Figure 11.7:** Market research companies often use online surveys

## Interviews

An interview involves an interviewer and an interviewee, and may take place at a business's premises, over the telephone or in the street. A trained interviewer asks questions to an interviewee and records their answers.

The main advantages of interviews are:

- the interviewer can explain any question that the interviewee does not understand
- follow-up questions can be asked.

> **TIP**
>
> To help you answer questions about market research, make sure you know the advantages and disadvantages of the different methods of research.

Disadvantages of interviews are:

- it is expensive to train interviewers
- the responses may be subject to bias as the interviewee may respond in a way that they think the interviewer wants them to.

> **ACTIVITY 11.2**
>
> You have just set up a business selling gaming headphones in your local area. You are planning to carry out interviews with some potential customers to find out what type of products they would like, how often they might buy the products and where they would like to buy the products from.
>
> Write down three potential questions you might ask in an interview to find out consumer preferences.
>
> Now work in pairs with someone in your class. Ask each other your three questions and then reflect upon:
>
> 1 How useful was each question in helping you to gather the information you required?
>
> 2 How might you adapt the questions to improve them?

# Methods of secondary research

The most commonly used sources of secondary data are shown in Figure 11.8.

> **TIP**
>
> Do not confuse primary and secondary research with primary and secondary sectors.

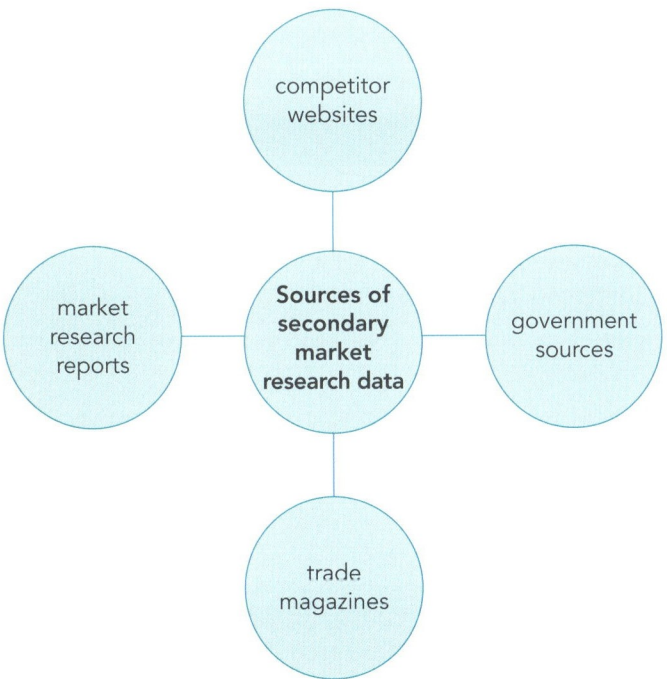

Figure 11.8: Sources of secondary market research data

## Competitor websites

Competitor websites are usually accessible via the internet. Businesses may find out information such as the type of products being sold by competitors and the price they are being sold for. They can also be used to see when competitors are running any promotional campaigns. Competitors' websites are free to access; however, a business will not have any information regarding the reasons behind decisions made by competitors.

## Government sources

Most governments publish data and information related to their own country; for example, population statistics and the support available for businesses. Increasingly, this information is available from official government websites, such as the Kenyan government's website. However, some government reports may not be publicly accessible or a fee may be charged to get access.

## Market research reports

Market research is often conducted by market research agencies. These are companies that collect and analyse market data, which they then sell to other businesses; for example, RNB Research, which has a Pan-Asia coverage including China, India and the UAE. A fee must be paid for this type of market report and not all the information included may be relevant to the business.

## Trade magazines

Trade magazines are specific to a particular industry; for example, the Oil and Gas Journal. This can help a business to gather information about the entire industry or market, which may be useful when making decisions. However, trade magazines may not be published regularly and therefore information may be out of date. All businesses in the industry also have access to the same information.

> ### ACTIVITY 11.3
>
> Choose an industry that you are interested in. You should access the websites of three businesses that operate in that industry. What information do you think that competitors would be interested in when looking at one another's websites? How might a business use the information from competitors' websites to inform their own decision-making?

11    Market research

**Figure 11.9:** Competitor websites are one method of secondary research a business might use

## Advantages and disadvantages of primary and secondary research

Table 11.1 considers the advantages and disadvantages of primary research.

**Table 11.1:** Advantages and disadvantages of primary research

| Advantages | Disadvantages |
| --- | --- |
| • Data is up to date.<br>• Data is collected for a specific purpose that is directly relevant to the business. This may lead to more informed decision-making.<br>• It is not available to other businesses. This may provide a competitive advantage. | • It is costly to collect. Therefore, there is an opportunity cost as this money could have been used in other areas of the business.<br>• It is time-consuming. This could lead to a delay in introducing new products to the market, for example.<br>• There is a risk of the data being inaccurate or containing bias; for example, if the interviewer asks a question that leads the interviewee to give an answer that they might not have intended. Also, if the sample chosen to be surveyed does not represent the whole population, the results will not reflect everyone's opinion. |

Table 11.2 shows the advantages and disadvantages of secondary research.

**Table 11.2:** Advantages and disadvantages of secondary research

| Advantages | Disadvantages |
|---|---|
| • It is often cheaper to obtain than primary research data. | • It may be out of date. This may lead to inaccurate decision-making. |
| • It is quicker to obtain than primary research data. This can increase the speed of decision-making. | • It has not been collected for the specific purpose required by the business, so may not be as reliable or as useful as primary research data. |

### CASE STUDY 11.2

**Sky Mavis seeks consumer feedback**

Sky Mavis is a software development company based in Vietnam. They develop online games, such as Axie Infinity, which has over 2 million players around the world.

Sky Mavis partners with game studios and creators when developing new products to ensure that the best games are created. Online games are popular worldwide. It is important to Sky Mavis to get feedback from its players. One type of feedback they receive relates to the game not working properly. Another type of feedback is related to general thoughts that players have on the game; what they like or dislike or what they might recommend to change.

Sky Mavis use primary research. Both types of feedback explained above are obtained via surveys that are available online. Sky Mavis describes the feedback it receives as 'top quality'.

**Discuss in pairs or groups:**

1. What is the difference between primary research and secondary research?
2. Why do you think Sky Mavis uses surveys to gather feedback from its players?
3. Explain one disadvantage to Sky Mavis of using surveys.

Figure 11.10: Online games are popular worldwide

## 11  Market research

# The need for sampling

When carrying out primary research, it is often unrealistic to be able to get the views of every consumer in the market. This would also be too expensive and too time-consuming for businesses.

This problem can be overcome by selecting a sample from the total market. **Sampling** means a business conducting market research on a small portion of their total market. This means they can gather information regarding the product, price, promotion and place and make informed decisions. It is also cheaper than interviewing the whole population and takes significantly less time.

There are different methods of sampling that a business can use; the method chosen must produce a sample that is representative of the whole population. If the sample chosen is not representative of the whole population this could lead to a business making the wrong decisions.

> **KEY TERM**
>
> **sampling:** it involves conducting market research on a small portion of the total market, which is representative of the entire market.

### ACTIVITY 11.4

You are going to carry out some market research involving students in your school.

Your class might choose their own research topic. For example, if you were setting up a shop selling food and drinks in school, what products would fellow students want to buy? How much would they spend in the shop per day/week? How many times a week would they use the shop? Alternatively, you could use the following questionnaire as a guide.

1  How often would you buy food in school, per week?

   Never     Once       Three or      Four or        Every day
             or twice   four times    more times

2  What type of food products would you like to buy?

   Crisps    Chocolates    Sweets    Fruits    Cereals    Other

3  How often would you buy drinks in school, per week?

   Once or twice        Three or four times        Every day

4  What type of drinks would you like to buy?

   Water    Fizzy drinks    Milkshakes    Juice    Other

5  How much would you be willing to spend on a drink?

   Less than $0.50    Between $0.50 and $1    More than $1

> **CONTINUED**
>
> You can add more questions or change the questions, but remember that people do not like answering questions that are too personal, for example, how much money they have to spend each week. As a class, you should survey between 50 and 100 students. Remember, the bigger the sample size, the more representative the results are likely to be of the whole school population. When you select your sample, you should also make sure that it is representative of the whole school, so it should include all ages.
>
> Once you have completed your survey, you need to present the results in tables, charts or graphs. You could publish your findings in your school magazine, if you have one, or on school noticeboards. Summarise the main findings of your research.

> **REFLECTION**
>
> When completing Activity 11.4, how did you select the sample you used? Do you think this sample was representative of your total market? How could this affect the accuracy of your market research findings?
>
> Did you have any problems when carrying out your market research? If you were to carry out the research again, would you do anything differently? If so, what and why?

## 11.2 Accuracy of market research data

We have seen how important it is for businesses to collect, record and analyse market research data to help in the decision-making process. However, it is important for users of market research data to recognise that the data may sometimes be inaccurate. This can be due to one or more of the following reasons:

- The sample chosen may be too small or may not be representative of the population.
- The business may choose the wrong type of method to collect the data.
- People who are interviewed as part of the market research process may not answer questions truthfully.
- In an interview, the interviewer may ask questions in a way that encourages the interviewee to give an answer that does not reflect their true view or that could lead to bias in the responses.

- The language used by the interviewer, or used in a questionnaire, may be unclear or difficult to understand.
- The data may be recorded incorrectly or numerical analysis may be carried out incorrectly.
- Secondary data may be out of date.
- Secondary data may have been collected for a different purpose to the one it is now being used for.

Any of these factors can result in market research data being inaccurate. If this is the case, then using the data is likely to result in poor or incorrect decisions being taken.

## 11.3 Analysis of market research results

Once market research has been carried out, the results need to be presented and analysed. Research could be presented in written reports, tables, charts and graphs. Businesses will use these research findings to make decisions.

Below is an example of how market research data might be used to make decisions:

**Scenario:** A school is thinking about hiring an external company to set up an after-school sports club. It needs to decide which sport(s) to offer in its club. The school has sought the opinions of its students using a questionnaire. Some of the research findings are shown below (see Figures 11.11 and 11.12):

Question 1: Which sports do you like to play?

> **TIP**
>
> To fully understand the topic of market research, you need to be able to explain the reasons why market research findings may be inaccurate.

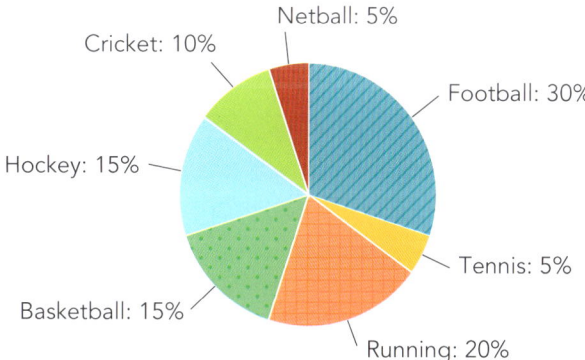

**Figure 11.11:** Pie chart showing the sports that students play

Question 2: How much would you be willing to pay per club?

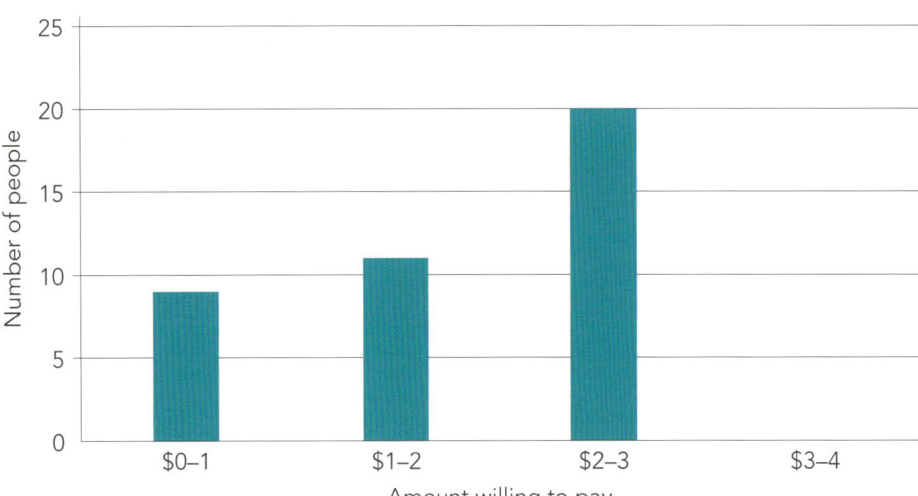

Figure 11.12: Bar chart showing how much students are willing to pay

As football and running are the two most popular sports, the school is likely to choose to offer one or both of these in the club. No one was willing to pay more than $3, which suggests that any price more than this is too high. However, $2–3 was the most popular response, so the school is likely to decide to charge this price.

### ACTIVITY 11.5

Joseph makes scented candles. He has carried out some market research about three new scents he is thinking of adding to his product range. He surveyed a sample of 50 existing customers to find out what they thought about the scent of these three new candles. The results of his research are presented in the bar chart in Figure 11.13.

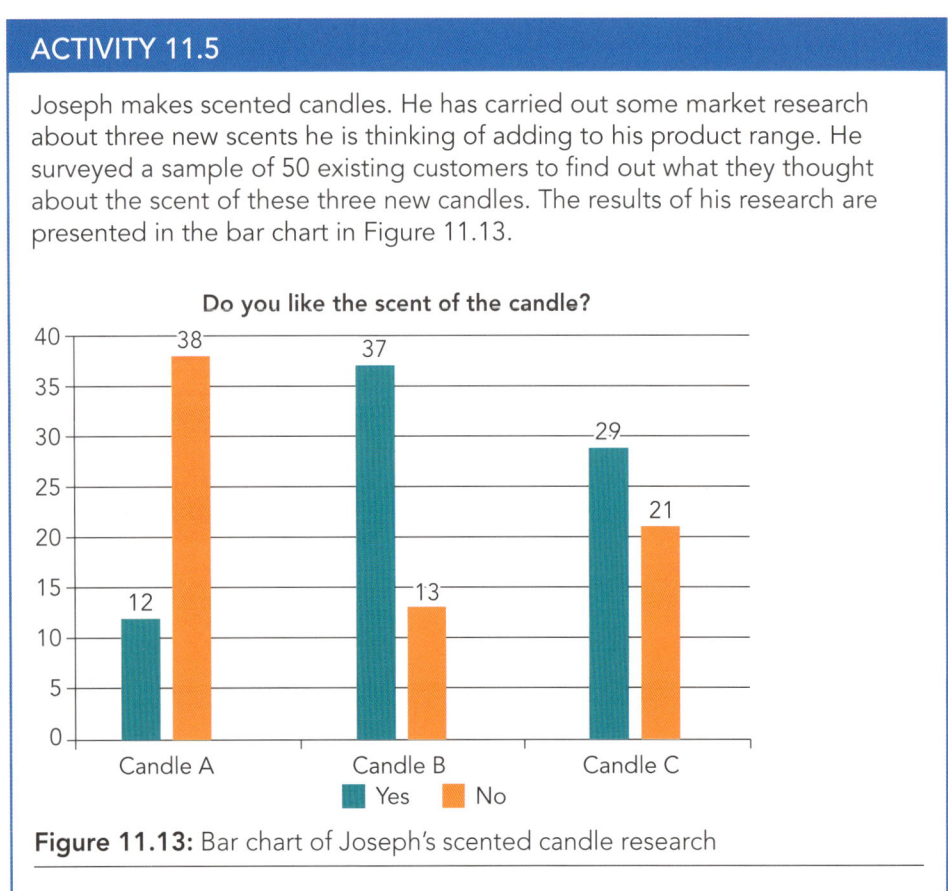

Figure 11.13: Bar chart of Joseph's scented candle research

## CONTINUED

1. Define 'sample'.
2. Which candle did the sample decide had the least popular smell?
3. Do you think Joseph's market research data is useful? What factors might affect the accuracy of the findings?

## BUSINESS IN ACTION

### JYSK

JYSK was established in Denmark in 1979. It sells furniture for the home and garden and has more than 3 200 stores in 48 countries. In May 2023, JYSK entered the Turkish market and opened three stores. In December 2023, JYSK announced that it would be opening its fourth store in Turkey during 2024.

**Figure 11.14:** A showroom for a furniture business

**Discuss in pairs or groups:**
1. Which methods of market research would you have recommended JYSK use before entering the Turkish market?
2. Would you recommend they use the same or a different method of market research before opening the fourth store? Explain your answer.

> BUSINESS FOR CAMBRIDGE IGCSE™ AND O LEVEL: COURSEBOOK

> **SUMMARY**
>
> You should now know:
>
> - Market research enables businesses to gather data about its customers, competitors and the market. This is used to make more informed decisions.
>
> - Market research can be either primary or secondary. Primary market research involves the collection of data first-hand that is specific to the needs of the business. Secondary market research is data which already exists and was collected for another purpose.
>
> - Advantages of primary research include that it is up-to-date and relevant to the business. However, it is often more time-consuming to collect and can be expensive.
>
> - Advantages of secondary research include that it is often quicker to collect than primary. However, it is not specific to the needs of the business.
>
> - Market research data needs to be presented in an appropriate way. This could be either a report or through tables and graphs. It will help the user of the market research to analyse the findings and make decisions.

# Chapter 11 practice questions

1. Bibi is thinking of setting up a children's nursery for children between 0 and 4 years of age. She knows she needs to carry out market research before opening her business, but is unsure whether this should be primary research or secondary research. She has a small market research budget. There are two competitors in the local area.

   a  Define 'market research'. [2]

   b  Outline **two** primary research methods Bibi could use to collect market research data. [4]

   c  Explain **two** advantages to Bibi of doing market research. [6]

   d  Bibi could use primary research or secondary research to collect data about her proposed business. Which method do you think she should use? Justify your answer. [8]

2. Company Y manufactures household cleaning products. It has been established in the market for five years. It has recently developed a new range of cleaning products for cleaning and polishing glass, wood and ceramic tiles. The Marketing Manager is deciding whether to sample the market using a focus group or questionnaire.

   a  Define 'sampling'. [2]

   b  Identify **two** factors which may affect the accuracy of the Company Y's market research. [4]

   c  Outline **two** advantages of sampling to Company Y. [6]

   d  Do you think Company Y should use a focus group or questionnaire to sample the market? Justify your answer. [8]

Total available marks: 40

## CHECK YOUR PROGRESS

How well do you think you have achieved the learning intentions for this chapter? Give yourself a score from 1 (still need a lot of practice) to 5 (feeling very confident) for each learning intention. Provide an example to support your score.

| Now I can … | Score | Example |
| --- | --- | --- |
| understand and explain the role of market research | | |
| identify primary and secondary methods of market research and explain the advantages and disadvantages of each | | |
| explain the factors affecting the accuracy of the market research | | |
| analyse simple market research data. | | |

> Chapter 12
# Marketing mix: product

**LEARNING INTENTIONS**

By the end of this chapter, you will be able to:

- explain the advantages and disadvantages of developing new products
- explain the importance of brand image
- explain the role of packaging
- identify the main stages of the product life cycle and understand a product life cycle diagram
- understand examples of extension strategies that a business could use, and explain their advantages and disadvantages
- recommend and justify an extension strategy to use in a given situation.

## Introduction

Over the next four chapters, you are going to learn about the different parts of the **marketing mix**. The marketing mix is the set of four key decisions that a business must take to market products effectively and help attract customers. These four decisions are often called the Four Ps. The first of these decisions you are going to look at is what product the business is producing and selling.

You will learn how each element of the marketing mix can influence sales.

> **KEY TERM**
>
> **marketing mix:** the four key marketing decisions that a business makes in order to market products effectively and help attract customers.

### BUSINESS IN CONTEXT

#### Oríré

All products have a life cycle. Some products are introduced into the market and sold for years and years. Other products are introduced and are withdrawn from the market after a very short period of time, possibly a few weeks or months. The life cycle of a product is determined by a range of factors such as the nature of the market and the level of competition. Decisions around marketing will be made based on the stage of the life cycle a product is in. For example, the price at which a product is sold will be determined, in part, by its stage in the product life cycle.

**Figure 12.1:** New products are regularly introduced into the clothing market

One market that is very fast paced is the clothing industry. New products are introduced into the market very frequently, sometimes due to changing weather conditions (e.g., selling more coats and jumpers during colder months), or sometimes because there are changes in what is in 'fashion' (see Figure 12.1).

Oríré was established in 2021. It is a fashion brand based in Nigeria that uses sustainable materials to manufacture clothes for a female target market. Oríré's ethos is to be creative and innovative with a commitment to its social and environmental responsibilities. It sells a range of products such as tops, dresses and trousers. Due to the fast-changing nature of the fashion market, Oríré regularly introduces new products to the market while also withdrawing others. It prides itself on the relationships it has developed with its suppliers and tailors, and ensures that everyone receives a fair wage and good working conditions.

#### Discuss in pairs or groups:

1. What are the benefits to Oríré of regularly developing new products?
2. How could Oríré's commitment to sustainability impact the price it charges for its clothes?

## 12.1 Product

A product can be either a good or service. A product is sold to satisfy consumer needs and wants. Consumers may be attracted towards a product, perhaps because of a low price or they may have seen it advertised. However, if the product does not meet the needs and expectations of customers, they will not buy it again. Successful products are bought again and again by customers. This helps to build the brand and develop customer loyalty.

> **TIP**
>
> Often people associate the word 'product' with a 'good', however, a product can be either a good or a service.

# Advantages and disadvantages of developing new products

Many businesses operate in very competitive and/or fast-changing markets. The survival and continued success of these businesses depends on either adapting existing products or developing new products to meet the changing needs and wants of customers. They may need to:

- develop new products
- change an existing product to meet the changing needs and wants of customers
- change an existing product to enter a new market.

> **LINK**
>
> More information about market research can be found in Chapter 11.

### ACTIVITY 12.1

Think of a product that you would like to introduce to the market. It could be a different version of a product that already exists, or something new entirely!

1. Draw a picture of the product and use labels to identify its key features.
2. Answer the following questions:
    a. Who is your target market?
    b. What price will you sell your product for?
    c. Where will you sell your product?
3. Present your idea to your class.

It can be very expensive to develop new products. It is also important to remember that even if a product is developed following market research, this does not guarantee success.

The advantages and disadvantages of developing new products are shown in Table 12.1.

> **LINK**
>
> Economies of scale occur when average costs per unit decrease, as output increases. More information can be found in Chapter 18.

**Table 12.1:** Advantages and disadvantages of developing new products

| Advantages of developing new products | Disadvantages of developing new products |
|---|---|
| • Developing a new product before competitors can helps to gain a competitive advantage. The business may be able to charge a high price for this new product which could increase profit margins.<br>• New products may appeal to a wider consumer base which can increase potential sales and revenue.<br>• Developing new products to add to those already being produced by the business spreads risk. This means if the sales of one product fall, they may be offset by rising sales of another product.<br>• The development of new products may help businesses benefit from economies of scale. | • Market research is likely to be carried out to identify customer needs. This can be very expensive and can also delay the time it takes to get the product to the market.<br>• The development of a new product requires expenses on the raw materials and labour required to produce the trial product. Not all businesses might be able to afford to do this.<br>• There is no guarantee that a new product will be a success; some products never make it to the market. This leads to a loss of both time and money.<br>• Advertising costs to inform consumers about the new product can be high. This creates an opportunity cost. |

## 12.2 Brand image

A brand is the name given by a business to its product or range of products. It allows a business to distinguish its products from those of its competitors. **Brand image** is the name, logo or identity of a product that distinguishes it from competitors. Brand image determines the perception that consumers have of a business. There are advantages to a business developing a brand image:

- Consumers are more likely to recognise the products of the business.
- Higher prices can often be charged for products with a brand image.
- It may be easier to launch new products in the market as consumers already know and trust the brand and so are more likely to try new products than if it was from an unknown brand – they have customer loyalty.

Each of these advantages can lead to an increase in sales and therefore revenue for a business.

> **KEY TERM**
>
> **brand image:** the name, logo or identity of a product that distinguishes it from competitors.

### DISCUSSION

Think of a business that has a strong brand image in your country. In pairs, discuss the following:

- Why does this business have such a strong brand image?
- What benefits are there to this business of having a strong brand image?

## 12.3 The role of packaging

Most products bought by consumers are packaged. In recent years, many businesses have started to use more environmentally friendly packaging and reduced the amount of single-use plastics being used in packaging. Many businesses use recycled materials in their packaging, or the packaging itself may be recycled. This is partly due to consumers becoming more aware of environmental issues.

The packaging used by a business may influence the perception that consumers have about the product. If the packaging is well designed and uses good quality materials, consumers are more likely to perceive the product inside to be of higher quality (see Figure 12.2). However, poorly designed or poor-quality packaging may influence consumers to think that the product inside is not very good.

Figure 12.2: Packaging can be used to protect a product or to provide information about a product

### DISCUSSION

What are the advantages to a business of using environmentally friendly packaging? Are there any disadvantages?

### ACTIVITY 12.2

In pairs, choose one of the following products:

- toothpaste
- coffee jar
- video game
- chocolate bar.

Look at the packaging of your chosen product. What do you think is the role of the packaging for the product you have chosen?

In Activity 12.2, you should have identified some of the following roles of packaging:

- to protect the product – if a product is damaged, it can increase waste
- to provide information about the product, which may be a legal requirement
- to help consumers recognise the product – this can lead to increased sales
- to promote the brand – this can help develop brand loyalty.

## 12.4 The product life cycle

All products have a life cycle. The **product life cycle** represents the volume of sales of a product over time. The product life cycle is divided into four main stages, as shown in Figure 12.3.

- **Introduction stage** – the product is launched into the market. Sales are low. The product might be making a loss in this stage due to the high cost of advertising needed to introduce the product to the market as well as high setup costs.
- **Growth stage** – the product is becoming more well known to consumers; the business may be developing a brand image. Sales are increasing. It is common for the product to start to earn profit during this stage.
- **Maturity stage** – the product is very well known. Sales are no longer growing but are not yet falling. This is the most profitable stage in a product's life cycle.
- **Decline stage** – sales are falling. The product eventually becomes unprofitable and has to be withdrawn from the market.

> **KEY TERM**
>
> **product life cycle:** the stages a product goes through over time, determined by the volume of sales made in each stage.

> **TIP**
>
> To fully understand the concept of the product life cycle, you should be able to identify and explain how each stage of the product life cycle might influence decisions about price, product, promotion and place.

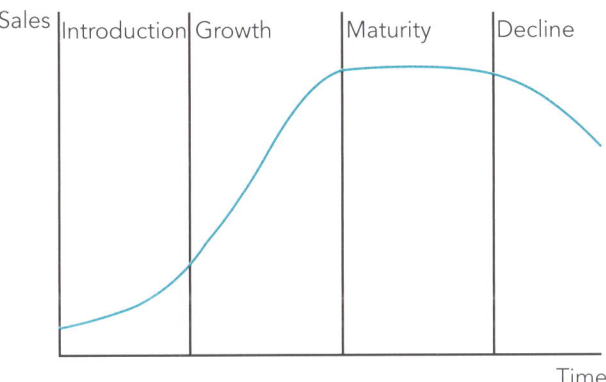

Figure 12.3: The stages of a product life cycle

The length of each stage of a product's life cycle varies from product to product. The overall life cycle of different products also varies. For example, when clothing retailer H&M release new clothes into the market, some of these products might be seasonal and spend very little time in the introduction and growth stages (see Figure 12.4).

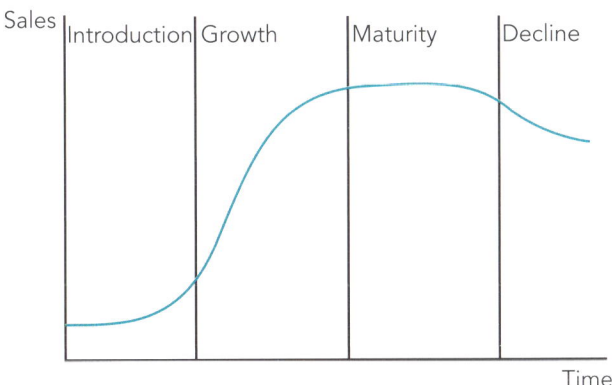

Figure 12.4: Example of a seasonal clothing product

Fashion clothing has a much shorter life cycle than a motor car (see Figure 12.5). Fashion clothing is introduced into the market and quickly grows and reaches maturity. It might only be in the market for a few weeks or months before it goes into decline as it is replaced with the 'latest' fashion.

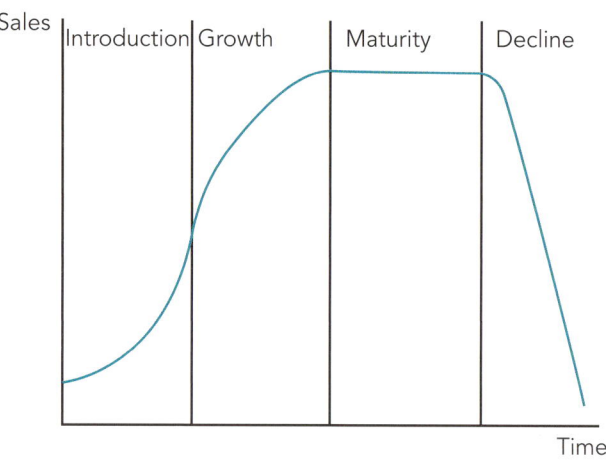

Figure 12.5: Example of a product lifecycle for fashion clothing

Motor cars will have a longer life cycle and will take longer to reach maturity (see Figure 12.6). They will eventually be replaced by a 'newer' model, but this could be 25 years after their introduction in the market.

Figure 12.6: Cars have a relatively long product life cycle

> **ACTIVITY 12.3**
>
> 1. Draw a product life cycle diagram labelling each stage.
> 2. Using newspapers, magazines, the internet or television, or your own experience as a consumer, identify one product for each stage of the product life cycle.
> 3. Draw the products onto the diagram at their life cycle stage.
> 4. Answer the following:
>    a. Explain why you believe these products to be at the stage of the life cycle you have identified.
>    b. Do you think that the products you have identified as being in the introduction stage will be a success? Why/why not?
>    c. Why has the product you have identified as being in the decline stage become less popular with consumers?

> **TIP**
>
> The product life cycle does not tell you how long a product will last in the market or how long it will spend in each stage. It only tells you the stages it might pass through.

> **REFLECTION**
>
> How easy was it to determine the stage of the product life cycle that each product is in? What factors did you consider when deciding upon an extension strategy? Do you think there is anything that the business could have done to prevent its product from entering the decline stage?

## How the product life cycle influences marketing decisions

Each stage of the product life cycle may require a different marketing mix. For example, when a product is being introduced to the market, is it likely that the business will spend more on promoting the product than it would when the product is in decline. At introduction, high promotional activity such as advertising is likely to be used to create product awareness and inform consumers that the product is on the market. However, at the decline stage, the only promotional activity is to advertise the lower price of the product or other promotions aimed at selling the remaining inventory.

## 12.5 Extension strategies

The maturity stage is the most profitable stage of a product's life cycle as sales of the product are at their highest. A business will want to keep the product in this stage for as long as possible (see Figure 12.7). It tries to do this by using **extension strategies**.

> **KEY TERM**
>
> **extension strategies:** actions taken by a business to keep a product in the maturity stage of the product life cycle to help maintain sales.

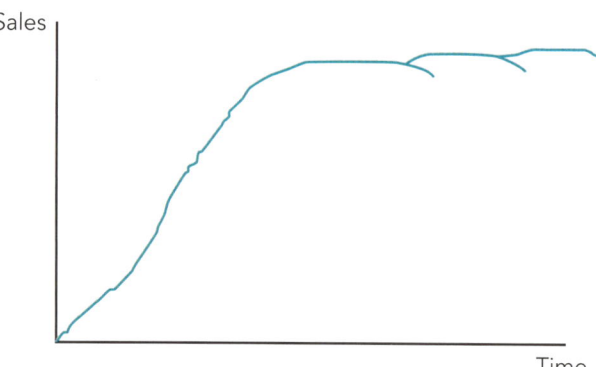

**Figure 12.7:** Diagram of extension strategies

Extension strategies include:

- **Finding new markets for the product** – this involves looking for other markets to sell the product in, perhaps by entering markets in other countries.

- **Finding new uses for the product** – sometimes products can have more than one use. This extension strategy may involve the research and development team looking to see if the product can be used for something other than what it was originally intended for; for example, a fizzy drink which is promoted as having benefits as a sports drink.

- **Adapting the product or the packaging to improve its appeal to consumers** – it may be the case that the packaging or product has become out of date. Therefore, the product or packaging may be adapted to meet current customer needs and wants.

- **Increased advertising and other promotional activities** – the marketing department may look for other ways to promote the product. This advertising could be intended to appeal to a new market or to remind the existing market that the product is still available.

### CASE STUDY 12.1

#### Michelin enters new markets

The Barbier-Daubree company was established in 1832. It sold a range of products made of rubber. In 1889, the business name changed to Michelin & Cie, still with the focus of developing new products made of rubber. It was in 1891 that the first modern day tyre was made and this was used in many bicycle races in France. Over time, the business entered the car market, now manufacturing tyres for cars. Product development continued for decades and it was in 1965 that the X tyre was produced.

Sales of the X tyre were high, and Michelin recognised the opportunity to grow the business internationally. They pursued an extension strategy of entering new markets (see Figure 12.8). In 1975, it built four production units in the USA; the X tyre was just as successful in other countries as it was in France. Michelin entered more markets during the 1980s and 1990s, again extending the maturity stage of the product life cycle. This time it entered emerging markets in Asia and Eastern Europe such as Thailand and Romania.

## 12 Marketing mix: product

### CONTINUED

Figure 12.8: Michelin tyres have entered new markets

**Discuss in pairs or groups:**

1. What is an extension strategy?
2. What were the disadvantages to Michelin of developing new products?
3. Were there any risks to Michelin in extending the maturity stage of the product life cycle by entering new markets?

### DISCUSSION

In pairs, discuss the following:

1. Of the extension strategies listed on the previous page, which extension strategy do you think is likely to be the most effective?
2. Are there any disadvantages of using any of the above extension strategies?

### LINK

New markets could be either in their own country or in another country. More information about entering markets in other countries can be found in Chapter 20.

### BUSINESS IN ACTION

**Tivoli Gardens**

Figure 12.9: Tivoli Gardens in Copenhagen

Tivoli Gardens is the second oldest amusement park in the world (see Figure 12.9). It is located in Copenhagen and has been operating since 1843. Tivoli Gardens has over 30 rides and 30 restaurants in its amusement park. Tivoli Gardens recognises the importance of adapting its product to suit changing consumer demands. One example of this is the adaptation of one of its rides, 'Odin Express'. The Odin Express rollercoaster has had over 30 million guest rides. Tivoli Gardens decided to adapt this rollercoaster into a new rollercoaster, 'The Milky Way Express'. This was to extend the product life cycle of the rollercoaster.

**Discuss in pairs or groups:**

1. What are the benefits to Tivoli Gardens of adapting one of its rollercoasters?
2. Are there any negatives to Tivoli Gardens changing the Odin Express to The Milky Way Express?

> BUSINESS FOR CAMBRIDGE IGCSE™ AND O LEVEL: COURSEBOOK

> **SUMMARY**
>
> You should now know:
>
> - The marketing mix is the four key decisions related to product, price, promotion and place that a business must take to market products effectively (the four Ps).
>
> - Successful businesses will develop customer relationships to build customer loyalty and develop brand image.
>
> - Packaging can help determine a consumer's perception of a product. It also fulfils roles such as protecting the product or providing information.
>
> - The product life cycle has four main stages – introduction, growth, maturity and decline. The stage of the product life cycle will influence decisions a business makes about its marketing mix.
>
> - Extension strategies, such as finding new markets, can be used to increase the amount of time a product remains in the maturity stage of the product life cycle.

# Chapter 12 practice questions

1. Cuts is a hairdressing salon. Its target market is females. It has 50 salons in Country X, each of which has an average of four full-time employees. Its labour turnover is high. The salon trains its employees using on-the-job training. It has been in the maturity stage of the product life cycle for a few years. The Managing Director is deciding on an extension strategy to extend the maturity stage of the product life cycle.

   a  Define 'extension strategy'. [2]

   b  Identify **four** extension strategies a business might use. [4]

   c  Explain **two** extension strategies Cuts could use. [6]

   d  Explain **two** ways Cuts could reduce labour turnover. Which one would you recommend it uses? Justify your answer. [8]

2. Carmel makes fashion jewellery which she sells at a local market. She does not use any packaging for her products. Some of her items have a short product life cycle so Carmel is always looking for jewellery to make and sell. Carmel's best-selling product, a necklace, is in the maturity stage of the product life cycle. Carmel needs to decide whether increasing advertising is the best way to increase sales of the necklace. She will use secondary market research to help her to decide which method to use. The market is very competitive.

   a  Identify **two** stages of a product's life cycle. [2]

   b  Identify **four** roles of packaging. [4]

   c  Explain **two** methods of secondary market research Carmel could use. [6]

   d  Do you think increasing advertising is the best way for Carmel to increase sales? Justify your answer. [8]

   **Total available marks: 40**

## 12 Marketing mix: product

### CHECK YOUR PROGRESS

How well do you think you have achieved the learning intentions for this chapter? Give yourself a score from 1 (still need a lot of practice) to 5 (feeling very confident) for each learning intention. Provide an example to support your score.

| Now I can … | Score | Example |
| --- | --- | --- |
| explain the advantages and disadvantages of developing new products | | |
| explain the importance of brand image | | |
| explain the role of packaging | | |
| identify the main stages of the product life cycle and understand a product life cycle diagram | | |
| understand examples of extension strategies that a business could use and explain their advantages and disadvantages | | |
| recommend and justify an extension strategy to use in a given situation. | | |

# Chapter 13
# Marketing mix: price

### LEARNING INTENTIONS

By the end of this chapter, you will be able to:
- identify pricing methods
- explain the advantages and disadvantages of pricing methods
- recommend which pricing strategy a business should use in a given situation.

# 13 Marketing mix: price

## Introduction

The next element of the marketing mix you are going to look at is price. Price is the amount the business is going to charge customers who want to buy the product. Businesses will decide which pricing method to use for their products; each of these have advantages and disadvantages.

### BUSINESS IN CONTEXT

**Reliance Jio**

Deciding on the price to charge for a product is a very important decision for a business to make. If the price is too high, customers may not be willing or able to buy the product; if it is too low then it may be perceived as being of low quality. There are many factors that influence the pricing method to be used by a business – level of competition in the market, uniqueness of the product and brand image of the business are just a few of these.

Reliance Jio is a mobile phone network in India that launched in 2016 (see Figure 13.1). Before Jio launched, India was ranked 155th in the world for mobile data consumption. In less than one year after Jio was introduced, it moved up to first in the world. Jio is now the largest operator in the country. Its products include mobile phones and network coverage, apps and fibre broadband. When Jio launched, its priority was to get as many customers as possible using its network. The market had established competition at the time and Reliance Jio had no real brand image to rely on. This led Reliance Jio to use penetration pricing to enter the market; setting a low price encourages consumers to try the product. In this case, Reliance Jio offered its services for a very low price; the price then gradually increased once a customer base and customer loyalty had been established. It is still the largest network provider in 2024, showing the success of this pricing method for the business.

**Discuss in pairs or groups:**

1. What are the benefits to Reliance Jio of using penetration pricing?
2. Are there any other pricing methods you would have recommended Reliance Jio to use instead? Why do you think this may have been more effective?

**Figure 13.1:** Reliance Jio launched in India in 2016

## 13.1 Price

### Does the price of a product influence whether or not you buy it?

Price is a very important part of the marketing mix because it is often the most important influence on customer demand for a product (see Figure 13.2). It can also influence the perception consumers have about the quality of a product – if price is very low then consumers may perceive the product to be of low quality and if price is high then consumers may perceive the product to be of high quality.

The market for many goods and services is very competitive. Consumers often base their buying decision, in part, on the price of the product. Here are some examples:

- If customers think that two products are very similar in quality then they are likely to buy the lower-priced product.

- Some consumers may not be able to afford to pay a higher price for a 'better' product so they will choose a product with a lower price.

- Some consumers may only buy products with a high price! For example, products that give the consumer a certain status, such as very expensive items of jewellery, one-off designer clothing and top-of-the-range sports cars.

Price may also be affected by supply and not just demand. For example, if a product becomes scarce, perhaps due to a poor harvest, then this will cause the price to rise.

**Figure 13.2:** Price is a very important part of the marketing mix

### ACTIVITY 13.1

Choose four products from an industry of your choice.

Rank the products from 1 to 4 (with 1 being the product you think is of the highest quality and 4 being the product you think has the lowest quality).

What factors have influenced your decision when ranking the products?

Now research the price of each of the four products. Is the most expensive product the one you decided was the highest quality? Is the cheapest product the one you decided was the lowest quality?

Describe the relationship between price and perceived quality in this industry.

# 13.2 Pricing methods

Businesses use several different methods for setting the prices of products. The most common pricing methods are shown in Figure 13.3.

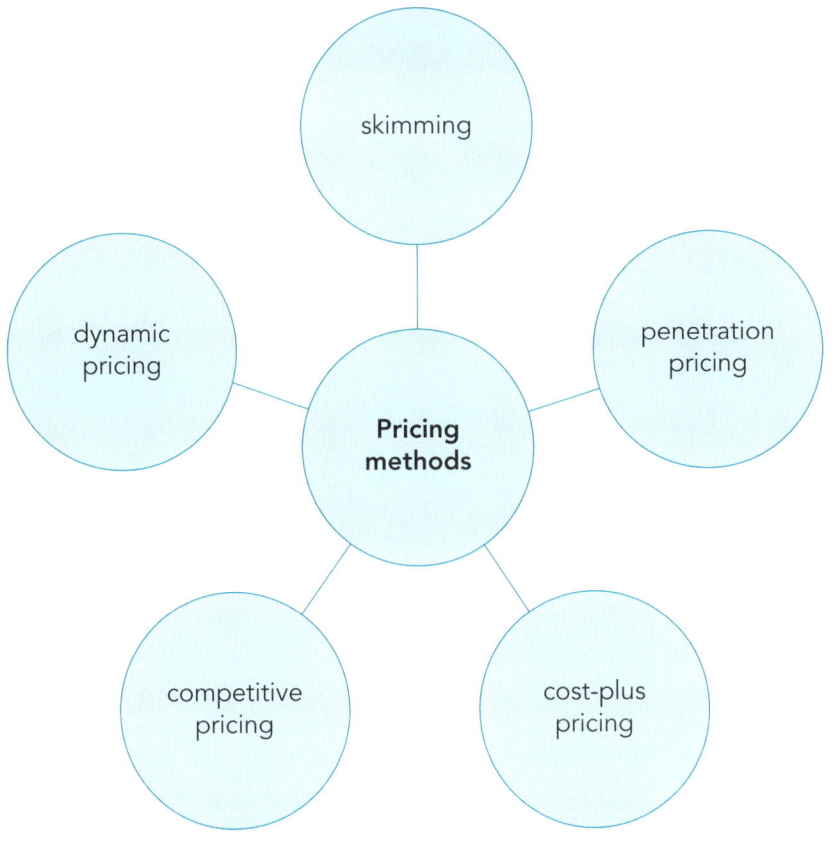

**Figure 13.3:** Pricing methods

## Skimming

A business may decide to set a high price for a new product that is unique or very different from anything on the market (see Figure 13.4). This is known as skimming. For example, when Google introduced its Google glasses, it was able to charge a very high price because it was a unique product and consumers were willing to pay more for the very latest technology. Consumers may also want the status of owning the latest version of a product and are prepared to pay a higher price for this.

The development of new medicines also attracts **(price) skimming**. The companies that develop these new medicines are given legal protection from any other company copying their product for a certain period of time. During this time, they can charge a very high price for the product they will have spent many millions of dollars researching and developing.

The profit earned when using market skimming is very high. Businesses sometimes need a large profit to get back the high costs of research and development of the product.

> **KEY TERM**
>
> **(price) skimming:** setting a high price for a new product that is unique or very different from any other product on the market.

Figure 13.4: Businesses can charge a higher price for the latest technology

## Penetration pricing

**Penetration pricing** is also used for new products. The price is set at a lower level from similar products already on the market to encourage consumers to try the product. Once the business has built up some customer loyalty for the product, it usually increases the price to a level similar to that of its main competitors. Businesses such as Netflix have very successfully used penetration pricing. The online streaming market is very competitive and therefore Netflix offered a low price initially to incentive consumers to use their product. Over time, the price charged for a Netflix subscription has increased.

> **KEY TERM**
>
> **penetration pricing:** setting a low price for a new product to attract customers to buy the product.

> **DISCUSSION**
>
> In pairs, discuss the following:
>
> - Are there any risks to a business of setting a low price when entering the market?
>
> - Are there any risks to a business of increasing its price once it is established?

## Competitive pricing

In many markets the level of competition is very high and firms selling in these markets will often charge similar prices to one another. This is because the products are often very similar with no strong brand advantage for any producers. If a business charges a higher price than its competitors, it is likely that consumers will not buy its product because they can get a similar product for cheaper. Taxi or car sharing can be booked online in countries all over the world using companies such as Bolt, Lyft or Uber (see Figure 13.5). These businesses use **competitive pricing**; the price charged by Bolt for a particular journey will be very similar to that charged by Lyft.

> **KEY TERM**
>
> **competitive pricing:** setting a price similar to that of competitors' products in the market.

**Figure 13.5:** Taxi businesses such as Lyft, Bolt and Uber use competitive pricing

## Dynamic pricing

Businesses that use **dynamic pricing** charge different prices for the same product at different times. Demand is a major factor that influences the price charged for a product. If a product is in high demand, then dynamic pricing means businesses will increase prices. If a product is in low demand, the price will be lowered to try and attract customers.

Airlines often use dynamic pricing. If there are no other airlines offering flights along the same flight route then the prices will be higher. If there are periods of time where demand is high, for example during school holidays, prices will also be high. When demand falls, so does the price.

> **KEY TERM**
>
> **dynamic pricing:** where different prices are paid for the same product at different times.

### CASE STUDY 13.1

**Airbnb's dynamic pricing model**

**Figure 13.6:** Airbnb uses dynamic pricing

Airbnb is used by consumers all around the world to book holidays or experiences. Individuals and businesses can 'list' accommodation on the Airbnb platform for users to search for and book. Airbnb uses a dynamic pricing model which means that users may pay different prices for the same accommodation at different times of the year. Airbnb bases its dynamic pricing on factors such as season, levels of demand and supply, the day of the week and whether there are any special events on nearby, such as a sporting event (see Figure 13.6).

**Discuss in pairs or groups:**

1 Define dynamic pricing.

2 Do you think using dynamic pricing is the best pricing method for Airbnb to use? Justify your answer.

## Cost-plus pricing

**Cost-plus pricing** is based on the cost of making the product or buying the product for resale to the final consumer. The price is set by adding a fixed amount, usually a percentage, to the cost of making or buying the product. It is common for supermarkets to use cost-plus pricing. As they sell a wide range of products for different prices, they can apply different mark-ups to each product.

**Example:**

Company X produces car batteries. The average cost of producing a battery is $8. It wants to make a profit of 150% per unit sold. The selling price of each battery will need to be:

$$\text{Cost} + 150\%$$

$$\$8 + (150\% \times \$8) = \$20$$

> **KEY TERM**
>
> **cost-plus pricing:** setting the price by adding a fixed percentage mark-up to the cost of making or buying the product in order to make a profit.

### ACTIVITY 13.2

1 Work in pairs and recommend which method of pricing might be the most suitable for the following business situations:

   a  The launch of a new electric car in your country.

   b  An airline offering both short-haul and long-haul flights.

   c  The room rate for a new luxury hotel in your country's capital city.

   d  A local supermarket that has seen a recent fall in sales due to the opening of a new store by a major competitor.

   e  A reusable water bottle to be sold to the mass market in your country.

> **REFLECTION**
>
> When completing Activity 13.2, how easy did you find it to recommend a pricing method? Were there any situations where you thought more than one pricing method might be appropriate? What extra information might be useful to help you to decide which is the best pricing method to use?

## 13.3 Advantages and disadvantages of pricing methods

A summary of the main features, uses, advantages and disadvantages of the pricing methods is shown in Table 13.1.

**Table 13.1:** Features, uses, benefits and limitations of the main methods of pricing

| Features | Uses | Advantages | Disadvantages |
|---|---|---|---|
| **(Price) skimming** | | | |
| <ul><li>A high price is set.</li><li>Price will fall when new competitors enter the market with similar products.</li></ul> | <ul><li>Used for new products that are unique or very different from other products on the market.</li></ul> | <ul><li>The high price enables the firm to recover research and development costs that are often very high.</li><li>The high price may help to create a quality image for products.</li></ul> | <ul><li>The high profits may attract new products to enter the market.</li><li>Some consumers may not be able to afford the high price. This can therefore limit potential sales.</li></ul> |
| **Penetration pricing** | | | |
| <ul><li>The price is set lower than similar products already on the market.</li><li>Price will be increased once consumer loyalty has been established.</li></ul> | <ul><li>Used for new products that are competing with similar products already established in the market.</li></ul> | <ul><li>Helps the product to become established in the market more quickly as consumers are attracted by the lower price. This can quickly increase sales.</li><li>Can increase market share quickly.</li></ul> | <ul><li>Revenue may be lower due to lower prices.</li><li>Development costs cannot be recovered quickly – if the product life cycle is too short, development costs might never be recovered.</li></ul> |

(Continued)

**Table 13.1:** (Continued)

| Competitive pricing | | | |
|---|---|---|---|
| • The price is set at a level similar to that charged by competitors. | • Existing products that have previously been priced using skimming or penetration (see above).<br>• New products where the business already has a good brand image and loyal customers. | • Prices are similar to those of competitors so the business can compete using non-price competition such as product quality or customer service. | • Need to find ways of competing to attract sales. |
| **Cost-plus pricing** | | | |
| • Price is set by adding the required profit percentage onto the cost of making the product. | • Retailers often use this method when deciding on the final price of the product to the consumer. | • Quick to work out the price.<br>• Makes sure that all costs are covered in the final price. | • Price might be set higher than those of competitors or than customers are willing to pay. This may reduce sales. |
| **Dynamic pricing** | | | |
| • Price is set according to factors such as level of demand and level of competition. | • Used by businesses to sell products that may have differing levels of demand at different times of the year. | • Increased revenue due to higher prices being charged during periods of high demand. This will also increase profit margin.<br>• Businesses can remain competitive by decreasing prices during periods of low demand. | • Some customers may be unhappy if other customers have paid less for the same product. This could worsen brand image. |

## Choosing a pricing method

There are a range of factors that a business will consider when deciding on the price of a product:

- **Is it a new or an existing product?** We have already seen how a new product could have a low price to enter the market (price penetration) or a high price if the product has a unique selling point or is differentiated (skimming). An existing product's price may be determined by its stage in the product life cycle. For example, when a product enters the decline stage its price might be lowered to sell the last remaining inventory.
- **Is the product unique?** A high price might be charged if a product has no close substitutes (alternatives). Once similar products enter the market, the competition will cause prices to fall.

> **TIP**
>
> Not all pricing strategies will be appropriate for all businesses or situations. Look at the context of the question before you decide which strategy is most appropriate.

## 13 Marketing mix: price

- **Is there a lot of competition in the market?** If the market is very competitive then it is likely that competitive pricing will be used. Similar products are likely to have similar prices; if they did not, the consumers would be likely to choose to purchase the cheapest product.

- **Does the business have a well-known brand image?** Companies such as Sony and Cadbury are able to charge a higher price for their products even though competitors have similar products on the market. This is because they have very high levels of brand loyalty and consumers trust the brand. It may also be the case that consumers consider the products to be of a better quality than the cheaper alternatives.

- **What are the costs of making and supplying the product?** A business needs to cover its costs of production and marketing. Therefore, the price charged must be higher than the cost of producing each unit so that the business can make a profit on each unit sold.

- **What are the marketing objectives of the business?** If a business has an objective of increasing market share, then it is likely that they will charge a lower price to encourage consumers to buy their product. However, if the objective is to maximise profit, then it might have a different pricing strategy, perhaps skimming.

> **TIP**
>
> You should consider each of the above factors if you are asked to recommend a pricing strategy for a business to use.

### BUSINESS IN ACTION

#### Grow Green Tea Company

Figure 13.7: A pot of green tea

Grow Green Tea Company successfully used skimming when entering the market in Singapore. Originating in Australia, Grow Green Tea Company sells high-end green tea. When entering the market in Singapore, there were low levels of competition and brand loyalty. This meant that Grow Green Tea Company could charge a high price when entering the market. The price was then reduced over time.

**Discuss in pairs or groups:**

1. What are the advantages and disadvantages of skimming?

2. Sometimes it can be risky for a high price to be set for a new product as consumers have no brand loyalty to the brand. Why do you think Grow Green Tea Company were able to be successful in using the skimming method?

> **BUSINESS FOR CAMBRIDGE IGCSE™ AND O LEVEL: COURSEBOOK**

### SUMMARY

You should now know:

- Pricing is an important influence on consumer demand and businesses have a number of pricing strategies they can use. The main pricing methods are skimming, penetration pricing, competitive pricing, dynamic pricing and cost-plus pricing.
- A number of factors will influence the pricing strategy used by a business; for example, whether the product is new or existing or the level of competition in the market.

## Chapter 13 practice questions

1. Debbie is a clothing designer. She designs unique and personalised dresses for people to wear on special occasions. Debbie is expanding her product range and entering a new market. She will make clothing for babies and young children. The clothing will be mass produced. Debbie has not yet decided on a pricing method for the new range of clothing.

   a  Define 'price'. [2]

   b  Identify **four** factors that might influence the pricing method used by a business. [4]

   c  Explain **two** methods of pricing Debbie might use for the new products. [6]

   d  Do you think the advantages to Debbie of developing new products outweigh the disadvantages? Justify your answer. [8]

2. HTB manufactures backpacks for children. It produces 200 units of output every day. Its backpacks are sold to the mass market in children's shops and other retailers. The market is very competitive. HTB uses competitive pricing. The Marketing Manager is considering whether to using cost-plus pricing instead.

   a  Define 'cost-plus pricing'. [2]

   b  Outline **one** advantage and **one** disadvantage to HTB of using competitive pricing. [4]

   c  Explain **two** advantages to HTB of using cost-plus pricing. [6]

   d  Do you think the advantages to HTB of operating in a mass market outweigh the disadvantages? Justify your answer. [8]

   **Total available marks: 40**

### CHECK YOUR PROGRESS

How well do you think you have achieved the learning intentions for this chapter? Give yourself a score from 1 (still need a lot of practice) to 5 (feeling very confident) for each learning intention. Provide an example to support your score.

| Now I can … | Score | Example |
|---|---|---|
| identify pricing methods | | |
| explain the advantages and disadvantages of pricing methods. | | |

# Chapter 14
# Marketing mix: place

**LEARNING INTENTIONS**

By the end of this chapter, you will be able to:

- identify different distribution channels
- explain the advantages and disadvantages of different distribution channels
- recommend an appropriate distribution channel for a business to use in a given situation.

## Introduction

In the previous two chapters you learnt about two elements of the marketing mix – product and price. In this chapter and the next, you will learn about the other two Ps: promotion and place. Place is where a consumer can buy products from a business; this can be either in a physical store or an online website.

> **BUSINESS IN CONTEXT**
>
> **Retailers**
>
>
>
> **Figure 14.1:** Retailers sell products on behalf of other businesses
>
> A key decision that producers need to make is how to get the company's products to the consumers. This is known as a channel of distribution. Should the business sell directly to the consumers themselves to keep all of the profit? Should they use an intermediary, such as a wholesaler or retailer and achieve benefits such as the intermediary advertising the product?
>
> Retailers sell products on behalf of other businesses (see Figure 14.1). As inventories are sold to the retailer, the retailer pays the costs involved in holding this inventory. This decreases costs for the business. Retailers are often located in areas that are readily accessible for consumers. This can lead to an increase in potential sales for a business – potentially more so than they might be able to make selling directly to the consumers themselves. However, retailers take a share of the profit and producers lose control over some of the marketing mix.
>
> There are many retailers all around the world and one such retailer is Metro Retail Stores Group Inc., based in the Philippines. It aims to provide its customers with value for money while providing an excellent customer experience in its 60 stores across the country. One of its store formats is a department store that offers a wide range of products from day-to-day items to children's toys to premium gift items.
>
> **Discuss in a pairs or groups:**
>
> 1. What are the advantages and disadvantages to businesses of using retailers such as Metro Retail Stores Group Inc.?
>
> 2. What are the reasons that a business might choose to sell directly to consumers rather than using an intermediary?

## 14.1 Place

There are two key decisions that a business will make for this element of the marketing mix:

- how to get the goods from the producer to the final consumer; this is known as the **channel of distribution**.
- where will the consumer be able to buy the goods or services, for example, in a shop or online.

> **KEY TERM**
>
> **channels of distribution:** the ways used to get a product from the producer to the final consumer.

Every business must decide the best way of getting its product to the final consumer. Businesses can use any of the channels of distribution shown in Figure 14.2 to achieve this.

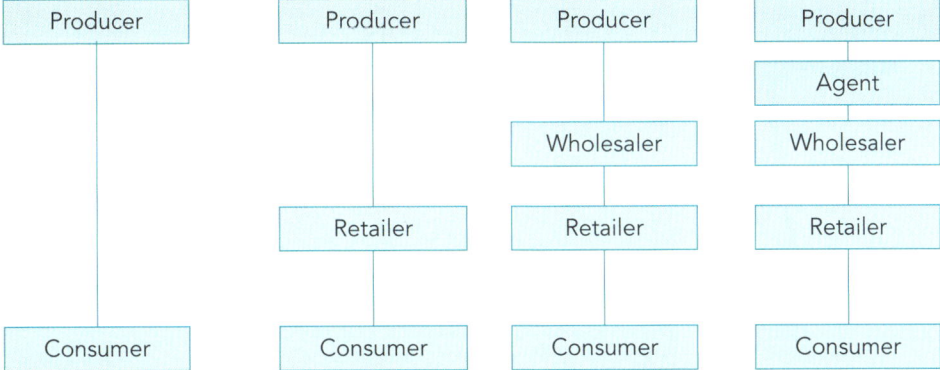

**Figure 14.2:** Channels of distribution

In the four channels of distribution shown in Figure 14.2, the agent, wholesaler, and retailer are known as intermediaries. They are also known as the 'middlemen' between businesses and the final consumers.

The four distribution channels are:

1  **Direct to consumers** (producer – consumer): this is where the producer sells the product directly to the consumer.

2  **Producer – retailer – consumer**: this distribution channel involves producers selling the product to retailers, who then sell the product to consumers.

3  **Producer – wholesaler – retailer – consumer**: the producer sells large quantities of the product to the wholesaler. The wholesaler then sells the product to retailers, who then sell small quantities of the product to the final consumers.

4  **Producer – agent – wholesaler – retailer – consumer**: this method is commonly used when a business is entering a market in another country. The producer will use an agent (someone with specialist knowledge about the country and its markets) who will help the producer to place the product with wholesalers and retailers.

### KEY TERMS

**wholesaler:** a business that buys products in bulk from producers and then sells them in smaller amounts.

**retailer:** a business that sells goods and services to the final consumer.

**direct to consumers:** where the product is sold by the producer directly to the final consumer without the need for any intermediaries.

### DISCUSSION

In pairs, discuss the following:

1  What are the benefits to a business of direct selling?

2  Why might a business choose to use an intermediary, such as a retailer?

### TIP

It is important that you learn the difference between a **wholesaler** and a **retailer**. A wholesaler will buy in bulk from a producer; they may then sell to retailers in smaller amounts.

## CASE STUDY 14.1

**Myntra**

**Figure 14.3:** Myntra launched a mobile phone app in 2015

Myntra is an online retailer based in India. It sells direct to consumers via its website. Myntra sells a variety of products such as clothes, shoes, accessories and beauty products. It sells products for men, women and children. Myntra describes itself as India's number one fashion destination; in just 5 years it had introduced over 350 local and international brands on its website. This is increasing year upon year. It developed a mobile phone app in 2015 to increase convenience even further for consumers (see Figure 14.3).

**Discuss in pairs or groups:**

1 What are the benefits to Myntra of selling direct to consumer?

2 Would you recommend Myntra to use an alternative method of distribution? If so, which one? What are the reasons for your decision?

# 14.2 Advantages and disadvantages of each channel of distribution

The advantages and disadvantages of each channel of distribution are shown in Table 14.1.

**Table 14.1:** Advantages and disadvantages of channels of distribution

| Channel of distribution | Advantages | Disadvantages |
| --- | --- | --- |
| Producer to consumer | <ul><li>All of the profit is earned by the producer.</li><li>The producer has full control over all parts of the marketing mix.</li><li>The producer has direct contact with the consumer – this could make it easier to obtain feedback from consumers that could help the businesses to improve products.</li></ul> | <ul><li>Delivery costs may be high if there are many customers located over a wide area.</li><li>All storage costs must be paid for by the producer.</li><li>All promotional activities must be paid for by the producer.</li></ul> |

(Continued)

**Table 14.1:** (Continued)

| Channel of distribution | Advantages | Disadvantages |
|---|---|---|
| Producer to retailer to consumer | • The cost of holding inventories of the product is paid, in part, by the retailer.<br>• The retailer will pay for advertising and other promotional activities.<br>• Increases potential sales for the business as a retailer is often located in areas that are accessible for consumers. | • The retailer takes some of the profit away from the producer.<br>• Producers lose some control of the marketing mix. |
| Producer to wholesaler to retailer to consumer | • The wholesaler buys in bulk from the producer.<br>• Wholesalers will advertise and promote the product to retailers and will pay for this.<br>• Wholesalers will pay for the storage costs of the products purchased from the producer.<br>• Distribution of goods through wholesalers helps the producer to sell the goods in a larger market. | • The wholesaler takes some of the profit from the producer.<br>• The wholesaler will make decisions around price and promotion, which means the producer loses control over these. |
| Producer to agent to wholesaler to retailer to consumer | • The agent has specialist knowledge of the market, especially a market in another country. They find wholesalers and retailers who are prepared to buy the product from the producer. This can save time for the producer when entering the market. | • The agent takes a share of the profit. |

### ACTIVITY 14.1

1. List three examples of the following in your country:
   - businesses that sell direct to consumers
   - retailers
   - wholesalers.
2. Can you think of any businesses that use more than one channel of distribution?

> **BUSINESS FOR CAMBRIDGE IGCSE™ AND O LEVEL: COURSEBOOK**

### ACTIVITY 14.2

Answer the following questions:

1. What is one advantage and one disadvantage to a business of direct selling?
2. Provide one advantage to a business of using a retailer.
3. Identify two benefits to a business of using a wholesaler.
4. What factors might a business consider when deciding upon a method of distribution to use?
5. A business currently sells products to consumers in the capital city of its country. It is planning to now increase its market and sell to consumers anywhere in the country. Which method of distribution would you recommend the business uses? Justify your answer.

## 14.3 Choosing a method of distribution

There are a number of factors that will influence the method of distribution a business uses:

- **The nature of the product** – if a good is perishable, such as milk, it will be important to get the product to the final consumer quickly and therefore a longer distribution channel may not be appropriate.
- **The market** – markets that cover a wide geographical area are best served through wholesalers who can buy the product in bulk from the producer and then sell to retailers.
- **Cost** – some methods of distribution are cheaper than others, and any that use an intermediary will take some of the profit away from the producer (see Figure 14.4). A business will need to consider if it has the resources available to deliver the goods to all of its customers itself. For example, does it own its own delivery vehicles or does it employ another firm to do this? If a business has limited resources, or if employing another firm is too expensive, then the business might choose to use a channel with an intermediary to reduce costs.

### TIP

In order to be able to recommend the method of distribution a business should use you need to understand the advantages and disadvantages of each method.

### LINK

There are costs to businesses of holding inventory. More information about the cost of holding inventory can be found in Chapter 15.

14 Marketing mix: place

**Figure 14.4:** Cost is one of the factors affecting the method of distribution used by a business

### ACTIVITY 14.3

You would like to launch a new business to teenagers in your country and need to decide the following:

1. the product you will be selling
2. the methods of advertising you will use
3. the pricing method you will use.

Now that you have made decisions about the other elements of the marketing mix, it is time to decide on the distribution channel to use. Which method is most appropriate for your product and why?

Create a poster summarising the key features of the marketing mix for your business (it might be a good idea to divide your page into four sections, with one area for each element of the marketing mix). You should be prepared to present this to your class.

### REFLECTION

When completing Activity 14.2, how did decisions for one element of the marketing mix influence decisions for other elements? How important was the target market being teenagers when making your decisions? What made you choose your distribution channel? Why was this more advantageous than the others?

## BUSINESS IN ACTION

**Trafigura**

**Figure 14.5:** Trafigura is a wholesaler that sells commodities around the world

Based in Singapore, Trafigura describes itself as one of the world's largest suppliers of commodities such as oil, petroleum and metals (see Figure 14.5). It is a wholesaler that was established in 1993. In 2024, it employed over 12 000 people worldwide and had commercial activities in more than 156 countries. It is actively trying to help the environment; it reduced its greenhouse gas emissions by 30% between 2020 and 2024.

### Discuss in pairs or groups:

1. Why might a business choose to use a wholesaler such as Trafigura?
2. What are the disadvantages to a business of using a wholesaler such as Trafigura?

## SUMMARY

You should now know:

- The marketing mix is the four key marketing decisions that a business makes in order to market products effectively and help attract customers.
- There are four methods of distribution a business might use, one of which is direct selling. The others involve intermediaries such as retailers, wholesalers and agents.
- There are advantages of direct selling such as the business keeps all the profit, but also disadvantages such as all storage costs must be paid for by the producer.
- Advantages of using a method of distribution involving a retailer, wholesaler or agent is that they will pay for advertising. However, the business loses control over its marketing mix.

14 Marketing mix: place

## Chapter 14 practice questions

1. JSL is an online retailer selling household items such as curtains to consumers in Country X. Its sales have increased since it started five years ago. JSL currently employs 50 employees to work in its warehouse. Employees find items in the warehouse and package them ready to send to consumers. JSL sells its product direct to consumers as its channel of distribution. It is considering opening a shop in the capital city of Country X.

    a   Identify **two** distribution channels (other than direct to consumers) that a business might use. [2]

    b   Outline **two** roles of packaging for JSL. [4]

    c   Explain **one** advantage and **one** disadvantage to JSL of opening a shop. [6]

    d   Do you think the advantages to JSL of selling direct to consumers are greater than the disadvantages? Justify your answer. [8]

2. The Regal Pottery Company (RPC) is a manufacturer of pottery, such as plates and cups, located in the UK. It produces high-quality items that celebrate events such as the Olympic Games and royal occasions as well as items celebrating different festivals. The market has become more competitive. RPC is thinking about using an extension strategy to extend the maturity stage of the product life cycle for some of its products. It distributes its products to the final consumer through wholesalers in its own country and abroad. RPC has recently invested in a new website. It wants to sell to its consumers using ecommerce.

    a   Define 'wholesaler'. [2]

    b   Outline **two** extension strategies RPC could use for its products. [4]

    c   Explain **two** advantages to RPC of using wholesalers to distribute its products. [6]

    d   Do you think the advantages to RPC of the market becoming more competitive outweigh the disadvantages? Justify your answer. [8]

    **Total available marks: 40**

### CHECK YOUR PROGRESS

How well do you think you have achieved the learning intentions for this chapter? Give yourself a score from 1 (still need a lot of practice) to 5 (feeling very confident) for each learning intention. Provide an example to support your score.

| Now I can … | Score | Example |
| --- | --- | --- |
| identify different distribution channels | | |
| explain the advantages and disadvantages of different distribution channels. | | |

# Chapter 15
# Marketing mix: promotion

## LEARNING INTENTIONS

By the end of this chapter, you will be able to:

- explain the reasons for sales promotion
- identify and explain methods of promotion and advertising
- recommend methods of sales promotion for a business to use in given situations
- identify examples of ecommerce
- explain advantages and disadvantages of ecommerce for businesses and for customers.

## 15 Marketing mix: promotion

# Introduction

You will now learn about the final element of the marketing mix – promotion. Promotion is about how businesses make consumers aware about their products and persuade them to buy them.

Although you will study each element of the marketing mix as separate concepts, it is important to remember that the four elements are linked, and that changes to one element of the marketing mix may lead to changes in at least one other element. For example, if a business decides to reduce the price of one of its products then this will have to be communicated to the consumer. Communication with consumers is one of the purposes of promotion.

You will also learn how technology has become a major influence on the way businesses market and sell products; this is known as ecommerce. You will consider the advantages and disadvantages to both businesses and consumers of ecommerce.

### BUSINESS IN CONTEXT

**Coconut Bowls**

Businesses must think of ways to increase awareness of products and of ways to incentivise customers to buy the products. There are many methods of sales promotion that a business can use. Sales promotions are incentives offered to consumers to encourage them to buy a product. A sales promotion will often cause a short-term increase in sales. A business will hope that customers become loyal and buy the products again and again.

Coconut Bowls is a business based in Australia. During a trip to Indonesia in 2015, the founder of Coconut Bowls realised that billions of coconut shells go to waste every year. These shells were often burned or thrown away. In Indonesia, it is common for coconut shells to be turned into handicrafts. The founder of Coconut Bowls saw an opportunity to use the shells and turn them into bowls (see Figure 15.1). A local Indonesian made some bowls that the founder took back to Australia. Coconut Bowls was established. The bowls were advertised using social media. Customers from all over the world wanted to buy the bowls. By 2024, Coconut Bowls has been reclaiming over 10 000 discarded coconut shells every month. It buys the shells from coconut farmers and the shells are cut, sanded and polished into bowls by skilled workers in its workshops in Vietnam and Indonesia. Every bowl made is unique and eco-friendly.

Coconut Bowls used sales promotion to increase brand awareness and increase the number of email subscribers it had to its brand. It ran a competition where customers could win one of its bowls as well as a Vitamix kitchen blender. Coconut Bowls generated 41 000 emails, 37 000 new followers and 15 000 social media shares within a week.

**Figure 15.1:** Discarded coconut shells can be transformed into bowls

#### Discuss in pairs or groups:
1. What are the benefits to Coconut Bowls of producing an environmentally friendly product?
2. Why was a competition an effective method of sales promotion for Coconut Bowls to use?

## 15.1 Promotion

**Promotion** informs consumers about a product and tries to persuade them to buy it. There are many methods of promotion that a business can use; you are probably already aware of some of these.

> **KEY TERM**
>
> **promotion:** a range of methods designed to encourage interest or raise awareness of products that a business is trying to sell.

### ACTIVITY 15.1

1. Think of different ways you have found out about the products a business is selling. In groups, make a mind map of all these ways.

2. Answer the following questions:

    a. Which of these methods was the most effective in informing you about a product?

    b. Did any of these methods encourage you to buy?

    c. Do you think any of these methods are likely to cost more than others?

## The aims of promotion

The main aim of promotion is to increase sales. Promotion does this by:

- making customers aware of the product or reminding consumers that the product is still on the market
- persuading consumers to buy the product
- explaining how a product is better than competitors' products
- creating and developing brand image
- encouraging wholesalers and retailers to stock the product
- reassuring consumers following a problem with the product.

## How promotion influences sales

Figure 15.2 shows the most common methods of promotion.

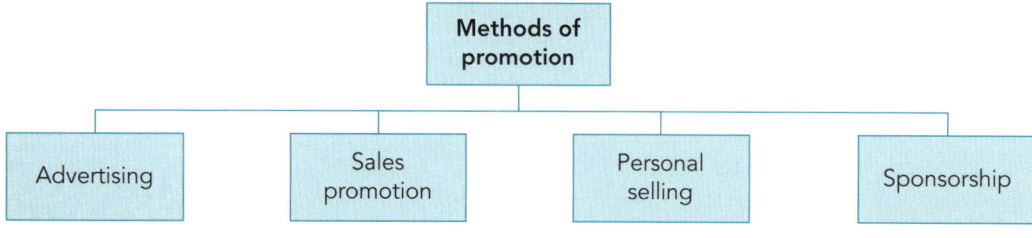

**Figure 15.2:** Methods of promotion

## Sales promotion

Businesses may choose to use a range of methods of **sales promotion**. The main advantage of sales promotion is that it is usually very specific to the business or its products. These could include:

- vouchers – vouchers give consumers money off the selling price of the product. This can be either a set amount or a percentage discount. This means that they can buy the product for a cheaper price than its usual selling price. The lower price may attract customers.

- reward schemes – loyalty reward points are given when customers spend money in the business. Often, when a customer has made a certain number of purchases, the business will give a product for free. For example, a coffee shop may have a reward scheme giving customers a free cup of coffee after they have bought ten cups of coffee themselves.

- competitions – a business may run a competition. If a customer buys something from the business or spends a minimum amount then they may be entered into a competition to win something. For example, a restaurant may enter customers into a competition if they spend a minimum amount on a meal. The winner of the competition may be entitled to a free meal at the restaurant.

- special offers – special offers can be very wide ranging, but could, for example, include customers receiving something in addition to the product they are buying or could include offers such as 'buy 2 get 20% off'.

> **KEY TERM**
>
> **sales promotion:** incentives used to encourage short-term increases in sales or repeat purchases.

### DISCUSSION

In pairs, discuss the following:

1. Which method of sales promotion do you think is most likely to increase sales?
2. Are there any disadvantages to a business of using this method of sales promotion?

### CASE STUDY 15.1

**The1**

**Figure 15.3:** Consumers can use The1's app every time they make a purchase

The1 provide a loyalty platform for shoppers in Thailand. The1 is Thailand's largest loyalty platform, with over 17 million members or about 25% of the population of Thailand. It strives to be the ultimate lifestyle platform that understands its customers and caters to every lifestyle through The1 business ecosystem with more than 1 000 partners and 20 000 service points. Consumers can download the app (see Figure 15.3) and show this every time they make a purchase at a partner's store of The1. Each time a purchase is made, the consumer collects points. Points can then be used to redeem rewards, transferred to a friend or be turned into a cash coupon.

> **CONTINUED**
>
> **Discuss in pairs or groups:**
> 1 What are the benefits to businesses such as The1 of using reward schemes as a method of promotion?
> 2 What are the benefits to The1 customers of the reward scheme offered by the company?

## Advertising

**Advertising** involves a business communicating with its customers. It can do this through a range of methods such as:

- social media – there are a range of social media platforms available for businesses to use to advertise their products. The platform used will depend upon the characteristics of the target market. Businesses may pay to run advertisements on social media platforms that will reach their target market. Examples of social media platforms include X, Weibo and Douyin. Social media reaches many people.

- direct/targeted emails – this involves sending emails to consumers who have either already bought products from the business or have signed up to a business newsletter, for example. This is a good way for a business to communicate with a large market over a wide geographical area. However, it is so widely used that there is a danger of it being considered 'junk mail' and not being read.

- leaflets – leaflets can be printed and distributed to customers in several different ways. Sometimes leaflets might be handed out on the street to customers passing by (see Figure 15.4). Leaflets may also be posted directly to the homes of potential customers or the offices of businesses. Leaflets can be eye-catching, which could encourage customers to read the information on the advertisement. However, just like targeted emails, there is a risk that they are seen as 'junk mail' and may be thrown away.

- billboards – billboards are large printed or digital images that are put up in areas where many people will see it. However, billboards cannot be personalised in the same way as using methods such as targeted emails can.

> **KEY TERM**
>
> **advertising:** the methods used by a business to inform customers about its products or persuade customers to buy its products.

> **ACTIVITY 15.2**
>
> Collect leaflets that have been delivered to your own home or ask the school office if it has any that you can have.
>
> Select one of the leaflets and write a brief report on what is being sold. Is the business local or national? What message is it trying to get across to consumers in its direct mail? Do you think the direct mail is effective? Justify your answer.

Most advertising is aimed at the final consumer. However, some advertising tries to persuade wholesalers and retailers to stock the product.

The advertising media used often depends on the available budget. Advertising on a billboard is more expensive than direct/targeted emails and may therefore only be used by businesses with a bigger marketing budget. The size of the firm will also influence

> **TIP**
>
> To fully understand the topic of promotion, make sure you know the difference between methods of advertising and methods of sales promotion.

## 15 Marketing mix: promotion

the method of advertising used, as well as the stage in the product life cycle that the product is at.

There are two main forms of promotional advertising:

- **Informative advertising** provides information to potential customers about the product. This can include information about the price of the product, what the product can be used for and the place where the customer can buy it. This form of advertising is often used when a new product is being launched in the market or enters a new market.

- **Persuasive advertising** is the most common form of advertising. A business uses this form of advertising to try to convince consumers that they need the product and that its product is better than the competitors' products.

Figure 15.4: Leaflets may be handed out to consumers on the street

### ACTIVITY 15.3

In pairs, design a magazine advertisement for a new electric car. You might want to look at newspaper and magazine advertisements to get some ideas about the layout and the sort of information you should include.

Present your advertisement to your class explaining the key features of your advert and why you think it would be effective in informing consumers about the product and persuading them to buy it.

### REFLECTION

When completing Activity 15.3, what was the most important feature of your advert? Will this be true for all advertisements? How confident did you feel when presenting to your class? Is there anything you would change about your presentation?

## The marketing budget and promotion decisions

The amount of money available to spend on sales promotion and advertising will influence the method used by a business. The marketing budget will determine how much money a business must spend on promotion. A marketing budget is the amount of money a business has allocated to spend on its marketing activities.

It is important to recognise that spending very large sums of money on promotion does not always guarantee success. Businesses will look at the relationship between sales and advertising and the level of sales made to see if the method used has been cost-effective and helped the business to achieve its marketing objectives.

> **TIP**
>
> Factors such as budget, size of the firm and stage in the product life cycle will influence the method of sales promotion or advertising that a business uses.

> **TIP**
>
> Remember that increased sales does not necessarily mean increased profits. It will depend on whether the revenue from the increased sales is greater than the cost of the promotion to generate the extra sales.

> **ACTIVITY 15.4**
>
> You are the Marketing Manager for a business selling equipment for school children such as pens, pencils and pencil cases. You and your team are developing a new range of products that are made entirely from recycled materials. The target market for the products is teenagers. You are creating a social media advert that will inform teenagers about your new product.
>
> Create a storyboard for your social media advert. Your storyboard should include six images that show the main scenes from your advert. Underneath, write a summary of each scene.

## 15.2 Ecommerce

The development of technology has affected many areas of business activity. The internet and social media networks have changed the ways that many businesses market and sell their products.

## Types of ecommerce

Many businesses, from sole traders to multinational companies, have websites. Websites provide businesses with the ability to sell their products over the internet. Customers must be willing and able to use the internet to buy the goods and services. There are some products that customers may prefer to buy in person, such as a car. This is because buying over the internet means customers cannot try the product before they buy it. Customers are becoming increasingly willing to buy products online, whether this be routine purchases such as the weekly family shopping or bigger purchases such as household furniture.

Examples of **ecommerce** are shown in Figure 15.5.

> **KEY TERM**
>
> **ecommerce:** the marketing, buying and selling of goods over the internet.

## 15 Marketing mix: promotion

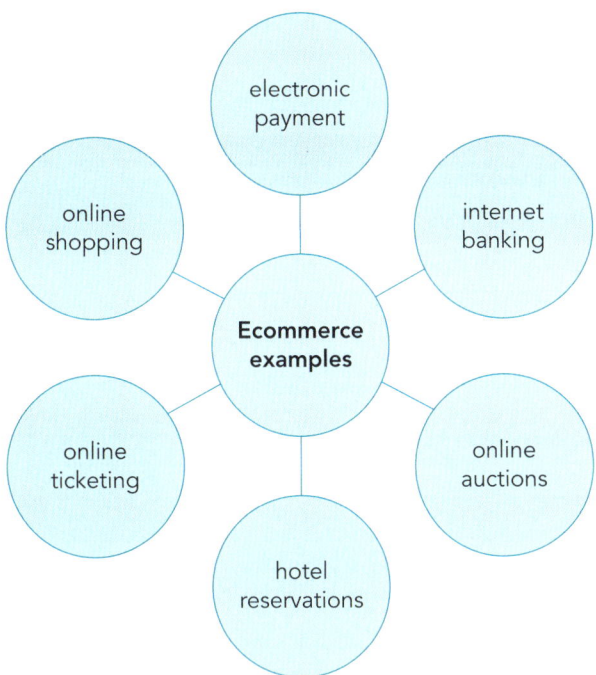

**Figure 15.5:** Examples of ecommerce

Examples of ecommerce include:

- mobile phone/internet banking – this involves consumers managing their bank accounts via their mobile phones, using either the bank's website or app
- online shopping – this involves consumers buying a product online
- online ticketing – this involves consumers buying online tickets for an event such as a music concert. This also means having paperless tickets; consumers can show a barcode or QR code on their phone to be scanned rather than having to show a physical ticket.

# Advantages and disadvantages of ecommerce

There are advantages and disadvantages of ecommerce to both businesses and consumers.

## Businesses

The advantages of ecommerce to a business are:

- **Increased potential number of sales** – the business can sell its goods and services to consumers all over the world and not just in its local area.
- **Reduced costs** – as there is no need for a physical shop, this saves costs such as staffing or rent.

However, there are also some disadvantages of ecommerce.

- **Increased competition** – competitors can now be from any part of the world, not just the local market.

> **LINK**
>
> There are two types of costs, fixed and variable. More information about types of cost can be found in Chapter 18.

- **Consumers may be unwilling or unable to buy online** – consumers may be less likely to buy the product as they cannot try before they buy, or may not have the ability to do so.

> **DISCUSSION**
>
> In pairs, discuss whether the benefits to a business of using ecommerce outweigh the risks? Justify your answer.

## Customers

The advantages and disadvantages of ecommerce to customers are shown in Table 15.1.

**Table 15.1:** Advantages and disadvantages of ecommerce to customers

| Advantages of ecommerce for customers | Disadvantages of ecommerce for customers |
|---|---|
| • **Convenience** – customers can order their products from the comfort of their own homes at any time of day.<br>• **Wider choice** – customers are now able to buy goods that they would not have had access to if they were only able to use their local shops.<br>• **Lower prices** – competition is worldwide and this reduces prices.<br>• **Better/more information** – consumers can read about the goods and services available from the websites of the different businesses and read reviews from customers who have bought products from businesses. | • **Risk of fraud** – a website might take a customer's money and not deliver the goods.<br>• **Risk of hacking** – a customer's personal details or bank account details might be 'stolen'.<br>• **Lack of personal service** – there is no face-to-face contact between the customer and the seller.<br>• **May be difficult to return items** – it can be inconvenient and expensive to return goods that do not meet the customer's needs, e.g., clothing that does not fit. |

> **CASE STUDY 15.2**
>
> **Ecommerce in Mexico**
>
>
>
> **Figure 15.6:** Ecommerce is used by many consumers and producers
>
> The use of ecommerce in Mexico increased significantly during COVID-19. The market for ecommerce is continuing to grow; however, at a slower rate than it was previously. In 2022, the ecommerce market was valued at $26.2 billion, with over 63 million ecommerce users in the same year. There are some challenges of using ecommerce in Mexico such as not all consumers have access to the internet to pursue ecommerce.
>
> **Discuss in pairs or groups:**
>
> 1. Define 'ecommerce'.
> 2. Explain **one** advantage and **one** disadvantage to consumers of using ecommerce.

# 15 Marketing mix: promotion

## BUSINESS IN ACTION

### Jumia

**Figure 15.7:** Many household cleaning products are sold on Jumia

Ecommerce has become increasingly popular in South Africa. Jumia is the largest ecommerce platform in South Africa, providing consumers with products at affordable prices. Many global brands are sold via Jumia, such as Dettol and Pampers. It uses delivery agents to deliver products to consumers.

**Discuss in pairs or groups:**

1. What are the advantages of ecommerce to Jumia's customers?
2. What are the advantages to Jumia of selling via ecommerce?

BUSINESS FOR CAMBRIDGE IGCSE™ AND O LEVEL: COURSEBOOK

> **SUMMARY**
>
> You should now know:
>
> - A business might use methods of sales promotion, such as vouchers, reward schemes, competitions and special offers, to increase consumer awareness about its products and persuade consumers to buy them instead of competitors' products.
>
> - A business might use methods of advertising such as billboards, social media, leaflets and targeted emails to communicate with its customers.
>
> - Ecommerce and social media networking provide huge marketing opportunities for businesses to promote and sell their products in global markets.
>
> - There are advantages to consumers of ecommerce such as more convenience, but also disadvantages such as the product cannot be tested before it is bought.
>
> - There are advantages to businesses of ecommerce such as higher potential sales, but also disadvantages such as an increase in the level of competition in the market.

# Chapter 15 practice questions

1. Excel Shoes is a manufacturer of footwear. It produces a range of shoes for children and adults. This market is very competitive. The Marketing Manager of Excel Shoes is considering entering the market for safety footwear. He is currently carrying out market research to find out consumer needs and wants. The safety footwear market is a niche market. The manager is also considering appropriate methods of advertisement for the potential product.

   a  Define 'niche market'. [2]

   b  Identify **four** methods of sales promotion that Excel Shoes could use for its new safety footwear. [4]

   c  Explain **two** benefits to Excel Shoes of carrying out market research. [6]

   d  Explain **two** methods of advertising Excel Shoes could use for its new product. Which method should Excel Shoes choose? Justify your answer. [8]

2. JWL is a theme park in Country X. Its target market is children and teenagers. JWL uses different methods of promotion to appeal to these markets. Attractions at the waterpark include rollercoasters, water rides and virtual reality experiences. Tickets to visit the theme park can only be bought via ecommerce. It sells tickets on its website. JWL has three main competitors in Country X. It uses competitive pricing. JWL's Marketing Manager is thinking about advertising using social media to increase awareness of the theme park.

   a  Define 'competitive pricing'. [2]

   b  Outline **two** benefits of ecommerce to consumers of JWL. [4]

   c  Explain **two** purposes of promotion to JWL. [6]

   d  Do you think JWL should use social media to advertise its products? Justify your answer. [8]

   Total available marks: 40

15 Marketing mix: promotion

## CHECK YOUR PROGRESS

How well do you think you have achieved the learning intentions for this chapter? Give yourself a score from 1 (still need a lot of practice) to 5 (feeling very confident) for each learning intention. Provide an example to support your score.

| Now I can … | Score | Example |
| --- | --- | --- |
| explain the reasons for promotion | | |
| identify and explain methods of sales promotion and methods of advertising | | |
| identify examples of ecommerce | | |
| explain advantages and disadvantages of ecommerce for businesses and for consumers. | | |

# Chapter 16
# Marketing strategy and legal controls

**LEARNING INTENTIONS**

By the end of this chapter, you should be able to:
- understand marketing strategies
- explain how legal controls influence marketing strategy
- explain the advantages and disadvantages of entering new markets in other countries.

# 16 Marketing strategy and legal controls

## Introduction

We have looked at the decisions that businesses make about price, product, promotion and place. Marketing decisions are not taken alone. In this chapter, you will learn how businesses combine the four marketing decisions into a marketing strategy.

### BUSINESS IN CONTEXT

#### Grab Holdings

It is important for businesses to get the right marketing strategy for their products. Businesses will consider who they are trying to sell their products to, what key features of their product they want to make customers aware of, what price is suitable for their target market and what differentiates their product from competitors. When deciding this strategy, businesses must consider the legal controls for each country they operate in.

In Singapore, there are legal controls over marketing such as:

- advertising must not be misleading
- messages cannot be sent to customers without their consent
- price must be displayed accurately and clearly.

Grab Holdings is a multinational technology company with its headquarters in Singapore. It provides an app where customers can book and pay for transport and food delivery online (see Figure 16.1). Grab Holdings advertises through social media and other event campaigns. The main focus of their advertising is to increase awareness of their USP of convenience for customers. About 4.8 million people use Facebook in Singapore and 94% of businesses on Facebook use paid advertisements.

Figure 16.1: Customers can order food online via an app

#### Discuss in pairs or groups:

1. What are the benefits to a business of advertising its products on social media?
2. How important is it for businesses to comply with legal controls over marketing?

## 16.1 Choosing a marketing strategy

Market research will be conducted and analysed before a **marketing strategy** is developed. A marketing strategy will also contain details of the marketing budget available to the business.

### The importance of the different elements of the marketing mix

If a marketing strategy is to achieve a business's marketing objectives, marketing decisions about product, price, promotion and place must be linked.

All decisions made must be relevant to the target market of the product. For example, the pricing method chosen should reflect a price that the target market is willing and able to pay for the product. However, if the product does not satisfy the needs and wants of the target market then it will not sell, even if the price is correct.

However, this does not mean that each part of the marketing mix is of equal importance. How important each part of the marketing mix is in influencing consumers varies depending on the situation.

> **KEY TERM**
>
> **marketing strategy:** a plan to achieve the marketing objectives of a business using a given level of resources.

> **DISCUSSION**
>
> Can you think of a business where price is the most important part of the marketing mix? Why is this the most important part for this particular business?

> **CASE STUDY 16.1**
>
> **Spotify**
>
>
>
> **Figure 16.2:** Spotify gives access to millions of songs from all over the world
>
> Spotify is a music streaming service that gives users access to millions of songs from all over the world. Spotify was founded in Sweden in 2006 and has expanded rapidly since then. Spotify advertised its service on social media to increase brand awareness. In 2021, Spotify undertook their biggest expansion to date by entering an additional 80 new markets (see Figure 16.2). During this expansion, they added 36 new languages to the platform to increase accessibility to the service. This helps Spotify with its aim of meeting the unique needs of each individual market. They also offer specialised payment formats for each market.
>
> The service they offer has also changed over time. Free and paid plans are available to its customers, and in some markets there are different types of membership, for example, a family membership. Spotify also now offer podcasts and music videos which may appeal to a new target market. In addition to paid memberships, Spotify also gain revenue from businesses advertising on their music streaming platform. They now gain a lot of customers via word-of-mouth promotion.

> **CONTINUED**
>
> **Discuss in pairs or groups:**
>
> Spotify's marketing strategy has changed over time. Think about how price, production, promotion and place have changed for Spotify since 2006. Complete the tasks below:
>
> 1 Give an example of how each area of the marketing mix has changed.
>
> 2 Explain why one of these changes may have happened.
>
> 3 Justify whether you think this change was a good idea or not. Explain your answer.

## Deciding marketing strategy

A business's marketing strategy is a plan to achieve its marketing objectives using a given level of resources.

Once a business has set its objectives, it will need to take decisions about product, price, promotion and place to achieve them. There are a range of factors that will influence these business decisions:

- the marketing budget available
- stage the product is at in its life cycle
- level of competition in the market
- characteristics of the target market.

> **LINK**
>
> More information about the product life cycle can be found in Chapter 15.

> **ACTIVITY 16.1**
>
> Choose a partner to work with. You are developing a marketing strategy for a children's toy. Individually, decide the following:
>
> - What is the marketing budget?
> - What stage in the product life cycle is the toy?
> - How much competition is in the market?
> - What are the characteristics of the target market?
>
> Swap your scenario with your partner. Now, develop a marketing strategy based on the responses your partner has given, including price, promotion and place, and anything else you think that might be relevant.
>
> Discuss both yours and your partner's marketing strategies. Is there anything you would change about each other's strategy?

> **DISCUSSION**
>
> How do you think the stage of the product life cycle could affect marketing strategy? Spending on promotion may be higher during the introduction phase than during the growth stage. How might this change the price?

> **TIP**
>
> Think about which factors affecting marketing strategy are most important for different forms of business. The budget available for a sole trader is likely to be smaller than that for a public limited company.

### ACTIVITY 16.2

JDB sells mobile phones to the mass market. Many of its customers have complained that the mobile phones are not working properly. JDB has had to replace 100 faulty mobile phones. The Production Manager is trying to identify why the product is faulty.

Discuss in pairs the answers to the below questions:

1   What are the advantages and disadvantages of selling to the mass market?

2   Could JDB have prevented faulty mobile phones being sold to customers? How?

3   How could the faulty mobile phones affect JDB in the short and long term?

### REFLECTION

When preparing your answers to Question 1 in Activity 16.2, did you and your partner have similar or different ideas or opinions? Were you able to justify these differences?

What factors did you consider when discussing the advantages and disadvantages of selling to the mass market? Do you think these benefits are applicable to all businesses? Could you think of different ways of preventing faulty products in Question 2? How did you differentiate between short- and long-term effects on JDB? Which do you think are the most significant?

## 16.2 Legal controls related to marketing

All areas of business are affected by legal controls (see Figure 16.3). These controls are the laws and regulations of the country in which a business operates. Legal controls vary from country to country, but most countries have laws that protect consumers from unfair or dangerous business activity. Examples of legal controls that influence the marketing of a product include:

- The advertised weights and measures of a product must be correct.

- Advertising must not mislead consumers by making false claims about the product.

- Goods that are faulty or dangerous must not be sold.

- Consumers must not be exploited in the market where there is little or no competition, for example, through prices being too high or product quality being too low.

16 Marketing strategy and legal controls

**Figure 16.3:** Legal controls are the laws and regulations of a country

## Effect of legal controls on marketing strategy

Table 16.1 shows the effect of legal controls on businesses.

**Table 16.1:** Effect of legal controls on businesses

| Legal control | Effect on business |
|---|---|
| Advertised weights and measures of a product must be correct/ advertising must not mislead consumers | Advertisements may have to be withdrawn and redesigned if they are found to contain misleading or inaccurate information. The business may have to advertise its product again. It may also be required to issue statements of apology in the newspapers, and in the worst case might be fined for deliberately misleading consumers. All of these actions increase a business's costs. |
| Faulty goods must not be sold | Products may need to be changed to meet minimum quality standards or prevent any health and safety issues. This will increase costs. |
| Consumers must not be exploited in a market where there is little to no competition | A large company that dominates a market may face legal controls, such as anti-trust or competition laws, if it is exploiting consumers by charging high prices or providing poor-quality goods and services. This can decrease brand image and potentially reduce sales. |

### ACTIVITY 16.3

Research examples of legal controls over advertising in your country, such as those given in Table 16.1.

1. State two of the legal controls you have researched.
2. How do these legal controls affect businesses in your country? Do they affect all businesses in the same way?

### TIP

When analysing points, try to use connectives such as 'this means' or 'therefore'. This will help to explain the impact of a point, rather than just state it. For example, products may need to be changed to meet minimum quality standards, therefore, business costs may increase.

### LINK

More information about competition can be found in Chapter 27.

## 16.3 Advantages and disadvantages of entering new markets in other countries

> **LINK**
>
> More information about ecommerce can be found in Chapter 15.

Developments in technology, for example, the internet, better transports and communication links have made it easier for businesses to enter new markets in other countries. Barriers to trade have reduced and therefore the financial costs of entering new markets in other countries are lower.

Selling direct to the consumer via ecommerce has enabled many businesses of all sizes to enter new markets in other countries. However, this expansion does not have to be through ecommerce, and there are many other examples of businesses that now export their goods and services to other countries using traditional distribution channels.

### Advantages of entering new markets in other countries

- Opportunity for increased sales which can increase revenue.
- To spread risk as the business is not relying on one country or market for its sales. For example, the home market may be in decline but demand for the product may still exist overseas (see Figure 16.4).
- Reduced barriers to entry.

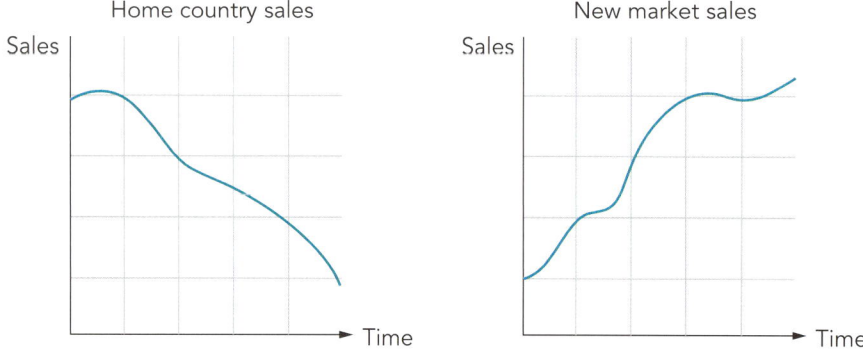

Figure 16.4: There may be the potential for increased sales in other countries

### Disadvantages of entering new markets in other countries

Although entering new markets in other countries offers huge marketing opportunities, there may also be problems for businesses entering these markets. Figure 16.5 identifies the main problems a business may face when making the decision to sell in markets in other countries.

# 16 Marketing strategy and legal controls

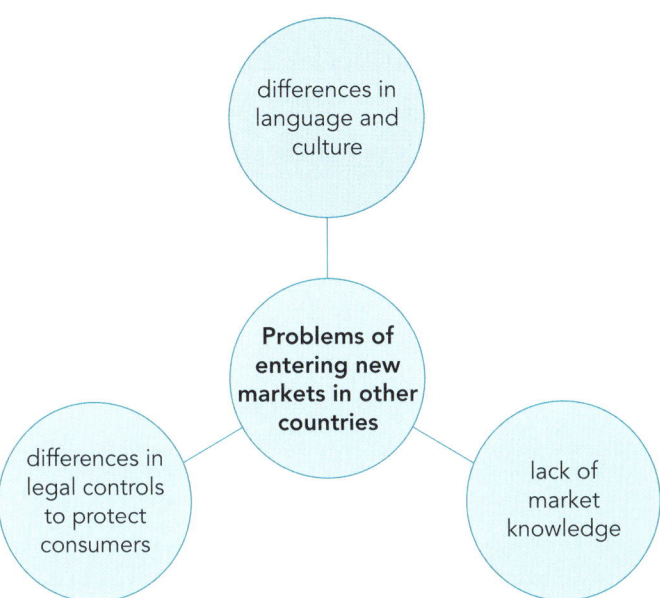

**Figure 16.5:** Disadvantages of entering new markets in other countries

## Cultural differences

Cultural differences can range from different languages between countries to how people dress to what they eat or value. It is important that cultural differences are addressed if a business wants to sell its goods and services in another country. Failure to do so could damage brand image.

For example, some words do not translate from one language to another, or may have a completely different meaning in another language. As a result, consumers may receive incorrect information about the product which could reduce sales. Countries where the population has a high proportion of young people, such as Indonesia, will have different needs and wants from countries where the population has a higher proportion of older people, such as the UK. A business may have to develop new products or adapt current products to suit these cultural differences. Product development or re-development will increase costs.

Businesses must also consider cultural differences. Colours, numbers, and symbols have different meanings and importance in different places. For example, in some cultures, it is rude to show the bottom of your feet, so this would need to be taken into consideration by a business. In some countries, for various reasons, it would not be appropriate to use certain images in advertisements.

## Differences in legal controls to protect consumers

As mentioned above, some countries have their own laws and regulations to protect consumers from unfair or dangerous business activity. These might be very different from the legal controls in the business's own country. Before a business decides to enter new markets in other countries, it must make sure that its products and the way it conducts business satisfy the laws of the countries it is looking to expand into. This may mean changing its product, packaging or advertisements, all of which increase costs.

> **TIP**
>
> Developing chains of analysis is important in longer questions. This means explaining the impact of your point, and then explaining the impact of this and then the impact of that and so on.

> BUSINESS FOR CAMBRIDGE IGCSE™ AND O LEVEL: COURSEBOOK

### BUSINESS IN ACTION

**Schweppes tonic water**

Schweppes tonic water is just one business that has failed to correctly translate words from one language to another. When entering Italy, Schweppes Tonic Water was translated to 'Schweppes Toilet Water'. This was not appealing to Italian customers.

**Discuss in pairs or groups:**

1. Why do businesses such as Schweppes want to enter new markets in other countries?

2. How could a translation error such as this affect the business? Is this likely to affect sales in other countries? Explain your answer.

**Figure 16.6:** A drink with tonic water

## Lack of market knowledge

Entering new markets for the first time presents two problems for most businesses:

- the business does not know the new market
- the market (consumers) does not know about the business or its products.

### ACTIVITY 16.4

Create a poster summarising the advantages and disadvantages of entering new markets in other countries.

Include at least three advantages and at least three disadvantages and try to use pictures to support your points. Examples of businesses that have been successful and unsuccessful in entering new markets could also be included in your poster.

You should be ready to present your poster to your class.

Some of the 'missing' knowledge relates to the factors discussed above. However, knowledge about market size, competitors, brand image, customer loyalty to existing products, consumer tastes and preferences, sources of media for promotion and channels of distribution is essential knowledge about the country and its markets.

### DISCUSSION

Choose two areas of required market knowledge stated on the previous page.

Why do businesses need to know each of these pieces of information for a successful entry into international markets?

# 16 Marketing strategy and legal controls

These problems need to be fully understood if a business is to succeed when entering a new market in another country.

The following case study is based on a business that has developed new products as a result of entering new markets.

## CASE STUDY 16.2

### GE HealthCare

It is common for a business to need to adapt its product when entering a new market in another country. India is a very large country and this can make it difficult for people living in rural areas to visit hospitals. GE HealthCare sells products, such as machines, that carry out ECG scans (this is a scan that records the activity of the heart). It recognised that its ECG machines were too expensive for many of the hospitals in India to be able to afford. So, GE HealthCare adapted its product and produced a portage scanning device that was small enough to fit inside a rucksack (see Figure 16.7). The price of this new product was only 5% of the price of the original machine. This allows Indian ambulances to use the machine to provide scans for people that would not previously have been able to receive a scan.

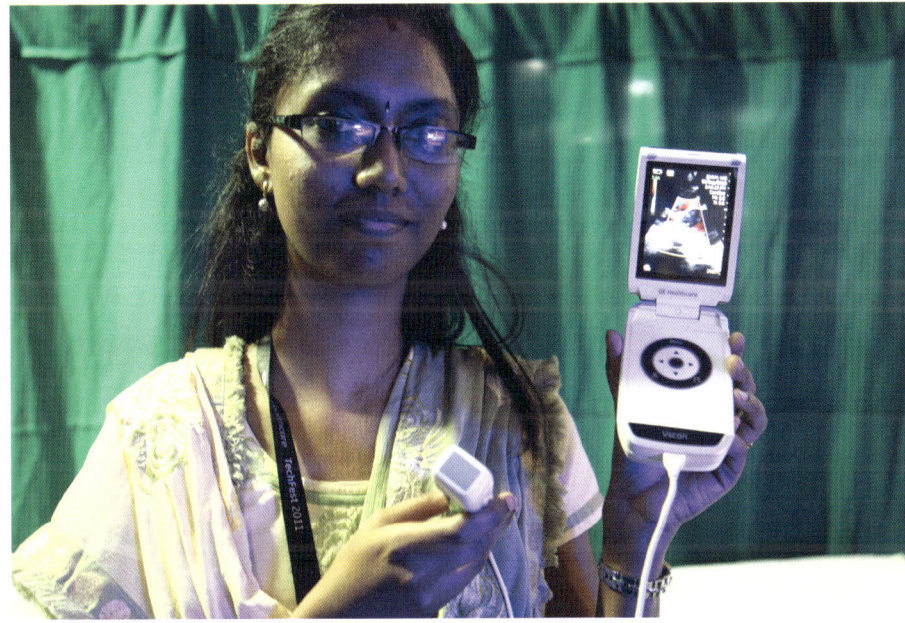

Figure 16.7: GE HealthCare developed portable ECG devices

**Discuss in pairs or groups:**
1 What advantages could the development of the portable scanning machine bring to GE HealthCare?
2 Are there any disadvantages to GE HealthCare of developing this portable machine?

> **TIP**
>
> Evaluation requires you to make a judgement that answers the question you have been asked. You should make a clear decision and not repeat points you have made earlier.

> **BUSINESS FOR CAMBRIDGE IGCSE™ AND O LEVEL: COURSEBOOK**

### SUMMARY

You should now know:

- Marketing strategy involves making decisions about price, product, promotion and place. These decisions complement each other.

- Legal controls influence marketing strategy – a common effect is an increase in costs for businesses.

- There are both advantages and disadvantages of entering new markets in other countries; the decision to enter will depend upon whether the advantages are greater than the disadvantages.

## Chapter 16 practice questions

1. Jim is a sole trader. He has three employees who manufacture handmade garden furniture using job production. Sales have decreased over the last two years. Jim is producing a new marketing strategy as new competition has entered the market. He knows that legal controls will affect his strategy.

   a. Define 'marketing strategy'. [2]

   b. Identify **four** elements of the marketing strategy. [4]

   c. Explain **two** legal controls that may affect Jim's marketing strategy. [6]

   d. Do you think that level of competition is likely to have the biggest influence on the marketing strategy for Jim? Justify your answer. [8]

2. ABC sells T-shirts to women in Country X. ABC is a franchise and it is considering entering a new market in another country. The Managing Director is concerned about the disadvantages of entering a new market in another country. The Marketing Director is thinking about the possible marketing strategy for the new market. He thinks price is the most important element of the marketing mix.

   a. Define 'franchise'. [2]

   b. Outline **two** advantages to ABC of entering a new market in another country. [4]

   c. Explain **two** disadvantages to ABC of entering a new market in another country. [6]

   d. Do you think price is the most important element of the marketing mix for ABC to consider when entering a new market? Justify your answer. [8]

   **Total available marks: 40**

## 16 Marketing strategy and legal controls

### CHECK YOUR PROGRESS

How well do you think you have achieved the learning intentions for this chapter? Give yourself a score from 1 (still need a lot of practice) to 5 (feeling very confident) for each learning intention. Provide an example to support your score.

| Now I can ... | Score | Example |
| --- | --- | --- |
| understand marketing strategies | | |
| explain how legal controls influence marketing strategy | | |
| explain the advantages and disadvantages of entering new markets in other countries. | | |

# Section 3 case study

## CASE STUDY

**Teen Fashions**

Teen Fashions is a manufacturer of clothing aimed at fashionable young people. The company has a strong brand image in Country X, which is where all its products are sold. Its current channel of distribution is shown in Appendix 1.

Shaun, the recently appointed Marketing Director, suggested in a recent board meeting that Teen Fashions should consider ecommerce for the business. 'Many of our competitors have an online presence and we are in danger of losing market share if we don't do the same,' he said.

The Operations Director was not in favour of Shaun's suggestion (see Appendix 2).

Sharee, the CEO of Teen Fashions, thinks that the company needs to consider expansion. She has identified two possible options:

**Option 1:** Manufacture clothing for people in the 25–40 age bracket. Many of these people will have bought clothing manufactured by Teen Fashions when they were younger so they are aware of the brand. Teen Fashions' Marketing Manager has been asked to carry out market research for this proposed new market.

**Option 2:** Enter new markets in other countries. Sharee has just returned from a trade mission organised by the government of Country X to several countries in the region. She has identified Country Y as a possible market for this expansion. An extract from her report to other members of the board is shown in Appendix 3.

## Appendix 1

**Current distribution channel**

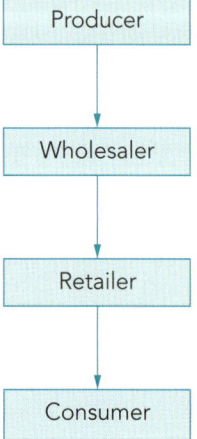

## Appendix 2

**Email from the Operations Director to Shaun**

In addition to operational factors, such as higher inventories and setting up a department to handle ecommerce sales, we will also require a new website to be designed and created. All of this will be very expensive, and I am not sure it will give our shareholders a good return on their investment.

## Appendix 3

**Extract from report on visit to Country Y prepared by Sharee**

- Country Y has a large percentage of the population under the age of 25.
- Despite the recession in most parts of the world, Country Y's economy has been growing rapidly and, as a result, consumers have high levels of disposable income.

The CEO is aware of the problems Teen Fashions might face when entering this new market, but feels that, with careful planning, these can be overcome.

1 a Explain **two** benefits to Teen Fashions of having a strong brand image.

   Benefit 1:

   Explanation:

   Benefit 2:

   Explanation: [8]

   b Consider how the following **three** factors influence the demand for Teen Fashions products.

   Which factor do you think is the most important? Justify your answer.

   Price of Teen Fashions' products:

   Consumer income:

   Quality of Teen Fashions' products:

   Conclusion: [12]

2 a Explain **one** advantage and **one** disadvantage to Teen Fashions of its current channel of distribution shown in Appendix 1.

   Advantage:

   Explanation:

   Disadvantage:

   Explanation: [8]

   b The Marketing Director and the Operations Director disagree about the benefits to Teen Fashions of ecommerce. Consider their views and recommend whether or not Teen Fashions should develop ecommerce activities. Justify your answer.

   Marketing Director's view:

   Operations Director's view:

   Recommendation: [12]

3 a  Explain **two** benefits to Teen Fashions of conducting market research.

   Benefit 1:

   Explanation:

   Benefit 2:

   Explanation: [8]

  b  The Board of Directors has agreed that Teen Fashions needs to expand the business.

   Consider Option 1 and Option 2.

   Which option do you think it should choose? Justify your answer.

   Option 1:

   Option 2:

   Recommendation: [12]

4 a  Explain **two** methods of promotion Teen Fashions might use if it chooses Option 1 to expand the business.

   Method 1:

   Explanation:

   Method 2:

   Explanation: [8]

  b  Explain how each of the following **three** factors might influence the success of Teen Fashions entering Country Y.

   Which of these factors do you think is likely to be the most important? Justify your answer.

   Social differences:

   Differences in language:

   Differences in legal controls to protect consumers:

   Conclusion: [12]

   Total available marks: 80

# Section 4
# Operations management

Many businesses in the private sector have profit as their main objective. To make a profit, businesses need to produce and sell products. In this section one of the things you will learn about is the production process – how businesses combine inputs to produce a saleable output. There are different methods of production a business may use to produce its output; you will look at the advantages and disadvantages of these methods. In order to be able to produce goods and services, a business must decide on a suitable location.

You will learn that there are many factors that affect location decisions, one of which is the role of legal controls. The concept of productivity and its importance will also be explored. Methods of improving labour and capital productivity will be considered. A business will incur different costs while manufacturing products. You will learn how to classify these costs and how to use them in break-even charts. Finally, you will learn about the importance of quality and how this might be achieved in different sectors of business activity.

# Chapter 17
# Production of goods and services

**LEARNING INTENTIONS**

By the end of this chapter, you will be able to:

- explain the production process
- explain why businesses need to hold inventories
- understand the concept of productivity, know how to calculate productivity, learn the benefits of increasing efficiency and identify ways to increase efficiency
- identify production methods and explain their advantages and disadvantages
- understand how technology influences production methods
- explain ways businesses can be more sustainable.

# 17 Production of goods and services

## Introduction

In this chapter, you will learn about the different **production** methods used by businesses and the factors that influence their choice. You will also learn how a business can measure its productivity, and methods of improving this. The importance of businesses holding inventory is also explored as well as the ways in which a business can be more sustainable and its advantages and disadvantages.

> **KEY TERM**
>
> **production:** the process of combining inputs together to turn them into product outputs.

### BUSINESS IN CONTEXT

#### Boogertman + Partners

Businesses must decide on a method of production to use when manufacturing products. Job, batch and flow production are three commonly used methods of production, each of which have advantages and disadvantages. There are various factors that influence the method of production a business uses, for example, the nature of the product and how many units will be produced.

Job production is used for one-off products that are produced specific to customer requirements. This means output is very low and it can often take a very long time to make one product. Specialised labour is often used, with raw materials used that are relevant to the particular product. Boogertman + Partners is just one business that uses job production. Boogertman + Partners is a studio for architecture, interior, graphic and urban design. Established in South Africa, it has now expanded and is completing projects throughout Africa and the Middle East. Boogertman + Partners work with their customers to create solutions for the specific requirements of an individual person or businesses. One of the projects Boogertman + Partners has worked on is the FNB Stadium in Johannesburg (see Figure 17.1). This stadium held the final of the 2010 FIFA World Cup. The reconstruction of this stadium was a unique project, with requirements specific to the product. The design for this stadium was based upon an African pot, known as the calabash. This was because Boogertman + Partners thought that the calabash would automatically be associated with the African continent. Textures, materials and colours were carefully chosen in the reconstruction of the stadium. Once completed, the stadium had a capacity of 88 460 spectators.

**Figure 17.1:** FNB Stadium in Johannesburg

#### Discuss in pairs or groups:

1. What are the benefits to Boogertman + Partners of using job production?
2. Is job production a suitable method of production for all businesses to use? What type of businesses would it not be suitable for?

## 17.1 What is production?

Production is the process of combining inputs together to convert them into product outputs. Examples of inputs include land, labour and capital. Output can be from either the primary, secondary or tertiary sector, and therefore includes both goods and services. Production can be measured by the number of units produced in a given period of time – this is the level of production.

# Managing resources to produce goods and services

## The production process

The production process is concerned with how a business turns inputs into outputs that can then be sold. Let us put the production process into context; a baker (labour) will take ingredients, such as flour and water, to their kitchen (land) and use mixers and ovens (capital) to make bread (the output), which will be sold to customers. In Figure 17.2, we can see various inputs (labour, land and capital) being converted into output (bread).

> **LINK**
>
> More information about factors of production and the primary, secondary and tertiary sectors can be found in Chapter 1.

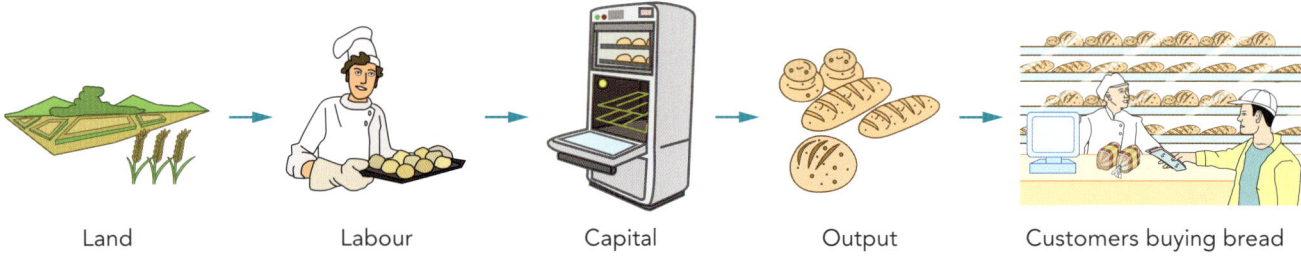

Land | Labour | Capital | Output | Customers buying bread

**Figure 17.2:** The production process

Operations management involves:

- overseeing the production process
- ensuring resources are being used as productively as possible
- producing the required output to meet consumer demand
- meeting the quality standard expected by consumers.

> **ACTIVITY 17.1**
>
> Using Figure 17.2 as a template, draw similar diagrams for three different products: one for primary, one for secondary and one for tertiary business activity. You should list the resources used and the good or service produced.

## Difference between production and productivity

Production is not to be confused with productivity. Productivity is a measure of how efficiently a business changes its inputs into outputs. It is the number of units of output produced by every worker in a given time period. One of the main methods of measuring business productivity is to calculate **labour productivity**. Labour productivity is the number of units of output produced for every unit of labour input in a given time period.

> **KEY TERM**
>
> **labour productivity:** the number of units of output produced for every unit of labour input in a given time period.

The productivity of labour (employees) is measured as follows:

$$\frac{\text{output per period (units)}}{\text{number of employees}} = \_\_ \text{ units per employee}$$

**Example**

A business has 100 employees and is currently producing 10 000 units of output per month. The calculation for labour productivity per month would be:

$$\frac{10000}{100} = 100 \text{ units per employee}$$

# Benefits of increasing efficiency and how to increase it

A rise in productivity will lead to a decrease in average costs. A fall in productivity will lead to an increase in average costs. Average cost is the cost of producing a single unit of output. A decrease in average costs results in a business becoming more efficient. Efficiency is a decrease in average costs as output increases.

There are some benefits to businesses of becoming more efficient:

- The cost savings could be passed on to consumers in the form of lower prices. This could increase business competitiveness and increase demand.
- A business could increase its profit margin if price remains the same.

## How to increase efficiency

To increase efficiency, a business might try to think of ways that it can increase its labour productivity. This means that they will try to increase the quantity of output produced per employee. Labour productivity could be increased by:

- improving the skill level of employees
- introducing more automation and technology.

### Improving the skill level of employees

Improving the skill level of employees could be achieved through training. As employees are more skilled, they might be less likely to make mistakes. This could lead to an increase in output per employee as there could be less time spent on remaking the product.

### Introducing more automation and technology

Machines can produce goods 24 hours a day (see Figure 17.3). They can also produce output faster than employees can. Therefore, introducing more automation and technology will result in more output being produced in the same amount of time, thereby increasing productivity.

> **LINK**
>
> More information about the types of training a business might use can be found in Chapter 6.

Figure 17.3: Machines are able to work 24 hours a day

### DISCUSSION

In pairs, discuss the following:

- What are the advantages and disadvantages of these two methods of increasing efficiency?
- What factors do you think might influence which method is used to increase efficiency?

### ACTIVITY 17.2

A manufacturing business currently has 100 workers. Its total output is 500 units per month.

1. Calculate the labour productivity per month.
2. In pairs, discuss how the business might increase its productivity. What is the biggest benefit to the business of increasing productivity? Share your ideas with another pair.

### REFLECTION

When completing Activity 17.2, what factors did you consider when deciding on how a business could increase its productivity? Did your partner agree with you or did they think something different? How might you approach this task differently next time?

### TIP

If you are asked to recommend ways a business could improve productivity, think about the type of business and what product it is making or selling. This will help you to decide which way would be most appropriate for the business.

### TIP

Points about productivity should always be linked to the effect on cost per unit of output.

Improving productivity will lead to an increase in costs for a business. For example, there will be costs arising from additional training or the purchase of new machinery. As the main benefit of improving productivity is to reduce average costs, the cost savings that result from improving productivity should outweigh the cost of achieving the improved productivity.

## Why businesses hold inventories

**Inventory** refers to the different items held by a business (see Figure 17.4). There are three types of inventory a business might hold:

1. **Raw materials and components** – these are the inputs needed for the production process.
2. **Work-in-progress** – these are goods that are not yet finished – they have not yet completed the production process.
3. **Finished goods** – these are goods that are ready to be sold or delivered to consumers.

> **KEY TERM**
>
> **inventory:** the stock of raw materials, work-in-progress and finished goods held by a business.

Figure 17.4: Inventories held by a business

Table 17.1 shows some of the reasons why a business might hold inventories.

**Table 17.1:** Reasons why a business might hold inventory

| Reason why it might hold inventory | Why it is important |
|---|---|
| • A business needs raw materials and components to be available to be used in the production process.<br>• A business may benefit from economies of scale if they are buying inventories in large quantities.<br>• Finished goods are required to be able to meet customer orders.<br>• Maintain or increase production. | • If this type of inventory is not available then production will stop and there will be a loss of output and productivity.<br>• Purchasing economies of scale means the cost per unit paid by the business decreases as the size of their order increases. A business may therefore place a larger order to benefit from a discount.<br>• If finished goods are not available the business could lose sales, perhaps to a competitor. It may also affect brand image.<br>• A business needs to hold inventories of work-in-progress so that it can continue with its production to ensure that demand can be met on time. |

There are disadvantages to holding too much inventory including cost of inventory, cost of storage, risk of damage and opportunity cost.

A business will therefore need to decide how much inventory to hold. Factors affecting the level of inventory held by a business include:

- **Warehouse space available** – If a business has little warehouse space then it is unlikely to hold high levels of inventory.
- **Cost of warehouse space** – If the cost of renting warehouse space is too high, a business might choose to hold lower levels of inventory.
- **Type of product being sold** – Some products are perishable and therefore it would be unwise for a business to hold high levels of such inventory due to the risk of waste.
- **Nature of demand for the product** – Some products operate in markets that are very fast-paced, such as technology. There is a risk to a business of holding high levels of inventory of finished goods as new products may enter the market, which could lead to a loss of demand for the product being held.
- **Liquidity of the business** – If a business holds inventory then it will have money tied up in stock. The business will therefore be unable to use this money for other purposes, such as paying its bills. Businesses that need to free up cash to pay bills are likely to hold lower levels of inventory.

### LINKS

More information about economies of scale can be found in Chapter 18.

Liquidity is the ability of a business to pay its day-to-day expenses. More information about liquidity can be found in Chapter 24.

## Lean production

Earlier in this chapter, we discussed how improving productivity can lead to a decrease in average cost, and how this can be passed on to customers in the form of lower prices. Lower prices can help to increase the competitiveness of a business. Another way that a business can improve its competitiveness is by using **lean production**. The main purpose of lean production is to minimise waste. Minimising waste can lead to a decrease in costs. The main sources of waste in business are shown in Figure 17.5.

> **KEY TERM**
>
> **lean production:** the production of goods and services while aiming to minimise the waste of resources.

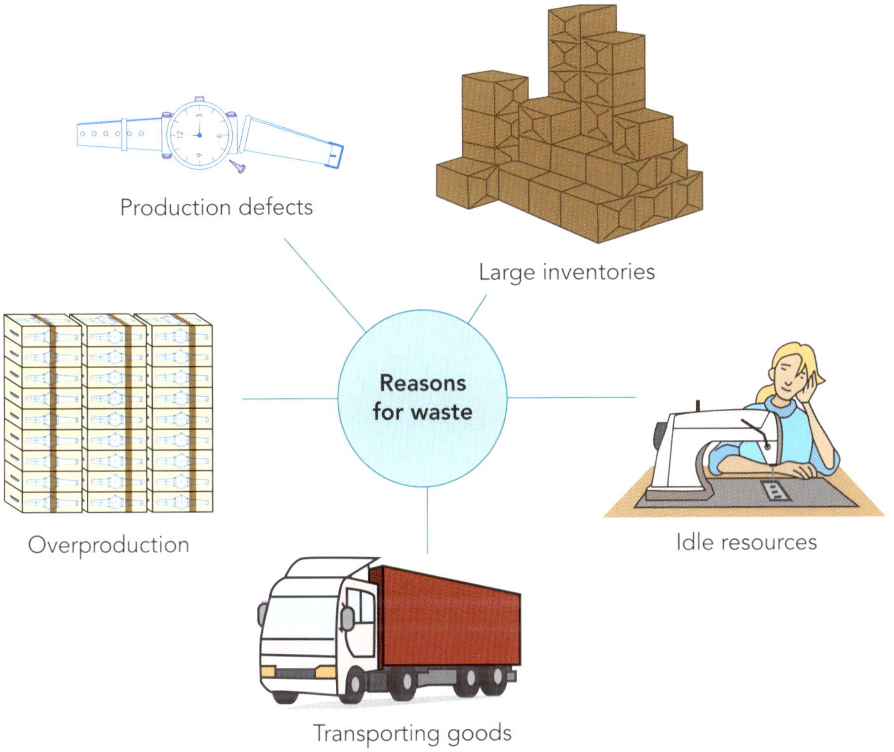

**Figure 17.5:** Sources of business waste

All these sources of waste increase a business's costs which, in turn, will reduce its competitiveness. Just-in-time (JIT) inventory control and Kaizen are two methods of lean production a business can use.

### Just-in-time (JIT) inventory control

Just-in-time (JIT) inventory control means that no inventories are held by the business. This system means that raw materials and components arrive from suppliers just as they are needed by the production process.

As soon as finished goods leave the production process, they are delivered to the customers.

The advantages and disadvantages of JIT inventory control are shown in Table 17.2.

Table 17.2: Advantages and disadvantages of JIT inventory control

| Advantages of JIT | Disadvantages of JIT |
|---|---|
| • Reduces inventory holding costs.<br>• Reduces the amount of cash tied up in inventory, which can improve liquidity.<br>• Prevents overproduction which can decrease storage costs or reduce the chances of products being wasted due to reasons such as obsolescence or no longer being in demand. | • May be difficult to cope with sudden changes in demand (as it may be difficult for suppliers to suddenly provide a certain amount of raw materials).<br>• The level of output may not be enough to meet demand, therefore a business might lose sales to competitors.<br>• Relies on raw materials being delivered on time. Factors outside the control of the business could lead to delays in raw materials being delivered, which will lead to delays in production. |

> **TIP**
>
> Try to learn a range of different advantages and disadvantages. This will help you to be able to use a range of different points, and also be able to select those which are most relevant for a particular question.

### ACTIVITY 17.3

The new Operations Director of Practical Plastic Products (PPP) wants to introduce JIT inventory control. He believes that it will bring important benefits to the company. At a recent board meeting, he said, 'The introduction of JIT inventory control will save $40 000 per year in warehousing costs and there will be other cost savings too.'

PPP's Marketing Director is worried about the risk to the company's reputation if it fails to meet customer deliveries. The Finance Director was concerned about the extra costs of new technologies required to improve communications with suppliers. The Human Resources Director wondered how the introduction of JIT could affect some employees.

1. What other costs savings do you think the introduction of JIT inventory control could bring to PPP?
2. Do you think the Marketing Director is right to be worried about the risk to PPP's reputation if JIT is introduced?
3. What are the 'new technologies' mentioned by the Finance Director and why are they needed to improve communications with suppliers?
4. How do you think the introduction of JIT could affect some of PPP's employees?

## Kaizen

Kaizen is a Japanese term meaning 'continuous improvement'. The Kaizen approach gives all employees the opportunity to make suggestions about how to improve quality or productivity. As employees are doing the tasks every day, they may know better than managers how to change the production process to make it more efficient. The changes suggested by individual employees may be very small, but all of these small improvements can lead to big improvements in efficiency, and hence decrease average costs.

Some of the advantages of using Kaizen are:

- it can improve employee motivation if they see their suggestions being implemented
- improving processes in the business can lead to a decrease in mistakes/increase in quality.

However, some of the disadvantages of using Kaizen are:

- employees may require training which can increase costs
- some employees in the business may be resistant to change, which can reduce the effectiveness of any change implemented.

### CASE STUDY 17.1

**Lockheed Martin holds successful Kaizen events**

**Figure 17.6:** Aircraft manufactured by Lockheed Martin

Lockheed Martin develop a range of products for the aerospace industry. One of the products it manufactures is military aircraft. It uses Kaizen to improve the production of this type of aircraft (see Figure 17.6), having successfully held a multi-day Kaizen event where the total production process was evaluated and areas for improvement identified. Changes made resulted in saving time moving the aircraft between stages of production as well as reducing labour costs. Lockheed Martin are continually looking for ways to improve all aspects of their business.

**Discuss in pairs or groups:**

1. What is Kaizen?
2. Explain how Lockheed Martin have benefited from using Kaizen in their business. What do you think is the biggest benefit they have experienced?
3. Think of a manufacturing company in your country. Can you think of any ways that they could improve their business to improve productivity and quality?

## 17.2 The main methods of production

The following methods of production may be used by businesses to produce goods and services:

- job production
- batch production
- flow production.

## Job production

In **job production**, one item is produced at a time. This method is normally used to produce single or one-off/unique items, such as a sports stadium or a tailored suit (see Figure 17.7).

> **KEY TERM**
>
> **job production:** the production of one-off items specific to customer requirements.

**Figure 17.7:** A tailored suit made using job production

> **DISCUSSION**
>
> In pairs, discuss the following:
>
> - Why might a business choose to use job production?
> - Can you think of any disadvantages to businesses of using job production?

## Batch production

Groups of items complete one stage of the production process at a time in **batch production**. Once one stage of production has been completed, the entire group passes through to the next stage. A good example of batch production is the making of bread in a bakery (see Figure 17.8). Once stage 1 of the process has been completed, the baker can use the mixer to start the production of another batch of products such as a different type of bread or a different product altogether such as doughnuts.

> **KEY TERM**
>
> **batch production:** where groups of identical products are made; each group passes through one stage of production before moving on to the next stage.

# 17 Production of goods and services

Stage 1    Stage 2    Stage 3

Stage 4    Stage 5

**Figure 17.8:** Stages of bread production

## Flow production

**Flow production** involves products moving continuously along a production line. This type of production is used when a large output of identical, standardised products is required, such as chocolate (see Figure 17.9). Flow production is also known as mass production.

> **KEY TERM**
>
> **flow production:** the continuous production of large quantities of identical goods.

**Figure 17.9:** Chocolate being produced using flow production

Each of these methods has advantages and disadvantages, as shown in Table 17.3.

**Table 17.3:** Advantages and disadvantages of job, batch and flow production

| Method of production | Advantages | Disadvantages |
|---|---|---|
| Job | • Unique, high-quality products are made.<br>• Employees are often more motivated.<br>• A higher price can usually be charged. | • Uses skilled labour, which increases costs.<br>• Production can take a long time.<br>• Economies of scale are not possible, increasing average costs. |
| Batch | • High level of output is produced.<br>• Provides flexibility as many different types of products can be made. | • Employees may be less motivated because the work becomes repetitive.<br>• Goods may be stored until they are sold, which can increase the cost of rent.<br>• Machinery may have to be reset between batches which can delay production. |
| Flow | • More capital intensive than job or batch production, which can lower the labour cost.<br>• Can benefit from economies of scale as materials can be bought in bulk.<br>• Machines can produce output 24/7, which means a high level of output can be produced. | • High capital investment.<br>• Employees may be demotivated due to repetitive work.<br>• If one part of the production line breaks down, the whole production process will have to stop until it is repaired.<br>• If a business does not use just-in-time inventory control then high levels of raw materials, work-in-progress and finished goods inventories are held. This increases business costs. |

# Choosing the method of production

A firm will choose their method of production based on a number of factors such as:

- the level of output it would like to produce
- the type of product it is making
- the level of flexibility required by a business; how much variety of products customers expect.

> **ACTIVITY 17.4**
>
> Work in a group with two other people. Research examples of businesses in your country that use flow, batch and job production.
>
> Each person in the group will now create a poster; one for flow production, one for batch production and one for job production.
>
> The poster should include:
>
> - a drawing of the product made using the method of production chosen
> - the advantages of the method of production chosen
> - the disadvantages of the method of production chosen
> - a judgement as to whether you think this method of production is the most suitable for this business to use, and an explanation of why.
>
> Present your poster to the others in your group. Are there any advantages or disadvantages which apply to more than one method of production?

# 17.3 How technology has changed production methods

Production methods have changed over time. A major factor causing this change is development in technology. Technology has changed production methods through automation (where the entire production process uses technology) and mechanisation (where part of the production process uses technology).

Two ways in which technology has changed production methods are computer-aided manufacturing (CAM) and 3D printing.

## Computer-aided manufacturing (CAM)

Technology enables products to be manufactured more quickly than if other methods were used. In CAM, computers control the machinery and equipment used in the production process. Manufacturing is more capital intensive, which reduces the need for labour and, therefore, reduces production costs (through a smaller wage bill).

In some industries, for example, car manufacturing, CAM has completely changed the production process. The use of robots and other technologies has enabled some manufacturers to have production lines or their entire factory controlled by computers. Computer-controlled robots can complete simple or complex task very quickly and more accurately than employees.

## 3D printing

3D printing has been used for some time to produce prototypes of products. Now, they are being used to produce finished products (see Figure 17.10) using materials such as metals, plastic and rubber. 3D printing could quickly customise products (such as prosthetic limbs and bespoke footwear). Production can also be much quicker, which means businesses are able to sell products sooner. 3D printing also enables firms to hold lower levels of inventories of finished products; this is because products can be printed on demand. Business may still need to hold stocks of materials used in printing such as rubber and plastic. 3D printing is used in industries such as healthcare and car manufacturing.

Figure 17.10: 3D printing is being used to produce finished products

## How technology is improving productivity in the service sector

Technology is also helping to improve productivity in the service sector, for example, through consumers being able to pay for products via contactless payments. This can make it much quicker for a business to serve each customer, as they do not need to exchange cash or calculate how much change is required to be given. Other businesses such as accountants and insurance companies can use technology and computer software to produce documents and help reduce the risk of mistakes.

> **TIP**
>
> You could be asked how new technology affects both businesses and employees; the impact on each group will be different. Make sure you know how both businesses and employees could be positively and negatively affected.
>
> Focus on how new technology affects businesses in terms of capital costs and opportunities for cost savings as well as how stakeholders such as employees and customers might be affected.

17 Production of goods and services

> **CASE STUDY 17.2**
>
> **Team UnLimbited design 3D printed arm devices**
>
>
>
> **Figure 17.11:** 3D printing can be used to make 3D printed limbs
>
> Team UnLimbited is a UK-based charity. It designs and produces 3D printed arms for children and adults. Its products are lightweight, customisable and very colourful. As they are 3D printed, they have a much lower production cost than other methods of production (see Figure 17.11). In 2024, the average production cost was £30 per arm. Team UnLimbited's designs are freely available to anyone in the world. Customers can download blueprints for free from the Team UnLimbited website, and use the blueprints to print the arm on their own 3D printer. It takes 24 hours to complete the production of a 3D-printed arm.
>
> **Discuss in pairs or groups:**
>
> 1 What are the benefits to consumers of downloading a blueprint from Team UnLimbited website?
>
> 2 What are the benefits to Team UnLimbited of offering its blueprints free of charge to consumers?

# Advantages and disadvantages of new technology

There are advantages and disadvantages to both businesses and its employees of new technology being introduced. The main ones are shown in Table 17.4.

**Table 17.4:** Advantages and disadvantages of new technology for businesses and employees

|  | Advantages | Disadvantages |
|---|---|---|
| **Businesses** | • Reduces the costs and time taken to design new products.<br>• Increases productivity.<br>• Reduces costs of production.<br>• Improves quality/reduces waste. | • Can be very expensive to buy.<br>• When technology is rapidly changing it may need to be changed often if the business is to remain competitive.<br>• May need to spend money training employees, which increases costs. |
| **Employees** | • Technology completes simple and repetitive tasks that employees find boring, which could increase motivation.<br>• May receive training that can increase skills. | • Technology often reduces the need for employees, resulting in redundancy.<br>• A smaller workforce could reduce the opportunities for promotion. |

A business is only likely to introduce new technology if the advantages of doing so outweigh the disadvantages. However, employees may be affected in different ways. Some employees may benefit through additional training and skills, whereas others may be made redundant.

> **DISCUSSION**
>
> In pairs, discuss the following:
>
> - What impact might creating redundancies have on the remaining employees?
> - What methods of communication would you suggest a business uses to inform its employees about redundancies?

## 17.4 Sustainable production of goods and services

If a business is being sustainable, it is trying to reduce the negative environmental impact of its operations. Many businesses are becoming increasingly focused upon becoming more sustainable when producing goods and services. There are many ways a business can become more sustainable. These are shown in Figure 17.12.

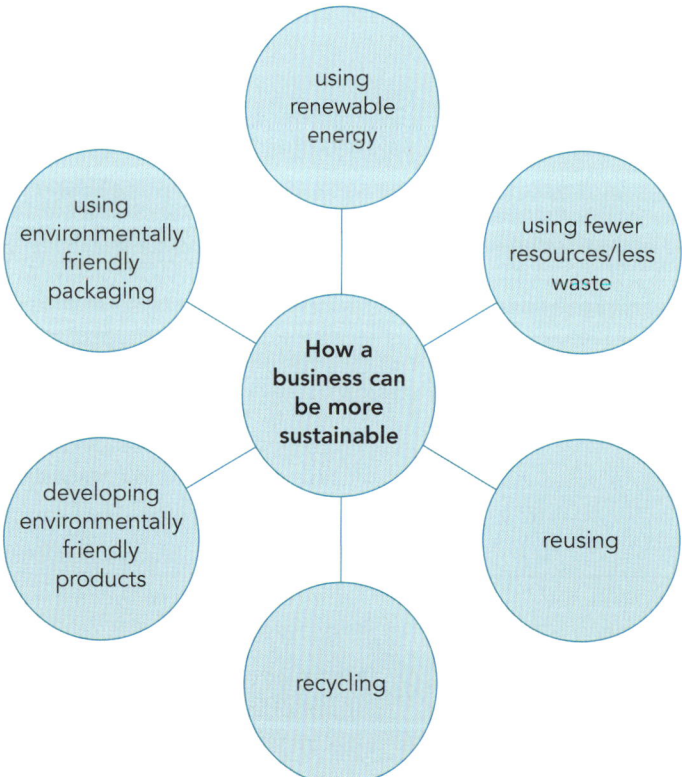

Figure 17.12: Sustainability in business

Table 17.5 shows the advantages and disadvantages to a business of becoming more sustainable.

Table 17.5: Advantages and disadvantages of sustainability to a business

| Advantages | Disadvantages |
|---|---|
| • May improve brand image, which can lead to an increase in sales.<br>• May provide a competitive advantage and therefore be able to charge higher prices.<br>• May help to attract employees who are environmentally conscious, which could increase the pool of applicants. | • May increase costs.<br>• May be difficult to find suppliers who can provide environmentally friendly raw materials.<br>• Competitors may imitate methods used. |

### LINK

More information about brand image can be found in Chapter 12.

### ACTIVITY 17.5

Produce a leaflet to put up in your school that provides details of the ways that students and teachers at your school can be more sustainable. Use pictures/drawings to make your leaflet more attractive.

### BUSINESS IN ACTION

#### Ryobi Limited aims to protect the environment

Figure 17.13: Manufacturers can reduce their environmental impact by recycling waste

Ryobi Limited is a Japanese manufacturer of components. These components are used in products such as cars and electrical goods.

The company aims to provide advanced technology which results in a higher standard of living for its customers. Ryobi Limited is increasingly focused on being a sustainable business and protecting the environment. It aims to reduce the environmental impact of its business activities through methods such as reducing waste, recycling waste and developing environmentally friendly products.

#### Discuss in pairs or groups:

1. Why might a business such as Ryobi Limited have a focus of sustainable development?
2. Are there any disadvantages to Ryobi Limited being sustainable?
3. Are there any other methods you could recommend Ryobi Limited to use to become more sustainable?

> **BUSINESS FOR CAMBRIDGE IGCSE™ AND O LEVEL: COURSEBOOK**

> **SUMMARY**
>
> You should now know:
>
> - The production process involves turning inputs such as land and labour into output, which is a finished product.
>
> - The process of converting inputs into outputs might use job, batch or flow production methods.
>
> - Lean production can help lower business costs through minimising waste, however, there are disadvantages of lean production.
>
> - New technology has advantages and disadvantages to both a business and its employees. Businesses may be able to produce a higher level of output using staff who have been trained, however, redundancies may have to be made and production may need to be stopped for machine maintenance.
>
> - Productivity measures the output per unit of labour. Improvements in productivity will decrease average costs in a given time period.
>
> - Most businesses hold inventories. Factors such as type of product will influence how much inventory is held.

# Chapter 17 practice questions

1   Company A manufactures printers to be used with computers. It uses flow production. The Production Manager is deciding whether or not to introduce new technology into the production process. She is also looking for ways to make the business more sustainable. Table 1 shows production data for Company A.

    **Table 1:** Production data

    | Production data | Company A |
    |---|---|
    | Units produced per week | 8 000 |
    | Number of employees | 25 |
    | Labour productivity | x |
    | Average weekly wage | $160 |
    | Profit per unit | $24 |

    a   Calculate the labour productivity for Company A. [2]

    b   Explain **two** advantages to Company A of becoming more sustainable. [4]

    c   Explain **one** advantage and **one** disadvantage to Company A of using flow production. [6]

    d   Do you think the directors of Company A should introduce new technology into the production process? Justify your answer. [8]

**2** NNS produces ready-made meals using batch production. The company has been asked to supply a large national supermarket chain with one of its most popular dishes. The supermarket would need 5000 units per week for the next 12 months and, if the product proved popular, further orders would be placed. NNS's Operations Director, Nasreen, knows this new order will increase the number of raw materials needs for production. She is thinking about introducing just-in-time inventory management.

   **a** Define 'batch production'. [2]

   **b** Outline **two** advantages to NNS of using batch production. [4]

   **c** Explain **two** factors influencing the level of inventory held by NNS. [6]

   **d** Do you think NNS should introduce just-in-time inventory management? Justify your answer. [8]

   Total available marks: 40

## CHECK YOUR PROGRESS

How well do you think you have achieved the learning intentions for this chapter? Give yourself a score from 1 (still need a lot of practice) to 5 (feeling very confident) for each learning intention. Provide an example to support your score.

| Now I can … | Score | Example |
|---|---|---|
| explain the production process | | |
| explain why businesses need to hold inventories | | |
| understand the concept of productivity, know how to calculate productivity, learn the benefits of increasing efficiency and identify ways to increase efficiency | | |
| identify production methods and explain their advantages and disadvantages | | |
| understand how technology influences production methods | | |
| explain ways businesses can be more sustainable. | | |

# Chapter 18
# Costs, scale of production and break-even analysis

## LEARNING INTENTIONS

By the end of this chapter, you will be able to:

- identify the different classifications of business costs and provide examples for these
- explain the usefulness of cost data in business decision-making
- explain economies and diseconomies of scale
- explain the concept of break-even, and be able to interpret, amend and complete a break-even chart
- explain the margin of safety
- calculate break-even and margin of safety
- explain the limitations of break-even analysis.

# 18 Costs, scale of production and break-even analysis

## Introduction

Businesses must take many decisions such as where to advertise products, which method of training to use and whether to develop a new product. Most business decisions require managers to have accurate data about the costs involved. This helps take more informed decisions.

In this chapter, you will learn about the different ways of classifying costs. You will learn how the classification of costs is important when using break-even analysis. This shows a business the total revenue and total costs that are associated with different levels of output. The margin of safety is an important business concept. You will learn why this is important and how to calculate it. You will also study the effect of the scales of production on average costs and how these might change as a business grows.

> **LINK**
>
> More information about business growth can be found in Chapter 1.

### BUSINESS IN CONTEXT

**Shoprite**

**Figure 18.1:** Shoprite Holdings is the largest supermarket retailer in Africa

Supermarkets are one example of a type of business that is likely to benefit from lower prices from suppliers as they are bulk buying (buying in large quantities). It is likely that a supermarket can negotiate a much lower cost per unit than another business that is buying a smaller quantity.

Shoprite Holdings is the largest supermarket retailer in Africa (see Figure 18.1). Established in 1979 with only eight stores, Shoprite Holdings has grown considerably since it started. In 1986, it had 33 outlets in South Africa; by 2024, it was serving over 27.8 million customers, either online or in-store. Shoprite Holdings works with many suppliers from across Africa.

**Discuss in pairs or groups:**

1. Bulk buying is one way that the average costs of a business might decrease as output increases. Can you think of any other ways in which average costs might decrease as the scale of output increases?
2. What are the disadvantages to a business of growing in size?

## 18.1 How are costs classified?

The main classifications of cost are:

- variable costs
- fixed costs
- total costs
- variable cost per unit
- average total cost.

## Fixed and variable costs

**Fixed costs** are those that do not change with output. Examples of fixed costs include rent on a business's premises or salaries of managers or employees. These are costs that must be paid regardless of the level of output. If a business is producing zero units, it must still pay its rent and workers' salaries. If a business is producing its maximum output, it will still pay the same amount of rent and workers' salaries.

**Variable costs** are those that change with output. Raw materials are an example of variable costs. The amount of raw materials a business buys will depend upon the level of output it is producing. If output increases by 50%, then the variable costs will also increase by 50%. It is calculated by multiplying the variable cost per unit by the number of units:

**Total variable costs** = variable cost per unit × number of units

**Total cost** is calculated by adding **total fixed costs** to total variable costs:

Total cost = fixed costs + total variable costs

It is the sum of all of the costs of making a certain level of output. If the fixed costs of producing 2 000 units of output is $3 000 and the total variable costs of producing 2 000 units is $5 000, then the total cost of producing 2 000 units is $8 000 ($3 000 + $5 000) (see Figure 18.2).

> **KEY TERMS**
>
> **fixed cost:** costs that do not change with output.
>
> **variable cost:** costs that change in direct proportion to output.
>
> **total variable cost:** all of the variable costs of producing the total output.
>
> **total cost:** all the variable and fixed costs of producing the total output.
>
> **total fixed costs:** all of the fixed costs of producing the total output.

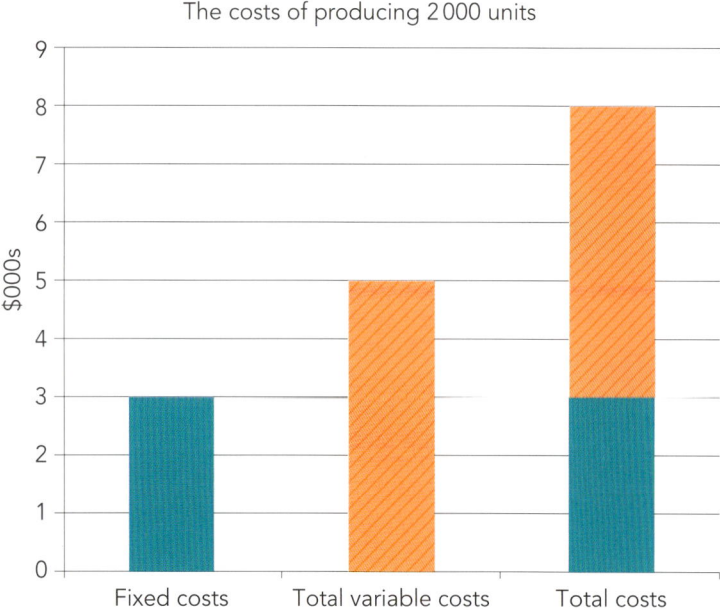

Figure 18.2: Total cost is calculated by adding fixed costs and variable costs

**Variable cost per unit** is calculated by dividing total variable costs by the quantity produced. It is the variable cost of producing one unit of output:

$$\text{Variable cost per unit} = \frac{\text{total variable costs}}{\text{number of units}}$$

**Average total cost** is calculated by dividing total cost by the quantity produced. It is the total cost of producing one unit of output:

$$\text{Average cost} = \frac{\text{total cost}}{\text{number of units}}$$

> **KEY TERMS**
>
> **variable cost per unit:** the variable cost of producing a single unit of output.
>
> **average total cost:** the total cost of producing a single unit of output.

# 18 Costs, scale of production and break-even analysis

> **DISCUSSION**
>
> In pairs, discuss the following:
>
> 1 Do you think it is easy to classify all costs as either fixed or variable?
> 2 Can you think of any costs that might have both a fixed or variable element?

> **ACTIVITY 18.1**
>
> Khaliq, the owner of The Casual Shoe Company (TCSC), knows that it is important to classify costs properly when making business decisions. He has asked you to help him classify the following costs. Copy and complete Table 18.1. The first cost has been completed as an example.
>
> Table 18.1: Classifying the costs
>
> |  | Fixed | Variable |
> | --- | --- | --- |
> | Factory rent | ✓ |  |
> | Leather used in making shoes |  |  |
> | Electricity used to power machinery |  |  |
> | Machinery maintenance |  |  |
> | Advertising |  |  |
> | Production workers' wages |  |  |
> | Operations Manager's salary |  |  |
> | Delivery of finished goods to customers |  |  |
> | Safety equipment for production workers |  |  |

**Example**

Table 18.2 shows cost and output data for TCSC.

Table 18.2: Cost and output data

|  | $ |
| --- | --- |
| Total fixed costs | 2 000 |
| Variable cost per unit | 3 |
| Output | 1 000 |

$$\text{Total variable costs} = \text{variable cost per unit} \times \text{number of units}$$
$$= \$3 \times 1\,000$$
$$= \$3\,000$$

$$\text{Total cost} = \text{fixed costs} + \text{total variable costs}$$
$$= \$2\,000 + \$3\,000$$
$$= \$5\,000$$

$$\text{Average total cost} = \frac{\text{total cost}}{\text{number of units}}$$

$$= \frac{\$5\,000}{1\,000}$$

$$= \$5$$

### ACTIVITY 18.2

Table 18.3 shows the costs of The Casual Shoe Company at different levels of output. It sells each pair of shoes for $43.

**Table 18.3:** The costs of The Casual Shoe Company

| Output (pairs of shoes) | Fixed costs ($) | Total variable costs ($3 per pair of shoes) | Total costs ($) |
|---|---|---|---|
| 0 | 2 000 | | |
| 1 000 | 2 000 | 3 000 | |
| 2 000 | 2 000 | | |
| 3 000 | | | 11 000 |
| 4 000 | | | |

1. Copy and complete the table.

2. Add an extra column to your table. Calculate the average total cost for each level of output.

## Using cost data to make simple cost-based decisions

In Chapter 12, you learnt about how cost data can be used to help make decisions about pricing methods. A business might also use cost data to decide whether to continue manufacturing a product or not. Later in this chapter, you will learn how cost data is used to calculate the break-even level of output.

**Example**

A business manufactures two products. The revenue, cost and profit data for each product are shown in Table 18.4.

> **LINK**
>
> More information about pricing methods can be found in Chapter 12.

## 18 Costs, scale of production and break-even analysis

Table 18.4: Revenue, cost and profit data for the manufacture of products A and B

|  | Product A | Product B | Total |
|---|---|---|---|
|  | $000 | $000 | $000 |
| Revenue | 20 | 50 | 70 |
| Fixed costs | 10 | 15 | 25 |
| Total variable costs | 12 | 18 | 30 |
| Total costs | 22 | 33 | 55 |
| Profit | (2) | 17 | 15 |

> **LINK**
>
> More information about revenue and profits can be found in Chapter 21.

**Note:** Profit is the difference between revenue – the amount a business earns from selling its products – and total costs.

We can see from the data in Table 18.4 that Product A has made a loss of $2000. The Marketing Manager thinks that the company should stop selling Product A, but the Finance Manager disagrees. Who is right?

You have already learnt that fixed costs do not change with output. Even when the output is zero, fixed costs still have to be paid. So, if the company stops producing Product A, it will still have to pay the fixed costs of $10 000. It will not have any variable costs, but it will lose the revenue from the sales of Product A.

The amended data for each product and the company in total is shown in Table 18.5.

Table 18.5: Revenue, cost and profit data for the production of products A and B

|  | Product A | Product B | Total |
|---|---|---|---|
|  | $000 | $000 | $000 |
| Revenue | – | 50 | 50 |
| Fixed costs | 10 | 15 | 25 |
| Total variable costs | – | 18 | 18 |
| Total costs | 10 | 33 | 43 |
| Profit | (10) | 17 | 7 |

We can see that if the company decides to stop producing Product A, total profit will fall from $15 000 to $7 000. Therefore, the accountant is right to suggest continuing the manufacture of Product A.

> **ACTIVITY 18.3**
>
> EasyAir is a budget airline operating internal flights in Tanzania. One of its most popular routes is Dar es Salaam to Kilimanjaro. Each aircraft used on this route has a capacity for carrying 140 passengers. The average price for a one-way ticket is $160. All passengers, adults and children must pay the same ticket price. EasyAir's fixed costs for a single journey are $14 000. The variable cost per passenger is $10.
>
> The number of flights and the passengers carried by EasyAir on this route during the first two quarters of 2025 are shown in Table 18.6.
>
> **Table 18.6:** The number of flights and passengers carried by EasyAir
>
> | Time period | Number of flights | Total passengers carried |
> | --- | --- | --- |
> | January–March | 25 | 1 925 |
> | April–June | 38 | 4 408 |
>
> 1. Define 'fixed costs'.
> 2. Calculate the average number of passengers per flight for the first quarter of 2025.
> 3. The average number of passengers carried on a flight in the second quarter was 116. Calculate:
>    a. the total variable cost per flight
>    b. the total cost per flight
>    c. the average cost per passenger per flight.
> 4. The average cost per passenger per flight in the first quarter was $191.82. Why does EasyAir continue flights when the average cost per passenger is less than the revenue per passenger?

## 18.2 Economies and diseconomies of scale

The term 'scale' simply refers to the level of output a business is making. As the scale of output for a business increases, it will often benefit from a decrease in average cost. This is because it is benefitting from **economies of scale**.

> **KEY TERM**
>
> **economies of scale:** the reduction in average costs as the scale of output increases.

### Economies of scale

Economies of scale occur when the total average cost decreases as the scale of output increases. Businesses may benefit from different types of economies of scale, as shown in Figure 18.3.

# 18 Costs, scale of production and break-even analysis

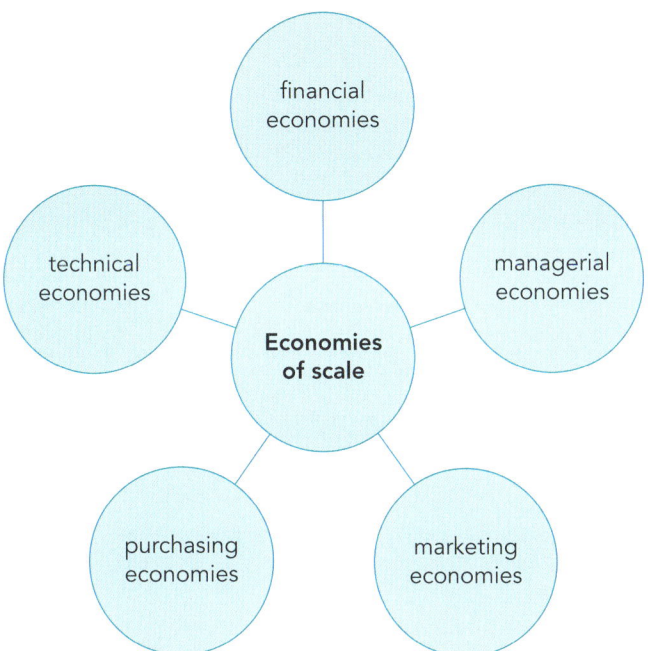

Figure 18.3: Different types of economies of scale

## Financial economies

It is common for banks to see larger businesses as less of a risk than smaller businesses. This could be due to the former making a higher volume of sales, which means they may find it easier to pay back loans. Thus, larger businesses are more likely to be able to borrow money and are also likely to benefit from a lower rate of interest than smaller businesses. A lower rate of interest is likely to result in lower cost than a higher rate of interest.

## Managerial economies

As a business grows, it often employs specialist managers for the different functional areas of the business, such as marketing, finance, operations and human resources (see Figure 18.4). Smaller businesses are more likely to have one person overseeing at least two of these areas. Specialist managers improve the quality of business decisions and make fewer mistakes than non-specialist managers.

## Marketing economies

While total marketing costs rise as a business gets larger, they do not rise at the same rate as sales output. So, if a business doubles its output and sales, it will not need to double its marketing costs. This means that the average cost of marketing falls as output and sales increase.

> **LINK**
>
> More information about interest rates can be found in Chapter 26.

## Purchasing economies

Large businesses usually buy greater quantities of raw materials and goods than smaller businesses. Suppliers often offer discounts on large, or bulk, purchases. Small businesses are less likely to benefit from discounts as they are likely to be making much smaller orders than large businesses.

## Technical economies

Larger businesses are likely to have the finance available to invest into new or better technology. One example of technology used by a business is computer-aided manufacturing (CAM). Technology can increase the productivity and efficiency of a business, which can decrease its average total cost.

> **LINK**
>
> More information about computer-aided manufacturing, productivity and efficiency can be found in Chapter 17.

> **DISCUSSION**
>
> In pairs, discuss the following:
> - Which economy of scale do you think has the potential to reduce average costs the most?
> - Is this true for all businesses?

> **TIP**
>
> You may be asked how a business might benefit from economies of scale as it expands. It is important to explain how each economy of scale will lead to a decrease in average costs.

> **CASE STUDY 18.1**
>
> **The Virgin Group**
>
>
>
> **Figure 18.4:** Virgin Money is one of the brands of the Virgin Group
>
> The Virgin Group has been operating for over 50 years. It has businesses in five sectors including Virgin Atlantic, Virgin Media and Virgin Money. The group operates all around the world with the aim of 'changing business for good'. Many of the Virgin brands have benefited from economies of scale as their scale of output has increased. One of these is marketing economies. As the Virgin Group increases the scale of its operations, its marketing expenditure is now spread over more units. As a result, the group experiences a decrease in average total cost.
>
> **Discuss in pairs or groups:**
>
> 1. How might Virgin Media benefit from the marketing of Virgin Atlantic?
> 2. Are there any other economies of scale the Virgin Group might benefit from as it increases its scale of operations?

## ACTIVITY 18.4

Choose a manufacturing business in your country. Choose three examples of economies of scale it might benefit from as it increases its scale of output.

Discuss your answers with another person in your class. Are some businesses more likely to benefit from some economies of scale than others? Can you think of any disadvantage to a business of increasing its scale of output?

## REFLECTION

When completing Activity 18.4, did you and your partner identify the same economies of scale that businesses might benefit from? What factors did you consider when deciding upon the economies of scale? Would your answers have been different if you had chosen a service business?

# Diseconomies of scale

A business might grow so large and increase its level of output so much that it starts to experience **diseconomies of scale**. Diseconomies of scale occur when the average total cost rises, as output increases. The main causes of diseconomies of scale are shown in Figure 18.5.

> **KEY TERM**
>
> **diseconomies of scale:** an increase in average costs as the scale of output increases.

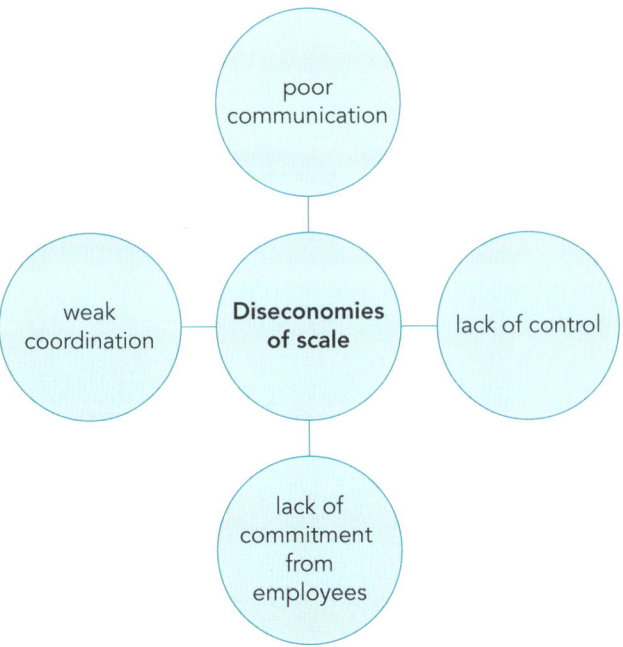

Figure 18.5: Diseconomies of scale

## Poor communication

If a business becomes too large, managers may no longer be able to communicate directly with all employees. Poor communication can lead to a decrease in quality or increase in mistakes, and can also lead to slow decision-making. Each of these impacts can lead to an increase in average total costs.

## Lack of commitment or loyalty from employees

As businesses grow in size, it is common for managers and employees to become more disconnected. For example, managers may no longer have day-to-day contact with employees.

This can lead to lack of commitment from employees who feel that they are no longer a valued part of the business. Employees may become demotivated (see Figure 18.6) and this can lead to high labour turnover, poor quality and a fall in productivity.

> **LINKS**
>
> More information about methods of communication and barrier to communication can be found in Chapter 6, and quality in Chapter 19.

**Figure 18.6:** Employees may become demotivated as a business grows in size

> **DISCUSSION**
>
> In pairs, discuss the following:
> - How would you recommend a business to improve the commitment of its employees?
> - Are there any disadvantages of trying to improve it in this way?

## Weak coordination

As a business grows, so too will the number of departments, products and production units. Coordinating each of these can become more difficult for managers; it may also become harder to ensure all raw materials are in the right place at the right time, which can lead to a delay in production. This represents a waste of time and lower levels of productivity which can increase average total costs.

Also, there is a greater risk that work will be duplicated and this, of course, is a waste of resources and increases costs unnecessarily.

## Lack of control

You have just learnt that as a business grows, so will the number of departments, products and production units. It can become more difficult to manage and control each of these areas. For example, managers in different departments or different production units may be working towards different objectives. In addition, there is a risk of duplication of work which represents a waste of resources and increases costs.

# The importance of economies and diseconomies of scale

Economies of scale reduce average total costs as output increases, and diseconomies of scale increase average total costs as output increases. The relationship between average costs and the scale of operation is shown in Figure 18.7.

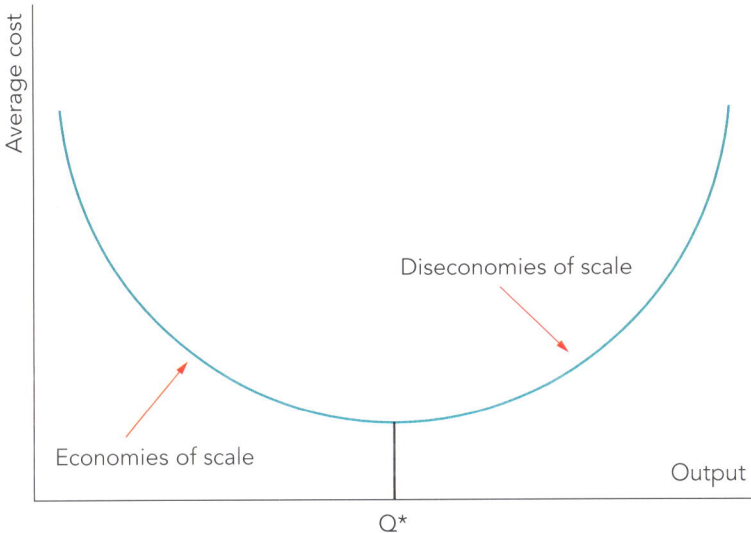

**Figure 18.7:** Average cost curve showing economies and diseconomies of scale

You can see that as output increases, unit costs fall and continue to do so until diseconomies of scale occur, and the unit costs begin to rise. Firms will often aim to produce at the level of output where average total costs are at a minimum; this is at the bottom of the curve at point Q*.

The fact that most businesses will eventually experience diseconomies of scale as the scale of operation grows explains why most industries are not dominated by just one or a few companies.

# 18.3 Break-even analysis

**Break-even** occurs when a business is not making a profit or a loss from the production and sale of its products. The total revenue earned by the business from the sale of its output is exactly equal to the total cost of producing the output. If the revenue a business earns from selling its output is greater than the total costs of producing it

> **KEY TERM**
>
> **break-even:** the level of output where revenue equals total costs; the business is making neither profit nor loss.

then the business earns a profit. However, if the revenue earned is less than the total costs then the business will make a loss. These three situations are shown in Figure 18.8.

**Figure 18.8:** Break-even, profit or loss

# The concept of break-even

Break-even analysis shows the total revenue and total costs associated with different levels of output. Break-even analysis can be used to help make decisions. For example, a business may use break-even analysis to:

- calculate how many units it needs to sell before it starts to make a profit
- calculate the effect on profits of increasing or decreasing the price of a product
- calculate the effect on profits of an increase or decrease in business fixed costs
- calculate the effect on profits of an increase or decrease in variable cost per unit.

## Calculating break-even

The break-even point can be identified by looking at a break-even chart, like in Figure 18.8. It can also be calculated by using the below formula:

$$\text{Break-even output} = \frac{\text{fixed costs}}{\text{contribution per unit}}$$

Contribution per unit is the difference between selling price and variable cost per unit:

$$\text{Contribution per unit} = \text{selling price per unit} - \text{variable cost per unit}$$

> **TIP**
>
> If you are drawing a break-even chart, remember that fixed costs do not start from zero, but variable costs do. This means that total costs will not start from zero either.

**Example**

Raaes is selling cakes to customers in his local area. He is currently producing 700 units of output. A summary of his cost and price data is shown in Table 18.7.

**Table 18.7:** Summary of Raaes' cost and price data

|  | $ |
|---|---|
| Fixed costs | 1 000 |
| Selling price | 5 |
| Variable cost per unit | 3 |

To calculate the break-even level of output, we need to divide fixed costs by contribution per unit.

$$\text{Break-even output} = \frac{\text{fixed costs}}{\text{contribution per unit}}$$
$$= \frac{1000}{(5-3)}$$
$$= \frac{1000}{2}$$
$$= 500 \text{ units}$$

# Simple break-even charts

A break-even chart shows the relationship between a business's revenue and costs at different levels of output. The chart shows the level of output that must be produced and sold where total revenue is equal to total costs. This is the break-even output.

To produce a break-even chart, a business needs to know its:

- revenue at zero output and at its maximum (capacity) output
- total costs at zero output and at capacity output
- fixed costs at zero output and at capacity output.

The revenue and cost information at these two output levels is then used to produce a break-even chart similar to that shown in Figure 18.9.

Once a break-even chart has been produced, it can be used to show the effect of changes in the business's revenue or costs. This could be useful if a business is considering changing its price or if it knows that it is likely to have a change in either its fixed costs or variable costs. For example, a supplier may increase the price of raw materials it supplies to the business, which would increase its variable costs.

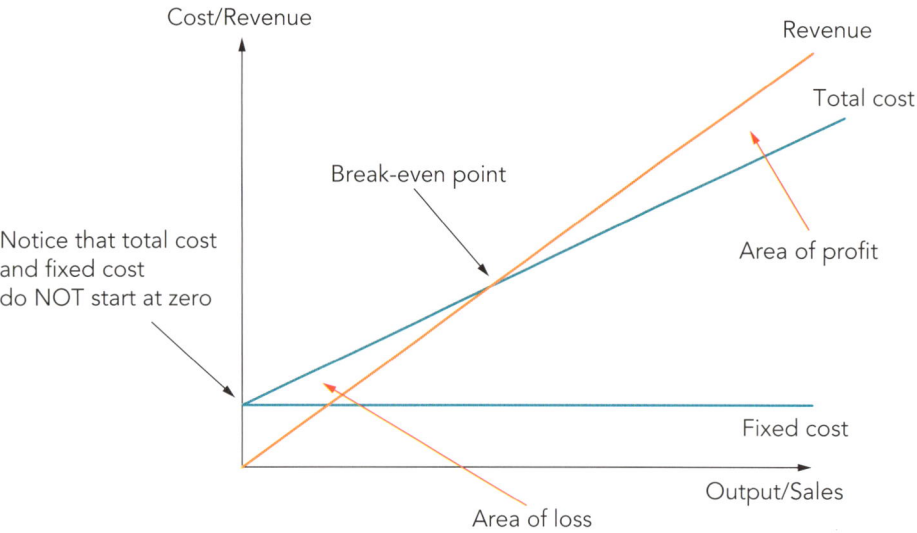

Figure 18.9: A simple break even chart

### CASE STUDY 18.2

**Peloton aims to break even**

Figure 18.10: Peloton uses technology to enable individuals to exercise in their own homes

Established in 2012, Peloton aims to make it easier for individuals to exercise in their own homes. It uses technology to do this (see Figure 18.10). Peloton offers a library of fitness classes that its customers can access at any time. It employs specialist instructors for the classes, and creates competition amongst users through the use of a user leaderboard. Peloton's revenue has declined for six consecutive quarters in the fourth quarter of 2022. Its aim was to break even during the second half of 2023.

**Discuss in pairs or groups:**

1. What is the break-even level of output?
2. If Peloton is operating at a level of output that is below the break-even level of output, they are making a loss. What potential problems might Peloton have if they are making losses?
3. What are the benefits to Peloton of using break-even analysis?

## 18 Costs, scale of production and break-even analysis

## Margin of safety

The **margin of safety** is the difference between the current level of output and the break-even level of output. It is calculated using the below formula:

Margin of safety = actual output – break-even level of output = _____ units

The margin of safety is measured in units. It is helpful for a business as it measures the amount by which output and sales can fall before losses are made. The higher the margin of safety, the lower the risk of a loss being made.

### Example

Look back at the examples of Raaes' cake business on page 305. You were told that Raaes is currently producing 700 units of output. His break-even level of output was calculated as 500 units.

Margin of safety = actual output – break-even level of output
= 700 – 500
= 200 units

### Example

Molly has decided to open a takeaway pizza shop in her local town. She has calculated that the average variable cost of producing each pizza will be $1. Molly estimates her fixed costs per week will be $600. She plans to sell her pizzas for $2.50 each. She has worked out that the maximum number of pizzas she could produce is 800 per week.

Molly carried out market research before setting up her business. She estimates that she will be able to sell 600 pizzas per week.

We are going to use the above information to draw a break-even chart for Molly's business. First, we need to calculate the following figures at zero output and at maximum (capacity) output:

- revenue – the amount earned from selling pizzas (price × output)
- fixed costs – these are $600 per week
- total variable costs – this will be $1 × output
- total costs – fixed costs + total variable costs.

**Note:** Molly's capacity is the maximum number of pizzas she can produce per week. We are told this is 800.

**Table 18.8:** Information for Molly's business

|  | Zero output | Capacity output (800) |
|---|---|---|
| Revenue | $2.50 × 0 = $0 | $2.50 × 800 = $2 000 |
| Fixed costs | $600 | $600 |
| Total variable costs | $0 | $1 × 800 = $800 |
| Total costs | $600 + $0 = $600 | $600 + $800 = $1 400 |

We now have the information needed to construct a break-even chart for Molly's business.

> **KEY TERM**
>
> **margin of safety:** the difference between the current level of output of a business and the break-even level of output.

### ACTIVITY 18.5

1. On a piece of graph paper:

   a. Draw and label:

      i. the x-axis from 0 to 800, labelled 'Output'.

      ii. the y-axis from $0 to $2 000, labelled 'Cost and revenue'. Make sure you use an appropriate scale for both axes.

   b. Plot the revenue at zero output and capacity output. Use a ruler to join these two points together.

   c. Repeat for both the total costs and the fixed costs data.

2. Now that you have a break-even chart for Molly's business, you can use this to work out how many pizzas she needs to sell each week for her business to break even. This will be where the total revenue line crosses the total cost line.

   a. Mark this on your chart as the break-even point.

   b. Using a ruler, draw a line down from the break-even point to the x-axis and read off the value of the break-even output/sales.

If you have drawn your chart correctly you should have a break-even output of 400 pizzas per week.

   c. Now draw a line from the break-even point to the y-axis and read off the value for the revenue and total costs at break-even.

If you have done this correctly you should have an answer of $1 000.

So, we can say that Molly needs to sell 400 pizzas per week to break even. Remember, at this output she will not make a profit, but neither will she be making a loss.

### ACTIVITY 18.6

Molly's first three months of trading have been disappointing. She realises that her price of $2.50 per pizza is more than competitors in the town. She has decided to reduce the price of her pizzas to $2 each.

1. Use this new price to draw a new revenue line on the graph you prepared earlier. (Remember to recalculate the revenue at zero output and the capacity output using the new selling price.)

2. How many pizzas must Molly now sell to break even?

3. What are the uses of break-even analysis to Molly's business?

## Uses and limitations of break-even analysis

Break-even analysis has uses and limitations for businesses. These are summarised in Table 18.9.

**Table 18.9:** Uses and limitations of break-even charts

| Uses | Limitations |
|---|---|
| • Shows the level of output that must be produced and sold where total revenue equals total costs.<br>• Shows the effect on profit of an increase or decrease in price.<br>• Shows the effect on profit of an increase or decrease in fixed costs.<br>• Shows the effect on profit of an increase or decrease in variable cost per unit.<br>• Shows changes in margin of safety as output/sales change. | • Assumes that all costs and revenues can be represented by straight lines.<br>• Some costs may be difficult to classify as either fixed or variable.<br>• Assumes that all output is sold. |

> **TIP**
>
> It can be easy to focus on remembering the formula for topics that include a calculation. However, it is just as important to understand the theory behind it too, for example, uses and limitations of break-even charts. This will mean you are able to answer calculation and extended-response questions.

### BUSINESS IN ACTION

**Air Asia**

**Figure 18.11:** Air Asia now has over 200 aircraft

Air Asia was established in 2001 with only two aircraft and 200 staff. It now has more than 200 aircrafts (see Figure 18.11) and 21 000 staff. It operates in countries such as Indonesia and the Philippines. One of the main aims of Air Asia is to provide affordable travel to its customers.

Like all businesses, airlines have costs to pay. Airlines have particularly high fixed costs (costs that do not change with output). One example of this is the fees that airlines must pay to airports for using runways and gates. Other examples include insurance and fuel. Airlines must pay these costs regardless of whether one person is on the flight or whether the flight is full.

**Discuss in pairs or groups:**

1. How does the number of passengers on a flight affect the average fixed costs of Air Asia?
2. Can you think of any examples of variable costs Air Asia might have?

> **BUSINESS FOR CAMBRIDGE IGCSE™ AND O LEVEL: COURSEBOOK**

> **SUMMARY**
>
> You should now know:
>
> - The costs of business can be classified into total fixed costs, total variable costs, total costs and average total cost and variable cost per unit. Knowledge of these costs is useful when making cost-based decisions.
>
> - A business experiences economies of scale when average total cost falls as output increases. Diseconomies of scale occur when average total costs rise as output rises.
>
> - Businesses can use break-even analysis to identify the level of output to be produced and sold where total revenue is equal to total costs.
>
> - Businesses can use break-even charts to identify the impact on profits of a change in price, change in fixed costs or change in variable cost per unit.
>
> - The margin of safety shows the difference between the current level of output and the break-even level of output.

# Chapter 18 practice questions

1. Company Y manufactures breakfast cereals for the mass market. It uses batch production. The company has 50 employees. An extract of Company Y's cost and revenue data is shown in Table 18.10.

    **Table 18.10:** Extract of Company Y's cost and revenue data

    |  | $ |
    |---|---|
    | Total fixed costs | 80 000 |
    | Variable cost per unit | 3 |
    | Selling price | 5 |

    a  Calculate Company Y's break-even level of output. [2]

    b  Outline how the following would affect the break-even level of output for Company Y:

        i  Increase in the price of Product X.

        ii  Decrease in variable cost per unit. [4]

    c  Explain **two** diseconomies of scale Company Y might experience as it expands. [6]

    d  Do you think the advantages of using batch production to Company Y are greater than the disadvantages? Justify your answer. [8]

## 18 Costs, scale of production and break-even analysis

2   Solar Enterprises (SE) is a manufacturer of solar panels. Its sales have increased for the last 5 years. In 2025 sales were 18 000 units and it expects a 15% increase in sales for 2026. This growth has enabled SE to benefit from economies of scale. SE's accountant is calculating total fixed costs and total variable costs. She uses cost information to produce break-even charts for its most popular products. The Managing Director thinks that the limitations of producing break-even charts are greater than the uses.

   a   Define 'break-even' point. [2]

   b   Outline **one** example of a fixed cost and **one** example of a variable cost that SE might have.

   Fixed cost:

   Variable cost: [4]

   c   Explain **two** economies of scale that SE might benefit from. [6]

   d   Do you think that benefits of using break-even charts are greater than the limitations? Justify your answer. [8]

   Total available marks: 40

### CHECK YOUR PROGRESS

How well do you think you have achieved the learning intentions for this chapter? Give yourself a score from 1 (still need a lot of practice) to 5 (feeling very confident) for each learning intention. Provide an example to support your score.

| Now I can … | Score | Example |
| --- | --- | --- |
| identify the different classifications of business costs and provide examples of these | | |
| explain the usefulness of cost data in business decision-making | | |
| explain economies and diseconomies of scale | | |
| explain the concept of break-even and be able to interpret, amend and complete a break-even chart | | |
| explain the margin of safety | | |
| calculate break-even and margin of safety | | |
| explain the limitations of break-even analysis. | | |

# Chapter 19
# Quality of goods and services

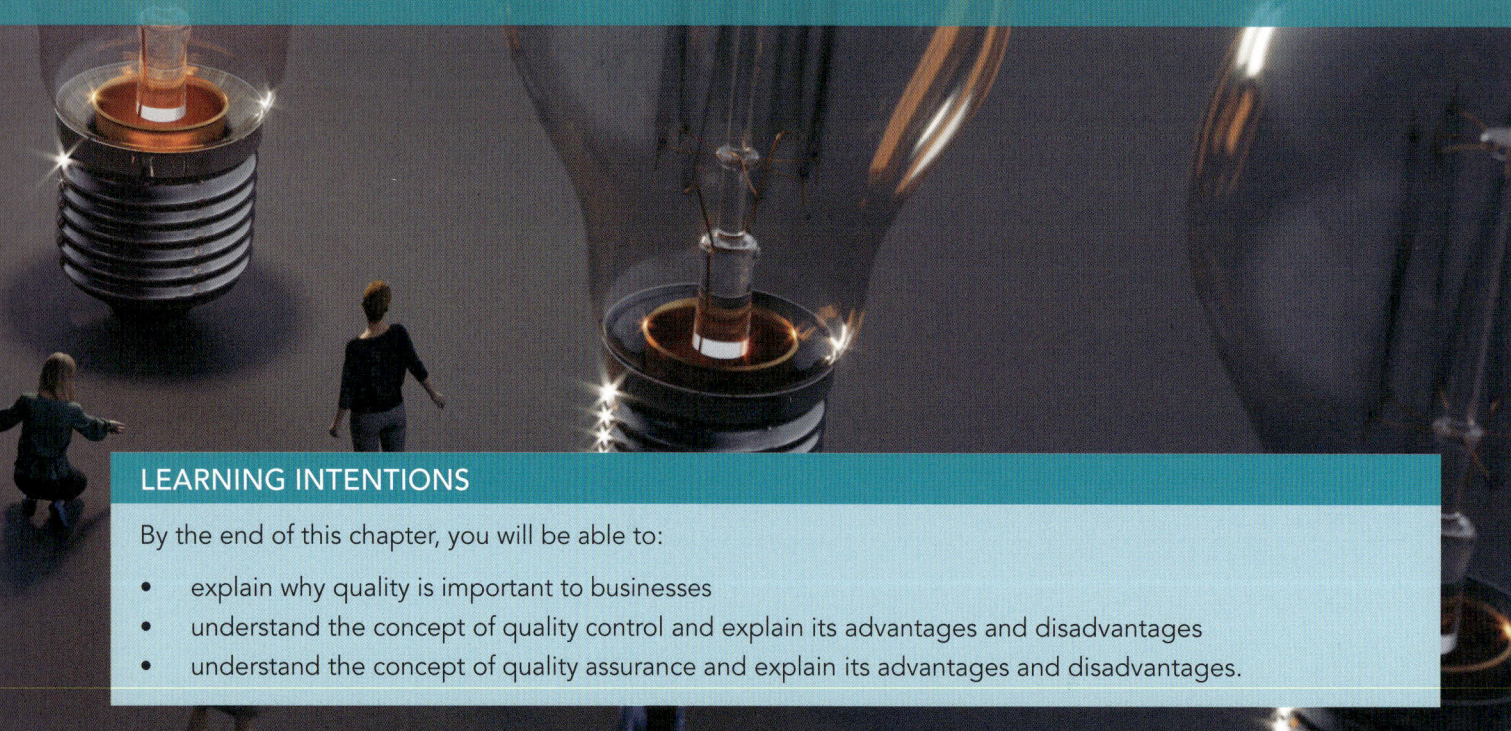

**LEARNING INTENTIONS**

By the end of this chapter, you will be able to:

- explain why quality is important to businesses
- understand the concept of quality control and explain its advantages and disadvantages
- understand the concept of quality assurance and explain its advantages and disadvantages.

# 19 Quality of goods and services

# Introduction

There are many factors that contribute to the reasons why customers develop loyalty or are attracted to a business. One of the most important factors is quality. If a business sells products of poor quality or provides poor customer service then it might experience a decrease in demand. High-quality products and good customer service can attract new customers to a business and help retain existing customers. In this chapter, you will learn the meaning and importance of quality and understand how businesses can achieve quality production. You will look at quality control and quality assurance.

## BUSINESS IN CONTEXT

### Fairsew Ethical Clothing

Fairsew is an ethical clothing manufacturer based in Phnom Penh, Cambodia. It provides a safe working environment for its employees while providing high-quality clothing to its customers. It is a very environmentally conscious business and engages in sustainable business activities such as reducing waste and recycling. Many of the materials used by Fairsew are local and recycled. It buys materials that would otherwise end up as waste in landfills. Fairsew is committed to providing high-quality products to its consumers, whether this be a newly designed T-shirt or a pattern to be used on the clothing.

Discuss in pairs or small groups:

1 Why is quality important to businesses such as Fairsew?

2 What are the benefits to Fairsew of being environmentally friendly?

**Figure 19.1:** Ethical clothing manufacturers can use materials that might otherwise end up in landfills

# 19.1 Why quality is important

## What quality means

Quality is a concept that means different things to different people. Individual customers have their own perceptions about quality. A high-quality product is not necessarily the most expensive nor the one manufactured using the most expensive raw materials. A good quality product is one that meets the expectations of customers, for example, it works in the way customers expect. It is also a product that is free from defects. For example, if you buy a calculator, you expect it to work out calculations correctly. In other words, a quality product is one that meets the needs and requirements of the customer.

### LINK

More information about methods of sustainable production can be found in Chapter 17.

Providing products of a high quality is an important part of running a successful business. Providing high-quality products can lead to benefits such as developing a good brand image. It can also mean that businesses may be able to charge higher prices. Quality is a concept based on the perceptions of individual customers. Market research can be used to determine what is important to customers in terms of the quality of a product. Businesses can use quality control (checking the product at the end of the production process through inspection) or quality assurance (employees checking the product at each stage of production) to check that products meet the quality desired by customers. There are advantages and disadvantages of both methods.

### DISCUSSION

In pairs, discuss the following:

1 Why might quality be important to a business?

2 Can you think of any ways that a business could ensure the quality of its products?

### ACTIVITY 19.1

Draw a table with two columns and six rows. In the first row of the first column, write the title 'Product', and in the first row of the second column, write the title 'Quality expectation'.

Complete the first column by writing each of the below products:

- Haircut
- Swimming lessons at a leisure centre
- Bentley car
- Children's swing
- Garden bench.

Complete the second column by writing down what quality expectations you would have for each of the products.

### REFLECTION

When completing Activity 19.1, were there any differences in your quality expectations across the different products? Did you have higher expectations for some products than others? What are the reasons for this?

The needs and requirements of customers can be found by a business conducting market research. Once customer needs have been identified, a business will be aware of the expectations that customers have regarding quality. The reasons why quality is important to businesses are shown in Figure 19.2.

### LINK

More information about market research can be found in Chapter 11.

19 Quality of goods and services

Figure 19.2: Why quality is important to businesses

## 19.2 The importance of quality to businesses

Quality is important to businesses for many reasons. These reasons are summarised in Table 19.1.

Figure 19.3: Retailers and wholesalers may stock items that are of high quality

Table 19.1: Reasons why quality is important to businesses

| Reason | Explanation |
|---|---|
| Helps to attract new customers/ develop customer loyalty | • New customers are likely to be attracted to buy products that have a reputation for being good quality.<br>• Existing customers are likely to return if they have bought a high-quality product or received high-quality customer service. |
| Reduces the number of customer complaints and the number of returns | • If a product does not meet the expectations of customers then they might return it. The product might have to be replaced or the customer might want a refund. Returns from customers increase costs.<br>• Customer complaints can damage the reputation of a business. This could lead to the loss of existing customers and make it more difficult to attract new customers. |
| Business may be able to charge a higher price | • Customers may be more likely to pay a higher price for a product deemed to be of high quality. Charging a higher price may lead to a higher profit margin. |
| Develop a strong brand image | • Products of high quality may improve the brand image of a business. This can help to attract new customers. In addition, it may make it easier for the business to introduce new products into the market. This is because customers may assume that a new product from the business will be of similar quality to those already available. |
| Encourage wholesalers and retailers to stock the product | • If a product is of high quality then it may be demanded by wholesalers and retailers as they know that customers will want to buy it (see Figure 19.3). This can increase revenue for the business. |

### ACTIVITY 19.2

Rank the reasons why quality is important in Table 19.1 from 1 (most important) down to 5 (least important) for a manufacturing business.

Do this activity again for a service sector business. Were there any differences in your rankings between manufacturing and service sector businesses? If so, what are your reasons for this?

### LINKS

More information about customer loyalty and brand image can be found in Chapter 10, profit in Chapter 23 and wholesalers and retailers in Chapter 14.

> **TIP**
>
> If you are asked why quality is important to a business, remember to provide different points rather than those which are repeating each other. For example, attracting new customers is the same as increasing sales, so only one of these points would be awarded.

## 19.3 How businesses achieve quality production

The purpose of any method of checking quality is to reduce the chances of faulty products reaching customers. Two methods that a business might use to achieve quality production are **quality control** and quality assurance.

### Quality control

Quality control involves inspecting products at the end of production process. Checking is completed by a trained quality inspector (see Figure 19.4). In quality control it is common for a sample of products to be checked. This is because it is often too expensive to check every single product.

> **KEY TERM**
>
> **quality control:** checking the quality of goods through inspection at the end of the production process.

Figure 19.4: A quality inspector at work

## Advantages and disadvantages of quality control

The advantages and disadvantages of quality control are summarised in Table 19.2.

**Table 19.2:** Advantages and disadvantages of quality control

| Advantages | Disadvantages |
|---|---|
| • Production does not stop while quality is being checked. This could make it more likely for a business to be able to meet customer demands.<br>• Production workers do not need to be trained to check quality. This can free up funds to be spent elsewhere in the business. | • It does not show where the problem occurred as problems are only spotted at the end. This means that it may take time to go back through the production process to identify where the error occurred.<br>• High level of waste or high cost of rework. Resources are wasted on completing a product that should have been rejected much earlier in the production process.<br>• Inspectors need to be recruited, which can increase costs. |

> **DISCUSSION**
>
> In pairs, discuss the following:
>
> 1 Are there any disadvantages to a business of using quality inspectors?
>
> 2 What type of products do you think would benefit from using quality control?

> **CASE STUDY 19.1**
>
> **R4R offers quality control services**
>
>
>
> **Figure 19.5:** R4R provides quality control for items such as clothing
>
> A business using quality control will hire quality control inspectors to check its products at the end of the production process. R4R is an example of a business that offers quality control services. Based in the UK, its experienced staff conduct quality control services for a range of clothing garments and other items, such as luggage and footwear. It provides businesses with a full report of the inspection once it has been completed.
>
> **Discuss in pairs or groups:**
>
> 1 Why might a business use R4R to carry out quality control on its products?
>
> 2 Are there any disadvantages to businesses using quality control?

## 19  Quality of goods and services

## Quality assurance

**Quality assurance** involves checking products at every stage of production. This means ensuring that raw materials and components are of the required standard before they enter the production process, and that quality standards are agreed for every stage of the production process. Employees are responsible for checking quality at every stage of production.

> **KEY TERM**
>
> **quality assurance:** where employees check the quality of products at each stage of the production process.

### ACTIVITY 19.3

Quality assurance is often used by shoe manufacturers.

Draw a flow diagram to show stages in the production process of a shoe manufacturer. Try to include at least four stages in the flow diagram. The first stage might be sourcing good quality leather to use for the shoes.

For each stage, identify what good quality would look like. It is only if the product meets this quality requirement that it will pass through to the next stage of the production process.

### Advantages and disadvantages of quality assurance

The advantages and disadvantages of quality assurance are summarised in Table 19.3.

Table 19.3: Advantages and disadvantages of quality assurance

| Advantages | Disadvantages |
|---|---|
| • Can increase motivation of employees as they have an important role in the production process. This can lead to higher levels of output for the business.<br>• Errors are spotted earlier in the process. This can reduce the cost of rework as resources are not wasted completing a product that will be rejected. | • Expensive to train all employees to check for errors. This means there may be less funds to invest elsewhere in the business.<br>• Not all workers may be able to spot problems in the production process. Therefore, some faulty products may go further through the production process than they should have done, increasing waste.<br>• Takes time to train all workers. This can lead to lower levels of output while workers are being trained. |

> **LINKS**
>
> More information about the benefits of a motivated workforce can be found in Chapter 9, and training in Chapter 6.

> **TIP**
>
> Think about a range of ways that you can develop your knowledge points. Knowing a range of points will help you to use those that are most relevant for a particular question and point.

## CASE STUDY 19.2

### Quality assurance at Hasbro

Figure 19.6: Hasbro manufactures toys and games

Hasbro manufactures toys and games (see Figure 19.6) for both children and adults. Hasbro Gaming, Nerf, Peppa Pig and Play-Doh are some of the branded products that Hasbro produce. Quality and safety are embedded into every product made by Hasbro. It meets all regulatory requirements and also sets itself its own quality standards. In 2021, Hasbro did not have to recall any of its products. The company uses quality assurance; products are checked at every stage of production from the design process right through to packaging.

**Discuss in pairs or groups:**

1. What is quality assurance?
2. What are the benefits to Hasbro of not having to recall any of its products?

## ACTIVITY 19.4

A biscuit manufacturer has just moved into your area. It manufactures different types of biscuits using batch production. Products are sold in supermarkets to the mass market.

1. What method of checking quality would you recommend the biscuit manufacturer to use? What are your reasons for this?
2. Are there any disadvantages to the biscuit manufacturer of using the method you have recommended? How could the business overcome these disadvantages?

## BUSINESS IN ACTION

### Hypnos

Figure 19.7: Beds undergo quality assurance before being sold to hospitality businesses

It is clear that quality is important to businesses for many different reasons. Hypnos is a UK-based manufacturer that sells beds to hospitality businesses. Its beds are 100% sustainable, foam-free and recyclable. Hypnos has won the Queen's Award for Enterprise for Sustainable Development; sustainable business is at the heart of its operations. Selling high-quality beds is a priority for Hypnos. It ensures that its products meet safety requirements using quality assurance. Every product is tested and checked throughout production, and is then checked again before it is sent to its customers.

**Discuss in pairs or groups:**

1. Why is quality important to Hypnos?
2. What are the advantages to Hypnos of using quality assurance?

> **SUMMARY**
>
> You should now know:
>
> - Quality is concerned with producing goods and services that meet consumer expectations. This helps a business to develop a strong brand image and can make it possible to charge higher prices.
>
> - Quality control involves checking the product at the end of the production process through inspection. This is beneficial as production does not stop for quality to be checked, however, there is a high cost of waste as some products are produced that should have been rejected earlier.
>
> - Quality assurance involves checking production at each stage of the production process. Employees must be trained to check quality, which can increase costs, however, not all employees will be able to spot errors.

## Chapter 19 practice questions

1. Zebtech produces components used in the manufacture of medical equipment. It uses flow production. Component Y is used in heart surgery. Zebtech uses quality control to check the quality of its products such as Component Y. It uses primary market research to identify its customer needs.

   a. Define 'quality control'. [2]

   b. Outline **two** disadvantages to Zebtech of using flow production. [4]

   c. Explain **two** advantages to Zebtech of using quality control. [6]

   d. Explain **two** methods of primary market research Zebtech could use. Which one should Zebtech use? Justify your answer. [8]

2. PP manufactures digital cameras for customers in a niche market. PP employs inspectors to check the quality of finished products. The quality control inspectors check a sample of all output. The senior managers of PP are concerned about the level of customer complaints. It has received complaints from 1.5% of its 10 000 customers over the last 6 months about the poor quality of its products. The Production Manager is considering introducing quality assurance.

   a. Define 'quality assurance'. [2]

   b. Identify **four** reasons why quality is important to a business. [4]

   c. Explain **two** benefits to PP of selling to a niche market. [6]

   d. Do you think PP should introduce quality assurance? Justify your answer. [8]

   Total available marks: 40

## CHECK YOUR PROGRESS

How well do you think you have achieved the learning intentions for this chapter? Give yourself a score from 1 (still need a lot of practice) to 5 (feeling very confident) for each learning intention. Provide an example to support your score.

| Now I can ... | Score | Example |
| --- | --- | --- |
| explain why quality is important to a business | | |
| understand the concept of quality control and explain its advantages and disadvantages | | |
| understand the concept of quality assurance and explain its advantages and disadvantages. | | |

> Chapter 20

# Location decisions

## LEARNING INTENTIONS

By the end of this chapter, you will be able to:

- explain the factors influencing the location decision of manufacturing and service businesses
- explain why businesses may decide to locate their operations in another country and identify the factors that would influence the choice of country to locate in.

# Introduction

Location decisions could be made when a new business is starting up or when an existing business is considering moving to a different place. The location of a business can affect costs and distribution. It is often difficult and expensive for a business to change its location.

There are a range of factors that will affect the location decision of a business. In this chapter, you will learn about these factors to better understand how businesses make decisions about location.

> ## BUSINESS IN CONTEXT
>
> ### Dyson in Singapore
>
> Dyson was established in the UK in 1991. It designs vacuum cleaners, electric cars and other items for households and businesses. It now sells to consumers in more than 100 countries worldwide. In 2019, Dyson announced that it would be moving its headquarters to Singapore (see Figure 20.1). One of the reasons for this was growth in the number of customers in Asian markets. The government in Singapore also offers tax incentives and benefits to businesses that locate there. There are also many skilled engineers in Singapore whom Dyson can employ, whereas there is a shortage of skilled engineers in the UK.
>
> ### Discuss in pairs or groups:
>
> 1 What are the potential disadvantages to Dyson of locating its headquarters to Singapore?
>
> 2 How would you recommend that Dyson manages the location to reduce the impact of the disadvantages you have identified?

**Figure 20.1:** Dyson located its headquarters in Singapore

## 20.1 Factors influencing location decisions for a business

A car manufacturer is planning to open a production plant in your area. Is there land available that the plant can be built upon? Is there infrastructure, for example, facilities such as transport services and power available to transport raw materials to the factory and finished goods from the factory? Are there skilled workers available in the areas? Likewise, a retailer may be planning to open a shop. Is there sufficient space for the shop as well as access to parking? How many potential customers are there in the area? These are just some of the questions that will be considered before a location decision is made.

The location decision is very important for a business. Location will affect a business in many ways: transportation costs, availability of labour and ease of access for consumers are just some of these ways. It is likely that a location has advantages and disadvantages. Those involved in decisions on the location of a business will have to consider all of these when making a final choice. It is also possible that a business might choose to move its business. The business might choose to move location to another part of the country in which it is currently operating or to another country entirely. Governments sometimes offer incentives for businesses to locate in a particular area or country.

> **DISCUSSION**
>
> In pairs, discuss the following:
>
> - What makes a 'good' location for a manufacturing business?
> - What makes a 'good' location for a service business?
> - What do you think is the most important factor contributing to a 'good' location?

## Factors influencing location decisions for manufacturing and service businesses

Businesses need to consider a variety of factors when choosing a location for a new business or an existing business.

It is likely that both manufacturing and service businesses will consider many of the same factors. However, there are some factors that may be more important for manufacturing businesses and others that are more important for service businesses. For example, a manufacturing business is likely to be interested in the ease of access to raw materials, whereas a service business will be concerned about whether there is parking available for its customers. Table 20.1 outlines factors that businesses are likely to consider.

> **ACTIVITY 20.1**
>
> Use the internet to research how the government in your country incentivises businesses to locate in particular areas.
>
> 1. What types of help does the government provide?
> 2. How effective do you think this help is in encouraging businesses to locate in these areas?
> 3. Are there any real-life examples of businesses that have located in these areas due to the support offered?

> **TIP**
>
> If you are asked to write about factors that affect the location decision, do not give two examples of the same type of factor. For example, water and power are both examples of infrastructure, so mentioning two of these will only be credited once.

> **LINK**
>
> More information about the ways governments can support business start-ups can be found in Chapter 3.

Table 20.1: Location factors that manufacturing and service businesses might consider

| Location factor | Explanation |
|---|---|
| Cost of site | How expensive the land and buildings are to rent or buy – this will increase costs. |
| Labour costs | What is the average wage paid to employees in the area? If there are low numbers of supply of labour then higher wages are likely to be paid. If workers are highly skilled, higher wages are likely to be paid. Likewise, if there are many businesses competing to employ labour, higher wages are likely to be paid. |
| Transport costs | How close to suppliers is the proposed site? What will be the cost of transporting goods to and from the site? How accessible is the location for customers? This last question is particularly important for service industries such as retail outlets, hotels, and cinemas. |
| Market (sales) potential | The market potential of a location will also be considered.<br>Service businesses such as restaurants and supermarkets will often need to be located close to customers to increase revenue. This is less likely to be a concern for manufacturing businesses. |
| Government incentives | Both local and national governments will often provide financial and other incentives to encourage businesses to locate in a particular area. These incentives can significantly reduce set-up costs. |
| The size of the available site | The site needs to be large enough to meet the current needs of the business. A business might also consider whether there is space to expand in the future. The availability of parking will also be a factor considered by service sector businesses. |
| Legal restrictions | There may be planning restrictions or other legal restrictions that prevent location in certain areas. For example, it would be unlikely that a manufacturing business would be allowed to locate very close to a residential sector because of noise and air pollution. |
| Quality of local infrastructure | How good are transport links such as road, rail, air and sea?<br>Does the location have good support services such as water, power and telecommunications? |
| Ethical issues and concerns | A business will need to consider the impact on its employees of moving from one part of the country to another or to another country entirely. The new location could lead to the redundancy. It could damage business reputation and decrease sales. |

> **DISCUSSION**
>
> In pairs, discuss the following:
>
> - Why might high labour costs represent a benefit to a business?
> - What factors could cause wages to be higher in one location than in another?

## 20 Location decisions

### CASE STUDY 20.1

**N.Bar expands into busy shopping malls**

**Figure 20.2:** Nail bars are very popular in the Middle East

N.Bar is one of the biggest nail bars in the UAE. It provides nail care and beauty services for women; it has developed a loyal customer base. In 2024, it had 27 nail bars. N.Bar has expanded by selling franchises across the UAE and in other countries such as the UK. Every time N.Bar opens another nail salon, it must choose a location for it. Many of the salons N.Bar have opened have been inside busy shopping malls (see Figure 20.2) and shopping districts, such as Rabwa Square, Riyadh, and West Walk, Doha.

**Discuss in pairs or groups:**

1. What is a franchise?
2. What are the benefits to N.Bar of growing its business by selling franchises?
3. Are there any disadvantages of selling franchises?
4. What factors do you think have led N.Bar to locate its nail salons in shopping malls and shopping districts?
5. Are there any disadvantages of choosing this type of location?

### ACTIVITY 20.2

Work in pairs. One person should choose a service business located in your country and the other person should choose a manufacturing business located in your country.

Create a mind map of all of the reasons why the business you have chosen may have located where it has. Use Table 20.1 to help you think about some of the factors that may have influenced the location decision.

Discuss your reasons with your partner. Are the reasons for the choice of location the same for both businesses? What are the differences?

Now swap your mind map with your partner. Can you think of any negatives of the location chosen by each of these businesses? Share your ideas with your class.

## 20.2 Why businesses locate their operations in another country

Sometimes, business may decide to locate their operations in another country (Figure 20.3). This could be for reasons such as:

- **To achieve growth** – if sales has reached its maximum level in the home market (the product is in the maturity stage of the product life cycle) then a business might choose to locate overseas to increase total sales.

> **LINK**
>
> More information about external costs can be found in Chapter 28.

- **To reduce production costs** – costs such as labour and rent are much lower in some countries than in others. A business can therefore reduce its total costs by locating in another country. This could increase profit margins or allow them to pass on the lower costs to customers in the form of lower prices. For example, Dyson, a UK manufacturer of vacuum cleaners, moved its production from the UK to Malaysia.

- **To locate production closer to the market** – this reduces delivery time to customers and reduces transport costs. Several multinational companies have located factories close to their international markets; for example, Coca-Cola has manufacturing operations in many countries throughout the world including Pakistan, Argentina, Costa Rica, Nigeria and Jordan.

- **To avoid legal barriers and import tariffs** – although many countries have removed or reduced their barriers to free trade, they still exist. One way around this is to locate in the country. The business then does not then have to pay import tariffs and will not be affected by legal restrictions on companies from other countries.

- **To benefit from government incentives** – governments around the world can see the benefits of attracting overseas businesses to locate in their country. In order to encourage businesses to locate in their country, governments may provide them incentives to do so.

> **LINKS**
>
> More information about the product life cycle can be found in Chapter 12, and import tariffs in Chapter 27.

> **TIP**
>
> When explaining why a factor is important, it is helpful if you can give reasons **why** you feel the factor is important. For example, do not just say that the location is cheaper; explain **how** it will save the business money. Identifying the specific type of cost that will be affected is also beneficial, for example, higher wages can increase variable costs.

Figure 20.3: There are several reasons for relocating a business overseas

There are some disadvantages to a business of locating their operations in another country:

- **Cultural differences** – products that are popular in one country may be less popular in some international markets due to different customer tastes or religious beliefs. There may also be differences in workplace culture.

- **Communication problems** – language differences may be a barrier to communication between employees, managers and suppliers. Communication problems may also arise if the head office of a business is located in a different country to its operations. For example, time differences may make it difficult to communicate.

- **Ethical concerns** – you have already learnt how a business will have to consider whether changing location could lead to redundancies of its existing employees. Another ethical concern could be related to working conditions and wages paid to employees. There have been several reported concerns about the exploitation of employees in low-cost economies, including issues of child labour. These issues could damage the reputation of a business.

- **Quality issues** – it might not be possible for the current suppliers of a business to continue to supply if the business is located overseas. A business may therefore need to find another supplier that may not have the same quality raw materials.

> **LINKS**
>
> More information about ethics can be found in Chapter 28, barriers to communication in Chapter 8 and quality in Chapter 19.

### ACTIVITY 20.3

Imagine that you have been employed as a consultant for a large international mobile phone manufacturer that is considering your country for the location of a new factory.

Write a report to the CEO of the company highlighting the advantages and disadvantages to the company of locating its new factory in your country.

## Choosing a location

The location decision is never easy. It is very likely that a location will have advantages and disadvantages. For example, the land on which to build a factory might be very cheap because it is located some distance from the nearest town. However, the business might find it difficult to recruit employees because of the distance employees would have to travel to get to work. Similarly, a business looking to locate in a low labour–cost country might need to balance the benefit of lower production costs with increased transportation costs for raw materials and finished goods.

Those faced with making the decision must balance location factors and choose the location where the advantages outweigh the disadvantages.

### ACTIVITY 20.4

Working in small groups, consider the following:

A fast food takeaway business is considering locating near your school. The owners of the business have asked your group to identify the advantages and disadvantages of this location for their business.

Each person has a piece of paper. Split your group in half – one half will think about the advantages of this location and the other half will think about the disadvantages.

1. Each person should write either an advantage or a disadvantage on their piece of paper (whichever they have been allocated).
2. Each person should pass their paper to the person on their right. The next person should explain the impact of this advantage or disadvantage, for example, state why this is good or bad for the business.
3. Again, each person should pass their paper to the person on their right. The next person should develop the point further to explain a further impact to the business.
4. You have worked together to develop chains of analysis. In your group, decide which advantages and which disadvantages you would like to share with your class.
5. Your teacher will write the chosen chains of analysis on the board that all of the groups have produced.

An example chain of analysis is below:

Person 1: The location has high labour costs.

Person 2: This can increase variable costs.

Person 3: This can decrease profit margin.

### REFLECTION

When completing Activity 20.4, how easy was it to develop the first point into analysis? Was it more challenging to develop the point a second time? Did your group come up with a range of advantages and disadvantages and a range of points of development? Would you be able to make a justified decision as to whether the location was a good choice for the business?

### CASE STUDY 20.2

**Agrid chooses base in South Africa**

Agrid South Africa, an offspring of Agrid International, was formed in July 1999. It manufactures diesel/petrol engines and agricultural implements for small-scale farmers.

Agrid has focused on exporting its products to Europe and other African countries such as Kenya, Nigeria, Angola and Uganda. However, it recently found a gap in the local market for its products. Agrid chose to locate in South Africa because of its established and proven manufacturing base, access to skilled labour (see Figure 20.4) and readily available management. Other attractions were the expansion of the local motor industry, excellent telecommunications and the accessibility of Sub-Saharan Africa, South America and Australia.

A spokesperson for the company said: 'I see South Africa as a low-cost manufacturing base for exporting products to the world.'

*Source:* Adapted from southafrica.info

## CONTINUED

Figure 20.4: South Africa has many skilled workers

**Discuss in pairs or groups:**

1 What are the benefits to Agrid International of locating its business in South Africa?

2 Do you think access to skilled labour or expansion of the motor industry was most significant in influencing Agrid International to locate in South Africa?

## BUSINESS IN ACTION

### New Balance

New Balance provide fashionable and functional footwear (see Figure 20.5) and clothing for athletes around the world. At the start of 2023, New Balance had six factories located in Indonesia. In May 2023, it announced that it planned to open another factory in the West Java region. One of the aims of this expansion is to provide employment for approximately 40 000 people. There has also been rapid growth in the footwear market in Indonesia. New Balance has over 300 suppliers. It exports its products from Indonesia to China, Japan, the USA and Europe.

**Discuss in pairs or groups:**

1 Why might New Balance decide to open a 7th factory in Indonesia?

2 The location of the 7th factory is intended to create 40 000 jobs. What are the benefits to New Balance of doing this?

3 Why would the Indonesian government support New Balance's decision to open a 7th factory?

Figure 20.5: New Balance provide fashionable and functional footwear

> **BUSINESS FOR CAMBRIDGE IGCSE™ AND O LEVEL: COURSEBOOK**

### SUMMARY

You should now know:

- There are several factors that owners or managers should consider when making a location decision.

- There are many factors that affect the location decision, such as cost of the site, access to the market (sales potential), size of the site and whether there are any legal restrictions.

- It is likely that a location will have some advantages and disadvantages; decisions around location must balance these factors; the advantages of the location chosen should outweigh the disadvantages.

# Chapter 20 practice questions

**1** Aisha is a sole trader. She is starting up her first hairdressing salon. She is considering two possible locations for her business. Aisha plans to employ two hairdressers. She understands the importance of training her employees and plans to use on-the-job training. Aisha is deciding whether to use skimming for her salon.

| | | |
|---|---|---|
| **a** | Define 'sole trader'. | [2] |
| **b** | Outline **two** benefits to Aisha of using on-the-job training. | [4] |
| **c** | Explain **two** factors Aisha should consider when deciding on the location for her business. | [6] |
| **d** | Do you think skimming is the best pricing method for Aisha to use? Justify your answer. | [8] |

**2** Triton Electrics (TE) is a public limited company. It manufactures electrical goods, such as microwave ovens, in Country X. It uses quality control to ensure the quality of its products. TE employs 500 workers. The directors of TE are considering moving the location of its factory to Country Y.

| | | |
|---|---|---|
| **a** | Identify **two** location factors a business should consider. | [2] |
| **b** | Outline two benefits to Aisha of using on-the-job training. | [4] |
| **c** | Explain **two** advantages to TE of locating its factory in Country Y. | [6] |
| **d** | Do you think quality control is the best way for TE to ensure the quality of its products? Justify your answer. | [8] |

Total available marks: 40

## CHECK YOUR PROGRESS

How well do you think you have achieved the learning intentions for this chapter? Give yourself a score from 1 (still need a lot of practice) to 5 (feeling very confident) for each learning intention. Provide an example to support your score.

| Now I can … | Score | Example |
|---|---|---|
| explain the factors influencing the location decision of manufacturing and service businesses | | |
| explain why businesses may decide to locate their operations in another country and identify the factors that would influence the choice of country to locate in. | | |

# Section 4 case study

## CASE STUDY

**Sunshine Foods**

Sunshine Foods (SF) manufactures a range of breakfast cereals. It purchases its ingredients from farms in Country Y. SF uses batch production for all of its products. However, the directors of SF have agreed to the introduction of flow production methods for its most popular products (see Appendix 1).

The company has grown over the past five years and this has meant that it has been able to benefit from economies of scale. It has developed a new chocolate-flavoured cereal, Choco-pops. The Marketing Manager has produced a break-even chart for Choco-pops based on cost information supplied by the Operations Department and a proposed selling price of $1.50.

The Operations Manager, who recently joined SF from one of its main competitors, wants to introduce a number of changes to SF's operations to improve productivity. He has suggested to the Operations Director a number of ways of achieving productivity improvements (see Appendix 2) and has also produced a report outlining the case for the introduction of just-in-time inventory management. In addition to these changes, The Operations Director is also thinking about relocating SF's factory.

The Marketing Manager is concerned about a recent email received from one of SF's major customers (see Appendix 3).

# Appendix 1

**Extract from the minutes of the most recent meeting of the Board of Directors**

Minute 3.1   The directors agreed to an investment of $500 000 over the next two years to finance new flow production methods.

# Appendix 2

**Extract from the report prepared by the Operations Manager**

The company needs to improve productivity. This may be achieved through:

- increasing the frequency and quality of training for production workers
- improving employee motivation, perhaps through non-financial incentives
- investing in new technology.

# Appendix 3

**Email message from Core Supermarkets:**

We have recently received complaints from some of our customers about the quality of cereal products manufactured by your company. Some customers have returned boxes of cereal purchased from our supermarkets claiming that the product does not taste very nice or contains material that does not look like cereal! If these complaints continue then we will have no option but to stop stocking your products and look for an alternative supplier.

# 20 Section 4 case study

1 a Explain **two** reasons why quality is important to Sunshine Foods.

Reason 1:

Explanation:

Reason 2:

Explanation: [8]

b Consider the advantages and disadvantages of quality control and quality assurance. Which method do you think Sunshine Foods should use? Justify your answer.

Quality control:

Quality assurance:

Conclusion: [12]

2 a Explain **one** advantage and **one** disadvantage to Sunshine Foods of introducing flow production.

Advantage:

Explanation:

Disadvantage:

Explanation: [8]

b The Operations Manager wants to improve productivity at Sunshine Foods. Explain how each of the following might help the Operations Manager to achieve this objective. Which method is likely to be the most effective? Justify your answer.

Training:

Improving employee motivation:

Investing in new technology:

Recommendation: [12]

3 a Explain **two** economies of scale Sunshine Foods may have benefited from.

Example 1:

Explanation:

Example 2:

Explanation: [8]

b Consider the advantages and disadvantages to Sunshine Foods of using break-even analysis. Do you think break-even analysis is useful for Sunshine Foods? Justify your answer.

Advantages:

Disadvantages:

Conclusion: [12]

335

**4  a**   Explain two factors that could affect Sunshine Foods relocation decision.

Factor 1:

Explanation:

Factor 2:

Explanation: [8]

**b**   Consider the advantages and disadvantages to Sunshine Foods of just-in-time inventory management. Do you think Sunshine Foods should introduce just-in-time inventory management? Justify your answer.

Advantages:

Disadvantages:

Recommendation: [12]

**Total available marks: 80**

# Section 5
# Financial information and decisions

Just as you need money to finance your purchasing decisions, so do businesses. Finance is an integral part of starting a business and its management is key in a business achieving its objectives. Decisions like how much to pay employees, how should a business fund the purchase of new machinery and how much to spend on advertising are all important financial decisions faced by a business.

Finance is needed for such things as start-up capital, to pay daily expenses and to finance growth plans. In this section, you will learn about:

- the different sources of finance available to businesses and how they might choose the most appropriate source for a given situation
- the importance of cash and how a business might use cash flow forecasts to effectively manage its cash balances
- the main elements of statements of profit or loss and statements of financial position and how different stakeholders might use the information contained in them
- using ratio analysis to interpret a business's financial statements so that you are able to make reasoned judgements about its performance.

> # Chapter 21
> # Business finance

**LEARNING INTENTIONS**

By the end of this chapter, you will be able to:

- understand why businesses need finance
- understand the difference between short- and long-term finance
- understand and calculate working capital
- identify and explain the main internal and external sources of finance
- understand the advantages and disadvantages of internal and external sources of finance
- outline the main factors to consider when selecting a source of finance
- recommend and justify an appropriate source of finance for a given situation.

# Introduction

The main activity of business is the production of goods and services. This activity cannot take place without the resources of land, labour, capital and enterprise. Finance is needed to start up a business and keep it running smoothly. When looking at raising money, businesses have to consider their needs and the available short- and long-term options to decide which of the many sources of finance is best for them.

In this chapter, you will learn about the different sources of finance available to businesses for funding a wide range of business activities. You will look at the factors that influence the choice of finance and how owners and managers may decide on the source of finance for their business needs.

## BUSINESS IN CONTEXT

### Jameela Tutoring

Jameela is 18 years old and is hoping to go to university next year. She has started thinking about how this could be financed and has arranged a meeting with a local bank to see if she can get a student loan.

She also wants to buy a laptop to help her with her schoolwork, but her savings are not enough to buy it. She plans on asking her older sister to lend her the money she needs. She also wants to enquire whether she could buy the laptop on credit and pay for it in monthly instalments.

To earn some pocket money, she has been tutoring children in maths and science since she was 14. She has become very popular and is not able keep up with the demand for her tutoring services. She is thinking of expanding her small tutoring business while continuing her own studies. She would like to hire some more tutors and rent a premise for a few hours where children could come for their lessons. She is now considering how she can get some start-up capital to set up her business.

People need money for expenditures that are necessary to live; businesses need finance to operate.

**Figure 21.1:** Jameela has been tutoring children to earn some pocket money

#### Discuss in pairs or groups:

1. Identify at least three things that Jameela would need money/finance for.
2. Where could she get the initial finance from?

## 21.1 Why businesses need finance

Finance is needed right from setting up a business to running daily operations to expansion. Businesses need finance for many different activities including:

- To set up the business. This is known as start-up capital.
- To pay day-to-day expenses of the business such as wages, payments for suppliers of raw materials and fuel expenses. This is known as **working capital**.
- To purchase buildings and other **non-current assets** such as machines to replace ones that are no longer working efficiently or are obsolete.
- To invest in the latest technology.
- To finance expansion of the business.
- To finance research into new products and/or new markets.

Capital expenditure refers to spending by a business on non-current assets, such as machinery and buildings. It is needed at the start of the business and as it expands.

> **KEY TERMS**
>
> **working capital:** the capital needed to finance the day-to-day running costs and pay the short-term debts of a business.
>
> **non-current assets:** resources owned by a business that are expected to last for more than one year.

## 21.2 Short- and long-term finance

Some business activities and decisions need large amounts of finance and the business will invest this money over several years – long-term finance; for example, building a new factory. Other activities need smaller amounts of money over a short period of time: short-term finance; for example, the purchase of raw materials. Most short-term finance is to help manage cash flow problems. If capital is needed to finance the purchase of items such as non-current assets, for example, machinery, then it is more likely to require long-term finance sources.

### ACTIVITY 21.1

Tebogo is considering opening a dessert cafe in your town/city. He plans to serve and make ice cream, milkshakes and some desserts from the same premises. He plans to develop his café's website to allow online orders and would also like to offer a home delivery service.

1. Make a list of all the resources Tebogo will need for setting up his business.

2. Identify the five most important items or resources that you think Tebogo will have to finance when setting up his business.

3. Use the internet, local newspapers and any other resources you think useful to find out the cost of each of these five items.

4. Compare your list with the lists of other members of your class and agree on a list of items and their cost (take an average of everyone's costs for each item).

5. Total the costs for each of the items the class has identified. This will provide an approximation of the minimum start-up capital that Tebogo needs when setting up his business.

## 21.3 Working capital

All businesses must have enough finance to pay for their daily expenses such as paying employees' wages and buying raw materials.

Many businesses offer their customers credit terms (an agreement between the buyer and seller about the timings of payment to be made for the goods bought on credit). The longer the credit period, the less cash the business has to operate. The amount owed to the business by its customers who bought on credit is known as **trade receivables**.

Working capital measures the **liquidity** of a business. Liquidity is the ability of the business to pay its short-term debts. A business that does not have enough working capital will be illiquid and cannot pay its short-term debts. If this happens the business may have to borrow the finance required. It will also have to pay interest on the amount borrowed and this increases the business's costs. However, if the business is unable to borrow the finance required then it may fail.

The amount of working capital needed by a business depends on the time it takes from buying raw materials, making these into goods for sale, finding customers for the finished goods and then receiving payment from them.

A business can improve its working capital by:

- reducing inventory levels
- delaying payments to its suppliers
- asking customers to pay quicker for goods bought on credit.

### Calculating working capital

The formula for working capital is:

Working capital = **current assets – current liabilities**

For example:

A business has the following current assets and current liabilities:

- Current assets: $150 000
- Current liabilities: $60 000

Working capital = $150 000 − $60 000 = $90 000

> **DISCUSSION**
>
> Finding the right balance between holding enough cash and liquid assets to meet short-term obligations while minimizing idle cash that could be invested elsewhere is important for effective working capital management.
>
> - What effect would increasing the current assets have on the working capital?
> - What are the advantages of a large amount of working capital?
> - Would a large amount of working capital always be good for the business?

**KEY TERMS**

**trade receivables:** the amount owed to the business by its customers who bought goods on credit.

**liquidity:** the ability of a business to pay its short-term debts.

**LINKS**

You can find more information about current assets and current liabilities and how to improve working capital in Chapter 25.

**KEY TERMS**

**current assets:** resources that the business owns, which it will have for less than one year.

**current liabilities:** short-term debts of the business, which need to be paid within one year.

> **TIP**
>
> Before working out the working capital, remember to add all the current assets to work out the total current assets and add all the current liabilities to work out the total current liabilities.

## CASE STUDY 21.1

### Shonaquip

**Figure 21.2:** Mobility devices such as wheelchairs and buggies support people with disabilities

Shonaquip was established in 1992 by Shona McDonald, when Shona and her family encountered challenges supporting her child with a disability. Shona drew on her sculpting background to design a mobility device, which made caring for her daughter safer, easier, and opened new possibilities for fun and learning.

After receiving many requests about the mobility device that she had designed and built for her daughter, Shona launched Shonaquip from her garage with a tiny team of two. It now manufactures and sells posture support and mobility devices such as wheelchairs and buggies for people with disabilities. Shonaquip's products and services have spread throughout Southern Africa, and as far as Iraq, Georgia, India and Uganda. Like all successful South African entrepreneurs, Shona had the ability to identify the bigger picture and take calculated risks, winning several prestigious awards for entrepreneurship ever since.

Shonaquip relies on government funding, grants and donations, and collaborations with other organisations to access funds. It has also been relying on its increasing revenue from the sale of its products and services as a source of finance as it invests all profits in social development. In 2022, it received loan funding from Inyosi Empowerment, an organisation that works on empowering the disadvantaged groups. This funding served as a working capital loan used to alleviate Shonaquip's cash flow pressures in order to fund the remaining costs needed to fulfil an order by the Botswana Ministry of Health & Wellness.

**Discuss in pairs or groups:**

1. Why is Shona McDonald a good example of an entrepreneur?
2. Identify two reasons why Shona would have needed cash for her business when she first started.
3. Why is working capital important to Shonaquip?
4. Discuss if Shonaquip is likely to raise a significant amount of money through grants and donations.
5. Why do you think Shonaquip has both short-term and long-term sources of finance?

# 21.4 Main sources of finance

Businesses can fund their activities using both internal and external sources of finance.

## Internal sources of finance

This is capital that can be raised from within the business itself. Figure 21.3 shows the possible internal sources of finance.

**Figure 21.3:** Internal sources of finance

### Owner's savings

This is the money that the owner put into the business from their personal savings. The advantages and disadvantages of using owner's savings as an internal source of finance are shown in Table 21.1.

**Table 21.1:** Advantages and disadvantages of using owner's savings

| Advantages | Disadvantages |
|---|---|
| • There is no need to pay interest, so there is no cost to the business.<br>• Convenient and quick to access. | • The savings may not be enough.<br>• The owner risks losing their personal savings if the business does not work. |

## Retained profits

The owners of a profitable business may decide to reinvest some of their profits they have made in the current or previous years back into the business instead of taking it themselves or paying dividends to shareholders. This source of finance is known as **retained profits**.

Retained profit is a source of internal finance that a business can use to improve working capital, increasing the capital available for day-to-day operations, such as paying suppliers, wages, and utility bills.

This source of finance is not available to new start-up businesses as they have not made a profit yet. The advantages and disadvantages of using retained profits as an internal source of finance are shown in Table 21.2.

> **KEY TERM**
>
> **retained profit:** profit made from current or past years, which can be reinvested into the business.

Table 21.2: Advantages and disadvantages of using retained profits

| Advantages | Disadvantages |
|---|---|
| • There is no need to pay interest, so there is no cost to the business.<br>• Convenient and quick to access.<br>• It does not affect the ownership of the business. | • It is only available when the business is profitable.<br>• There may not be enough retained profits to fund large investment projects.<br>• New businesses do not have this source of finance.<br>• There is an opportunity cost involved in the use of internal finance, because once retained profit is used it is not available for other purposes. |

## Sale of non-current assets

The sale of non-current assets is another possible source of internal finance. The business can sell old or unwanted machinery or other assets to raise funds. The advantages and disadvantages of using the sale of unwanted non-current assets as an internal source of finance are shown in Table 21.3.

Table 21.3: Advantages and disadvantages of using the sale of unwanted non-current assets

| Advantages | Disadvantages |
|---|---|
| • There is no direct cost to the business.<br>• The sale of some assets can raise a lot of capital. | • Not all businesses will have unwanted assets to sell, especially new businesses.<br>• Not all assets are likely to raise money, as they may not have any commercial value (e.g., specialised machinery can only be sold as scrap metal). |

> **DISCUSSION**
>
> The sale of non-current assets is an important source of internal finance for companies. However, not all non-current assets offer the same value.
>
> Discuss with other students in your class why:
>
> 1. The sale of an unused building is likely to raise more money than the sale of a piece of machinery.
> 2. The sale of a 3-year-old motor vehicle is likely to raise more money than the sale of ten 3-year-old computers.
> 3. The sale of a very large item of machinery that cost $1 million when bought new three years ago might only raise a much smaller sum of money if sold today.

## Working capital

Businesses may be able to use their working capital to fund their day-to-day expenses, short-term debts and unexpected expenditure.

Improving working capital involves managing current assets and current liabilities more efficiently to enhance liquidity and ensure the business has enough resources to cover its day-to-day expenses. Some ways a business can improve their working capital are:

- reducing their inventory levels
- reducing trade receivables
- delaying trade payables.

### Reducing inventory levels

The business may decide to reduce the quantity of raw materials and components or finished goods it holds. For example, if a business has inventories valued at $60 000 and it is able to reduce this to $50 000, then this will mean that $10 000 less cash is tied up in inventories. This cash is now available for other more profitable uses.

### Reducing trade receivables

Most businesses sell goods to customers on credit. These used to be referred to as debtors. This means that customers receive the goods but pay for them at an agreed date in the future; for example, 30 days after delivery. A business can reduce the length of time it has to wait (trade credit period) for payment by making sure that customers pay on time or by offering discounts on early payment. By reducing the total accounts receivable in this way the business's cash balances increase and this provides a possible source of internal funds for short-term requirements.

Table 21.4 looks at the advantages and disadvantages of using working capital as a source of internal finance.

### Delaying trade payables

Negotiate with suppliers to extend the time you have to pay (e.g., from 30 days to 60 or 90 days). This keeps cash in your business for a longer period.

> **LINK**
>
> For more information about inventories, see Chapter 17.

**Table 21.4:** Advantages and disadvantages of using working capital

| Advantages | Disadvantages |
|---|---|
| • By shortening their trade credit period, a business will have received cash from its customers more quickly.<br>• By reducing inventory levels, the cost of storing inventory is reduced.<br>• Cash balances of the business are quick to access. | • A shorter trade credit period may discourage customers and so the business may have reduced sales.<br>• The business would be unable to meet a sudden increase in demand resulting in a loss of sales.<br>• Working capital is limited to the amount of cash, trade receivables, and inventory that the business has on hand. If it uses too much working capital, it can quickly run out of resources to pay day-to-day expenses, which could threaten the survival of the business. |

The amount of finance raised by reducing working capital cycle depends on the size of the business because larger businesses are likely to have higher levels of inventory and credit sales than small businesses. But reducing the value of working capital is risky because it may reduce the business's liquidity and its ability to pay short-term debts.

### ACTIVITY 21.2

Invicta Engineering (IE) is a small private limited company that manufactures mechanical components. Its main customers are other businesses that manufacture domestic appliances such as washing machines, vacuum cleaners and refrigerators.

The owners of IE are considering how to finance an unexpected expenditure of $14 000 for repairs and maintenance of its premises which needs to be paid by the end of the month. IE's current liabilities are $45 000. The directors of IE want to use internal sources of finance to fund this unexpected expenditure. They have asked Kasinda, the company's finance manager, to provide them with relevant financial data as of 30th April 2024. This is shown in Table 21.5.

**Table 21.5:** Extract from IE's most recent quarterly financial statement as of 30th April 2024

|  | $000 |
|---|---|
| Raw material inventories | 18 |
| Finished goods inventories | 15 |
| Trade receivables: 30 days | 9 |
| Bank balance | 14 |

### LINK

For more information about liquidity, see Chapter 21.

> **CONTINUED**
>
> Notes:
> - IE holds enough raw material inventories for three weeks' production.
> - IE gives customers 30 days credit.
>
> The Finance Director has suggested reducing the raw material inventories so that IE only holds enough for one week's production. The Operations Director disagrees. He proposes reducing the level of finished goods inventories by 50%. The Marketing Director disagrees with this proposal.
>
> 1. Explain why the directors of IE decided against using any of the current bank balance to pay for the unexpected expenditure.
>
> 2. Explain one limitation to IE of the Finance Director's proposal to reduce raw material inventories.
>
> 3. Explain why you think the Marketing Director disagrees with the Operation Director's proposal for finished goods inventories.
>
> 4. Assuming none of the trade receivables have come through yet, calculate IE's working capital as of 30th April 2024?
>
> 5. Discuss how the directors of IE might raise the $14 000 from within its working capital.

# External sources of finance

This is capital that is raised from outside the business. External sources of finance are usually divided into short- and long-term sources. The different types of external finance are shown in Table 21.6.

Table 21.6: The different types of external sources of finance

| Short-term finance (less than 1 year) | Long-term finance (more than 1 year) |
|---|---|
| • Overdrafts<br>• Trade credit | • Bank loans<br>• Hire purchase<br>• Leasing<br>• Crowdfunding<br>• Share issue<br>• Venture capital<br>• Government grants |

## Short-term sources

Businesses sometimes need to borrow finance for a short period of time. If the finance is needed for less than one year it is classified as short term.

## Overdrafts

Most businesses will have an **overdraft** agreement with their bank. This allows them to withdraw a sum of money from their account that is greater than the balance in their account. This is a very flexible source of finance because businesses only borrow what they need, so it may work out cheaper than a bank loan. However, the interest rates charged for this type of borrowing is often higher than most other sources of borrowing. For this reason, overdrafts are usually used only to meet short-term cash shortages. The advantages and disadvantages of using a bank overdraft as an external source of finance are shown in Table 21.7.

**Table 21.7:** Advantages and disadvantages of using a bank overdraft

| Advantages | Disadvantages |
| --- | --- |
| - No need for security.<br>- It is flexible – as businesses only borrow what they need and pay interest accordingly.<br>- It is readily available to acquire, so it is useful for overcoming short-term liquidity problems and emergency requirements.<br>- Interest only needs to be paid when account is overdrawn; otherwise, there are no regular charges. | - Can be expensive as interest rates are usually variable and higher than bank loans.<br>- Bank can ask for the overdraft to be repaid at a short notice, which can cause cash flow problems for the business.<br>- The overdraft limit/amount that can be overdrawn is usually low for small businesses.<br>- There might be a transaction fee when an overdraft is needed. A business will be charged a fee every time it withdraws more than what it has in its account. |

> **KEY TERM**
>
> **overdraft:** an agreement with the bank that allows a business to spend more money than it has in its account up to an agreed limit. The loan has to be repaid within 12 months.

> **TIP**
>
> You must show that you understand the difference between an overdraft and a bank loan. A bank loan describes loans over 12 months, so generally anything described as a 'bank loan' without any time span cannot be accepted as a short-term measure.

## Trade credit

Businesses usually buy most of their resources such as raw materials and components from their suppliers on credit. Trade credit is a source of finance as the supplier is really lending the money for the cost of the goods for the length of the agreed credit period.

If a business can negotiate longer credit terms with suppliers it will increase short-term finance. For example, if a business can buy $5 000 of raw materials from its supplier on credit terms of 40 days instead of 30 days, then this means that the business has $5 000 available for an extra ten days.

The advantages and disadvantages of using trade credit as an external source of finance are shown in Table 21.8.

Table 21.8: Advantages and disadvantages of using trade credit

| Advantages | Disadvantages |
|---|---|
| - It allows businesses to undertake jobs that require materials without cash at the start.<br>- There is no interest cost. | - Any discount offered by the supplier for prompt or early payment will be lost.<br>- The supplier may refuse further deliveries to the business until the outstanding payment has been made.<br>- If delayed payment occurs too often, then the supplier may demand payment before delivery. |

## Long-term sources

Any source of finance that is required for more than one year is classified as long-term. Some long-term finance might be needed for buying non-current assets with a relatively low value; for example, a motor vehicle. The amount needed will be quite small compared to the finance needed for non-current assets such as a new production line or factory extension. The main sources of long-term finance are venture capital and bank loans.

### Venture capital

**Venture capital** is a source of finance provided by individuals or companies (venture capitalists) to start-up companies that are innovative, have huge growth potential and are likely to give high returns. In return for their investment, the venture capitalists get a stake in the company, so they become shareholders of the company. Though venture capital mainly provides the initial start-up funding, it can also provide funding at different stages of a company's growth. The advantages and disadvantages of using venture capital as an external source of finance are shown in Table 21.9.

Table 21.9: Advantages and disadvantages of using venture capital

| Advantages | Disadvantages |
|---|---|
| - Accessible to new start-ups.<br>- No monthly payments have to be made.<br>- If venture capitalists are interested, large sums of money can be borrowed.<br>- Venture capitalists can offer their expertise. | - It is difficult to obtain as the process is highly competitive and there are not many venture capitalists.<br>- Reduces ownership and control of the founders of the business. |

### Bank loans

A **bank loan** is the most common source of external business finance. The amount borrowed is offered with either a fixed or variable rate of interest. If the rate of interest is fixed, then the business can be certain as to how much interest it will have to pay over the whole life of the loan. This reduces the risk to the business of increased

> **LINK**
>
> For more information about trade receivables, see Chapter 24.

> **KEY TERM**
>
> **venture capital:** a source of finance provided by individuals or companies to start-up companies that have huge growth potential and are likely to give high returns.

> **KEY TERM**
>
> **bank loan:** provision of finance by a bank that the business will repay with interest over an agreed period of time.

costs if interests on borrowing rise in the future. A variable rate of interest can rise or fall depending on economic factors. The advantages and disadvantages of using bank loans as an external source of finance are shown in Table 21.10.

Table 21.10: Advantages and disadvantages of using bank loans

| Advantages | Disadvantages |
| --- | --- |
| • Once the application is successful, the money becomes immediately available.<br>• Repayment of loan and interest payments are made at regular intervals, which helps with cash flow planning and management.<br>• Once approved, large sums of money can be borrowed. | • Businesses have to pay back more than what they borrowed as interest has to be paid on the amount borrowed.<br>• It is more difficult for small businesses to obtain bank loans as they are seen as a greater risk of not being able to repay the loans when due. If they are able to obtain a loan then this is often at a higher rate of interest than might be charged to larger businesses.<br>• Security/collateral has to be provided to obtain the loan. This puts the owners at risk of losing the assets put up as security. |

## CASE STUDY 21.2

### Twiga Foods

Figure 21.4: A stall holder in Kenya checks her mobile phone for a purchase order made to Twiga Foods

When Twiga Foods was first started in 2014 with its start-up capital, it used to supply bananas from small farms to retailers in a neighbourhood in Nairobi, Kenya.

With more start-up capital, it developed an internal technology platform to track orders. As it grew, it expanded the line of produce, added more farmers and suppliers, and improved its technology and distribution each step of the way. It also has a mobile application that helps both parties exchange money. Twiga Foods is said to be one of the best-funded tech start-ups on the African continent, securing US$10 million funding in 2018, and much more after that.

Today, Twiga Foods is a technology-driven company that connects consumers, vendors and suppliers, providing access to high-quality foods, products and retail services in Africa. In the last nine years, Twiga has done business with over 140 000 small retailers across Kenya – about 25% of the entire industry. In 2022, it started selling everyday consumer goods under its own brand.

Discuss in pairs or groups:

1  Define 'start-up capital'.

2  What do you think were the two main uses of Twiga Foods' start-up capital when they first started their operations in 2014?

3  Why do you think Twiga Foods was successful in attracting so much funding?

4  How did Twiga Foods spend its additional funding on expansion over the years?

## Leasing

**Leasing** is used as a source of finance for non-current assets, in particular, motor vehicles and machinery. In return for having use of the asset, the business pays the leasing company a fixed amount over a set period of time.

This payment is usually paid monthly or quarterly. The asset is not owned by the business, and at the end of the lease term, it can give the asset back to the leasing company. The leasing company is usually responsible for the maintenance and repair of the asset. The advantages and disadvantages of using leasing as an external source of finance are shown in Table 21.11.

Table 21.11: Advantages and disadvantages of using leasing

| Advantages | Disadvantages |
|---|---|
| The business can acquire and use assets without investing a large sum of money. | There is an interest charge as part of the payment. |
| The maintenance and repair of leased assets are often managed and paid for by the leasing company. | The total cost of leasing over a long period of time can be very expensive and well above the price of the asset. |
| Leases are generally easier to obtain than loans. | The business never gets to own the asset that it leases. |
| The leased assets can be updated regularly so the business benefits from using the latest technology. | |
| The cost is spread over time – usually one to five years – and this can be financed out of working capital. | |

> **KEY TERM**
>
> **leasing:** obtaining the use of a non-current asset by paying a fixed amount per time period for a fixed period of time. Ownership remains with the leasing company.

## Hire purchase

Like leasing, **hire purchase** is used to finance non-current assets such as motor vehicles and machinery. However, the main difference is that the business will own the asset once all payments have been made and it is responsible for any maintenance or repairs to the asset. The advantages and disadvantages of using hire purchase as an external source of finance are shown in Table 21.12.

Table 21.12: Advantages and disadvantages of using hire purchase

| Advantages | Disadvantages |
|---|---|
| The business can acquire and use assets without investing a large sum of money. | There is an interest charge as part of the payment. |
| The cost is spread over time – usually one to five years – and this can be financed out of working capital. | The total cost over a long period of time can be very expensive and well above the price of the asset. |

> **KEY TERM**
>
> **hire purchase:** the purchase of an asset by paying a fixed repayment amount per time period over an agreed period of time. The asset is owned by the purchasing company on completion of the final repayment.

> **ACTIVITY 21.3**
>
> Research the financial and other support the government provides for businesses in your country. Your research should consider the type and level of support available, the purpose of the grant/support, whether the grant has to be repaid and why the government is providing the grant/support.

### Share issue

This source of finance is only available to limited companies as they are the only form of legal structure allowed to raise finance through a **share issue**. The company can offer to sell shares up to a maximum number. Private limited companies can only sell shares to existing shareholders or private investors. Public limited companies can offer their shares for sale to the public. The amount of capital raised through a share issue becomes permanent capital and never has to be repaid unless the business ceases to trade. The advantages and disadvantages of using share issue as an external source of finance are shown in Table 21.13.

> **KEY TERM**
>
> **share issue:** a source of permanent capital available to limited liability companies.

Table 21.13: Advantages and disadvantages of using share issue

| Advantages | Disadvantages |
|---|---|
| • This is a form of permanent capital, so there is no obligation to repay it unless the business ceases to trade.<br>• The business does not have to pay dividends if it has not made enough profits.<br>• In the case of a private limited company, owners of shares have a say in how the business is run.<br>• Large amounts of finance can be raised.<br>• The business can benefit from the expertise of shareholders who have more ownership and control of the business. | • The increase in shareholders 'dilutes' the ownership of the company. This can slow down decision-making.<br>• The business becomes vulnerable to the threat of a takeover when an individual or a group buys enough shares.<br>• In the case of a public limited company, producing a prospectus to offer the shares for sale is expensive. |

### Government grants

The governments of many countries support businesses in their country by providing grants and other financial assistance to encourage new business start-ups, or to assist business growth and development. The advantages and disadvantages of using government grants as an external source of finance are shown in Table 21.14.

Table 21.14: Advantages and disadvantages of using government grants

| Advantages | Disadvantages |
|---|---|
| • It does not need to be paid back.<br>• Available to small businesses. | • Business needs to meet certain criteria in order to qualify for the grant.<br>• It can be time-consuming to complete the paperwork required to apply for grants. |

# Alternative sources of capital: crowdfunding

**Crowdfunding** is an alternative source of external short-term finance and it can be raised through obtaining small amounts of capital from a large number of people, most often using the internet and social media networks.

Entrepreneurs publish their idea for a project on the internet or through social media networks. They say how much finance they need, what they will do with the capital raised and how any investor might benefit in the future. They invite anyone who is interested to invest in their business idea. Often the finance is raised from a large number of people each investing a small amount of money. The advantages and disadvantages of using crowdfunding as an external source of finance are shown in Table 21.15.

> **KEY TERM**
>
> **crowdfunding:** financing a business idea by obtaining small amounts of capital from a large number of people, most often using the internet and social media networks.

**Table 21.15:** Advantages and disadvantages of using crowdfunding

| Advantages | Disadvantages |
|---|---|
| • Available for individuals who would like to start up a business when they do not have access to other sources of funding.<br>• It helps to test the appeal and success of a business idea – if people do not invest then the business idea is not likely to do well.<br>• Access to large numbers of investors.<br>• Funds can sometimes be raised fairly quickly. | • Making the business idea public can increase competition.<br>• It can be difficult to attract investors and reach the funding target, in which case the money has to be returned to the investors. |

### CASE STUDY 21.3

**PetSnowy**

PetSnowy was founded in the USA in 2020 to create convenient, time-saving products so that pet owners can maximize their time with pets. In 2023, it raised $1.8 million from the crowd-funding platform, Indiegogo. You can find some media coverage below about PetSnowy's latest innovation – a self-cleaning litter box.

> The SNOW, self-cleaning litter box, revolutionizes cat waste disposal by improving the convenience, sanitation and cleanliness of one of the most undesirable parts of cat parenting.
>
> Cat parents cite the SNOW litter box's innovative design, cleanliness and ability to monitor litter box behaviours and status as winning features.
>
> The Most Popular Pet Project on Indiegogo

> In February 2023, we took Indiegogo by storm, fully funding our project in just one hour.

**Discuss in pairs or groups:**

1 Why do you think PetSnowy was successful in getting crowdfunding?

2 Why might PetSnowy have found it difficult to raise the finance it needed for its business from banks and other lenders?

3 State two advantages of crowdfunding.

4 Explain one advantage and one disadvantage to PetSnowy of making its proposed design public and raising finance through crowdfunding.

> BUSINESS FOR CAMBRIDGE IGCSE™ AND O LEVEL: COURSEBOOK

### ACTIVITY 21.4

Mr. See Lim is the owner of Gold Gym, a private limited company, and is looking at expanding the company's operations by building a spa. He has made good profits this year and has enough retained profits to fund this expansion. However, he also needs to invest in new fitness equipment in his gym. Mr. Lim is considering if he should get a loan for the spa and is evaluating whether to get an internal or external source of finance for building the spa.

1. What are the advantages of internal finance?
2. What are the disadvantages of internal finance?
3. What should Mr. Lim consider before deciding whether to use the retained profits or a loan to fund the spa.

### TIP

You must be able to describe the main sources of finance, but more importantly, you must know which source would be suitable in a given situation.

## 21.5 Factors influencing the choice of finance

Choosing the right source of finance will require consideration of a variety of factors, as shown in Table 21.16.

**Table 21.16:** Factors influencing the choice of finance

| Factor | Reasons why the factor needs to be considered |
|---|---|
| Size and legal form of business | • Unincorporated businesses such as sole traders and partnerships are unable to raise finance by issuing shares. Additionally, they find it more difficult to borrow from banks and other lenders because they are considered at greater risk of not being able to pay back the amount borrowed. The business's legal status may therefore influence the sources of finance available to it.<br>• Smaller businesses may find it more difficult to borrow from banks and other lenders because they have limited financial history and are considered to be of greater risk. Even when small businesses are able to borrow from banks, they are often charged a higher rate of interest. |
| Purpose of the finance | • Different sources of finance may be suitable depending on whether the finance is needed for start-up capital, for expansion or for additional working capital. For example, for start-up capital, venture capitalists may be able to give the largest amount of funds. Some sources of finance are usually only available for very specific uses. For example, mortgages are only available for the purchase of land or buildings. Leasing is only available for financing physical assets such as cars, machinery and property; it could not, for example, be used to finance a major advertising campaign. |
| Amount required | • If a large capital amount is required then share issues are more appropriate. A smaller amount might be financed through bank loans or leasing and hire purchase. |

(Continued)

**Table 21.16:** (Continued)

| Factor | Reasons why the factor needs to be considered |
|---|---|
| Length of time | • If a business needs long-term finance then it may want to consider share issues.<br>• In the short term, an overdraft may be the most flexible solution.<br>• The longer the period of time finance is borrowed for, the more costly it will be because of interest payments. |
| How quickly the money is required | • If a business needs money quickly in order to solve a short-term cash flow problems then it may go for the quickest source of finance even if it is more expensive. |
| Existing borrowing | • If a business already has existing borrowing then it might find it more difficult to borrow further amounts from banks and other lenders. This is because it will be seen as a greater risk. |
| Use of finance | • Some sources of finance are usually only available for very specific uses. For example, mortgages are only available for the purchase of land or buildings. Leasing is only available for financing physical assets such as cars, machinery and property; it could not, for example, be used to finance a major advertising campaign. |
| Cost of the finance | • This is the extra money that needs to be paid to secure the initial amount – the typical cost is the interest that has to be paid on the borrowed amount.<br>• The cheapest form of money to a business comes from its trading profits. |

## BUSINESS IN ACTION

### Shark Tank

**Figure 21.5:** Several popular TV shows have entrepreneurs making business presentations to venture capitalists to gain investment

Shark Tank India is a popular TV show that shows entrepreneurs making business presentations to a group of venture capitalists (investors in start-ups), called "sharks" on the program, in order to convince them to invest in their business ventures. Other countries have similar TV shows that provide a platform for entrepreneurs to showcase their business ideas and seek investment; Dragons' Den is another such program.

Discuss in pairs or groups:

1. Explain the benefit to a new business of obtaining finance from one of the investors on a TV show.

2. Working in groups, come up with a business idea that you would like to launch with them. Identify the main characteristics of the product or service your business will be offering.

3. Make a business plan and consider the following:

    - the objectives of the business
    - the skills and expertise of the employees that will be needed
    - work out the costs involved and come up with an estimate of how much start-up capital would be required.

### CONTINUED

4   In your groups, discuss and prepare a presentation you would give in front of a panel of venture capitalists to impress them and win their investment.

5   Assume you only receive part of the start-up capital you need. What other source of finance could you use to raise the remaining amount?

### ACTIVITY 21.5

Working with a partner, consider the following scenarios and identify which source of finance may be the most suitable in each scenario and explain why.

#### Scenario 1

Mr. Pule wants to start up his own internet cafe, but he needs some finance to set up his business. He is considering the following sources of finance.

| Source of finance | Reason why the source is suitable |
| --- | --- |
| Owner's capital | |
| Hire purchase | |
| Bank loan | |

#### Scenario 2

Tika shoes is a private limited company that manufactures sports shoes. Its Finance Manager, Mr. Kapil, has forecasted a negative balance next month. The company needs to find a suitable source of finance to fund the additional working capital needs. Mr. Kapil is considering the following sources of finance.

| Source of finance | Reason why the source is suitable |
| --- | --- |
| Owner's capital | |
| Overdraft | |
| Selling non-current assets | |
| Trade credit | |

#### Scenario 3

Genoia Enterprises is a public limited company that manufactures electric cables. It wants to expand its operations and set up another factory in a different part of the country. Its management team is considering the following sources of finance.

| Source of finance | Reason why the source is suitable |
| --- | --- |
| Retained profits | |
| Venture capitalists | |
| Share issue | |
| Bank loan | |

### TIP

When selecting the most suitable source of finance, carefully consider the financial information that is presented within the case study/question and look for clues in the information provided, such as the personal circumstances of the business owner or the nature of the business itself.

Then give a justified reason about why one particular source of finance is likely to be most suitable in this situation compared to the other option(s) discussed.

> **REFLECTION**
>
> In choosing a source of finance in Activity 21.5, how did you evaluate the factors that led you to your conclusion? Discuss your conclusion with another group. Did they reach the same conclusion? If not, how would you justify your choice? How did their approach to this task differ from what you did? Can you learn any ideas from how they approached this task?

> **SUMMARY**
>
> You should now know:
>
> - Businesses need funds for a number of different reasons and these reasons will influence whether they use short- or long-term sources of finance.
>
> - The advantages and disadvantages of various internal and external sources of finance.
>
> - In some countries crowdfunding has become a popular way for entrepreneurs to borrow small amounts of finance for business start-ups.
>
> - When choosing which source of finance is the most appropriate to use, businesses will consider a number of factors such as cost, legal status, amount required and level of existing borrowing.

# Chapter 21 practice questions

1. Roy is a sole trader who owns Super Sports, a shop selling sporting goods. Roy wants to expand his business by having a sports injury and rehab clinic close to the shop. He will need to rent an office space for the clinic and buy some equipment. Roy estimates that he will need $20 000 to rent, fit and equip the clinic and a further $2 000 to buy inventories: a total of $22 000. Roy is considering using external finance, for example, asking his bank for a loan, an overdraft or leasing the equipment.

    a  Define 'overdraft'. [2]

    b  Outline **two** disadvantages to Roy of using external sources of finance to fund the expansion of his business. [4]

    c  Outline **two** pieces of financial information the bank manager might want to know when considering Roy's application for a bank loan. [6]

    d  Explain **two** external sources of finance, other than a bank loan, that Roy might consider for raising all or part of the $22 000 needed to finance the expansion of his business. Which source of finance do you think is more suitable? Justify your answer. [8]

**BUSINESS FOR CAMBRIDGE IGCSE™ AND O LEVEL: COURSEBOOK**

2   BE is a private limited company. It manufactures ceiling fans and air conditioners. BE has been very profitable over the past two years and this year is expecting profits to be $400 000. BE has just received a large order for its products from a holiday resort being constructed in the area which it wants to have ready on time. Instead of using internal sources of finance BE has applied for an overdraft to meet its working capital needs. BE also needs finance to buy land to set up a new factory in order to meet the growing demand.

   a   Define 'working capital'. [2]

   b   Outline **two** internal sources of finance BE might use. [4]

   c   Explain **two** factors that might influence BE's choice of finance when buying the land. [6]

   d   Explain **two** sources of finance BE could use for the new factory. Which is the best source of finance for BE to use? Justify your answer. [8]

   Total available marks: 40

## CHECK YOUR PROGRESS

How well do you think you have achieved the learning intentions for this chapter? Give yourself a score from 1 (still need a lot of practice) to 5 (feeling very confident) for each learning intention. Provide an example to support your score.

| Now I can … | Score | Example |
| --- | --- | --- |
| outline why businesses need finance | | |
| explain the difference between short- and long-term finance | | |
| calculate and explain the importance of working capital | | |
| identify and explain the main internal and external sources of finance | | |
| outline the advantages and disadvantages of internal and external sources of finance | | |
| outline the main factors to consider when selecting a source of finance | | |
| recommend and justify an appropriate source of finance for a given situation. | | |

# Chapter 22
# Cash flow forecasts

**LEARNING INTENTIONS**

By the end of this chapter, you will be able to:

- understand the importance of cash to businesses
- understand what a cash flow forecast is and its importance
- identify the key features of a cash flow forecast
- amend, complete and interpret a cash flow forecast
- understand how businesses deal with short-term cash flow problems.

# Introduction

Cash flow refers to the money coming in and going out of a business. Businesses manage their cash flow to ensure that there is enough cash on hand to meet their day-to-day needs, such as paying bills, employees' salaries and other expenses and to make use of investment opportunities of surplus cash, if any. An accurate cash flow forecast forms the basis of effective cash flow management. A cash flow forecast is an estimate of when money will be received from sales, investments or other sources, as well as when payments will need to be made for expenses such as rent, utilities, salaries and loan repayments.

Making a profit is good, but it is cash that will pay the bills. If there is not enough cash to meet the day-to-day needs of a business, it will eventually fail.

In this chapter, you will study the importance of cash to a business, and how it can be effectively managed. You will also look at what businesses might do if faced with the problem of temporary cash shortages.

## BUSINESS IN CONTEXT

### Rattan furniture

**Figure 22.1:** A selection of rattan bags

A rattan furniture and accessory maker, Abigeal Akinrinade is the founder of Rattan by Abbie. It all began in Nigeria in 2019 when Abigeal came across someone who sold rattan (the thin jointed stems of a palm tree, used to make furniture or other items) bags. She bought one with her pocket money, took a picture and posted it on social media. Two of her friends showed interest in the bag and she sold it at double the price at which she had bought it. She then went back to where she had bought it to buy more bags. More people began requesting her for the bags but some of them wanted to pay her on delivery. So, she asked her father for some money to start her business and used it to buy ten rattan bags.

In March 2020, she started her own brand where she designed the logo herself and wrote out the vision and mission statement for the brand. She has been selling handmade and sophisticated rattan items to Nigerians and people outside the country for more than three years now.

Her love for African fashion items along with her love for unique things made her go into this business. She aspires to have her own showroom someday.

### Discuss in pairs or groups:

1. Was selling the first bag at double the price a good decision?
2. What could Abigeal have done if she was not able to borrow money from anyone to buy more bags?

## 22.1 Why cash is important to businesses

Cash is the physical money in notes and coins, or money in the bank, which is readily available to be spent by the business. A business needs cash. Without it, the business will not be able to pay:

- its employees' wages
- its suppliers for goods and services
- rent, heating and lighting and other costs for its premises.

Without cash, a business will fail.

How does a business make sure it has enough cash to pay its bills? Most businesses operate cash flow management, which means that they have the finance whenever they need it to pay their employees, their suppliers and so on. Managing a business's cash flow involves making sure that enough cash is coming into the business to cover the cash that goes out of the business. For example, is there enough cash from the sale of goods to cover the amount needed to pay suppliers?

Many businesses have failed because their owners did not manage the business's cash flow well. For example, The VanMoof Group, a major Dutch ebike retailer, failed in July 2023 after running successfully for a decade. This was because of little cash coming in due to slow growth and failure to cut costs or raise funds.

## 22.2 What is a cash flow forecast?

All business activity results in either a flow of cash into the business or a flow of cash out of the business.

The main sources of cash inflow in a business are:

- share capital/owner's capital
- sales revenue
- loan.

The main sources of cash outflow are:

- payment to suppliers
- utilities, such as electricity and water
- wages and salaries
- loan repayments
- mortgage payments or rent.

The survival of any business depends on it having a positive cash flow where the **cash inflows** are greater than the **cash outflows**, as shown in Figure 22.2.

It is better to have a positive cash flow as any temporary cash shortage may cause problems for the business and result in an increase in borrowing costs.

To prevent a negative net cash flow, businesses need an accurate forecast of the size and timing of cash inflows and outflows. A **cash flow forecast** enables businesses to identify any future time periods when cash shortages may occur.

> **TIP**
>
> Cash is not the same as profit so make sure you understand the difference. A profitable firm can run out of cash. If so, and the business cannot pay its debts, then the firm may not be able to survive even though it is profitable. In the short run, cash is more important than profit.

> **KEY TERMS**
>
> **cash inflow:** the money coming into the business.
>
> **cash outflow:** the money going out of the business.
>
> **cash flow forecast:** an estimate of the future cash inflows and outflows of a business.

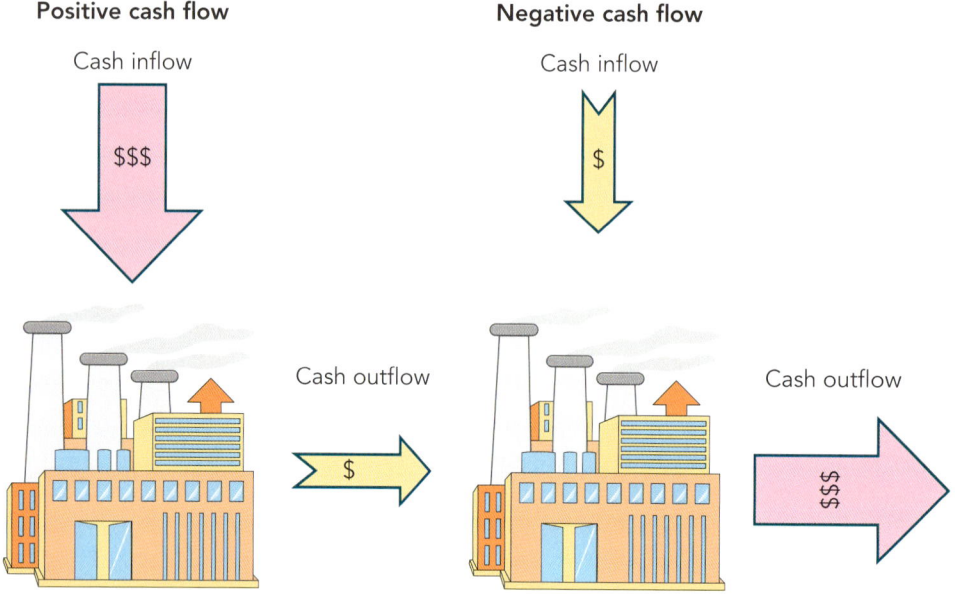

Figure 22.2: Positive and negative cash flow

> **ACTIVITY 22.1**
>
> Give examples of the possible cash inflows and outflows for the following businesses:
>
> - café
> - cinema
> - dance studio.

## 22.3 The main features of a cash flow forecast

The cash flow forecast shows how much cash the business expects to have at the end of each month. A cash flow forecast statement has five main parts:

- **Cash inflow:** This is the estimated/projected money coming into the business for a specific period, such as a month. For example, cash received from sale of inventory and non current assets and cash received from loan will be included here.

- **Cash outflow:** This is the estimated/projected money going out of the business for a specific period, such as a month. For example, expenditure or payment of cash made by a business for expenses, interest and loan repayments and taxes will be included here.

- **Net cash flow**: This is the difference between total cash inflows and total cash outflows. A positive net cash flow indicates that there will be more cash coming into the business than going out. A negative net cash flow indicates that there will be more cash going out than coming in.

> **KEY TERM**
>
> **net cash flow:** cash inflow minus cash outflow.

- **Opening balance**: This is the amount of cash a business expects to have at the beginning of a specific period.
- **Closing balance**: This is how much cash the business expects to have at the end of a specific period, e.g., a month. If the closing balance is forecast to be negative then this tells management that the business will have a cash shortage.

## 22.4 Completing and amending a cash flow forecast

Consider the main components of a cash flow forecast when completing or amending an existing cash flow forecast. Follow the below steps to calculate the closing balance at the end of a specific period of time:

1. Estimate the cash inflows and add them together to calculate the total cash inflows for that time period.
2. Estimate all the cash outflows and add them together to calculate the total cash outflows for that time period.
3. Calculate the net cash flow by subtracting the total cash outflows from the total cash inflows for that time period.

    Net cash flow = Total cash inflows − Total cash outflows

4. Add the net outflows to the opening balance to give you the closing balance.

    Net cash flow + Opening balance = Closing balance

5. Remember that the closing balance at the end of a period is the opening balance for the next.

The cash flow forecast in Table 22.1 shows the amount of cash inflows and outflows in thousands each month, the net cash flow and the opening and closing balances every month for the months of January, February and March. For example, in January:

- The business expects to receive $10 000 in revenue and $5 000 in loan, making the total cash inflows to be $15 000.
- It anticipates paying wages and salaries of $6 000 and payment to suppliers for $7 000, making the total cash outflows to be $13 000.
- This means that in January, there will be a net cash flow of total cash inflows minus total cash outflows: $15 000 − $13 000 = $2 000.
- The closing balance is the net cash flow + the opening balance = $2 000 + $5 000 = $7 000.
- The closing balance for January is the opening balance for February.

> **KEY TERMS**
>
> **opening balance:** the projected bank balance at the start of a specific period.
>
> **closing balance:** how much cash the business expects to have at the end of a specific period, e.g., a month.

Table 22.1: Sample cash flow forecast showing values (in thousands $)

|  | Jan | Feb | Mar |
|---|---|---|---|
| **Cash inflows** |  |  |  |
| Revenue | 10 | 19 | 28 |
| Loan | 5 |  |  |
| Total cash | 15 | 19 | 28 |
| **Cash outflows** |  |  |  |
| Payments to suppliers | 7 | 27 | 12 |
| Wages/salaries | 6 | 7 | 8 |
| Total cash outflow | 13 | 34 | 20 |
| **Net cash flow** | 2 | (–15) | 8 |
| Opening balance | 5 | 7 | (–8) |
| **Closing balance** | 7 | (–8) | 0 |

> ### ACTIVITY 22.2
>
> Look at the cash flow forecast above.
>
> 1 In which month is there going to be a negative closing balance?
>
> 2 What has caused the balance at the end of this month to become negative?
>
> 3 What could the business do to reduce the cash outflows in February?
>
> 4 How much should the business reduce the cash outflows by to not have a negative closing balance?

# Interpreting cash flow forecasts

Interpreting a cash flow forecast accurately will help businesses manage their cash and alert them to possible cash shortages in the future. This will help them take action beforehand and prevent a situation where they cannot pay their immediate bills and expenses. Here are some key steps to consider for interpreting a cash flow forecast effectively:

- Analyse the cash inflows and outflows and identify which inflows and outflows are the most significant/largest. Look for any seasonal patterns or trends, or irregularities that may have affected cash flow projections.
- Calculate the net cash flow by subtracting total cash outflows from total cash inflows.
    1 A positive net cash flow means that there were more cash inflows than outflows during the period which suggests a healthy cash flow position. A positive net cash flow can result from factors such as strong sales revenue, efficient collections from debtors, or reduced expenses.
    2 A negative net cash flow means that there were more cash outflows than inflows during the period. A cash shortage may occur if the opening balance does not cover the net negative cash flow. A negative net cash flow can result from factors such as high expenses, low sales revenue or large investments in assets or expansion projects.

- Check the closing balance: A positive closing balance indicates that, at the end of a given period (such as a month or year), there is a surplus or positive amount of funds. A negative closing balance means the opposite.
- Compare the cash flow forecast to historical cash flow data, if available. Check whether the current cash forecast follows a similar pattern to the past performance. If not, then explore why.

By carefully interpreting a cash flow forecast, it is possible to gain valuable insights into the expected movement of cash, identify potential risks or opportunities and make informed decisions to manage cash flow effectively and ensure financial stability.

> **TIP**
>
> You will not be expected to draw up a cash flow forecast for IGCSE/O Level Business, but you might be asked to fill in missing numbers.

## CASE STUDY 22.1

### Jet Airways

**Figure 22.3:** Jet Airways was India's premium airline

Once India's premium private-owned, Jet Airways (India) Limited was set up in 1993. In 2002–2004, thanks to its superior quality, the full-service airline (provided in-flight meals and economy luggage allowance while charging a higher price) reached 44% of the domestic passenger market share. In 2005, Jet Airways made its first long-haul flight to London.

Jet airways like most other airlines, leased planes to cut costs. This let them explore new routes at minimal additional costs too. It also allowed them to return the aircraft once demand fell.

With the growth of low-cost airlines (offers bare minimum services but has low ticket prices) in 2000, Jet Airways started losing market share. So, it decided to try to establish its own low-cost brand. However, air carriers operate at a fixed cost. This means that the cost of flying a plane on a certain route is the same, whether the plane is full or half-empty.

In 2007, Jet Airways incurred debt to fund its expansion and its profitability started going down. Slowly, its fleet started getting smaller and the air carrier that once boasted a fleet of 120 aircraft had only seven planes in April 2019. Unfortunately, the burden of the debt coincided with the 2008 financial crisis. Demand fell and oil prices surged. In India, fuel accounts for 34% of the total costs for Indian carriers due to taxes. A rise in fuel costs may prove fatal for a company.

In 2013, Jet Airways started a price/fare war with low-cost carriers IndiGo and SpiceJet. The airline's market value fell and it started posting losses. Due to cash flow problems, employees had not been paid for months. Operational creditors and lessors were looking to recover their dues. In 2019, lenders had decided to seek their money back under the insolvency and bankruptcy laws.

**Discuss in pairs or groups:**

1 Define the terms 'cash inflow' and 'cash outflow'.
2 Explain how leasing the aeroplanes would have been beneficial for Jet Airways.
3 What would be the sources of cash inflows for an airline such as Jet Airways?
4 What would be the possible cash outflows for an airline such as Jet Airways?
5 Why do you think the company's fleet started getting smaller as profitability fell?
6 How would operating at fixed cost affect the net cash flow of an airline?
7 List all the factors that you think contributed to Jet Airways becoming illiquid.

## ACTIVITY 22.3

The cash flow forecast shown in Table 22.2 has been produced by the Finance Manager of Crystal Paints.

**Table 22.2:** Cash flow forecast for Crystal Paints (in thousands $)

|  | Jan | Feb | Mar | Apr | May | Jun |
|---|---|---|---|---|---|---|
| **Cash inflows** | | | | | | |
| Revenue | 10 | 14 | 14 | 18 | 26 | 29 |
| Loan | 2 | | | | | |
| Total cash inflow | 12 | 14 | 14 | 18 | 26 | 27 |
| **Cash outflows** | | | | | | |
| Payments | 10 | 12 | 12 | 14 | 14 | 16 |
| Electricity and water | 6 | 6 | 6 | 6 | 6 | 6 |
| Total cash outflow | 16 | 18 | 18 | 20 | 20 | 22 |
| **Net cash flow** | (–4) | (–4) | (–4) | (–2) | | |
| Opening balance | 10 | 6 | 2 | (–2) | | |
| **Closing balance** | 6 | 2 | (–2) | (–4) | | |

1. Calculate the closing balance for both May and June.
2. Comment on the forecast cash flow for Crystal Paints between January and June.
3. How could the Finance Manager use the cash flow forecast to better manage Crystal Paints' cash flow?

Remember, the most important line in any cash flow statement is the one containing the 'closing balance'. If a business's cash position is forecast to become negative for a short period of time, management might decide to finance this with an overdraft. However, overdrafts can be a very expensive source of finance. Before deciding to use an overdraft, managers should consider ways of removing or reducing the cash shortage. Even if they only reduce the size of the forecast cash shortage, this will at least reduce the size and cost of any required overdraft.

### TIP

Look at the trend (change) in the individual items that make up the total cash inflows and total cash outflows to identify the reasons for cash flow problems. This will help you identify how a business might overcome them.

## ACTIVITY 22.4

The cash flow forecast shown in Table 22.3 has been prepared for the next four months for AGO.

**Table 22.3:** Cash flow forecast for AGO

|  | Month 1 $000 | Month 2 $000 | Month 3 $000 | Month 4 $000 |
|---|---|---|---|---|
| **Cash inflow** |  |  |  |  |
| Cash from sales | 35 | 42 | 36 | 47 |
| Total cash inflow | 35 | 42 | 36 | 47 |
| **Cash outflow** |  |  |  |  |
| Expenses | 33 | 46 | 53 | 35 |
| Total cash outflow | 33 | 46 | 53 | 35 |
| Net cash flow | 2 | (–4) | (–17) | 12 |
| Opening balance | 11 | 13 | 9 | (–8) |
| **Closing balance** | 13 | 9 | (–8) | 4 |

Having discussed the cash flow forecast, the management of AGO plan to take the following actions:

- Offer an early payment discount to some of their most important customers. They expect that this will improve the cash inflow by $1 000 in months 1 and 2 and by $2 000 in months 3 and 4.
- In month 3 they were planning to replace one of their delivery vehicles with a newer model. They have decided to look at other ways of financing this purchase. They are considering leasing the vehicle instead of an outright cash purchase. This will reduce cash outflows in month 3 by $8 000, but increase the cash outflow in month 4 by $2 000, when the first quarter lease payment will be due.

1. Use the information above to amend AGO's cash flow forecast.
2. Comment on your amended cash flow forecast.
3. Do you think the management of AGO were right to use a lease to finance the new delivery vehicle? Justify your answer.

## CASE STUDY 22.2

### Toys"R"Us

**Figure 22.4:** Toys"R"Us used to sell baby furniture but then changed to specialise in toys

Founded in the 1950s, Toys"R"Us originally sold baby furniture until the focus of the company changed to toy sales. The company grew and stores carried the brands families demanded, such as the Star Wars franchise, which helped fuel the remarkable growth of this company.

In 2017, however, Toys"R"Us filed for bankruptcy (a legal process where a court creates a plan for selling off assets to repay the company's debts over time) as they had run out of cash. Financial experts give many reasons as to why this could have happened.

One reason relates to the seasonal nature of the toy business where more than 40% of the company's sales comes in during the last four months of the year. In 2013, snow and rain caused a nearly 9% decline (compared to the previous year) in US store foot traffic. So, they tried to compensate for it and attract tourists by keeping their Times Square store open every day for 24 hours from 1st December to Christmas Eve.

However, this required an additional 45 000 seasonal workers to help keep the stores open. Combined with lower sales due to bad weather, this caused a financial disaster that was hard to overcome.

Other contributing reasons include the changing nature of what children wanted and the growing popularity of ecommerce. As toys and entertainment were becoming more electronic, they had to be innovative in designing new products and smart in marketing them to keep up with the growing competition from retailers, such as Target and Walmart. They also had to keep up with the changing technology and start embracing ecommerce.

**Discuss in pairs or groups:**

1. How do you think the seasonal nature of the toy business affected Toys"R"Us' cash flow in 2013?

2. What impact did hiring 45 000 additional workers have on the cash flow of the company at the time?

3. How would changing market trends like electronic toys have impacted Toys"R"Us' cash flows at the time?

4. How did the growing popularity of ecommerce have affected their cash flows at the time?

5. How did growing competition from retailers have affected Toys"R"Us' marketing strategies? How did this impact their cash flow at the time?

6. Which of the above reasons do you think was the most important in the company filing for bankruptcy? Explain your reasons to your partner.

## 22.5 Financing a short-term cash shortage

If a business knows in advance that there is going to be a period of cash shortage, it can take action to try to prevent this from happening. If possible, managers need to find some solutions. There are several ways a business can overcome a short-term cash flow problem, including:

- delaying payments to suppliers: negotiating longer credit terms with suppliers would reduce cash outflows in the short term, but the business may miss out on discounts offered for prompt payment.
- reducing the credit period for customers: the business will receive cash sooner, which will increase cash inflows, but this could upset customers, who may decide to shop elsewhere.
- obtaining overdraft from the bank, which will allow the business to spend more cash than is currently in its bank account, allowing it to pay some cash outflows.
- delaying the purchase of non-current assets: this would delay cash outflows until the cash flow position improves.

Any solution to cash flow problems may have possible negative effects on the business. For example, obtaining a bank overdraft would help with the cash flow position but there will be an interest cost as well.

**Example**

As shown in the cash forecast in Table 22.1, greater outflows than inflows in February contribute to a negative closing balance.

Let us assume that the payments for February include the purchase of a new delivery van at a cost of $16 000. If the decision to buy this vehicle is delayed by one month, then the amended cash flow forecast will look like the one shown in Table 22.4.

**Table 22.4:** Amended cash flow forecast (in thousands $)

|  | Jan | Feb | Mar |
|---|---|---|---|
| **Cash inflows** | | | |
| Revenue | 10 | 19 | 28 |
| Loan | 5 | | |
| Total cash inflow | 15 | 19 | 28 |
| **Cash outflows** | | | |
| Payments to suppliers | 7 | 11 | 12 |
| Wages/salaries | 6 | 7 | 8 |
| Total cash outflows | 13 | 18 | 20 |
| **Net cash flow** | 2 | 1 | 8 |
| Opening balance | 5 | 7 | 8 |
| **Closing balance** | 7 | 8 | 16 |

Delaying the purchase of the delivery vehicle improves the cash flow by removing the negative cash balance in February. If the business cannot delay the purchase of the delivery van by one month it has two options:

- Use another source of finance for the purchase of the van, for example, hire purchase, leasing or a bank loan.
- As the cash shortage is forecast to be very short term, the business may arrange an overdraft with the bank to cover the shortfall.

Both options are costlier than delaying the purchase of the vehicle until March.

> **LINK**
>
> You can find more information about hire purchase, bank loans and overdrafts in Chapter 19.

## BUSINESS IN ACTION

### Business ideas

**Figure 22.5:** Selling cakes at a school event is one possible business idea

Shark Tank India is a popular TV show that shows entrepreneurs making business presentations to a panel of venture capitalists (investors in start-ups), called "sharks" on the program, in order to convince them to invest in their business ventures. Other countries have similar TV shows that provide a platform for entrepreneurs to showcase their business ideas and seek investment; Dragons' Den is another such program.

Working in groups, come up with a business idea. You could even use the business idea that you came up with in Chapter 21 or think of a simple business idea to raise funds for your school in one of your school events, for example, selling food and drinks or old books and toys.

**Discuss in pairs or groups:**

1. Use the internet to estimate your revenue and payments.
2. Work out the costs involved and come up with an estimate of how much start-up capital would be required.
3. Using the template shown in Table 22.5, fill in the estimated receipts and payments for the cash forecast. There are empty rows in the cash inflows and cash outflow sections for you to add your own items.
4. What is the total cash outflows?
5. What is the total cash inflows?
6. What is the net cash flow in the first month?
7. How could you improve the net cash flow?

You could use the template below or create a similar one using spreadsheet software.

**Table 22.5:** Cash forecast for the first month

|  | Month 1 |
|---|---|
| **Cash inflows** |  |
| Revenue |  |
|  |  |
| Total cash inflow |  |
| **Cash outflows** |  |
| Payments |  |
|  |  |
| Total cash outflow |  |
| **Net cash flow** |  |
|  |  |

## ACTIVITY 22.5

Betsy has a bookshop in Lilongwe, Malawi. The cash flow forecast (in thousands $) shown in Table 22.6 shows that her revenue mainly consists of the sales of her books. She bought a huge stock in November, just before the Christmas season, and received 30 days credit for the books she bought.

Table 22.6: Cash flow forecast for Betsy's bookshop

|  | November | December | January | February |
|---|---|---|---|---|
| **Cash inflows** | | | | |
| Cash sales | 6000 | 12000 | 2000 | 2000 |
| Bank loan | | | | 2000 |
| Sale of unused assets | | | 2000 | |
| Total cash inflow | 6000 | 12000 | 4000 | 4000 |
| **Cash outflows** | | | | |
| Stock | 2000 | 5100 | 3000 | 2000 |
| Rent | 500 | 500 | 500 | 500 |
| Gas and electricity | 200 | 400 | 200 | 200 |
| Wages | 2500 | 4000 | 3000 | 3000 |
| Total cash outflow | 5700 | 10000 | 6700 | 5700 |
| **Net cash flow** | 300 | 2000 | (2700) | (1700) |
| Opening balance | 200 | 500 | 2500 | (200) |
| **Closing balance** | 500 | 2500 | (200) | (2000) |

Discuss with a partner:

1. Why do you think the sales are the greatest in December?
2. Why do you think the money spent on wages is higher in December?
3. Why is there a greater outflow of cash on buying stock in December when the books are bought in November?
4. Why do you think she sold her unused assets in January?
5. Why is rent an easy item to forecast?
6. Why is the February closing balance a worry for Betsy?
7. Betsy has a negative closing balance in February. What could she do to solve the cash flow problem?
8. Why is this cash flow forecast useful for Betsy?

> BUSINESS FOR CAMBRIDGE IGCSE™ AND O LEVEL: COURSEBOOK

### REFLECTION

How did completing this activity support you in improving your ability to interpret cash flow forecasts? How did relating Betsy's forecast cash inflow and forecast cash outflow to real-life scenarios such as Christmas help your understanding of how cash inflows and cash outflows can vary and how they can be better managed? Discuss your answers with another pair. Did they have similar answers?

### SUMMARY

You should now know:

- The management of cash is important to a business because it must have enough cash coming in to cover the cash leaving the business.
- Cash flow forecasts can be used to show the timing of cash inflows and cash outflows and identify any periods of time when the business might have a cash shortage.
- There are several ways a business can solve or reduce cash flow problems including measures to increase cash inflows or delay cash outflows.

## Chapter 22 practice questions

1. Mark and Jack are brothers and business partners. In September 2023, they opened a stationery shop, MJS. Although the business has been profitable in its first two months, the business does not always have enough money to pay its suppliers. Their younger sister, Lydia, has produced the cash flow forecast, as shown in Table 22.7, for the first two months of 2024. She has told her brothers that this will help them avoid cash flow problems. Mark does not think the business has a cash flow problem as it is making a profit.

   a Use the cash flow forecast to calculate the value of **A** and **B**. [2]

   b Identify **two** ways a business can increase cash inflows and **two** ways it can decrease cash outflows. [4]

   c Explain how **two** of MJS's stakeholder groups might be affected by its cash flow problems. [6]

   d Explain **two** ways MJS could overcome its cash flow problem. Which way should MJS use? Justify your answer. [8]

**Table 22.7:** MJS's cash flow forecast for January–February 2024 (in thousands $)

|  | Jan | Feb |
|---|---|---|
| **Cash inflows** | | |
| Cash sales | 160 | 80 |
| **Cash sales** | | |
| Owner's capital and loans | 550 | 810 |
| Total cash inflows | 710 | 890 |
| **Cash outflows** | | |
| Cash purchases | 520 | 800 |
| Shop rent | 150 | 150 |
| Other expenses | 30 | 30 |
| Total cash outflow | 700 | 980 |
| **Net cash flow** | A | (90) |
| Opening balance | (70) | (60) |
| **Closing balance** | (60) | B |

2  Mobil Phones (MPL) sells mobile phones. The Finance Manager has produced a cash flow forecast for the next three months of trading for MPL. An extract is shown in Table 22.8. He has not completed the forecast for February and March. MPL buys its goods from a new supplier and is trying to negotiate a 15 days' credit period on the items. The Finance Manager is confident that MPL is doing well because in March, the demand increased, the sales nearly doubled and the business is making profits. MPL allows 30 days' credit on all items purchased by customers.

**Table 22.8:** Simplified cash flow forecast for MPL for the next three months of trading (in thousands $)

|  | Month 1 | Month 2 | Month 3 |
|---|---|---|---|
| **Cash inflow** | | | |
| Credit sales | 230 | 250 | 400 |
| Cash sales | 200 | 230 | 200 |
| Total inflow | 200 | 230 | 200 |
| **Cash outflow** | | | |
| Payments | 160 | 250 | 350 |
| **Net cash flow** | 40 | (20) | B |
| Opening balance | 20 | 60 | C |
| **Closing balance** | 60 | A | D |

a   Explain **one** problem that may be caused by poor cash flow in MPL.  [2]

b   Calculate the values of A, B, C and D to complete the cash flow forecast for Month 2 and Month 3.  [4]

c   Explain **two** reasons why MPL might be facing cash flow problems.  [6]

d   Explain **two** ways the Finance Manager might use this forecast to improve MPL's cash flow over the coming months. Which is the best way? Justify your answer.  [8]

**Total available marks 40**

## CHECK YOUR PROGRESS

How well do you think you have achieved the learning intentions for this chapter? Give yourself a score from 1 (still need a lot of practice) to 5 (feeling very confident) for each learning intention. Provide an example to support your score.

| Now I can … | Score | Example |
|---|---|---|
| explain the importance of cash to businesses | | |
| discuss what a cash flow forecast is and why it is important | | |
| identify the main features of a cash flow forecast | | |
| amend, complete and interpret a cash flow forecast | | |
| outline how businesses deal with short-term cash flow problems. | | |

# Chapter 23
# Statement of profit or loss

## LEARNING INTENTIONS

By the end of this chapter, you will be able to:

- understand what profit is and why it is important
- understand the main features of a statement of profit or loss
- make calculations based on a statement of profit or loss
- make decisions based on a statement of profit or loss.

## BUSINESS IN CONTEXT

### The Body Shop

**Figure 23.1:** The Body Shop faced a lot of competition from emerging natural beauty brands

The Body Shop was set up by Dame Anita Roddick in 1976 with a promise to sell natural cosmetics that were sustainable and had not been tested on animals. However, after years of success, what was once The Body Shop's unique selling point became a norm in the cosmetics industry. So The Body Shop started facing a lot of competition from the emerging natural beauty brands, including Lush, Rituals and L'Occitane and its profits started to fall.

Despite being bought by a famous brand like L'Oréal in 2006, The Body Shop's performance continued to decline and it was sold to the Brazilian cosmetics group Natura in 2017. At the time, The Body Shop's gross profits had plunged 38% with sales down 5%. However, under Natura's ownership, the struggling brand came out with new products, new store concepts, international expansion, a revamped look and refillable stations across its stores in the UK and the US. Despite these efforts, soaring production costs, consumers struggling with affordability, weakness in its US operations and challenges faced by the retail industry, it suffered a loss of millions. In 2023, Natura sold The Body Shop to Aurelius.

In March 2024, however, The Body Shop filed for bankruptcy (the business owed more money than it had available for payment), failing to pay its suppliers, employees and creditors. The next step for The Body Shop is to restructure its operations by cutting costs and it is doing this by letting go of some of its staff and closing some shops.

**Discuss in pairs or groups:**

1. What were the main reasons for The Body Shop's success when it first started?
2. What were the main reasons for The Body Shop's reducing profits and then eventually making losses?

# Introduction

The main objective of all private sector businesses is to earn a profit.

In this chapter, you will learn what is profit and why it is important. You will look at the main features of a statement of profit or loss and how the information it contains is used in decision-making by the business to see how well the business is doing. The statement of profit or loss is also used when applying for finance.

## 23.1 What is profit and why is it important?

Profit is the difference between total **revenue** and **total costs**.

There are three types of profit:

- **Gross profit** – the difference between the revenue earned from selling products and the cost of making those products.

### KEY TERMS

**revenue:** the amount earned from the sale of products or services.

**total cost:** all the variable and fixed costs of producing the total output.

**gross profit:** the difference between revenue and cost of sales.

- **Profit** – the difference between the revenue from sales and total costs or the difference between gross profit and expenses. Profit used to be called 'net profit'.
- Retained profit – the owners of a profitable business may decide to reinvest some of the profits in the business.

## The difference between profit and cash

In Chapter 22, we looked at the importance of cash to a business, and in this chapter, we look at the importance of profit. Many new businesses make a profit, but they will not survive very long if they do not manage their cash well. Businesses often fail because their owners do not understand the difference between cash and profit.

The business scenarios in Table 23.1 highlight some of the differences between cash and profit.

> **KEY TERM**
>
> **profit:** the difference between revenue and total costs.

> **LINKS**
>
> For more information on retained profit, see Chapter 22, and total cost see Chapter 16.

Table 23.1: The differences between cash and profit

| Business scenario | Impact on profit | Impact on cash flow |
|---|---|---|
| Money is invested in a business, or borrowed by a business | Does not increase profit | There is a cash inflow and so the net cash flow value increases |
| Sale of goods (produced by the business) on credit | Revenue is recorded in the statement of profit or loss as soon as the goods are sold, increasing the profit | Cash inflow does not increase until the buyer pays for the goods. |
| Raw materials bought on credit | Cost of raw materials is recorded in the statement of profit or loss as soon as the goods are sold, decreasing the profit | There is no cash outflow until the business pays for the raw materials |
| Interest payment on loan | Interest payment is recorded in the statement of profit or loss as soon as it is paid decreasing the profit | There is a cash outflow as soon as the interest is paid |

It is important for owners and managers to remember that cash pays the day-to-day expenses, not profit. Cash is always important for the business; profit becomes more important for the long-term success of the business.

## The importance of profit to private sector businesses

Profit is one of the main objectives of private sector businesses and is important for several reasons.

- **Measure the success of a business** – A profitable business generates more revenue than it spends on expenses, which helps in ensuring its success in the long term.

> **LINK**
>
> For more information on private sector businesses, see Chapter 2.

- **As a source of finance** – For the purchase of non-current assets and investing in the business.
- **Reward for risk-taking** – Profit can act as an incentive to the owners to take the risk to start up the business. It can help attract new investors and encourage existing investors to provide capital to the business for further investment and growth.

### ACTIVITY 23.1

Consider the information contained in Table 23.2.

**Table 23.2:** Information for companies A, B and C

|  | Revenue | Profit | Dividend per share | Retained profit |
| --- | --- | --- | --- | --- |
| Company A | $340 000 | $95 000 | $2.00 | $15 000 |
| Company B | $260 000 | $101 000 | $1.60 | $27 000 |
| Company C | $570 000 | $130 000 | $1.30 | $76 000 |

Work in small groups to discuss the following:

1. Which of the three companies do you think has been the most successful and why?
2. Assume you are a shareholder in one of these companies. Giving reasons:
   a. Which company would you choose as a short-term investment?
   b. Would you choose a different company if you were looking for a long-term investment?

## 23.2 Statement of profit or loss

A **statement of profit or loss** is a financial record of business revenue, costs and profit over a period (usually a year). It must be produced at least once a year by all businesses, but it may be produced more frequently for use by managers.

### Features of a statement of profit or loss

The statement of profit or loss (see Table 23.3) contains the main components that are required for calculating profit.

> **KEY TERM**
>
> **statement of profit or loss:** a financial statement that records the revenue, costs and profits of a business for a given period.

Table 23.3: Sample statement of profit or loss

| Statement of profit or loss of XYZ for the Year 2024 | |
|---|---|
| Revenue | $150 000 |
| Cost of sales | $70 000 |
| Gross profit | $80 000 |
| | |
| Expenses | $30 000 |
| | |
| Profit | $50 000 |

## Revenue

The total amount of money a business earns from selling its products is called revenue.

The formula for calculating revenue is:

$$\text{Revenue} = \text{selling price per unit} \times \text{number of units sold}$$

## Total cost

For a statement of profit or loss, the total cost to a business of supplying its goods and services can be divided into **cost of sales** and **expenses**. The formula for the total cost is:

$$\text{Total cost} = \text{cost of sales} + \text{expenses}$$

## Cost of sales

These are the direct expenses incurred by a business in producing goods or services, for example, the cost of raw materials and labour costs.

## Gross profit

This is the difference between the revenue earned from selling products and the cost of making those products. The formula for calculating gross profit is:

$$\text{Gross profit} = \text{revenue} - \text{cost of sales}$$

## Expenses

Also known as overheads, these are the costs incurred by the business that are not directly related to the production or selling of goods and services. The expenses that can be incurred by a business are shown in Figure 23.2.

## Profit

A business earns a profit by selling its products to customers at a price that is higher than the total cost of making and supplying those products.

The profit formula is:

$$\text{Profit} = \text{revenue} - \text{total costs}$$

or

$$\text{Profit} = \text{gross profit} - \text{expenses}$$

> **KEY TERMS**
>
> **cost of sales:** the cost of purchasing the raw materials/goods and packaging for producing or selling of products and services.
>
> **expenses:** the costs that are not directly linked to the production or the selling of products and services.

Statements of profit or loss are usually more detailed including the components of cost of sales and expenses as shown in Activity 23.2.

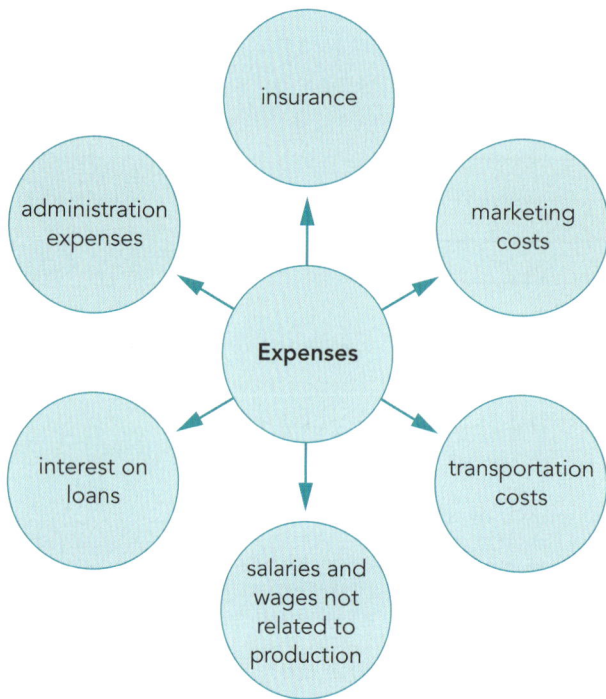

Figure 23.2: Expenses that can be incurred by a business

> ### DISCUSSION
>
> Chata owns a small bakery. He only makes bread. Chata's main items of expenditure are listed below. Discuss whether each of these items would be classified as 'cost of sales' or 'expenses':
>
> - flour
> - electricity
> - yeast
> - rent
> - advertising
> - water
> - machinery repairs
> - salt
> - insurance for the bakery.

# 23 Statement of profit or loss

### ACTIVITY 23.2

Table 23.4: Statement of profit or loss of XYZ for the year 2024

| Statement of profit or loss of XYZ for the year 2024 | |
|---|---|
| Revenue | $150 000 |
| Cost of sales | $70 000 |
| Gross profit | $80 000 |
| Rent | $15 000 |
| Insurance | $7 000 |
| Advertising expenses | |
| Expenses | $30 000 |
| Profit | $50 000 |

1. Fill in the missing value for advertising expenses.
2. How can the additional information in the detailed statement of profit or loss be useful to a business?

When interpreting the statement of profit or loss, it is useful to compare the business' performance over a period or with competitors.

## Making simple calculations based on a statement of profit or loss

The example below shows how the different components of the statement of profit or loss can be calculated using the specified formulae.

**Example**

Chata sells the loaves of bread he makes in his bakery for $0.30 each. In June, Chata sold 1500 loaves of bread. He has calculated his cost of sales for June to be $150 and his expenses for the month to be $100.

We can use this information to calculate Chata's gross profit or loss for June.

Chata's revenue will be calculated using the formula:

$$\text{Revenue} = \text{selling price per loaf} \times \text{quantity of loaves sold}$$
$$= \$0.30 \times 1\,500$$
$$= \$450$$

> **LINKS**
>
> For more information on stakeholders, see Chapter 5, and retained profit as a source of finance see Chapter 19.

Chata's gross profit will be calculated using the formula:

Gross profit = revenue − cost of sales
= $450 − $150
= $300

Chata's profit will be calculated using the formula:

Profit = gross profit − expenses
= $300 − $100
= $200

**Note:** If we only wanted to calculate Chata's profit without calculating gross profit, then we could have used the formula:

Profit = revenue − total costs
Profit = $450 − ($150 + $100)
= $200

### ACTIVITY 23.3

Table 23.5 shows Chata's sales and costs for the first six months of 2024.

**Table 23.5:** Chata's sales and costs, January–June 2024

|  | January | February | March | April | May | June |
|---|---|---|---|---|---|---|
| Revenue ($) | 1 600 | 1 580 | 1 550 | 1 530 | 1 520 | 1 500 |
| Cost of sales ($) | 160 | 158 | 155 | 153 | 152 | 150 |
| Expenses ($) | 100 | 100 | 100 | 100 | 100 | 100 |

1. Calculate Chata's revenue for the six-month period from January to June.
2. Calculate Chata's gross profit and profit for the same six-month period.
3. Explain why Chata's cost of sales changes each month but the expenses remain the same.
4. Give two reasons that might explain why Chata's sales of bread have fallen between January and June.

> **TIP**
>
> You will not be asked in IGCSE/O Level Business to construct a statement of profit or loss, but you must know how to interpret one and make simple calculations based on it.

## CASE STUDY 23.1

**Canva**

Figure 23.3: Canva is an online design and publishing tool

Canva was founded in 2012 in Australia by Melanie Perkins, her husband Clifford Obrecht and others. It is an online design and publishing tool with a mission to empower everyone in the world to design anything and publish anywhere. In its first year, Canva had more than 750 000 users and it now has users in more than 190 countries.

It has reached profitability for the sixth year in a row and achieved high growth for several years. The company is a private limited company and has been reinvesting its profits into the business for expansion. The graphic design market globally is growing steadily and currently stands at about $45 billion, and in 2023, Canva's revenue was $1.7 billion. In 2023, Melanie and her husband were named among the wealthiest people in Australia.

Looking to growth in the future, in March 2023 Canva announced its new artificial intelligence (AI) enabled Assistant tool, which makes recommendations on graphics and styles that match the user's existing design. It is also hoping to offer shares to the public and become a public limited company by 2025–2026. Investment from venture capital firms from time to time has helped with its expansion.

**Discuss in pairs or groups:**

1  Define profit.
2  Explain two reasons why profit has been important to Canva.
3  How have the founders and shareholders of Canva benefitted from the company's success?
4  Would investment from venture capital firms affect Canvas' profitability?
5  How would Canva benefit from becoming a public limited company?

# Uses of statements of profit or loss to make decisions

The main aim of many private sector businesses is to increase profits. Reviewing their statements of profit or loss can help businesses with their decision-making so that they can achieve their targets. The statement of profit or loss is used in the following ways to inform business decision-making.

1  To assess how well the business has performed: To see if the business has made the revenue it aimed to achieve.
2  To review the costs and take corrective action: If a business feels that the cost of sales is very high or if the expenses are very high then it can take actions to control expenses and improve profitability.
3  To identify which products or services are generating the most revenue for the business. A business might decide to stop manufacturing products that are not generating enough revenue. This will also help them make informed decisions about pricing.

> **TIP**
>
> Think of why things happen in real life when explaining why there may have been changes in profits, revenue and costs for a business.

4   To compare performance over time.
5   To compare performance against competitors.
6   To calculate gross profit margin.
7   To calculate profit margin.

> **LINK**
>
> You will learn about gross profit margin and profit margin in Chapter 25.

## CASE STUDY 23.2

**BUA Cement**

**Figure 23.4:** BUA Cement is Nigeria's second larger cement producer

BUA Cement, Nigeria's second-largest cement producer, saw its profit drop in the first nine months of 2023. Though the firm's revenue grew by 27.8% in the same period of 2022 due to increase in price per tonne in the cement industry, it had high operating costs and finance expenses.

The cost of sales was up by 30.5%. Energy cost accounted for 44% of the cost of sales, which reflects the worldwide increase in energy costs and the cost of materials increased by 47.3%. High interest rates have led to an increase in finance costs.

**Discuss in pairs or groups:**

1   Define cost of sales.
2   Define expenses as they may appear in the statement of profit or loss of BUA Cement.
3   What could have caused an increase in revenue for BUA Cement?
4   What are the two main reasons for an increase in the cost of sales for BUA Cement?
5   What are the main reasons for the decrease in profits of BUA Cement from 2022 to 2023 despite the increase in revenue?

## BUSINESS IN ACTION

**Alibaba**

**Figure 23.5:** Alibaba is one of the most successful ecommerce service providers in China

The internet was still new to most Chinese consumers and businesses when the Alibaba Group was founded in 1999. However, it has profited a lot from the rapid development of the internet and the ecommerce in the last 20 years and has become one of the most successful ecommerce service providers in China.

Since 2023, however, its revenue is not growing at the same rate. Table 23.6 shows the value (in billions) as well as percentage change in the revenue and gross profit from the previous year.

Due to new regulation in the technology sector by the Chinese government and ecommerce becoming more competitive in China, Alibaba is

### CONTINUED

**Table 23.6:** Showing the change in revenue and gross profit for Alibaba

| Financial indicator | 2021 (in billions) | 2022 (in billions) | 2023 (in billions) |
|---|---|---|---|
| Annual revenue | $110 (52% increase) | $135 (23% increase) | $126 (6% decline) |
| Gross profit | $45 (41% increase) | $49 (9% increase) | $46 (6% decline) |

also exploring new areas for its revenue increase. For instance, it invested in the Chinese courier company STO Express in 2019. It did this to pursue its goal of 24-hour delivery anywhere in China and 72 hours globally.

Alibaba's growth strategy now focuses on affordability, improving the user experience and connecting small- to medium-sized merchants with customers. They are hoping that when this is fully in place it will also make them more competitive.

**Discuss in pairs or groups:**

1. Define revenue.
2. Define gross profit.

In groups, discuss the questions below, applying the information provided above to your understanding of profit and its importance to various stakeholders:

3. What world event do you think would have caused an increase in revenue of 52% for Alibaba? Explain your answer.
4. Why do you think Alibaba's revenue declined in 2023?
5. What impact has the decrease in revenue had on the gross profits in 2023?
6. Do you think the costs would have increased in 2023 as compared to 2022?
7. What impact would the decline in revenue and gross profit have on the following Alibaba stakeholders?
   a  Shareholders
   b  Employees
   c  Lenders
8. What steps is Alibaba taking to increase its revenue?

## ACTIVITY 23.4

Below are the statements of profit or loss of Company X that produces cheese. Half way through the year, it had to take an overdraft of $5 000 to meet its cash flow needs.

**Statements of profit or loss for Company X for 2022 and 2023**

|  | 2022 (in $) | 2023 (in $) |
|---|---|---|
| Revenue | 80 000 | 75 000 |
| Cost of sales | 39 000 | 41 000 |
| Gross profit |  |  |
| Electricity | 2 000 | 2 000 |
| Transportation | 1 000 | 1 500 |
| Interest costs | 500 | 2 000 |
| Total expenses | 3 500 | 5 500 |
| Profit |  |  |

Working in a group, discuss the following:

1. Calculate the values for the gross profit and the profit for both years.
2. Why is profit important to a business such as Company X?
3. Why do you think Company X had to take an overdraft?
4. What is the difference between cash and profit?
5. What will be the impact of increasing expenses on the net cash flow of Company X?

## REFLECTION

Think about Activity 23.4. What did you learn from completing the activity? Did it encourage you to think about the uses of a statement of profit or loss? Can you think of any ways of memorising the formulae for calculating gross profit and profit?

> **SUMMARY**
>
> You should now know:
>
> - Profit is the difference between the revenue earned from sales and all the costs of producing and distributing the goods and services sold.
>
> - Profit is the return to owners/shareholders as a reward for risking their investment in the business. Some of the profit will be paid to owners and some will be retained in the business to finance future operations and plans.
>
> - The statement of profit or loss shows how the gross profit and the profit of a business have been calculated. This information is useful when making decisions.

# Chapter 23 practice questions

1. Consider the information provided below for Amber Trading, a manufacturer of LED lights, which use less electricity and are longer-lasting. It has had sustained growth in the last five years and now has over 200 employees. It has the most market share in the LED lights industry and wants to expand next year. It is hoping to raise finance by issuing shares.

    **Statement of profit or loss ($)**

    |  | Previous year | Current year |
    |---|---|---|
    | Revenue | 83 000 | 95 000 |
    | Cost of sales | 32 000 | 35 000 |
    | Gross profit | A | 60 000 |
    | Expenses | 20 000 | 20 000 |
    | Profit | 31 000 | B |
    | Retained profit | 13 000 | 20 000 |

    a. Define 'gross profit'. [2]

    b. Calculate the value of A and B in the statement of profit or loss above. [4]

    c. Explain **two** uses of Amber Trading's statement of profit or loss to any **two** stakeholder groups. [6]

    d. Do you think investors will see buying shares of Amber Trading as a good investment? Justify your answer. [8]

2  Bathware is a manufacturer of highly priced modern bathroom fittings. It uses different suppliers to obtain components or parts that it needs. Bathware is considering being loyal to just one supplier to get bulk discounts and reduce cost. The data below shows Bathware's revenue and profit data for the various products it manufactures. The market for modern bath fittings was $1 200 000 in 2023 and in 2024 it rose to $1 500 000.

|  | Bathware's financial data in 2023 | Bathware's financial data in 2024 |
|---|---|---|
| Revenue | 10% share of the market $120 000 | 5% share of the market $75 000 |
| Cost of sales | $50 000 | $20 000 |
| Gross profit | $70 000 | $55 000 |
| Expenses | $25 000 | $11 000 |
| Profit |  |  |

a  Identify **two** expenses a business might have. [2]

b  Calculate the profit for Bathware for 2023 and 2024. [4]

c  Explain **two** possible reasons for the decrease in Bathware's profits between 2023 and 2024. [6]

d  Do you think reducing costs is the best way for Bathware to increase its profit? Justify your answer. [8]

Total available marks: 40

## CHECK YOUR PROGRESS

How well do you think you have achieved the learning intentions for this chapter? Give yourself a score from 1 (still need a lot of practice) to 5 (feeling very confident about this) for each learning intention. Provide an example to support your score.

| Now I can … | Score | Example |
|---|---|---|
| explain what profit is and why it is important |  |  |
| outline the main features of a statement of profit or loss |  |  |
| make calculations based on a statement of profit or loss |  |  |
| make decisions based on a statement of profit or loss. |  |  |

# Chapter 24
# Statement of financial position

**LEARNING INTENTIONS**

By the end of this chapter, you will be able to:
- understand the main parts of a statement of financial position
- outline the difference between assets and liabilities
- calculate the total assets, the total liabilities and the working capital from the statement of financial position
- understand the concept of capital employed
- make decisions based on statements of financial position.

## Introduction

As the name suggests, a statement of financial position is a snapshot of a business's financial position at a certain point in time. In this chapter, you will study the main parts of a statement of financial position and understand what stakeholders can learn about the business from the information contained in this statement. The statement of financial position is a record of a business's assets and liabilities and the amount of money the owners have invested (owner's/shareholder's equity). The statement also shows how a business finances its operations. Limited companies must, by law, produce a statement of financial position at the end of every financial year, but other types of business often choose to do so too. It provides useful information about a company's financial position at a point in time, which helps the company's stakeholders assess the company's ability to meet its financial obligations and make decisions accordingly.

> **LINK**
>
> You can find more information about stakeholders in Chapter 5.

### BUSINESS IN CONTEXT

**Mark Wang**

Figure 24.1: Solar panels and wind turbines are green technologies

Mark Wang believes in improving and protecting the quality of the natural environment and wants to invest some money in companies that focus on climate concerns and improving the environment. He believes that investing in companies that have a positive social impact is not only moral but also a smart investment decision in our changing world. With growing awareness of how business decisions affect our environment, companies that are more environmentally friendly are likely to do better.

Mark has been gathering information on companies that are involved in green technology, renewable sources of energy and providing solutions to environmental problems. Mark has also been looking at the statement of financial position for various companies to understand their financial health and evaluate their potential as an investment. He has looked at some key components of the statements of financial position such as:

- the amount invested in property and equipment to assess how much is the investment in non-current assets
- the amount of non-current liabilities, such as mortgages and other long-term loans, in order to evaluate the company's ability to pay its debts and the terms of its debt agreements.

Mark also feels that it is important to look at the current assets and current liabilities that are shown in the statement of financial position. He wants to make an investment decision after looking at the future prospects as well as non-financial information about a company.

**Discuss in pairs or groups:**

1. Why it is important for Mark to look at the current assets and liabilities of a business before investing in it?
2. Why should Mark not just rely on the statement of financial position before investing?

# 24.1 The main parts of a statement of financial position

The main elements of a **statement of financial position** are **assets** and **liabilities** as shown in Figure 24.2. The statement reflects the company's assets and how they are financed by liabilities, as well as showing the overall value of the business. This ensures that all the resources of the business are accounted for and nothing is missing.

> **KEY TERMS**
>
> **statement of financial position:** an accounting statement that records the assets, liabilities and owners' equity of a business on a particular date.
>
> **assets:** resources that are owned by a business.
>
> **liabilities:** debts of the business that will have to be paid sometime in the future.

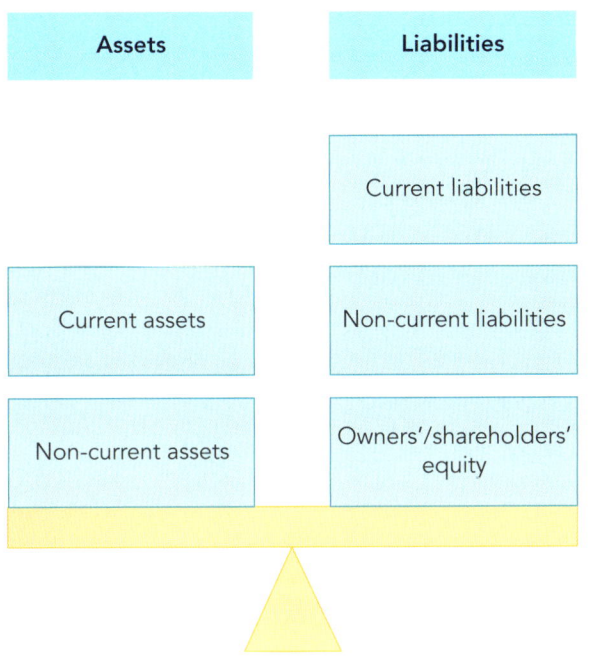

**Figure 24.2:** Main elements of a statement of financial position

The layout and main parts of a statement of financial position that you need to know for IGCSE/O Level Business are shown in Table 24.1.

**Table 24.1:** Extract from Tang Toys' Statement of financial position at 31 December 2023 (in thousands $)

| | |
|---|---|
| Non-current assets | 100 |
| Current assets | 50 |
| Current liabilities | (30) |
| | 20 |
| **Net assets** | **120** |
| Financed by: | |
| Owner's equity | 90 |
| Non-current liabilities | 30 |
| **Capital employed** | **120** |

> **TIP**
>
> Think back to your understanding of cash flow management in Chapter 22 in order to understand the significance of current assets and current liabilities.

> **DISCUSSION**
>
> Using the statement of financial position shown in Table 24.1, discuss the following with your partner and share your ideas with the class:
>
> 1 Explain why a statement of financial position is sometimes called a 'balance sheet'.
>
> 2 Which other financial term shows the difference between current assets and current liabilities?

## Assets

Assets are any resources that a business owns. They can be divided into non-current assets and current assets, as shown in Figure 24.3.

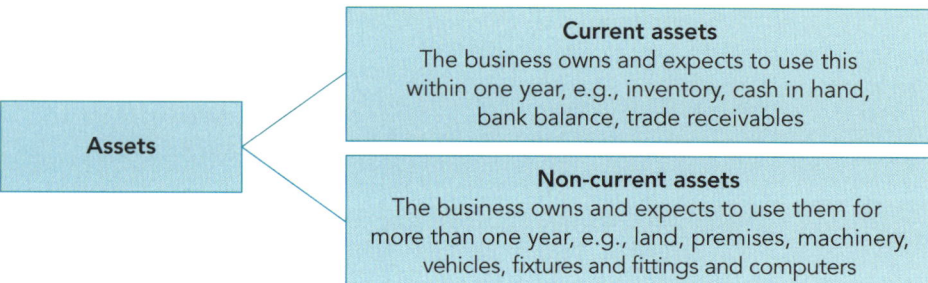

Figure 24.3: Different types of current and non-current assets

> **LINKS**
>
> You can find more information about trade receivables in Chapter 19, and liquidity in Chapter 23.

### Current assets

**Current assets** are cash or any other resources owned by the business that it expects to convert into cash within the next 12 months. The most common examples of current assets are inventories, **trade receivables** and cash. Current assets are very important to businesses because they are an important source of liquidity.

### Non-current assets

**Non-current assets** are resources that the business owns and expects to use for more than one year. These are longer-term or one-time buy items, including property, machinery, computers and vehicles.

Total assets is the sum of non-current assets and current assets. For example, using the data from Table 24.1, present as formula:

Total assets = non-current assets + current assets

Total assets = $100 000 + $50 000 = $150 000

> **KEY TERMS**
>
> **current assets:** resources that the business owns, which it will have for less than one year.
>
> **trade receivables:** the amount of money owed to the business by customers who have been sold goods on credit.
>
> **non-current assets:** resources that a business owns and expects to use for more than one year.

## Liabilities

Liabilities are the amounts owed by the business to stakeholders such as suppliers and lenders.

**Owner's equity** is the amount of money that has been invested in the business by the owners. This includes money brought into the business by the owners plus any retained profit. For a limited company these amounts are also known as **shareholders' equity** or shareholders' funds. Owner's equity is considered a liability because it represents the company's obligation to its owners. Owners expect a return on their equity, whether through dividends or retained profits. It is different from liabilities like loans or payables where the company owes money to an external party but it is still a claim on the company's assets—making it part of the broader category of liabilities. The liabilities of a business which it owes to external creditors can be divided into current liabilities and non-current liabilities, as shown in Figure 24.4.

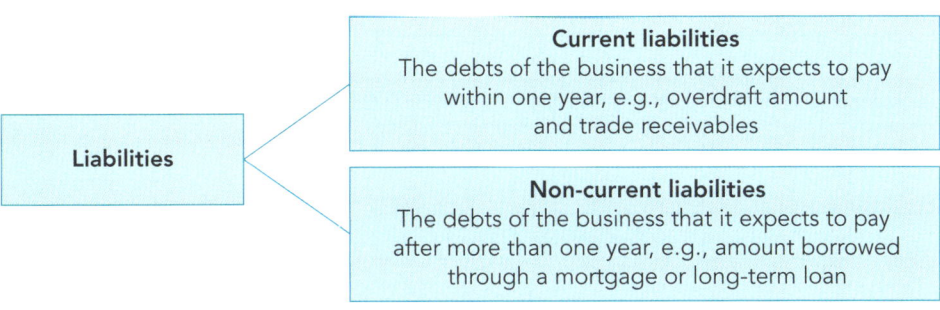

**Figure 24.4:** Different types of current and non-current liabilities

- **Current liabilities** are the short-term debts of a business that it expects to pay within the next year. Examples include **trade payables** (these used to be called 'creditors') and bank overdraft. A business may have to use these to help manage their cash flow.
- **Non-current liabilities** are the debts of a business that it does not expect to repay within the next year, for example, bank loans.

Total liabilities is the sum of current liabilities and non-current liabilities. For example, using the data from Table 24.1:

Total liabilities = non-current liabilities + current liabilities

Total liabilities = $30 000 + $30 000 = $60 000

## Capital employed

**Capital employed** is the total amount of capital invested in a business for the purpose of generating profits. It is the long-term funds used by a company to finance its operations and assets and it is the total of the non-current liabilities and the funds contributed by the owners (or shareholders, for limited companies).

Capital employed = shareholders'/owners' equity + non-current liabilities

### KEY TERMS

**owner's equity:** the amount invested in the business by the owners.

**shareholders' equity:** alternative term for owner's equity, but can only be used by limited liability companies.

**current liabilities:** short-term debts of the business which need to be paid within one year.

**trade payables:** the amount a business owes to its suppliers for goods bought on credit.

**non-current liabilities:** debts of the business which will be payable after more than one year.

**capital employed:** the total amount of capital invested in a business for the purpose of generating profits.

### ACTIVITY 24.1

Copy out Table 24.2.

**Table 24.2:** Categories and elements of a statement of financial position

| Statement item | Non-current asset | Current asset | Current liability | Non-current liability |
|---|---|---|---|---|
| Inventories | | ✓ | | |
| Bank loan | | | | |
| Machinery | | | | |
| Overdraft | | | | |
| Trade receivables | | | | |
| Property | | | | |
| Trade payables | | | | |

Place a tick in the correct column for each statement of financial position item shown in the table. The first has been done for you.

> **TIP**
>
> Statements of profit or loss, statements of financial position and cash-flow forecasts are all referred to as 'financial statements', so if a question simply refers to the 'financial statements', you could refer to any one or all of them depending on which one is given.

## 24.2 Calculations and decisions based on statements of financial position

A statement of financial position can be used to gain a better understanding of the value of a business. This can then be used to make informed decisions about the business. It gives different stakeholders useful information about a business. It shows:

- the value of assets the business owns
- what the business is owed
- the value of liabilities
- what the business owes
- how the business finances its activities.

It also helps to:

- calculate working capital
- calculate current ratio
- calculate acid test ratio
- compare performance with other years
- compare performance against other businesses.

> **TIP**
>
> Learn the definitions of key terms for both the statement of financial position and the statement of profit or loss. Using an example for each will help you explain your understanding.

> **LINKS**
>
> You can find more information about working capital in Chapter 22, and current ratio and acid test ratio in Chapter 25.

Remember that a statement of financial position is only a snapshot of a business's financial position at a particular point in time – the date of the statement. The individual figures can change a lot in a short space of time. Therefore, the statement is not a reliable measure of how much a business is worth.

### ACTIVITY 24.2

Consider the following extract from JB Plastics' statement of financial position (see Table 24.3) as of June 2024.

**Table 24.3:** Statement of financial position for JB Plastics as of June 2024

| Non-current assets | Amounts (in thousands $) |
|---|---|
| Vehicles | 10 |
| Machinery | 60 |
| Property | 30 |
| **Current assets** | |
| Inventory | 15 |
| Trade receivables | 30 |
| Cash | 5 |
| Total current assets | ? |
| **Current liabilities** | |
| Trade payables | 16 |
| **Non-current liabilities** | |
| Bank loan | 30 |

1. What is the value of the amount owed to JB Plastics?
2. What is the value of the amount JB Plastics owes to its suppliers?
3. What is the value of the total current assets owned by JB Plastics?
4. What is the value of the current liabilities of JB Plastics?
5. What is JB Plastics' working capital as of June 2024?
6. What is the statement value of all of the assets that are owned by JB Plastics that it expects to use for more than one year?

### CASE STUDY 24.1

**Chow Tai Fook Jewellery Group**

**Table 24.4:** Extract from Chow Tai Fook Jewellery's Group statement of financial position at 31 December 2023

| Non-current assets | Value in HKD in Millions |
| --- | --- |
| Property | 1 490 |
| Machinery and equipment | 330 |
| Other non-current assets | 8 250 |
| **Current assets** | |
| Cash | 11 734 |
| Trade receivables | 6 243 |
| Inventories | 59 290 |
| **Current liabilities** | |
| Trade payables | 993 |
| Other current liabilities | 50 029 |
| **Capital employed** | 36 319 |

Founded in 1929, Chow Tai Fook Jewellery Group is widely recognised and renowned for its product design, quality and luxury jewellery. The Hong Kong, China (SAR) based company's vision is to become the most trusted jewellery group in the world. Table 24.4 shows the statement of financial position of Chow Tai Fook Jewellery for 2023.

**Discuss in pairs or small groups:**

1. Define 'non-current liabilities'.
2. Explain the difference between current and non-current assets.
3. Calculate the value of total assets.
4. Calculate the value of the working capital for 2023.
5. Explain how trade payables can act as a source of finance for a business.
6. Identify two internal stakeholders that might be interested in the company's financial position.
7. Explain the term 'capital employed'.

**Figure 24.5:** Chow Tai Fook Jewellery Group produces quality, luxury items

## 24 Statement of financial position

### BUSINESS IN ACTION

**Lux Island Resorts**

Figure 24.6: Lux Island Resorts owns and manages properties in the Indian Ocean region

Lux Island Resorts (LIR) owns and manages a portfolio of 4- and 5-star luxury properties and leisure resorts. With its headquarters in Mauritius, this company operates throughout the Indian Ocean region. The company's objective is to build shareholder value.

The information in Table 24.5 is an extract from LIR's statement of financial position as of 31 December 2022 and 2023.

Table 24.5: Extract from LIR's statement of financial position at 31 December 2022 and at 31 December 2023

|  | as of 31 December 2022 (in millions $) | as of 31 December 2023 (in millions $) |
|---|---|---|
| **Assets** | | |
| Non-current assets | 367.4 | 308 |
| Current assets | 52.8 | 57.2 |
| Total assets | 420.2 | 365.2 |
| **Liabilities** | | |
| Non-current liabilities | 165 | 174.8 |
| Current liabilities | 68.2 | 50.8 |
| Equity | 187 | 139.6 |
| Total equity and liabilities | 420.2 | 365.2 |

**Discuss in pairs and groups:**

Using the information above:

1. Explain how the assets the business owns have changed from 2022 to 2023.
2. Explain how the amount the business owes has changed from 2022 to 2023.
3. Explain how the business financed its activities in 2023.
4. Explain how the business financed its activities in 2022.
5. What are the limitations of using a statement of financial position?

## ACTIVITY 24.3

Analyse the information in the statement of financial position for Ezy, a private limited company, for the year 2023 (see Table 24.6), and answer the following questions with your partner.

Table 24.6: Extract from Ezy's statement of financial position for 2023

| Non-current assets | Amounts in $ |
| --- | --- |
| Vehicles | 10 500 |
| Machinery | 2 000 |
| Property | 200 000 |
| **Current assets** | |
| Inventory | 2 000 |
| Trade receivables | 4 000 |
| Cash | 8 000 |
| Total current assets | 14 000 |
| **Current liabilities** | |
| Trade payables | 4000 |
| **Non-current liabilities** | |
| Bank loan | 50 000 |

1. What is meant by a statement of financial position?
2. Calculate the value of total assets.
3. Calculate the value of total liabilities.
4. Explain the difference between current assets and current liabilities.
5. Why do you think Ezy is holding a high amount of inventory?
6. Explain how suppliers might use the statement of financial position.

## REFLECTION

Share your answers to Activity 24.3 with a partner or as a part of a small group. Reflect on the activity as a pair/group. Did your answers differ? Were you surprised by the answers your partner gave? Were you able to defend your answers?

## 24 Statement of financial position

> **SUMMARY**
>
> You should now know:
>
> - The statement of financial position records all of the assets (what a business owns) and liabilities (what a business owes) on a particular date.
> - Assets can be divided into non-current assets and current assets. Similarly, liabilities can be divided into non-current liabilities and current liabilities.
> - The statement of financial position shows the amount of capital invested in the business by the owners and how much the business owes the owners.
> - The capital employed is the total amount of capital invested in a business for the purpose of generating profits.
> - The statement of financial position can be used to make decisions including calculating working capital.

# Chapter 24 practice questions

1. The data below has been extracted from the statement of financial position of Rayner Furnishings (RF) which produces curtains, rugs and cushions. It has taken out a mortgage to buy its factory and used the shareholders' capital to buy the required machinery.

|  | 30 June 2023 | 30 June 2024 |
|---|---|---|
|  | (in thousands $) | (in thousands $) |
| Non-current assets | 2 500 | 2 900 |
| Current assets | 330 | 350 |
| Current liabilities | 100 | 200 |
| Non-current liabilities | 800 | 900 |

   a  Calculate the working capital of RF as of 30 June 2024.  [2]

   b  Outline **two** reasons why RF might need non-current assets.  [4]

   c  Explain how **two** stakeholder groups of RF might use the data shown in the table above.  [6]

   d  Do you think RF's managers should be concerned about the change in current liabilities between 2023 and 2024? Justify your answer.  [8]

2   Below are extracts from the statements of financial position of Top Ice Cream, a private limited company that produces ice cream, as of June 2023 and 2024.

|  | 2023 (in millions $) | 2024 (in millions $) |
|---|---|---|
| Non-current assets | 2.7 | 2.9 |
| Current assets | 0.5 | 0.8 |
| Current liabilities | 0.3 | 1.0 |
| Non-current liabilities | 1.0 | 1.1 |
| Owner's equity | 1.9 | 1.6 |

a   Identify **two** non-current assets a business may have. [2]

b   i   Define 'working capital'. [2]

   ii   Calculate Top Ice Cream's working capital in June 2024. [2]

c   Explain **two** differences between Top Ice Cream's statement of financial position data between June 2023 and 2024. [6]

d   Do you think Top Ice Cream's financial performance has improved? Justify your answer. [8]

Total available marks: 40

## CHECK YOUR PROGRESS

How well do you think you have achieved the learning intentions for this chapter? Give yourself a score from 1 (still need a lot of practice) to 5 (feeling very confident) for each learning intention. Provide an example to support your score.

| Now I can ... | Score | Example |
|---|---|---|
| understand the main parts of a statement of financial position | | |
| outline the difference between assets and liabilities | | |
| calculate the total assets, the total liabilities and the working capital from the statement of financial position | | |
| understand the concept of capital employed | | |
| make decisions based on statements of financial position. | | |

# Chapter 25
# Analysis of accounts

## LEARNING INTENTIONS

By the end of this chapter, you will be able to:
- understand the concept of profitability
- understand the concept of liquidity
- calculate profitability ratios and liquidity ratios
- explain how stakeholders might use financial information to help make decisions
- outline the limitations of using accounts and ratio analysis.

# Introduction

In Chapters 23 and 24, you learnt how information contained in statements of profit or loss and statements of financial position can be used by business stakeholders. While these are useful, it is essential to take care when interpreting financial data. A simple comparison of the change in revenue, costs, profits and assets or liabilities of a business from one year to the next can provide stakeholders with misleading information.

Consider the following accounting data (see Table 25.1) for two companies that are competitors in the clothing industry.

**Table 25.1:** Financial data for Companies X and Y

|  | Company X (in thousands $) | Company Y (in thousands $) |
|---|---|---|
| Revenue | 200 | 500 |
| Profit | 140 | 200 |
| Capital employed | 50 | 300 |

A simple comparison of these results might conclude that Company Y has performed better than Company X. This is because both the revenue and the profits for Company Y are higher than they are for Company X. Since Company Y has a higher profit, shareholders in Company Y may expect to receive a higher dividend than shareholders in Company X.

This shows that simple interpretation of accounting data, though useful, needs to be used with some caution.

In this chapter, you will find out how to analyse business accounting information using ratios. You will learn how to calculate and interpret ratios that measure:

- business profitability
- business liquidity.

# 25 Analysis of accounts

## BUSINESS IN CONTEXT

### BYJU'S Learning

**Figure 25.1:** BYJU'S is passionate about teaching

Taking a closer look at BYJU'S, the Indian education technology company mentioned in Chapter 7, shows that its revenue from operations came from the sale of video lectures on SD cards and tablets (forming 57% of the total revenue) and course fees. Together with other income, the company saw an increase of about 120% in total revenue in 2022 as compared to 2021.

The company's operational costs and other expenses included the cost of recording lectures, streaming, advertising, employee benefits, travel, legal and IT. The total costs increased by 94.51% to $1.6 million in financial year 2022 from about $850 000 in financial year 2021.

BYJU'S started facing financial difficulties in 2020 and losses grew significantly from 2021 to 2022. With continuing losses and a $1.2 billion loan, the survival of the company is very uncertain.

**Discuss in pairs or groups:**

1. What were the different ways BYJU'S earned revenue?
2. What are the main causes of BYJU'S Learning's financial troubles and uncertainties?

## 25.1 Why measure business performance?

A business must check its performance regularly as this can help to:

- identify its strengths and weaknesses, so it can decide which, if any, of its policies or strategies need to be changed
- show whether the business is meeting its objectives
- improve future business performance.

> **LINK**
>
> For more information on stakeholder groups, see Chapter 5.

### ACTIVITY 25.1

The performance of a business will be of interest to its internal and external stakeholders. They may want to know such things as:

- Will the business have profits to reinvest in the business?
- Will the business continue to exist in the future?
- Will future profits rise or fall?
- Will it be able to pay its debts?
- Will it be able to repay long-term borrowing?

Explain why each of these statements might be important to one or more business stakeholders.

### LINKS

For more information on the difference between profit and cash, see Chapter 21.

For more information on the importance of profit see Chapter 21.

## Measuring business performance

Since the main objective of all businesses in the private sector is to make a profit, profitability is an important indicator of how well a business is performing. As you learnt earlier in Chapter 22, a business needs more than just profit to survive. It must also have enough cash to pay its short-term liabilities and also have some cash in reserve for any unexpected expenses. So, when looking at a business's performance you also need to consider how well it manages its **liquidity**.

The information on statements of profit or loss and statements of financial position can be analysed using profitability and liquidity ratios. These provide stakeholders with important information to help them assess both the profitability and liquidity of a business and help to improve their decision-making.

### KEY TERM

**liquidity:** the ability of a business to pay its short-term debts.

## 25.2 Profitability

You have already learnt about the importance of profit to business growth and survival. You are now going to learn how to calculate and use the following ratios to analyse a business's profitability:

- gross profit margin
- profit margin
- return on capital employed.

These ratios measure profit in relation to the sales revenue or the amount of capital employed. When using profitability ratios to judge performance, it is important to look at trends and to see how well a business has performed over a number of years – as was the case when analysing statements of profit or loss.

To help with your understanding of these ratios we are going to use an extract from the accounting statements of Tang Toys (TT) (see Table 25.2).

### TIP

You must learn the formula for all five ratios in this chapter and remember to include the % sign where appropriate.

Table 25.2: Extract from the financial statements of Tang Toys

|  | 2022 (in thousands $) | 2023 (in thousands $) |
|---|---|---|
| Revenue | 420 | 500 |
| Gross profit | 189 | 240 |
| Profit | 63 | 70 |
| Capital employed | 120 | 120 |

# Gross profit margin

The gross profit margin ratio shows gross profit as a percentage of revenue. This ratio tells us how much gross profit is earned per $1 of revenue. It is calculated as:

$$\text{Gross profit margin \%} = \frac{\text{gross profit}}{\text{revenue}} \times 100$$

The gross profit margin is useful, as it considers the cost of sales to a business to see if these are what is expected by the business as compared to previous years and competitors.

> **LINK**
>
> For more information on gross profit and profit, see Chapter 21.

## Example

Using the data from Table 25.2, the 2022 gross profit margin for TT is:

$$\text{Gross profit margin \%} = \frac{189}{420} \times 100$$

$$= 45\%$$

This result tells us that every $1 of revenue earned $0.45 gross profit.

Since gross profit is the difference between revenue and cost of sales, you can see that the gross profit margin is influenced by both revenue and cost of sales. The gross profit margin can be improved by:

1. Increasing revenue without a similar increase in cost of sales. This can be done by:
   a. increasing price
   b. increasing the number of sales by
      - extending the product range
      - improving quality
      - increasing promotional activities, such as using new advertising media
      - selling the product in different countries
      - selling the product using different distribution channels.

2. Reducing cost of sales without a similar decrease in revenue by:
   a buying cheaper supplies
   b reducing labour costs by
   - reducing the number of workers
   - replacing some of the jobs with technology
   - locating in a country where labour costs are lower.

## Profit margin

The profit margin is a more effective ratio to use to analyse a business's financial performance, as it takes into account all of the costs the business has to pay.

The profit margin shows profit as a percentage of revenue. This ratio tells us how much profit is earned per $1 of revenue. It is calculated as:

$$\text{Profit margin \%} = \frac{\text{profit}}{\text{revenue}} \times 100$$

### Example

Using the data from Table 25.2, the 2022 profit margin for TT is:

$$\text{Profit margin \%} = \frac{63}{420} \times 100$$

$$= 15\%$$

This result tells us that every $1 of revenue earned $0.15 of profit.

This ratio measures the performance of the business in converting revenue into profit. Since profit is the difference between revenue and total costs, it is:

$$\text{Profit} = \text{revenue} - (\text{cost of sales} + \text{expenses})$$

To improve the profit margin, a business should:

- improve the gross profit margin
- reduce expenses.

### Interpreting the gross profit margin and the profit margin

Both the gross profit margin and the profit margin can be used to measure how well the business can increase added value and/or controls costs.

- Any improvement in the gross profit margin from one year to the next may indicate an improved added value. Also, if a business has a higher gross profit margin than a competitor, the business may have achieved a higher added value for its products than its competitor.

- Since profit will always be lower than gross profit, this means that the percentage profit margin will always be lower than the percentage gross profit margin. The difference between these two ratios is the effect that expenses have on the profits of a business. Therefore, the profit margin is also a good measure of how well the business has controlled its expenses.

> **TIP**
> 
> Do not confuse gross profit margin and profit margin. You could think of "gross" as representing the overall or raw profit before additional expenses.

> **LINK**
> 
> For more information on adding value, see Chapter 1.

## 25 Analysis of accounts

When analysing profit ratios, it is important to look at trends and to see how well a business has performed over a number of years (as we did when we analysed the statement of profit or loss) or compared with that of competitors.

> ### ACTIVITY 25.2
>
> Table 25.3 shows the gross profit margin and the profit margin for two companies in the same industry over the three years, 2021–2023.
>
> **Table 25.3:** Information for companies A and B
>
> |  | Company A ||| Company B |||
> |---|---|---|---|---|---|---|
> |  | 2021 | 2022 | 2023 | 2021 | 2022 | 2023 |
> | Gross profit margin (%) | 23 | 24 | 25 | 30 | 28 | 26 |
> | Profit margin (%) | 8 | 8.5 | 8 | 10 | 9.5 | 9 |
>
> 1. Comment on the change in Company A's gross profit margin between 2021 and 2023.
> 2. Compare the change in gross profit margin of Company A and Company B between 2022 and 2023.
> 3. Explain why you think the profit margin for Company A has decreased in 2023 despite an increase in the gross profit margin.
> 4. Which company do you think has performed best over the period 2021–2023? Justify your answer.

# Return on capital employed

The return on capital employed (ROCE) ratio shows profit as a percentage of capital employed. It tells us how much profit is earned for every $1 invested in the business. This ratio is the most used measure of efficiency and is often considered to be the most important way of analysing a business's profitability.

Capital employed is the amount invested in the business by the owners, for example, sole traders, partners or shareholders. Any long-term borrowing, such as bank loans, should also be included as capital employed. The money is usually borrowed to purchase profit-earning assets, such as buildings and machinery.

$$\text{Return on capital employed \%} = \frac{\text{profit}}{\text{capital employed}} \times 100$$

## Example

Using the data from Table 25.2, the 2022 ROCE for TT is:

$$\text{Return on capital employed \%} = \frac{63}{120} \times 100$$

$$= 52.5\%$$

This measure tells us that every $1 of capital invested in TT earned a return to the shareholders of $0.525.

## ACTIVITY 25.3

Copy out Table 25.4.

**Table 25.4:** Profitability ratios for 2022 and 2023

| Profitability ratio | 2022 | 2023 |
|---|---|---|
| Gross profit margin | 45% | |
| Profit margin | 15% | |
| Capital employed | 52.5% | |

1. Use the data in Table 25.2 to calculate the profitability ratios for 2023 and fill in your copied out table.
2. Using your results, comment on the financial performance of TT in 2023 compared to 2022.
3. Explain how the following stakeholders of TT might view these results:
   a. shareholders
   b. employees
   c. suppliers
   d. government.
4. Based on the information, do you think a bank would lend money to TT to finance expansion plans? Justify your answer.

As with the other ratios you have studied so far, the ROCE ratio has limited use unless it is compared with the business's ROCE results from previous years or with the ROCE results of similar businesses in the industry. As a general rule, if the ROCE increases from one year to the next the business's profitability has improved.

## CASE STUDY 25.1

**Wilko**

**Figure 25.2:** Wilko was originally a hardware store

Wilko was founded by James Wilkinson as a hardware store in 1930. It grew into a successful retail discount chain selling homewares, garden wares, household goods and DIY products. Wilko remained under the ownership of the Wilkinson family and is one of the largest privately owned retail companies in the UK. At its peak, Wilko earned $2 billion in revenue in 2018. After that, however, it suffered from declining revenue and profits.

Wilko collapsed in August 2023, closing down 400 stores and letting go of more than 12 000 employees. Factors such as high rents, tough competition leading to reduced sales and the

> **CONTINUED**
>
> decision to pay out $3.2 million in dividends in 2022 and $950 000 in early 2023, despite losses and a bleak outlook for the company, all contributed to its decline. COVID-19 was also a significant contributing factor to reduced sales when shoppers used online shopping and Wilko could no longer rely on customers browsing their stores in person and purchasing items in addition to those they had come in intending to buy. Sudden changes in economic policies in the UK in 2022 stopped an important loan from coming through. Management at the company stated that Wilko 'ran out of cash' before its turnaround efforts were able to take effect.
>
> While an uncertain future awaits Wilko, experts suggest that discount companies from other countries may purchase parts of Wilko as a way to enter the UK market.
>
> **Discuss in pairs or groups:**
>
> 1. Explain the difference between cash and profit.
> 2. What were the main reasons for Wilko's financial troubles?
> 3. Outline the impact of Wilko's failure on two stakeholders of the business.
> 4. Explain how the company 'running out of cash' would have been a problem for Wilko.
> 5. Do you think declining profitability or declining liquidity was more significant in Wilko's financial troubles?

## 25.3 Liquidity

If a business does not have enough cash to pay for its immediate expenses or short-term liabilities (business debts), and has no access to cash from internal or external sources, it will not be able to continue trading. A business's liquidity is its access to cash.

Current assets are important to a business because they indicate how much cash a business can access to meet its short-term liabilities.

Liquidity is so important to a business's survival that it must be carefully managed at all times. One way of monitoring a business's liquidity is using the following liquidity ratios:

- current ratio
- acid test ratio.

To help with our calculation and understanding of these ratios we are going to use a further extract from the accounting statements of TT (see Table 25.5).

> **LINK**
>
> For more information on assets and liabilities, see Chapter 22.

**Table 25.5:** Extract from the statements of financial position of Tang Toys

|  | 2022 (in thousands $) | 2023 (in thousands $) |
|---|---|---|
| Current assets | 60 | 50 |
| Current assets – inventories | 20 | 30 |
| Current liabilities | 40 | 30 |

## Current ratio

The current ratio is the ratio between current assets and current liabilities.

$$\text{Current ratio} = \frac{\text{current assets}}{\text{current liabilities}}$$

- Current assets represent things owned by the business that are already in the form of cash, or are easy to convert into cash within 12 months.
- Current liabilities are the short-term debts of a business, which are expected to be paid within 12 months.

Therefore, it is important that the level of current assets is greater than the level of current liabilities. If this is not the case, then the business risks liquidity problems. There is not enough cash coming into the business to pay its short-term liabilities and have spare cash for unexpected expenses.

### Example

Using the data from Table 25.5, the 2022 current ratio for TT is:

$$\text{current ratio} = \frac{60}{40}$$

$$= 1.5:1$$

(Note that the result is always shown as a ratio.)

For every $1 of current liabilities, TT has $1.5 of current assets, that is, it has access to more cash than it needs to meet its short-term liabilities to pay for any unexpected expenses.

There is no perfect ratio as it depends on the business and industry. As a general guide, the current ratio should be at least 1.5:1, otherwise there is a risk of running out of cash to pay short term debts.

However, it should be no greater than 2:1, since it may suggest there could be too much idle cash and inventory.

A business will compare the current ratio from one year to the next. If it increases, then current ratio has improved so the business is better able to pay its short-term debts. If it decreases from one year to the next, the business is less able to pay its short-term debts.

## Acid test ratio

The main problem with the current ratio as a measure of liquidity is that some current assets are more difficult to turn into cash than others. Inventories are the least liquid of the current assets because:

- the finished goods inventories have to be sold
- when they are sold on credit, the business has to wait for customers to pay.

The acid test ratio excludes inventories from current assets. It shows the most liquid current assets as a ratio of current liabilities. For this reason, the acid test ratio is often considered to be a better measure of a business's liquidity.

$$\text{Acid test ratio} = \frac{\text{current assets} - \text{inventory}}{\text{current liabilities}}$$

## Example

Using the data from Table 25.5, the 2022 acid test ratio for TT is:

$$\text{current ratio} = \frac{60 - 20}{40}$$

$$= 1:1$$

An acid test ratio of 1:1 is generally viewed as satisfactory. If it is lower than this, there is a risk of the business not having enough cash to pay its short-term liabilities. If it is too high, then cash is being tied up in unprofitable assets.

### ACTIVITY 25.4

Copy out Table 25.6.

**Table 25.6:** Liquidity ratios as of June 2022 and 2023

|  | 2022 | 2023 |
| --- | --- | --- |
| Current ratio | 1.5:1 |  |
| Acid test ratio | 1:1 |  |

1. Using the data in Table 25.5, calculate the liquidity ratios for 2023 and fill out your copied table.
2. Using your results, comment on the liquidity position of TT in 2023 compared to 2022.
3. Explain two ways of improving TT's liquidity.

### CASE STUDY 25.2

**Bogawantalawa Tea Estates**

**Figure 25.3:** A worker picking tea on a plantation in Sri Lanka

The Sri Lanka-based Bogawantalawa Tea Estates, a public limited company, aspires to be the world's best tea growing and marketing company. Its vision is to be a company where people share the responsibility and commitment to attain excellence in managing the resources on a sustainable basis by providing customers with high-quality products and services while developing their employees and protecting the environment.

The tea sector experienced a rise in production costs in 2022 due to the higher prices of chemical fertilizers and other agricultural inputs along with a domestic shortage of those inputs. Despite this, the company achieved a sales revenue of ₹5.4 billion

## CONTINUED

and the profit before taxation was recorded at ₹1.4 billion. The average price of tea increased notably by 105.2% to ₹1 270.50 per kg during the year, from ₹619.15 per kg recorded in 2021.

Tables 25.7 and 25.8 show the profitability and liquidity ratios for Bogawantalawa Tea Estates for two consecutive years.

Table 25.7: Profitability ratios for the years 2021–2023

| Profitability ratios | 2021–2022 | 2022–2023 |
|---|---|---|
| Gross profit margin | $\frac{0.2}{3.4} \times 100 = 5.9\%$ | $\frac{1.6}{5.4} \times 100 = 29.6\%$ |
| Profit margin | $\frac{0.1}{3.4} \times 100 = 2.9\%$ | $\frac{1.2}{5.4} \times 100 = 22.2\%$ |
| ROCE | $\frac{0.1}{5.2} \times 100 = 1.9\%$ | $\frac{1.2}{6.7} \times 100 = 17.9\%$ |

The liquidity ratios for the years 2021–2023.

Table 25.8: Liquidity ratios for the years 2021–2023

| Liquidity ratios | 2021–2022 | 2022–2023 |
|---|---|---|
| Current ratio | 0.9:1 | 3:1 |
| Acid test ratio | 0.6:1 | 2:1 |

**Discuss in pairs or groups:**

1. What could be a possible reason for the increase in revenue in 2022–2023.
2. What were the main reasons for the increase in cost of sales?
3. Why do you think the gross profit margin increased so much despite the increase in the cost of sales?
4. Using the ratios above, comment on the liquidity of the business in 2021–2022.
5. Using the ratios above, comment on the liquidity of the business in 2022–2023.
6. Given this information, can it be concluded that 2022–2023 was a more successful year for Bogawantalawa Tea Estates?

# 25.4 Use of accounts and ratio analysis

Businesses use financial statements such as the statement of profit or loss and the statement of financial position in the following ways:

- To disclose and report a company's financial information in a reliable and consistent way.
- To help track progress towards financial goals.
- To evaluate a company's financial position and performance by calculating its profitability and liquidity.
- To enable analysis of its financial performance over time.

- To enable comparison with its competitors.
- To provide relevant information to make some informed decisions related to investments, lending and budgeting.

Both internal and external stakeholders are interested in the financial statements of a business, although they may not need to calculate any of the performance or liquidity ratios. The main uses of financial statements and ratio analysis by business stakeholder groups are summarised in Table 25.9.

Table 25.9: Main uses of accounts and ratio analysis by business stakeholder groups

| Stakeholder | Use of accounts and ratio analysis | Useful ratios/information |
|---|---|---|
| Owners/shareholders | • They will want to know how well the business is performing and whether they are getting a good return on their investment.<br>• Compare the profits with previous years and/or with similar businesses to decide whether to continue investing or not.<br>• Shareholders of limited companies will compare the dividends they receive with previous years' and with the returns they could get if their money was invested elsewhere. | • Profit<br>• Profitability ratios |
| Managers | • Has the business met its targets?<br>• Has the revenue increased?<br>• How well have costs been controlled?<br>• Are profits rising?<br>• Do they have sufficient funds to pay suppliers and other creditors? | • Profit<br>• Profitability ratios<br>• Liquidity ratios |
| Employees | • Interested in the profitability of the business as a business that continues to make good levels of profit is likely to offer greater job security.<br>• Could be used by the employees or their trade union to support their claim for higher wages.<br>• Employees will be interested in liquidity ratios as this will indicate a business' ability to pay wages. | • Profit<br>• Profitability ratios |
| Suppliers | • Interested in the liquidity of the business to know that the business has sufficient cash to pay its debts when they become due.<br>• Interested in the profitability of a business. A business that is making good profits and expanding will continue to need raw materials and other supplies. This will help suppliers to increase their own revenue and profits. | • Liquidity ratios<br>• Profitability ratios<br>• Profit |

(Continued)

**Table 25.9:** (Continued)

| Stakeholder | Use of accounts and ratio analysis | Useful ratios/information |
|---|---|---|
| Lenders/Banks | • Banks and other lenders will be interested in the profits and liquidity of the business as they would want to know: <br>   • that they will receive the interest on any money they have loaned the business <br>   • that the business will be able to repay its borrowing when it becomes due. | • Profit <br> • Liquidity ratio |
| Government | • Companies have to pay tax on their profits. The higher the profits, the higher the tax revenue received by the government. <br> • Also, a business that is performing well and earning profits to expand will provide employment. This will reduce government spending on support for the unemployed. | • Profit |

## 25.5 Limitations of accounts and ratio analysis

Ratio analysis is not perfect, so care must be taken not to rely too heavily on the results. The main limitations for users of financial statements and profitability and liquidity ratios are:

- Ratios compare past data and may not reflect current market conditions. Users of accounts – stakeholders – are much more interested in what the future holds for the business.
- Financial statements do not include all the strengths and weaknesses of a business, for example, the quality and skills of employees. These factors are also likely to affect business performance, especially profitability.
- Statements of profit or loss and statements of financial position are not always prepared in the same way by different businesses as they may use different accounting methods and industry practices. Therefore, the ratios do not compare like with like.
- Businesses are affected by external factor, such as legislation, exchange rates and economic factors, but these will not be shown in the financial statements.

Despite these limitations, along with other sources of information, a company's statements of accounts are very useful for assessing a company's performance.

> **TIP**
>
> Each stakeholder group will want to know different information. You will need to be able to explain how each group would use the accounts. Remember too that not all the information the stakeholders want will be in the accounts.

## BUSINESS IN ACTION

### Shamsi

**Figure 25.4:** Shamsi needs to decide which technology company to invest in

Shamsi has $100 that he wants to invest in a technology company. He has used Microsoft products, such as the Windows operating system and the Microsoft Office Suite, on computers at home and in school since he was a young age. His family also uses some Apple products, such as iPads and iPhones. He considers some of the key financial ratios for these two popular technology companies, as shown in Table 25.10.

**Table 25.10:** Showing some financial ratios for two companies for 2022–2023

| Financial performance | Apple | Microsoft |
|---|---|---|
| Gross profit margin (from December 2022 to December 2023) | 45% | 69.8% |
| Profit margin (from December 2022 to December 2023) | 26.1% | 36.3% |
| Current ratio (December 2023) | 1.07 | 1.22 |

**Discuss in pairs or groups:**
1. Which of the three ratios do you think is the most useful in assessing the companies' financial performance?
2. Why is this information not enough to make a well-informed investment decision? What other information would Shamsi need to consider?

## ACTIVITY 25.5

Southern Gas Company (SGC) is a distributor of natural gas. The information in Table 25.11 has been extracted from the company's accounts for 2021–2022 and 2022–2023.

Table 25.11: Showing financial information for SGC for 2021–2022 and 2022–2023

|  | 2021–2022 | 2022–2023 |
|---|---|---|
|  | $ | $ |
| Capital employed | 533 670 | 590 000 |
| Revenue | 1 162 340 | 1 328 300 |
| Gross profit | 114 217 | 117 998 |
| Profit | 56 002 | 41 458 |
| Current assets | 805 394 | 1 087 365 |
| Current liabilities | 784 856 | 1 066 017 |

1. Calculate the gross profit margin and the profit margin for both years.
2. Calculate the return on capital employed for both years.
3. Using your results to Questions 1 and 2, comment on the company's performance in 2022–2023 compared to 2021–2022.
4. Calculate the current ratio as of Dec 2022 and Dec 2023.
5. Using your results to Question 4, comment on the company's liquidity in both years.
6. Explain how any **five** of the company's stakeholder groups might use this information.
7. Do you think potential investors would consider the SGC a good investment? Justify your answer.

## REFLECTION

Reflect on Activity 25.5 in a small group. Did you remember the formulae to calculate the various ratios? Share your approach to learning them with your group. Note down any approaches that you think might be useful to you too.

Compare your answers with your group. Did everyone in the group conclude that Southern Gas Company was a good investment? If not, how would you defend your decision? Listen carefully to their justifications too and modify/strengthen your conclusion.

## SUMMARY

You should now know:

- The calculation of profitability and liquidity ratios helps stakeholder groups to interpret financial statements and assess the importance of these results in meeting their own objectives.
- Although profit is the primary objective of all private sector businesses, they must not ignore the importance of liquidity to business survival.

# Chapter 25 practice questions

1  Two years ago, Jacob was made redundant from his job. He decided to invest his $35 000 redundancy payment and $15 000 life savings into his own catering business. He used the $50 000 to buy machinery and equipment, rent suitable premises and buy the inventories needed to set up the business. The table below shows an extract from Jacob's financial statements for the first two years of trading.

|  | Year 1 | Year 2 |
|---|---|---|
|  | $ | $ |
| Revenue | 36 000 | 42 000 |
| Profit | 10 000 | 12 000 |
| Return on capital employed | ? | 24% |

    a    Calculate the return on capital employed for Year 1. [2]

    b    Outline **two** factors that might influence Jacob's revenue. [4]

    c    Explain the usefulness of Jacob's financial data to any **two** of his business' stakeholders. [6]

    d    Do you think Jacob should be pleased with the performance of his business during the first two years? Justify your answer. [8]

2   Figure 25.5 shows the gross profit margin and the profit margin for three industries in Country Y.

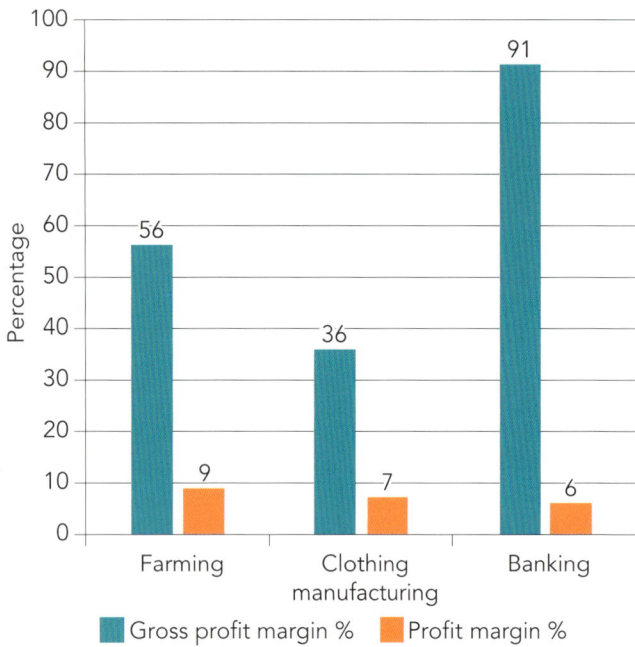

**Figure 25.5:** Bar chart of profit margins

a   Define 'profit margin'. [2]

b   Outline **two** ways that a clothing manufacturer could improve its gross profit margin. [4]

c   Explain **two** reasons why the difference between gross profit margin and profit margin is greater for banking than for either of the other two industries shown. [6]

d   Do you think that all clothing manufacturers in Country Y will have a profit margin of 7%? Justify your answer. [8]

Total available marks: 40

25 Analysis of accounts

## CHECK YOUR PROGRESS

How well do you think you have achieved the learning intentions for this chapter? Give yourself a score from 1 (still need a lot of practice) to 5 (feeling very confident) for each learning intention. Provide an example to support your score.

| Now I can … | Score | Example |
|---|---|---|
| understand the concept of profitability | | |
| understand the concept of liquidity | | |
| calculate profitability ratios and liquidity ratios | | |
| explain how stakeholders might use financial information to help make decisions | | |
| outline the limitations of using accounts and ratio analysis. | | |

# Section 5 case study

## CASE STUDY

### The S-Mart Group

The S-Mart Group is a public limited company in Country A. The company is an international supermarket chain that sells quality groceries at affordable prices across ten countries in Africa. Although company profits have grown rapidly over the past two years, the Operations Head, Lefoko Morris, is concerned about the performance of one of the S-Mart supermarkets recently opened in Country B, which he feels has performed less well than the others in the group. He has asked Bosena Ngosi, who works in the Finance Department, to provide him some financial data on how the S-Mart supermarket in Country B is performing. He is given the data as shown in Appendix 1 for the supermarket in Country B and Country A.

There has been increasing government regulation aimed at making businesses more environmentally friendly by reducing waste and pollution and using renewable sources of energy. Therefore, one of the main aims of the company is to make its operations more sustainable. The management of the company recognises that making its operations more sustainable may be costly at first but that new ideas could lead to cost efficiency and competitive advantage in the longer run.

The S-Mart Group wants to make its operations technology enabled so that sourcing its products can be more cost efficient, minimise waste and still keep the prices of its products affordable. A team of experts have estimated the cost of doing this to be $1.2 million. The Finance Department is now considering how best to finance this investment.

Bosena has raised concerns about the S-Mart Group's cash position as the current liabilities shown on the statement of financial position increased from $1.4 million in 2022 to $1.8 million in 2023. With sustainability and investment in technology being a focus, Bosena feels that there may be unexpected costs and expenses. She is planning to prepare a cash flow forecast for the next six months to ensure the company will have enough liquidity to meet unexpected costs. Lefoko has acknowledged Bosena's concerns, but believes that since the profit and profit margin have both been increasing every year for the last two years, there is nothing to worry about.

Lefoko has sent the memorandum shown in Appendix 3 to all other directors of the S-Mart Group. However, the other directors are not convinced about the advantages of a share issue and support the CEO's view that as interest rates are likely to fall, a long-term bank loan is the better option.

# Appendix 1

**Financial data for the S-Mart in Country B and Country A for 2022–2023**

|  | S-Mart in Country B | S-Mart in Country A |
|---|---|---|
| Revenue | $1 million | $8 million |
| Gross profit | $0.5 million | $4 million |
| Profit | $0.1 million | $2 million |
| Capital employed | $0.5 million | $5.7 million |

# Appendix 2

**Extract from the financial statements of the S-Mart Group of Supermarkets**

|  | 2022 (in millions $) | 2023 (in millions $) |
|---|---|---|
| Profit after tax | 2.1 | 2.5 |
| Dividends paid | 1.5 | 1.8 |
| Non-current assets | 5.5 | 5.9 |
| Current assets | 1.1 | 2.1 |
| Current liabilities | 1.4 | 1.8 |
| **Net assets** | **5.2** | **6.2** |
| Share capital | 1.0 | 1.0 |
| Retained profits | 2.1 | 2.8 |
| Non-current liabilities | 2.1 | 2.4 |
| **Capital employed** | **5.2** | **6.2** |

# Appendix 3

**Memorandum:**

From: Lefoko Morris

To: All directors

As interest rates are high, taking a loan will be expensive. I think using our retained profit will be the best source of capital to finance the upgrade of our technological infrastructure.

1. a. Explain how any **two** external stakeholders of the S-Mart Group might use the financial data provided in the text and Appendix 2.

    Stakeholder 1:

    Explanation:

    Stakeholder 2:

    Explanation: [8]

    b. Calculate the gross profit margin for S-Mart in Country B and in Country A. Calculate the profit margin for S-Mart in Country B and in Country A.

    Do you think The S-Mart supermarket in Country B is as successful as it is in Country A? Justify your answer using the two profitability ratios. [12]

**2** **a** **i** Use Appendix 2 to calculate S-Mart's liquidity in 2022. [2]

    **ii** Use Appendix 2 to calculate S-Mart's liquidity in 2023. [2]

    **iii** Explain whether S-Mart's liquidity has improved or declined from 2022 to 2023. [4]

  **b** Consider the advantages and disadvantages of the following methods that could be used to finance the purchase of City Budget Supermarkets.

    Which source should the Board of Directors use? Justify your answer.

    Retained profit:

    Long-term bank loan:

    Recommendation: [12]

**3** **a** Explain **two** ways the company's accountant, Bosena Ngosi, might use the cash flow forecast she has prepared to better manage the S-Mart Group's cash position.

    Use 1:

    Explanation:

    Use 2:

    Explanation: [8]

  **b** Lefoko Morris believes that since the profit and profit margin have both been increasing every year for the last two years, there is nothing to worry about. Explain why each of the following is important to the S-Mart Group. Which do you think is the most important? Justify your answer.

    Cash:

    Profit:

    Conclusion: [12]

**4** **a** Explain **two** ways the S-Mart Group could increase its profits.

    Way 1:

    Explanation:

    Way 2:

    Explanation: [8]

  **b** Explain how the following **two** financial documents might be useful to the S-Mart Group's directors when choosing a source of finance. Which statement do you think is the most useful to the S-Mart Group's directors? Justify your answer.

    Statement of profit or loss:

    Statement of financial position:

    Conclusion: [12]

**Total available marks: 80**

# Section 6
# External influences on business activity

This section covers how governmental, international and environmental factors influence and shape business decision-making.

You will learn about the various stages of the business cycle and their impact on business activity.

The government of a country has the job of organising funds for the common needs of the people in areas such as education and health. They do this by setting relevant policies to help achieve their aims and objectives. You will learn how the policies that involve taxation and interest rates affect businesses.

The global recognition of brands is a sign of the growth in international trade and the growth of globalisation. You will learn about the advantages and disadvantages of globalisation and how the international business environment and its considerations such as exchange rates also influence business activity.

The positive and negative impact of businesses on the physical environment and society around them greatly influences business operations and success. You will learn how pressure groups and legal controls exert influence to control the negative impact of business activity. When making decisions, businesses need to bear in mind their environmental and ethical responsibilities.

# Chapter 26
# Economic issues

## LEARNING INTENTIONS

By the end of this chapter, you will be able to:

- explain the main stages of the business cycle and how each stage of the business cycle might affect a business
- describe the effects of changes in the levels of employment, inflation and economic growth on a business
- describe the effects of government policy: changes in government spending and interest rates as well as taxes on business profit and people's incomes
- understand how businesses respond to changes in taxes and interest rates.

# 26 Economic issues

## Introduction

The level of economy in a country fluctuates over time and is known as the business cycle. In this chapter, you will learn about the different stages of the business cycle and their impact on business activity.

All governments have objectives. They try to achieve their objectives by introducing or changing policies. These policies influence government spending, interest rates and taxation in the country, which in turn affect businesses. In this chapter, you will look at how government policies affect business activities. Businesses are affected differently depending on the good or service they are selling, the industry they are in and the size of the business.

### BUSINESS IN CONTEXT

#### Unemployment in South Africa

**Figure 26.1:** South Africa has one of the most industrialised economies in Africa

Despite South Africa having one of the most industrialised economies in Africa, it has one of the highest unemployment rates in the world. The official unemployment rate in South Africa was 33% in 2023, which does not include those who have given up on finding work. As per official data, roughly 24 million adults out of a population of 60 million are either unemployed or not involved in any economic activity and youth unemployment is at 46.5%, as those in the 15–34 age range account for over half the country's employable population of 40.6 million aged between 15 and 64. The situation is described as 'a ticking time bomb' by the UN.

While South Africa's unemployment problem has been building up for many years, according to government statistics, the COVID-19 pandemic left an additional 2 million South Africans unemployed. A low economic growth, which is not producing enough jobs for those entering the workforce every year, is another contributing factor to the high unemployment rate. The government has set up policies to help young entrepreneurs start their own business, but this is nowhere near enough to reduce the unemployment problem.

The power crisis is having a huge negative impact on households and businesses and is putting additional pressure on firms that are struggling to stay open in an economy faced with problems such as poverty, low economic growth and crime. So, unemployment is only expected to increase further. A report by the UN states how rising unemployment is threatening the country's stability and the future of the young generations.

#### Discuss in pairs or groups:

1. What impact would rising unemployment have on individuals and businesses in South Africa?
2. Why do you think rising unemployment is a problem for the government of a country?

## 26.1 The business cycle

The economy of a country is unlikely to grow by the same amount over a period of time. The change in the economic activity as the economy grows and shrinks over a number of years is known as the business cycle. This plays a vital role in shaping the policies of the government.

The business cycle has four main stages. Each stage may last for months or even years. The stages, as shown in Figure 26.2, are:

- growth – an increase in the value of goods and services produced by an economy over time
- boom – the period of time where gross domestic product (economic growth) is at its highest
- recession – two consecutive quarters (six months) of negative economic growth
- slump – a sustained period of negative economic growth.

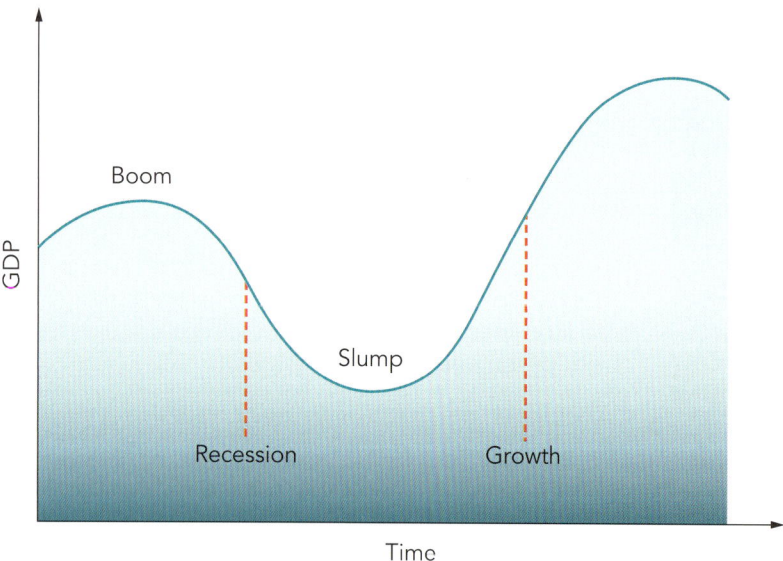

Figure 26.2: The stages of the business cycle

Table 26.1 shows how each stage of the business cycle might affect a business.

**Table 26.1:** How each stage of the business cycle might affect a business

| Growth | Possible effect on business |
|---|---|
| • A positive outlook for new businesses.<br>• Growth in economic activity until it reaches a maximum (boom).<br>• Falling unemployment as there are more jobs due to businesses doing well.<br>• Raised standards of living as more people are employed. | • Increase in new start-ups may lead to increase competition.<br>• Existing businesses grow and make more sales which may lead to increase in profits (if sales greater than costs).<br>• May be difficult to find employees, leading to increased labour costs. |
| **Boom** | |
| • Business investments and profit are likely to be at their highest levels.<br>• Most sectors of the economy are performing at their best.<br>• High levels of demand for goods and services causing prices to rise (inflation).<br>• Very low unemployment rates and people have better jobs to choose from. | • High business profit.<br>• Increased demand/sales leading to an increase in revenue.<br>• Higher wage demands could increase labour costs.<br>• Shortage of skilled labour which may lower output/quality. |
| **Recession** | |
| • Business confidence falls.<br>• Decline in economic activity until it reaches a minimum (slump).<br>• Falling demand by consumers leads to falling sales.<br>• Unemployment rises as businesses are not doing well and have to cut costs. | • Less investment in new and existing businesses.<br>• Lower sales could lead to less revenue.<br>• May have to make some employees redundant.<br>• Some businesses even close down. |
| **Slump** | |
| • Very low business confidence.<br>• Low production of goods and services, leading to many businesses close down.<br>• Low demand for goods and services.<br>• High unemployment due to low business activity. | • Leads to little/no investment in new and existing businesses.<br>• Low/no sales but fixed costs still need to be paid.<br>• Businesses may close down.<br>• Labour costs may reduce as many people looking for jobs. |

> **TIP**
>
> Do not confuse the business cycle with the product life cycle of a particular business. A business cycle shows the ups and downs in the growth of an economy over time – this affects all businesses. The product cycle only refers to a product of an individual business.

# 26.2 Effects of changes in the levels of unemployment, inflation and economic growth on a business

All governments want their country to have economic growth and low unemployment and low inflation. The government of every country will set and adjust its policies to achieve these aims. These will have a significant influence on business activity.

## Effects of changes in inflation on business activity

**Inflation** is the price increase of goods and services over time. When there is inflation, the prices of goods and services are increasing.

When inflation is low:

- People enjoy a better standard of living as they can afford to pay for goods and services. They can also afford to pay for non-essential (luxury) items. This ensures that businesses make usual or higher sales and earn revenue. It becomes easier for companies to set up new ventures and expand.
- Businesses also benefit from stable or lower costs of raw materials and energy, keeping their production costs low.

When inflation goes up:

- People may not be able to afford to buy local goods and instead may buy goods from other countries (which may be cheaper). This can affect local businesses in the country as they make fewer sales.
- The production costs for businesses would increase too.

> **KEY TERMS**
>
> **inflation:** an increase in the average price level of goods and services over time.
>
> **level of unemployment:** the percentage of the population that are willing and able to work, but are unable to find work.

## Effects of changes in level of employment on business activity

The level of employment in a country refers to how many people who are able to and want to work are currently employed.

All governments want their country to have a low **level of unemployment**.

### Reasons why a government wants as many people to have jobs as possible

Here are the main reasons why a government would want as many people to have jobs as possible.

- They contribute to the total output of the country and improve economic growth.
- The higher the level of employment, the more income tax a government receives.
- The people can earn money and have a better standard of living.
- The government does not have to spend money on unemployment benefits and can instead spend it on improving the country's infrastructure.

While low unemployment is beneficial for the government, it poses both advantages and disadvantages for businesses.

The disadvantages of low unemployment for a business are:

- Increase in the labour cost as businesses may have to pay higher wages to retain workers.
- Difficulty in recruiting skilled workers as there are fewer people to recruit from.

The advantages of low unemployment for a business are:

- Increase in sales as most people are employed and may have more disposable income to spend on goods and services.
- Increased use of automation and technology as workers become harder to recruit. This leads to improvements in efficiency.

## CASE STUDY 26.1

**Unemployment rates in the Philippines**

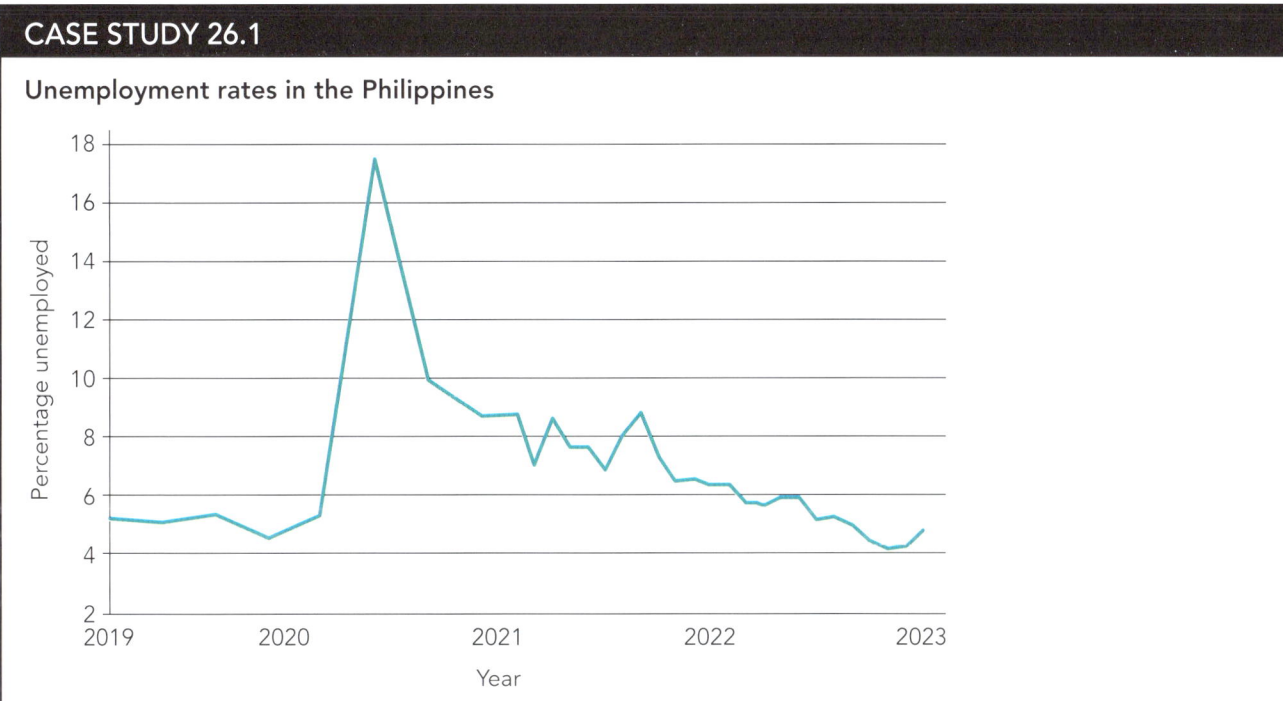

**Figure 26.3:** The Philippines' unemployment rates from 2019 to 2023

*Source:* www.tradingeconomics.com, Central Agency for Public Mobilization & Statistics.

Most of the population of the Philippines works in the service industry, which also significantly contributes to the country's economic growth. Unemployment rates are low and there is a shortage of skilled workers. To address this problem, the government has introduced vocational training programs to improve the ICT and technical skills of its workforce. Look at Figure 26.3 that shows the Philippines' unemployment rates over five years from 2019 to 2023.

**Discuss in pairs or groups:**

1 What has been the highest rate of unemployment in the Philippines between 2019 and 2023?

2 Why do you think the rate of unemployment was so high then?

3 What was the highest rate of unemployment in the Philippines in 2019?

4 What was the highest rate of unemployment in the Philippines in 2023?

5 What has been the percentage change in the unemployment rate from 2019 to 2023?

6 Why is it important for the unemployment rate to be low for

　a  the country's economy

　b  the people of the country?

# Effects of changes in economic growth on business activity

**Economic growth** is one of the main government objectives. One measure of economic growth of a country is gross domestic product (GDP), which is the value of all goods and services produced by a country in a year. This measure allows us to analyse the economic growth of a country from one year to the next between years and to compare its performance with other countries' economies.

If GDP increases, there is economic growth and it means more goods and services have been produced in the country and there is more income earned by people and businesses compared to the previous year. Higher income means more salaries for workers which helps them have a better standard of living.

A growing economy has many benefits for a business:

- more business opportunities for new and existing businesses
- increased consumer demand
- increased sales revenue
- more profitability due to higher sales revenue
- more innovation as increased competition due to growth in businesses encourages firms to innovate and improve efficiency.

However, if GDP falls, this is bad for the economy and the businesses and people in it. For example, it would mean lower output so fewer employees are needed, and generally people experience a lower standard of living as they cannot afford to buy as many goods and services.

> **KEY TERM**
>
> **economic growth:** an increase in the value of goods and services produced by an economy over time.

Figure 26.4: A government wants as many people as possible to have a job

## 26 Economic issues

### CASE STUDY 26.2

**The Malaysian economy**

Figure 26.5: Malaysia is a well-diversified economy

Malaysia is a well-diversified economy (produces a variety of goods and services) and experts say it has the ability to adapt to the changing global environment. In the last quarter of 2023, the economy grew by 3.9% and, based on other economic data, it is expected to grow further.

Analyse and explain how the data on inflation and unemployment levels for Malaysia for the last few years leading up to 2023 as shown in Figures 26.6 and 26.7, support the statement above.

Note: When analysing the data, consider the following for each set of data:

- What has been the trend in inflation and unemployment over the last five years?
- What is the inflation and unemployment in 2023?
- What does this value indicate about the country's economy?

**Inflation**

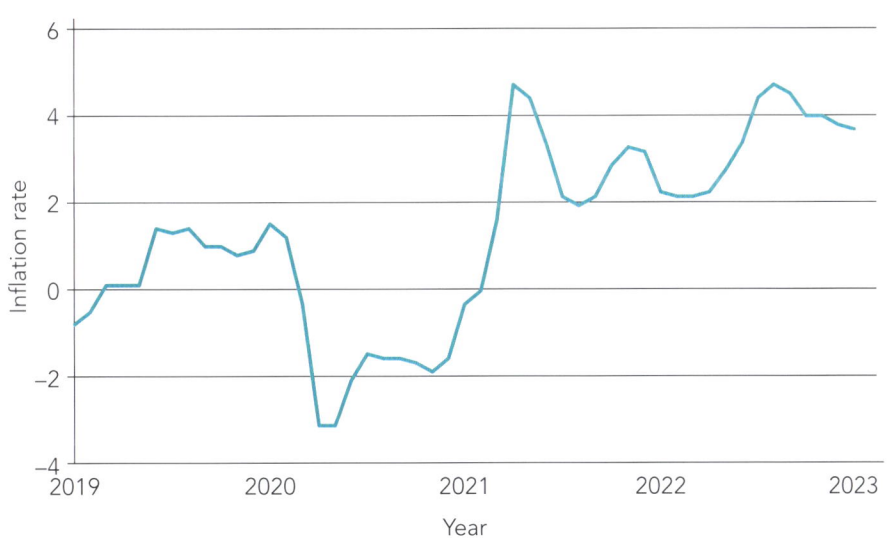

Figure 26.6: Malaysia's inflation rate from 2019 to 2023

*Source:* tradingeconomics.com

> **CONTINUED**
>
>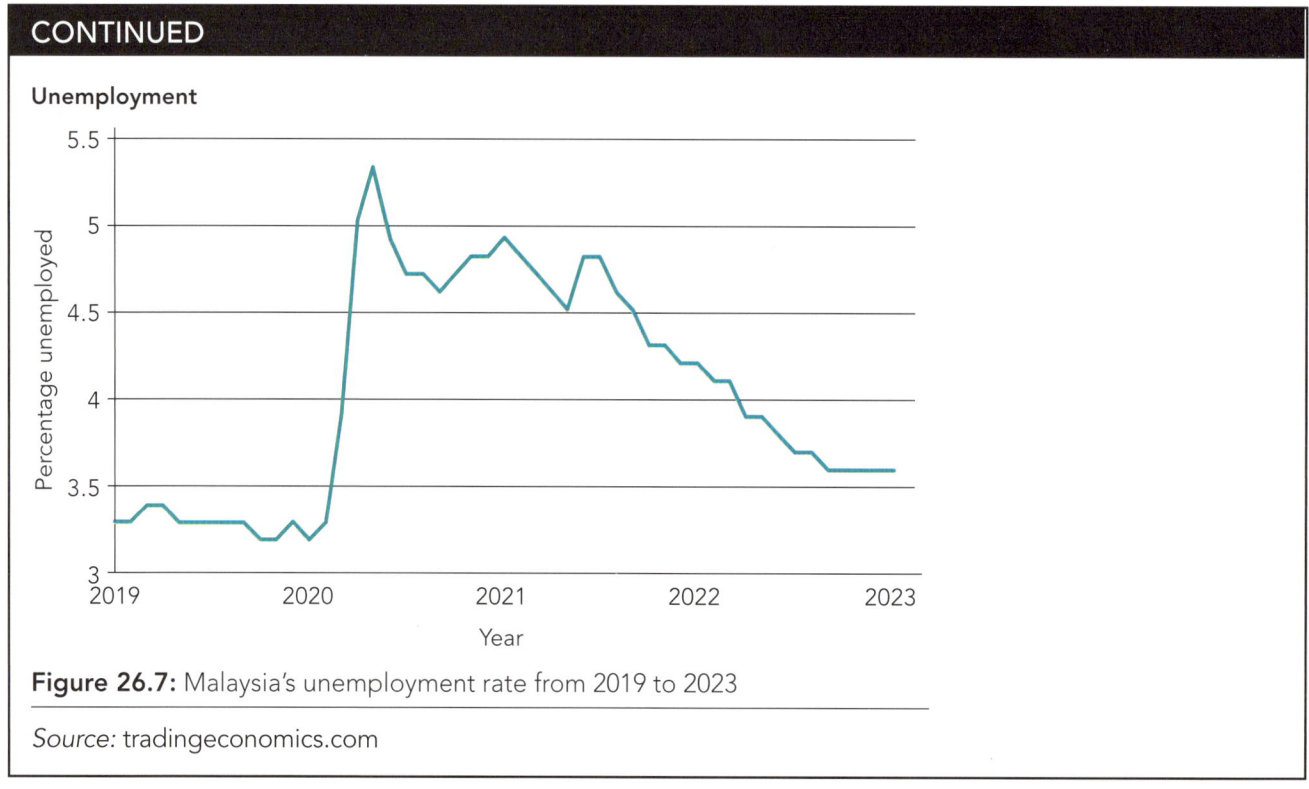
>
> Figure 26.7: Malaysia's unemployment rate from 2019 to 2023
>
> *Source:* tradingeconomics.com

> **DISCUSSION**
>
> 1. Why would the government of a country want a low inflation rate?
> 2. Why would the government of a country want a low unemployment rate?

## 26.3 Effects of government policy

Governments mainly get their income from **taxes** and they spend this income fulfilling the common needs of the people in areas such as education, infrastructure and health. But tax rates can only be altered to a certain extent, so governments may need to borrow funds to pay for all their spending.

Figure 26.8 shows the components of how a government earns and spends its income.

> **KEY TERM**
>
> **tax:** a charge/fee paid to the government on individual's income, business profit or its goods and services.

# 26 Economic issues

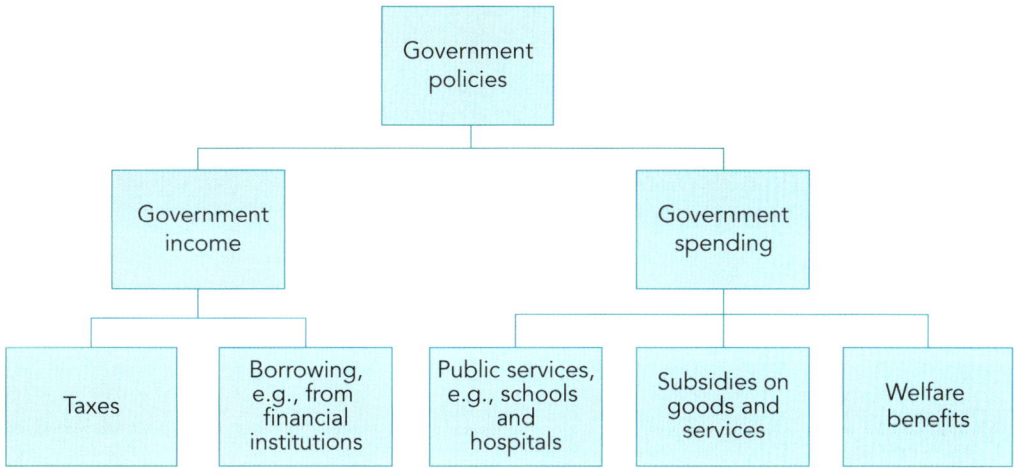

**Figure 26.8:** Government policies

Through its policies, the government uses taxes, **interest rates** and government spending to influence the economic conditions of a country.

For example, a steady growth in the economic activity of a country is what most governments aim for. If the growth is too fast, it may not be long-lasting as the infrastructure to support this growth may not exist. A slow growth rate will increase unemployment levels as there will be fewer jobs. In this situation, governments may change their economic policies to encourage growth.

> **KEY TERM**
>
> **interest rate:** the cost to a person or business of borrowing money from a lender such as a bank.

### ACTIVITY 26.1

1. What should the government use tax money for?
2. What expenses should a government cover for members of society who have no money?
3. Do some research to find out what the government in your country spends most of its money on.
   a. In what areas should spending go up?
   b. In what areas should there be less spending?

## How changes in taxes affect business activity

Taxes are used by governments to pay for investments they make in public services, such as education, health and transportation. Taxes affect both businesses and people.

### Types of taxes

There are two main types of taxes that can be paid by an individual or a business.

- Tax on people's income (sometimes known as income tax).
- Tax on business profit (sometimes known as corporation tax).

**Tax on people's income**

The amount of tax charged depends on the amount of income. The higher the income tax rate, the smaller the disposable income of individuals – the amount of income left over for individuals after taxes have been paid.

If the economy is in recession, the government may decide to invest in certain sectors to encourage growth. This investment may be partly funded by higher tax rates. Figure 26.9 shows the effects of increasing income tax rates on consumers and businesses, as well as how businesses respond.

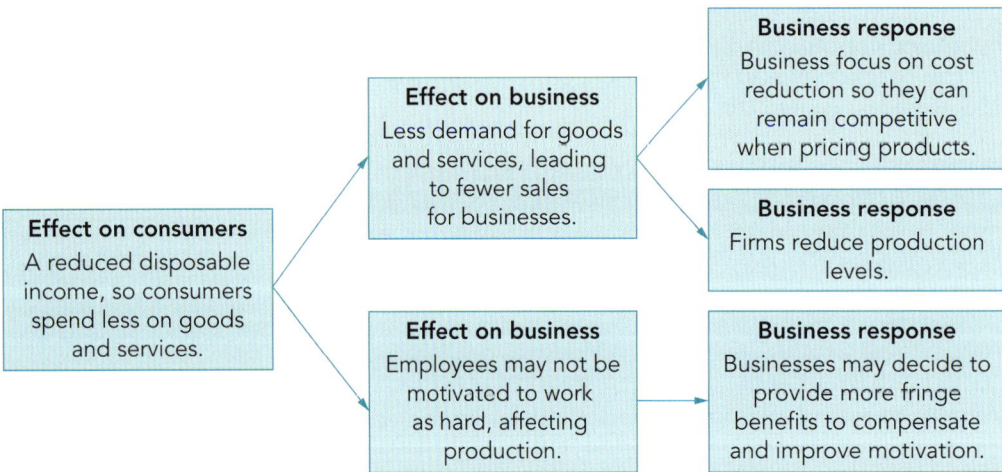

**Figure 26.9:** The effects of an increase in income tax rates

## ACTIVITY 26.2

Hasan Ahmed is a computer software engineer for a technology company in Country Z. He has a monthly salary of $5 000. His income level is taxed at the rate of 20%.

1. How much disposable income would Hasan have after paying tax on his income?

2. The government of Country Z has raised the tax rate to 25%. What would be the impact on Hasan's disposable income and his spending habits?

**Taxes on business**

This is the tax paid by businesses on the profits they make. The higher the business tax rate, the smaller the profits after tax available to businesses.

If a country is in recession and the government's objective is to encourage economic growth, it can lower the tax rate on business profit.

## ACTIVITY 26.3

Kanta Enterprises wants to expand its operations in another country. It looks at the corporation tax rates in Countries A, B and C to see which country offers the best business environment for them.

| Country | Tax rate on businesses (on revenue less than $1 000 000) | Tax paid ($) |
| --- | --- | --- |
| A | 28% | |
| B | 26% | |
| C | 32% | |

1. Assuming a profit of $600 000, copy and complete the table to show the tax that Kanta Enterprises may have to pay in each of these countries.

2. Which country should Kanta Enterprises expand its operations in based on the corporation tax rate?

3. What is the tax rate on businesses in your country?

   a. Do you think it is competitive with neighbouring countries in order to attract overseas investment? (Hint: Use the internet or ask your teacher to provide you with business newspapers or journals to do your research.)

   b. Consider how a decrease in the tax rate on businesses can affect the businesses in a particular industry that is dominant in your country.

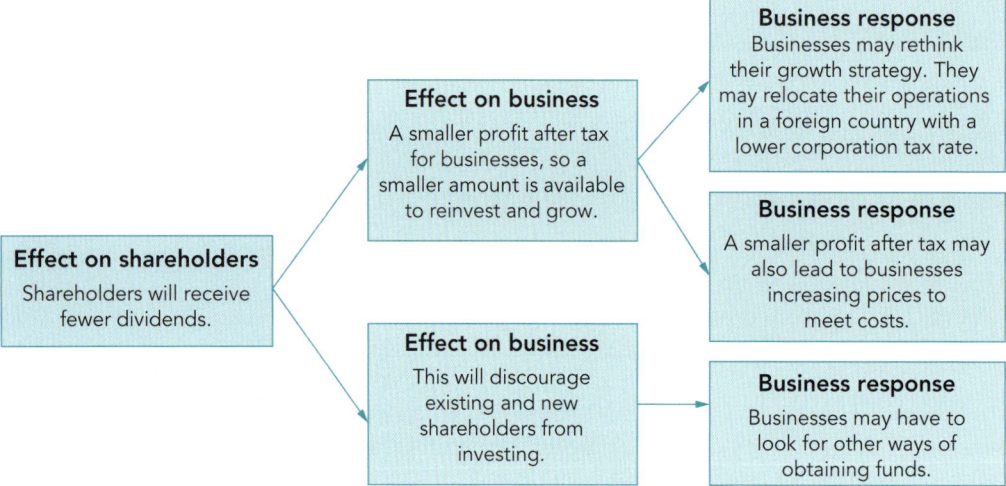

Figure 26.10: The effects of an increase in corporation tax rates

An increase in the tax rate on businesses will lead to a smaller profit after tax for businesses. Figure 26.10 looks at the impact of this on shareholders and businesses and how businesses may respond to this.

## How changes in government spending affect business activity

The money raised through taxes is used by the government to improve the infrastructure of its country.

The government can affect economic growth by controlling its own spending. If growth is slow, the government can increase its spending in areas such as schools, hospitals and transportation. This will create more jobs in these and other dependent sectors. For example, if the government spends more on roads, then construction firms that build and repair the road network will benefit. This will encourage businesses to think about growth. Alternatively, the government can affect the level of business activity by reducing its spending or discouraging businesses from expansion.

## 26.4 How businesses might respond to changes in taxes and interest rates

The government or central bank uses interest rates to maintain economic growth and keep inflation low.

Interest rates determine:

- the money that an individual or a financial organisation can gain when they deposit money with a bank
- the cost of borrowing money from a bank.

26 Economic issues

Some Islamic countries follow Sharia law, which does not permit financial gain on loan of money. These countries combine standard and Islamic banking principles (which are based on profit sharing and non-interest-based lending and borrowing).

### ACTIVITY 26.4

Below is a newspaper article published in a national newspaper of Country X.

**Country X's economy remains in recession**

Country X's economy has been in recession since late 2018 and is unlikely to return to growth before 2024. The unemployment rate has hit an all-time high of 27%. Although inflation has remained steady, economic growth rate has massively declined. The government has tried to encourage growth and investment by keeping interest rates at 0.5%. It has put together a committee of economic and financial experts to recommend further measures to improve economic growth.

1 Make a list of the economic factors that reflect the state of the economy of Country X.
2 What measures has the government of Country X taken to help the economy?
3 What problems might businesses in Country X face in a recession?

Figure 26.11 explains the effects of increase in interest rates on consumers and businesses and how businesses respond to this.

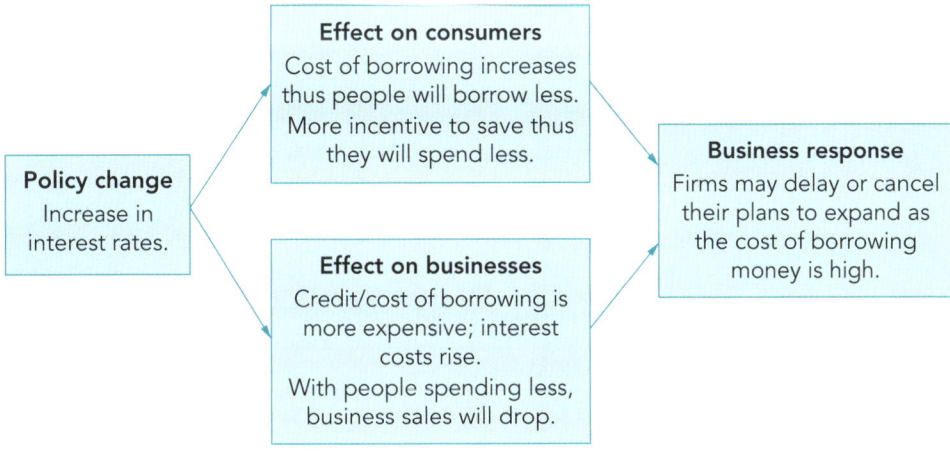

Figure 26.11: The effects of an increase in interest rates

In the long term, an increase in interest rates may lead to the following effects on the economy:

- Reduced business activity leading to slow economic growth.
- High rate of return from savings will encourage individuals and financial institutions from other countries to invest their money with the banks in that country. This strengthens the national currency and leads to exchange rate appreciation. This will make imports cheaper.

### TIP

Make sure you understand what happens when interest or tax rates change. If rates rise, what does this mean for businesses and consumers? How could you explain it?

Changes in taxation and interest rates affect businesses differently. Generally, businesses that produce non-essential/luxury goods and services (such as electronic gadgets and the tourism industry) are affected the most by changes in taxation policies. Businesses that produce essential goods and services, such as food and health-related products, are less affected by such changes. People cannot do without essential goods and must buy them no matter how expensive they are.

### CASE STUDY 26.3

**The changing interest rates in Botswana**

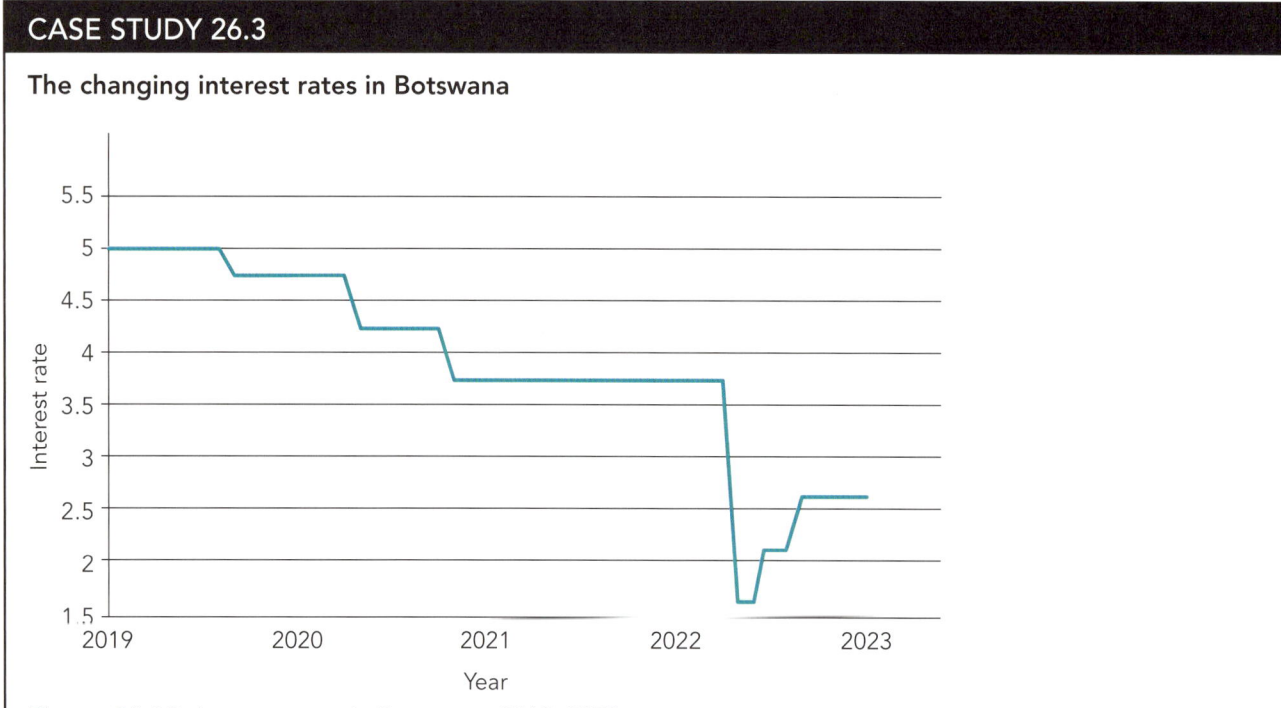

**Figure 26.12:** Interest rates in Botswana, 2019–2023

*Source:* www.tradingeconomics.com, the Bank of Botswana.

**The interest rate in Botswana**

The interest rate changes made by the Bank of Botswana from 2019 to 2023 are shown in Figure 26.12.

The interest rate in Botswana was at a record high of 5% in 2019 and was 2.65% in 2023.

Patience Naledi is thinking about buying a house. She met with the Bank Manager to apply for a housing loan/mortgage. The Bank Manager explained how changes in interest rates could affect how much she has to spend each month. She did this by analysing the changes in interest rates (assuming these are the lending rates too) and their impact over the last few years on a borrowed amount of 700 000 pula.

| Year | Interest rate | Annual interest payment (pula) | Monthly payment (pula) |
|---|---|---|---|
| 2019 | 5% | 35 000 | 2 917 |
| 2020 | 4.8% | | |
| 2021 | 3.8% | | |
| 2022 | 1.65% | | |
| 2023 | 2.65% | | |

**Discuss in pairs or groups:**
1  Copy and complete the table provided above.
2  Use the graph to describe how interest rates have changed over the last five years.
3  Do you think it is a good time for Patience Naledi to take up a loan/mortgage in order to buy a house? Explain your answer.

## BUSINESS IN ACTION

### Expansion into Southeast Asia

Figure 26.13: Textile industry worker sorting fabrics

Imagine you have your own manufacturing company and are looking at expanding into Southeast Asia. You have collected some useful economic information on three countries (see Table 26.2).

### Discuss in pairs or groups:

Using the information below, which of the three countries would you prefer to expand your operations in?

Table 26.2: Economic information about countries in Southeast Asia

| Country | Corporation tax rate | Interest rate | Unemployment rate | Inflation |
|---|---|---|---|---|
| Indonesia | 22% | 6% | 5.3% | 2.6% |
| The Philippines | 25% | 6.5% | 4.5% | 4.9% |
| Singapore | 17% | 3.6% | 2% | 4.1% |

The following sentence stems may be useful to analyse the significance/impact of each factor on business activity.

- _____ has the lowest inflation rate. The advantage of a low inflation rate is that _____
- _____ has the highest unemployment rate. The advantage of a high unemployment rate is that _____
- _____ offers the lowest corporation tax rate. The advantage of a low corporation tax rate is that_____
- _____ offers the lowest interest rate. The advantage of a low interest rate is that _____
- What other factors would you need to consider?

### ACTIVITY 26.5

Working in pairs, use the internet to develop your understanding of your country's economy. Identify what stage of the business cycle your country is in.

Use the questions in the table below to analyse and understand the key economic factors and record your findings in a suitable table, as shown below:

| Economic factor to be considered | Trend – has this factor gone up or down? | Consider the following to analyse and understand the economic factors | |
|---|---|---|---|
| Inflation | | What is the current level of inflation? | |
| | | Has there been a noticeable change in the inflation, i.e., did you notice the change in your daily life? | |
| Unemployment | | What is the current level of unemployment? | |

**Discuss in pairs or groups:**

1. What stage of the business cycle is your country's economy in? What are its key characteristics?

2. Analyse the above two economic factors. Do you think there will be low, medium or high economic growth in your country?

3. What other factors do you think will affect your country's economic growth?

4. Identify and explain what steps could be taken by the government to encourage more business activity.

### REFLECTION

Think about Activity 26.5. What did you learn from completing this activity? Did it encourage you to think about your country's economy? What is the benefit of applying your learning to a relevant example? Share you answers with a partner or as a small group and reflect on your analysis and understanding of your country's economy. Did your answers differ?

> **SUMMARY**
>
> You should now know:
>
> - There are four stages in the business cycle: growth, boom, recession and slump. These can affect business activity in different ways.
>
> - Economic growth, low inflation and low unemployment are the key objectives of any government.
>
> - Governments aim to achieve these objectives by changes to tax and interest rates and also by controlling how much they spend on public services.

# Chapter 26 practice questions

1.  The economy of Country P has been in recession for the past six months. Things have become worse as unemployment rate in Country P has risen from 4.2% to 7.1% in the past year; the inflation is said to have gone up and the economic growth is decreasing. Country P is a very small country and relies heavily on imports from other countries. Retail businesses have been affected the most as their import costs are rising.

    a  Identify **two** stages (other than recession) of the business cycle. [2]

    b  Outline **two** types of taxes (one type of tax a business has to pay, and one type of tax a consumer has to pay) that the businesses in Country P may have to pay. [4]

    c  Explain **two** effects that the rising unemployment levels may have on a retail company in Country P. [6]

    d  Explain **two** ways that the government of Country P can help stimulate growth in the economy. Justify your answer. [8]

2.  Country M is experiencing an economic boom with increasing demand for goods and services. The country is a major exporter of agricultural produce and copper. It is also a popular tourist destination. However, Country M is heavily dependent upon imports of fuels for its energy needs, which is very expensive. The government wants to accelerate economic growth further, so it is considering how it can adjust the interest rates to attract more investment from both local and overseas companies.

    a  Define 'economic boom'. [2]

    b  Explain **one** benefit of low unemployment and **one** benefit of low inflation on businesses in Country M. [4]

    c  Explain the effect of a decrease in both corporation tax and income tax rates in attracting new companies to invest in Country M. [6]

    d  Do you think an increase in interest rates in Country M will be helpful to businesses? Justify your answer. [8]

    **Total available marks: 40**

> **TIP**
>
> Always answer the longer questions in context. For example, when explaining the impact of tax and interest rates on businesses, make sure you relate it to the business or country mentioned in the question.

## CHECK YOUR PROGRESS

How well do you think you have achieved the learning intentions for this chapter? Give yourself a score from 1 (still need a lot of practice) to 5 (feeling very confident) for each learning intention. Provide an example to support your score.

| Now I can … | Score | Example |
| --- | --- | --- |
| explain the main stages of the business cycle and how each stage of the business cycle might affect a business | | |
| describe the effects of changes in the levels of employment, inflation and economic growth on a business | | |
| describe the effects of government policy: changes in government spending and interest rates as well as taxes on business profit and people's income | | |
| understand how businesses respond to changes in taxes and interest rates. | | |

# Chapter 27
# Business and the international economy

**LEARNING INTENTIONS**

By the end of this chapter, you will be able to:

- understand the reasons for globalisation and its opportunities and threats for businesses
- discuss import tariffs and import quotas and their effects on businesses
- understand what a multinational company (MNC) is and the advantages to a business of becoming an MNC
- discuss the advantages and disadvantages for a country where an MNC is located
- understand and analyse the external costs and external benefits of business decisions
- explain the impact of appreciation and depreciation of exchange rates on importers and exporters of products and services.

# Introduction

Countries that trade with each other contribute to the process of **globalisation**. Rapid developments in technology have made it possible to connect cultures, societies and economies across the world, making international expansion much easier for companies. For many businesses, expansion into international markets is an important growth strategy.

The international business environment and things such as tariffs and exchange rate fluctuations greatly influence business activity.

> **KEY TERM**
>
> **globalisation:** the process by which countries are connected with one another because of the trade of goods and services.

## BUSINESS IN CONTEXT

### Globalisation

Figure 27.1: Globalisation enables us to share goods and services, ideas, language and culture

Have you ever wondered how many of the products and services that you use are from abroad? Check where your phone, tablet, gaming console, computer or your family/friend's car was manufactured. If you are on any social media, then you are using a service provided from abroad. Do you enjoy food or music from other countries? Globalisation is the reason why we can share goods and services, ideas, language and culture from different countries. Coca-Cola is one such global brand.

Founded in 1886 and headquartered in Atlanta in the USA, Coca-Cola is one of the most popular multinational beverages in the world. Coca-Cola marketing and advertising campaigns through television, print, digital, and social media platforms have been very impactful and have resulted in strong brand recognition and consumer loyalty.

The company's products are sold under 500 brands catering to diverse needs and preferences of consumers in more than 200 countries. It is important for Coca-Cola to understand the needs, preferences and tastes of consumers in different regions as well as cater to the latest lifestyle trends to ensure its products appeal to a diverse audience. Therefore, it offers a wide variety of products from water, juices, ready to drink teas and coffees, sugar-free drinks, sports drinks and, of course, the original soft drink. Its most popular brands include Coca-Cola, Diet Coke, Coca-Cola Zero, Fanta, Sprite, Minute Maid, Dasani, Powerade and Honest Tea.

Due to its global presence, Coca-Cola must comply with local and international regulations of trade and taxation and adapt to the changing political climate of the countries it operates in. As a multinational corporation, which operates in many different countries, it must conduct business in multiple currencies. Fluctuations in exchange rates can impact the company's revenues, costs and profitability.

### Discuss in pairs or groups:

1. Are there other brands like Coca-Cola that have a global presence and have impacted your life or your community?
2. What do you think are the main factors that have led to the growth of globalisation?
3. What factors do you think Coca-Cola would have considered before expanding operations in other countries?

27 Business and the international economy

## 27.1 The importance of globalisation

In the past, goods and services were often produced in one country and sold locally. Nowadays, goods and services may be produced by a business in one country and then exported to countries all over the world. One type of business is the **multinational company (MNC)**, where a company has its headquarters in one country and branches and factories in other countries around the world. The result has been a huge increase in international trade which has led to globalisation. Globalisation has a great impact on the people and the countries involved. For example:

- people benefit from a wider variety of products available to them at a lower cost
- reduction in prices contributes to greater exports and incoming currency from other countries
- attracting more businesses to invest in their country can help governments achieve their economic objectives, such as lower unemployment and increase economic growth.

With greater cultural, technological, social and political interaction between countries (globalisation) and fewer barriers and regulations, there is greater trade (exchange of goods and services between countries). This makes the world a single market – where there is free movement of goods, services and people – with the economies of different countries being dependent upon one another. Brands become recognised globally and products and services are easily accessible anywhere in the world. Figure 27.2 shows the key characteristics of globalisation.

> **KEY TERM**
>
> **multinational company (MNC):** an organisation that has operations in more than one country.

**Characteristics of globalisation:**
- growth in international trade
- dependency on the global economy
- greater movement of products, services, people and money
- companies operating in more than one country
- global recognition of brands

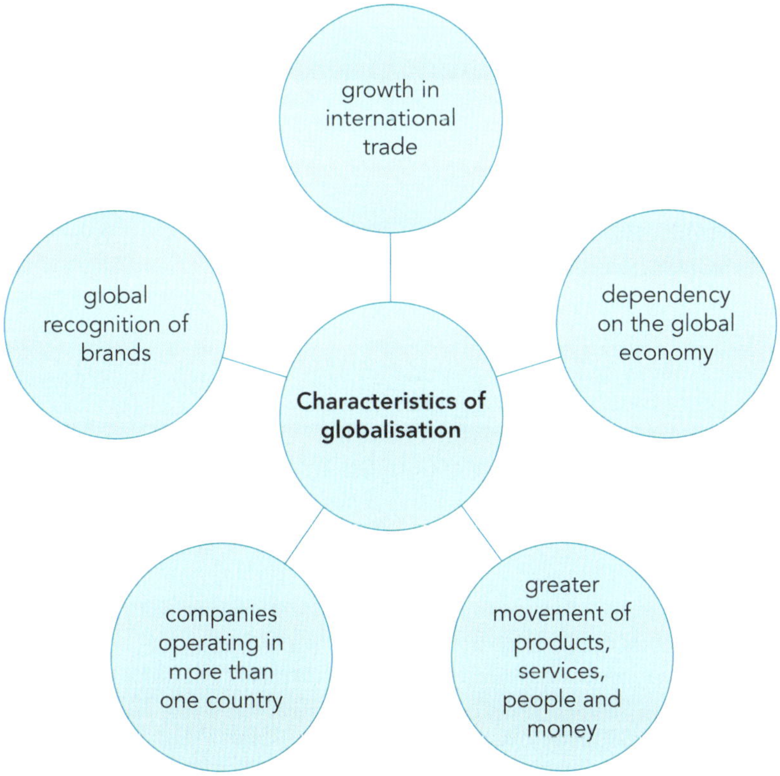

Figure 27.2: Characteristics of globalisation

## Reasons for globalisation

There have been many reasons for globalisation in recent years. All the factors mentioned below have made international expansion easier for companies.

1   **Improved transport links** – Improved transport links such as container shipping and air travel have reduced costs, increased connectivity and decreased the time taken to move goods from one country to another.

2   **Technological change** – Innovations in technologies such as the internet have made immediate communication easier through emails, video conferences and mobile phones. This has allowed people to work remotely from anywhere in the world. Digital payment systems and the digitisation of information has helped information, knowledge and services to be provided easily across borders.

3   **Free trade agreements** – To allow easy movement of goods, services and people across borders, governments have actively implemented policies to reduce trade barriers (restrictions) and signed free trade agreements.

4   **Newly industrialised countries** – Countries such as Republic of Korea, Singapore and Malaysia in Asia, as well as Brazil and Mexico in Latin America have experienced rapid economic growth and development in the last decade leading to an increase in globalisation. Various factors such as government policies to attract investment support from other countries' export-oriented industries and provide incentives for innovation and entrepreneurship along with technological and infrastructure development have contributed to the economic growth of these countries.

> **LINK**
>
> For more information on economic growth, see Chapter 26.

### DISCUSSION

Which reason do you think is the most important for the growth of globalisation?

### ACTIVITY 27.1

Carlos owns a manufacturing business. He buys the raw material locally but is concerned that it has become expensive and the quality is not as good as before. He has found a supplier of better quality raw material in a neighbouring country. He currently sells his products to the local market but would also like to sell them to other countries. His country's government is planning to sign a free trade agreement with the neighbouring countries. The government says this would encourage more trade between the countries.

1   What do you think are the main reasons for Carlos going for a global expansion strategy?

2   How might joining the free trade agreement help Carlos with the raw materials that he needs for his business?

3   What would be the benefit of Carlos's country joining a free trade agreement? Would there be any disadvantages?

## Opportunities and threats of globalisation

Globalisation provides many opportunities to businesses, such as being able to expand into global markets and benefits from increased sales and possible reduced labour costs. There are, however, threats of globalisation too, increasing competition causing local businesses to suffer being one of the main ones. Table 27.1 outlines the key opportunities and threats of globalisation for businesses.

**Table 27.1:** Advantages and disadvantages of globalisation for businesses

| Advantages | Disadvantages |
|---|---|
| • **Access to more markets** – Businesses can enter more markets, which may lead to an increase in sales.<br>• **Lower labour costs** – Labour may be cheaper in some countries so businesses can benefit from lower costs.<br>• **Access to cheaper and better range of resources** – Businesses may operate in countries that have better raw materials or technological infrastructure, giving them a competitive advantage.<br>• **Global brand recognition** – May make consumers perceive products to be of higher quality and hence more desirable.<br>• **Economies of scale** – Having large-scale operations across many countries allows businesses to benefit from economies in marketing and possibly production and distribution too.<br>• **Spread risk** – Operating in different countries/markets with varying economic conditions and business cycles reduces risk, so businesses benefit from presence in different markets. | • **Increased competition for local businesses** – Local businesses may lose sales as other businesses start to sell their products at a cheaper price.<br>• **Currency fluctuations** – If currency appreciates, imports may become more expensive which increases business costs, so businesses may have to increase prices leading to decrease in demand or profit margins.<br>If currency depreciates, exports become relatively more expensive, which decreases demand and could necessitate lowering production levels or reducing the number of employees. For more on currency fluctuations see Section 27.6.<br>• **Increase in marketing and distribution** costs due to markets being spread across the world. |

With more trade between countries due to globalisation, there is an increase in demand and supply of goods and services. To meet the increasing demand, businesses produce more goods and services, which leads to economic growth in that country.

Despite the advantages and disadvantages mentioned in Table 27.1, entry to international markets for some businesses is an important objective, as it will enable them to grow. Starbucks, Nike and Samsung are examples of companies that have grown because of their expansion into other countries.

> **LINK**
>
> For more information about economies of scale, see Chapter 18.

### CASE STUDY 27.1

**Is Tesla a globalisation success story?**

**Figure 27.3:** More affordable electric vehicle cars will attract a broader customer base

Tesla Inc is an American multinational automotive and clean energy company headquartered in Austin, Texas. Roadster was the first car produced by Tesla in 2008 in California. Tesla cars can now be found on roads around the world. It is pushing for global expansion and wants to open more factories around the world. It aims to create more affordable electric vehicle (EV) options to attract a broader customer base and produce the first fully self-driving car. The EV market is set to reach 35 million by 2030 with China and Europe being the two big EV markets.

Tesla has a global presence, with production facilities in China and the United States, as well as 438 stores and 100 service centres in various countries.

As part of its expansion strategy, Tesla is also setting up factories around the world – aiming to expand manufacturing capacity quickly, the strategy being to open factories where there is market potential. It also opened a factory in Berlin, Germany in 2022. This is the first European factory designed to produce 500 000 vehicles per year. This factory allows them to sell directly to European countries instead of importing them from China and the United States. Tesla is also planning to set up a factory in Mexico.

Tesla faces a lot of challenges in building factories in new countries:

- Elon Musk, the co-founder and CEO of Tesla, has a hands-on approach and likes to work one-on-one with his engineers. He feels that it is essential to build good products, but this slows down decision-making.

- The company develops most of its own components/parts inhouse, which makes it difficult for Tesla to increase production as compared to other automakers making EVs, such as Toyota and Volkswagen. Tesla may have to source its products from other companies to keep up with the competition.

- Other automakers, such as Toyota and Volkswagen, already have factories across the world and vast distribution networks. While they are converting their existing manufacturing plants into EV plants, Tesla must start from scratch, which is expensive.

- Working within the legal and regulatory environment of other countries requires keeping in close contact with the legal requirements.

It also needs to keep in mind a low carbon emission approach and its environmental impact.

**Discuss in pairs or groups:**

1 How is Tesla growing globally?
2 Which countries are its biggest market?
3 Which countries does it have factories in?
4 What challenges has Tesla faced when setting up factories abroad?
5 Do some research with your partner to see Tesla's performance currently. Evaluate if Tesla is a globalisation success story.

## 27.2 Why governments introduce import tariffs and import quotas

Globalisation offers consumers a wider choice of products and services, but this may cause problems for businesses in the host country – this is the overseas country where a business sets up its operations. Multinational companies can often supply products and services at cheaper prices than local businesses. Smaller businesses sometimes cannot compete and may have to close with a loss of jobs. If MNCs start to take over the trade in the host country, this can have a damaging effect on the local economy. As local businesses and shops close, there will be less choice for consumers and unemployment may rise. For these reasons, governments often try to control the amount of international trade. Two of the main ways they use are tariffs and quotas.

### Import tariffs

An **import tariff** is a type of tax paid on goods that are imported from other countries.

A government may place a tariff on imports to reduce imports into the country. The tariff increases the cost of the imported goods, and businesses then must sell the goods at a higher price. This reduces local demand for the goods and benefits local businesses as they have less competition.

Tax on imports is important because this can be expensive for a country. The import tariff also earns revenue for the government.

> **KEY TERM**
>
> **import tariff:** a tax applied to the value of imported goods into a country.

### Quotas

An **import quota** is a physical limit on the quantity of goods that can be imported into a country. Quotas on imports benefit local producers as there are fewer goods from other countries in the market and they face less competition. However, customers might be disappointed as there are limited supplies of popular products. Quotas are set on the import of certain commodities, either from specific countries or globally. Exporting countries may suffer as they will only be able to sell a limited amount of goods to the country that has a quota.

> **KEY TERM**
>
> **import quota:** physical limit on the quantity of goods that can be imported into a country.

> **ACTIVITY 27.2**
>
> With globalisation, we can now communicate, trade and share each other's cultures around the world in minutes. There is however an ongoing debate on whether globalisation is indeed beneficial to the economy of a country and its people's lives. What do you think?
>
> **Discuss in groups:**
>
> In groups of three or more, consider the following motion for a debate: *Globalisation is beneficial to the economy of a country and its people's lives.*
>
> 1. Decide which country you would like to base this on. Do some research on this country first.
> 2. Decide who would like to speak in favour of and against the motion.
> 3. Decide who would like to chair and judge the debate.

### CONTINUED

4. Research and prepare: Identify all the arguments in favour/against, decide which is the strongest in favour/against and emphasise this more in your debate.

5. Challenge yourself by justifying your main argument.

6. Have the debate; take in turns to put forward your arguments in favour of and against globalisation.

7. Once both sides of the arguments have been heard, the chair will decide which side wins and justify their choice.

### TIP

- To identify the positive and negative impacts, it may be useful to think from the perspective of an environmentalist, a trade unionist, a business owner, a consumer, an employee or the government.
- Using examples of businesses in your country will make your arguments stronger.
- If you are in favour of the motion, consider the positive impacts of globalisation. If you are against the motion, consider the negative impacts of globalisation.

### TIP

Remember, for a business to be called 'multinational' it must produce goods and services in more than one country. The term does not apply to a business that only sells its products in other countries.

## 27.3 Multinational companies

A multinational company is a business that has operations in more than one country. Whether a business decides to expand internationally or become an MNC will depend on what its objectives are. The home country is where an MNC first sets up its operations – this is where it is likely to have its head office. The host country is the other country where an MNC sets up its operations.

### CASE STUDY 27.2

**Mauritius attracts multinational companies**

**Figure 27.4:** Port Louis in Mauritius is an attractive place for MNCs

In the last decade, Mauritius has emerged as one of the most attractive countries in Africa for businesses looking to expand their operations. Some of the factors that have contributed to it being so attractive for MNCs are:

- a stable democracy
- availability of a skilled workforce – well educated and multilingual
- competitive labour costs compared to other countries
- a growing economy with a consistent GDP growth

> **CONTINUED**
>
> - low corporate tax rates
> - located on a shipping route in the Indian Ocean
> - excellent port facilities
> - a safe living environment
> - modern telecommunications networks and reliable internet services
> - efficient transportation system.
>
> **Discuss in pairs or groups:**
>
> 1. Choose three of the factors and explain why they are important in making Mauritius an attractive place for MNCs.
> 2. Rank the three factors you chose in Question 1 from the most important to the least important. How did you decide which factor was the most important?
> 3. Why might some businesses in Mauritius oppose globalisation?

# 27.4 Advantages to a business of becoming a multinational company

Most businesses benefit from expanding their operations in other countries. The advantages are shown in Figure 27.5.

> **TIP**
>
> The coming of an MNC has both positive and negative effects on a country.

> **ACTIVITY 27.3**
>
> A company decides to set up operations abroad and become a multinational company. Before deciding on this expansion strategy, the company wants to consider the effect on all stakeholders. Look again at Chapter 5 to remind yourself of the different business stakeholders and their objectives. Copy the table and add two more stakeholders to the table. See the example on the positive impact on shareholders. Working with a partner, identify the positive and negative impact on different stakeholders of this decision.
>
> | Stakeholder | Positive impact | Negative impact |
> | --- | --- | --- |
> | Shareholders/Owners | Potential to increase dividends and the value of shares if the multinational increases overall profits. | |
> | Employees/Managers | | |
> | Customers | | |
> | | | |
> | | | |

Easier access to raw materials – By setting up operations where the raw materials are easily available, businesses can reduce transportation time and costs and maybe even avoid trade barriers. This will lower production costs and improve reliability of supply.

Premium pricing – MNCs may be able to charge higher prices for globally recognised brands.

Economies of scale – By selling in many countries, businesses can benefit from economies of large-scale production. This makes them very competitive.

Lower cost of labour – If there is plenty of labour in the host country then it is likely to be available cheap.

Spreading of risk – MNCs are not dependent on one market. Their business may not be badly affected even if one of their markets is in decline, politically unstable or has a natural disaster.

Lower production costs – Energy costs and the purchase or renting of business sites may be cheaper in host countries. If there is a local market then companies can save on transportation costs also.

Access to bigger markets – Mergers and joint ventures with companies in the host country can lead to increases in revenue.

Figure 27.5: Advantages of becoming a multinational company

## Advantages of a multinational company to the host country

The host country benefits from multinational companies that set up operations in its country. The advantages are shown in Table 27.2.

### LINK

For more information on opportunities and problems of entering new markets in other countries, see Chapter 14.

# 27 Business and the international economy

Table 27.2: Advantages of a multinational company to the host country

| Advantage of a multinational company to the host country | Impact of the advantage |
|---|---|
| Increases the choice and quality of goods and services | The local market has access to a greater variety of goods. Due to competition and better production methods, the quality of goods may be higher too. |
| Increases job/employment opportunities | The local workforce will be employed to work in the MNC. Governments of host countries provide incentives to MNCs to set up in areas with high unemployment and a plentiful supply of labour. |
| Generates tax revenue for government | The profit generated by the MNC will be taxable in the host country; this government revenue can be spent on important services such as healthcare, infrastructure and education. |
| Reduces imports | Imports, which can be expensive, may reduce as the MNC may be able to provide the products that were previously imported. Exports may increase as the MNC has a global presence. |
| Improves the country's reputation | Companies from another country investing in the host country indicate that the country has a positive economic environment. This may encourage other MNCs to set up there. |
| Improves infrastructure | The MNC may have to invest in transportation and communication networks. This may benefit everyone in the host country. |

# Disadvantages of a multinational company to the host country

Multinational companies also have some disadvantages to the host country. These are shown in Table 27.3.

Table 27.3: Disadvantages of a multinational company to the host country

| Disadvantage of a multinational company to the host country | Impact of the disadvantage |
|---|---|
| Exploitation of labour | If the host country has high unemployment, then MNCs may pay low-skilled employees low wages and recruit skilled workers from other countries for high-skilled jobs. |
| Undue influence on the government | The investments made by MNCs can be huge, greatly affecting the economic conditions of the host country. In exchange for this, MNCs may try to influence government policies that affect them. This may not be good for the host country in the long term. |
| Increased competition | Since MNCs are large and maybe experts in their area of operation, they are cost-efficient and can provide better-quality goods at lower prices. Local companies that provide the same goods may suffer in such a case. |
| Repatriation of profit | Many MNCs repatriate (send back) the profits that they earn to their home country, leaving the host country with very little financial benefit. |

(Continued)

**Table 27.3:** (Continued)

| Disadvantage of a multinational company to the host country | Impact of the disadvantage |
| --- | --- |
| Environmental damage | MNCs aim to produce goods as quickly and as cheaply as possible, and in doing so, they may ignore their impact on the environment. |
| Exploitation of natural resources | Sometimes, MNCs set up their operations in host countries so they can have access to their natural resources. This may lead to scarcity of that natural resource in the host country. |

### BUSINESS IN ACTION

**LG in India**

**Figure 27.6:** LG Electronics opened a megastore in Mumbai, India

As an expansion strategy, LG Electronics of Republic of Korea established LG Electronics India, a private limited company, in January 1997 and it is now one of the most popular brands in India for home appliances, consumer electronics and IT hardware. It has manufacturing plants in Noida and Pune and plans to set up another one in a new location to increase the production of its most popular items. Today, most of the company's products are manufactured locally, which has helped it cut costs.

Another reason for LG's success in the Indian market is its strategy to customise its products to suit the Indian market. For example, LG India designed and produced refrigerators with a shelf for spices, an essential for Indian cooking. Its low-priced, good-quality products have helped LG remain competitive in India and tap into its huge population and market potential.

India has a growing population of high-income earners. The country also has the strongest demand for premium electronics than any other market. As of 2023, LG dominated the country's TV sector with a market share of more than 70% and it ranked first in the washing machine sector with a market share of 34.8%. The company's sales in India continue to grow.

**Discuss in pairs or groups:**

1. Identify the main reasons for LG's success in India.
2. What characteristics of the Indian market have been beneficial for LG?
3. How do we know that LG's expansion strategy in India has been successful?

## 27.5 External costs and benefits of business decisions

A business's activities can have a negative or positive impact on individuals, the community and the environment; these are known as its external costs and benefits. Some business activities are more environmentally friendly than others. How a business uses energy, disposes of waste or creates pollution and its impact on everyday life may have far-reaching effects on the local community and other businesses in the area, considering external costs are important for sustainable and responsible business practices.

## External costs

The negative impact of business activity on the environment and its effects on individuals and society is its **external cost**. For example, environmental pollution caused by a factory manufacturing goods is an external cost because the cost of the pollution (such as health problems or environmental damage) is not paid by the factory or its owners, but rather by society. Some examples of external costs are:

- **Traffic congestion** – A business decision that leads to increased traffic congestion can create external costs for local residents and other road users because of the time wasted in traffic jams.
- **Pollution** – Business activity that creates a lot of noise or air pollution can create external costs for local residents or businesses by reducing their quality of life or lead to health risks.
- **Using up natural resources** – Business activities such as mining can use up natural resources, so future generations may not have access to those resources.
- **Loss of land or space** – Factories or operations reduce the amount of land or green spaces for people or nature.

> **KEY TERM**
>
> **external cost:** where a business decision has a negative impact on a third party.

## External benefits

An **external benefit** of a business activity is a benefit that is gained by another party. It contributes to the protection and preservation of the environment and betterment of society. For example, the construction of a new hospital in a residential area will create more jobs and the local community will have easier access to healthcare. Some examples of how business decisions can provide external benefits are:

- **Job creation** – Businesses will often need employees which provides incomes for people who may be able to increase their standard of living.
- **Improved infrastructure** – A business decision to invest in infrastructure (such as roads and bridges) for its operations can benefit the wider community by improving transportation connectivity.
- **Technological advancements** – Businesses that invest in research and development can generate new technologies that benefit other businesses or industries, which reduce waste and/or improve efficiency.
- **Environmental benefits** – Some business decisions can lead to environmental benefits such as reduction in waste and greenhouse gases, recycling and investment in renewable energy sources. This benefits society by reducing pollution and conserving natural resources.

Despite the financial cost to the business, some businesses try to do what is right for the environment and the community in which they operate. This might be in terms of production processes used, charitable actions or what they produce.

> **KEY TERM**
>
> **external benefit:** where a business decision has a positive impact on a third party.

> **TIP**
>
> When considering the impact of a business decision, remember to evaluate both the external costs and external benefits, and that the external benefits must outweigh the external costs.

## ACTIVITY 27.4

Loreli Handa wants to set up a factory that manufactures eco-friendly packaging products close to a nature reserve (protected area). The nature reserve is also a popular tourist spot. She likes the site because it is cheap and close to a good supply of water. The nearest city also has a high unemployment rate.

Before putting her proposal to the government, she analyses the potential costs and benefits of this project (see Table 27.4). She hopes her proposal will be approved as she has invested a lot in research and development and is willing to work with the government to help improve the infrastructure of the area (to benefit the community as well as herself).

Help Loreli evaluate the potential impact of this project by sorting her proposal list correctly into external cost or external benefit and analysing their impact. One positive and negative impact has been analysed for you. There are four external benefits and three external costs.

Copy and complete the table below:

| |
|---|
| Production of environmentally friendly packaging. |
| The business will provide employment for the local people. |
| Visual pollution caused by having a factory close to the nature reserve. |
| Air pollution caused by fumes created by manufacturing plant. |
| Road congestion caused by delivery trucks. |
| Due to research and development, consumers can have access to improved products at possibly reduced costs. |
| The business may improve the infrastructure in the area by having a reliable power supply, better transportation network, schools and hospitals. |
| Destruction of ecology in the area due to sound, light and air pollution from the factory. |
| New production technique. |

**Table 27.4:** The potential environmental impact of setting up a factory to manufacture eco-friendly packaging products near to a nature reserve

| External benefit | Analyse why this is a benefit |
|---|---|
| Production of environmentally friendly packaging. | This is more sustainable and provides a benefit to the society as a whole. |

| External cost | Analyse why this is a problem |
|---|---|
| Visual pollution caused by having a factory close to the nature reserve. | This will spoil the natural beauty of the place and discourage visitors from coming to the nature reserve. |

1. In groups, analyse and evaluate whether the impact of the environmental benefits is greater than that of the environmental costs.

2. Should the government approve the proposal? In your groups, present a report to your class evaluating the above factors that you have considered and justify your decision.

## TIP

Explaining the impact of each factor will help you understand how important each factor is. This will help you evaluate the factors and come to a justified conclusion.

# 27.6 The impact of exchange rate changes

The success of international trade depends a lot on the **exchange rate** between currencies. The main factors affecting exchange rates are demand and supply. If demand for a currency is high, the exchange rate will rise. For example, if investors from Argentina want to invest in Singapore or buy Singapore's exports, then the demand for the Singapore dollar will rise. This also affects the value of the Argentine peso as it will have to change its Argentine peso to Singapore dollars. This will increase the supply of the Argentine peso in the currency market. The increase in supply may lead to a drop in the value of the Argentine peso.

## The significance of exchange rates on international trade

The exchange of money when trading goods and services internationally is closely linked to the exchange rates between currencies. The exchange rate between currencies depends on demand and supply and varies on a day-to-day basis.

## Depreciation and appreciation of an exchange rate

Exchange rate changes can have a significant effect on a business in terms of sales, costs and profits. Changes in exchange rate affect the levels of exports and imports. This in turn can influence the whole economy. The impact of appreciation and depreciation of the exchange rate on importers and exporters is analysed in greater detail below.

### Effect of depreciation of currency on importers and exporters

A currency is said to **depreciate** if the value of the currency decreases with respect to another. When this happens, the exchange rate of that currency falls. Figure 27.7 explains how a fall in exchange rate affects businesses.

A currency is said to **appreciate** if the value of the currency increases with respect to another. When this happens, the exchange rate of that currency rises. Figure 27.7 shows how a rise in exchange rate affects businesses.

> **KEY TERM**
>
> **exchange rate:** the price of one currency in terms of another.

> **TIP**
>
> You will be expected to know how appreciation or depreciation of the currency will affect the prices paid by importers and exporters. How will this affect their sales and profit? To help remember this, use the acronym 'MADE': iMporters benefit from Appreciation, while Depreciation benefits Exporters in terms of lower prices.

> **KEY TERMS**
>
> **depreciation:** a fall in the value of a currency against another currency.
>
> **appreciation:** a rise in the value of a currency against another currency.

### Depreciation of exchange rate

- Import will appear to be cheaper.
- Businesses selling imported goods or relying on imported materials will benefit from reduced costs.

- Exports are relatively more expensive overseas: this may decrease their demand.
- Businesses that export will suffer from reduced sales.

### Appreciation of exchange rate

- Import will appear to be more expensive.
- Businesses that rely on imports will have to pay more.

- Exports are relatively cheaper overseas: this should increase the demand for them.
- Businesses that export will benefit from increased sales.

**Figure 27.7:** The impact of depreciation and appreciation of a currency on importers and exporters

## ACTIVITY 27.5

A multinational company, XYZ, wants to set up operations in your local area. All residents in the area have been informed of this by the authorities as they would like to consult/know whether the local residents are in favour or not. Do you think the MNC XYZ should be allowed to set up operations in our area?

1. With your partner, discuss the pros and cons of an MNC setting up operations in your local area.
2. Make a list of the pros and cons.
3. Decide whether you are in favour of or against this.
4. Identify your strongest points in favour of or against this.
5. Think of evidence and explain your points to strengthen it.
6. Use the above to justify your opinion.
7. Write a persuasive letter to the local authority indicating your opinion and giving reasons why.

### Example
Dear Sir/Madam,

*Introductory paragraph:* Most people believe that permitting the MNC to set up operations here will be an advantage to the local economy and community. However, there may be disadvantages too, so analysing the impact of the advantages is crucial to make the right decision.

*You could use the PEEL technique to help structure your argument in favour of the MNC:*

P Many people/I believe that the MNC will improve the lives of the local people.

E First, there will be more job opportunities available and….

E This will help improve their living standards and….

L As a result, the MNC will have a positive impact on….

**Alternatively:**

*Introductory paragraph:* Some people believe that permitting the MNC to set up operations here will be an advantage to the local economy and community. This could be true to some extent but there are also significant disadvantages that need careful consideration.

*You could use the PEEL technique to help structure your argument in against of the MNC.*

P I believe that the MNC will not do much to improve the lives of the local people.

E First, the company will send most of its profits back to….

E So, there will not be any, or much, money invested back into the local economy

L Therefore, the MNC will not have a positive impact on….

## 27 Business and the international economy

> **REFLECTION**
>
> What helped you identify the strongest arguments? How has giving evidence and explaining (analysis) your point helped to evaluate and justify your opinion? Would you do things differently next time?

> **SUMMARY**
>
> You should now know:
>
> - Globalisation is the process by which countries are connected with one another because of trade of goods and services.
> - There are many opportunities posed by globalisation, the main one being businesses have access to more markets and an opportunity to grow and become more profitable.
> - The main threat of globalisation is that there is increased competition which may lead local businesses to suffer or even close.
> - Governments often set tariffs and quotas to protect local businesses from the effects of globalisation.
> - Companies that set up operations in other countries to expand their businesses are called multinational companies.
> - When setting up operations in another country, an MNC needs to consider various factors of the host country such as availability of good infrastructure, skilled labour, access to raw materials, tax incentives and political stability.
> - When considering the impact of a business decision, you should evaluate both the external costs and benefits.
> - The exchange rate of a country is the value of one currency compared to another.
> - An appreciation of exchange rate is an advantage to importers but is not good for exporters.
> - A depreciation of exchange rate is an advantage to exporters but is not good for importers.

# Chapter 27 practice questions

1   Adaku Wires is an electrical wires manufacturer based in Nigeria. It buys some of its raw materials from Zambia in Africa. The company sells its wires all over the world, with Germany being its biggest market. The company has faced some barriers to trade and needs to keep a close eye on the exchange rates between the Nigerian naira (NGN) and other currencies it trades in. The value of the Nigerian naira (NGN) has recently appreciated against both the German currency, the Euro (EUR), and the Zambian kwacha (CNY).

   a   Define 'appreciation' of exchange rates. [2]

   b   Outline **one** advantage and **one** disadvantage to Adaku Wires of selling their products worldwide. [4]

    c    Explain **two** barriers to trade that Adaku Wires could have faced when trading internationally. [6]

    d    Do you think the appreciation of the Naira has been beneficial for Adaku Wires? Justify your answer. [8]

2    Pita Station is a fast-food chain based in the UAE. Profits have grown in the last five years and the business wants to grow by setting up a new operation in another country. With increased globalisation, one of its main objectives is to become a multinational company. It has identified Greece and Morocco as two possible host countries that it would like to begin operations in.

    a    Define 'multinational company'. [2]

    b    Identify **four** advantages to Pita Station becoming a multinational company. [4]

    c    Explain **two** factors Pita Station should consider when choosing a suitable host country. [6]

    d    Do you think that the host country will benefit from Pita Station setting up its operations there and if becoming a multinational company will be beneficial for Pita Station? Justify your answer. [8]

**Total available marks: 40**

## CHECK YOUR PROGRESS

How well do you think you have achieved the learning intentions for this chapter? Give yourself a score from 1 (still need a lot of practice) to 5 (feeling very confident) for each learning intention. Provide an example to support your score.

| Now I can ... | Score | Example |
| --- | --- | --- |
| outline the reasons for globalisation | | |
| discuss the opportunities and threats of globalisation for local businesses | | |
| discuss import tariffs and import quotas and their effects on businesses | | |
| explain what a multinational company is and the advantages to a business of becoming an MNC | | |
| discuss the advantages and disadvantages for a country where an MNC is located | | |
| discuss and explain the external costs and external benefits of business decisions | | |
| explain the impact of appreciation and depreciation of exchange rates on importers and exporters of products and services. | | |

# Chapter 28
# Environmental and ethical issues

**LEARNING INTENTIONS**

By the end of this chapter, you will be able to:

- discuss how business activity can negatively affect the environment
- understand how and why businesses might respond to environmental issues
- outline the effects of legal controls over business activity affecting the environment
- understand the ethical issues that might affect businesses
- understand how businesses respond to ethical issues and the advantages and disadvantages of being ethical
- understand the role of pressure groups and how they can influence business decisions.

# Introduction

Business activity has an impact on the environment in which it operates. This chapter looks at the positive and negative impact businesses have on the environment and society around them. The impact on the environment as well as many ethical issues must be considered in business decision-making. In dealing with environmental and ethical concerns, businesses face many threats as well as opportunities. The chapter also looks at the role of pressure groups and government controls on business activity.

## BUSINESS IN CONTEXT

### How toxic air is affecting our physical and mental health

**Figure 28.1:** Air pollution can affect our health

The World Health Organization (WHO) claims that residents of the Italian city of Rome are exposed to pollution levels three times higher that it deems to be safe. A study carried out in the city in 2023 has revealed a link between air pollution and its negative effects on our mental health. It found that people living in areas with higher particle pollution had a greater chance of developing mental disorders, including depression and anxiety. The data was backed-up by analysis of drug prescriptions, where people aged between 30 and 64 had the clearest association with air pollution.

Air pollution is all around us. Very tiny pollutants in the air can get into our bodies and penetrate deep into our respiratory and circulatory system, damaging our lungs, heart and brain. While operating, nearly every business contributes to air pollution, including the emissions from burning fuels used to heat buildings, emissions from cooking and harmful gases released via distribution and delivery vehicles.

Data from the study suggests it could be possible to predict the benefits of improvements to the city's air quality - if particle pollution is reduced by 10%, it could reduce mental health conditions by a similar amount. Greater improvements would be achieved by meeting the WHO guidelines.

**Discuss in pairs or groups:**

1. As per the study mentioned in the text, what is the impact of air pollution on our physical and mental health?
2. What do you think are the main contributors to air pollution?
3. What environmental impact of human and business activity have you noticed in your daily lives?

# 28.1 How business activity can negatively affect the environment

Many businesses are increasingly aware of the need to deal with the environmental issues related to their activities. Failure to recognise this may lead to bad publicity and loss of sales for a business. Equally, a business that is environmentally friendly can lead to an improved image and an opportunity to increase sales. Businesses try to work in such a way that their environmental impact is minimal.

> **LINK**
>
> For more information on primary, secondary and tertiary sector, see Chapter 2.

Every business activity, whether it is from the primary, secondary or tertiary sector, has an impact on the environment and society. While some business activities can help solve environmental challenges by innovation and the use of technology in areas such as waste management and using renewable sources of energy, there is far more of a negative impact. Table 28.1 analyses how industries in all three sectors of the economy can have a negative impact on the environment.

**Table 28.1:** The environmental impact of industries in all three sectors of the economy

| Sector and industry | Impact on the environment |
|---|---|
| Primary (e.g. mining) | **Deforestation and loss of habitat** as some types of mining methods often require large areas of land to be cleared, leading to deforestation, soil erosion and loss of biodiversity. |
| | **Air pollution** caused by dust emissions and **water pollution** caused by leaching of toxic chemicals from the mining operations. |
| | **Water scarcity** where irrigation for crops as well as mining consumes vast amounts of freshwater, using up the water from rivers, lakes and underground water which can cause water scarcity in some areas. |
| Secondary (e.g., manufacturing) | **Air and water pollution** caused by gaseous emissions and wastewater discharge from factories, and littering caused by improper disposal of solid waste, such as packaging materials. |
| | Greenhouse gas emissions, mainly through the burning of fossil fuels for energy and transportation. |
| | **Resource depletion** as manufacturing activities require large amounts of natural resources such as energy, water, minerals and raw materials which may eventually run out. |
| | **Deforestation and loss of biodiversity** due to the production of wood-based products such as paper and furniture can drive further deforestation, which reduces biodiversity and destroys habitats. |
| Tertiary (e.g., tourism) | **Increased pollution** through littering, noise, air and visual pollution. For example, development of infrastructure such as public transport made to support tourism can spoil people's ability to enjoy natural views. |
| | **Overuse of a country's natural resources** such as water (used in swimming pools, hotels and golf courses). |
| | **Soil erosion and loss of habitats** caused by construction of buildings such as hotels and resorts. |

Business activity can affect us and our environment in many ways, including:

- pollution and emission of greenhouse gases
- waste
- use of energy
- depletion of natural resources.

## Pollution

Figure 28.2: Business activity can result in pollution

Business activity is responsible for a range of pollutions, as shown in Table 28.2.

Table 28.2: Types of pollution

| Air pollution | Caused by fumes from manufacturing units and exhaust fumes created by vehicles. Can lead to respiratory disorders in humans, and affect plants and animals. Corrosive (harmful) chemicals in the air can damage buildings. |
| --- | --- |
| | By burning fossil fuels such as coal and oil, the amounts of greenhouse gases in the atmosphere greatly increase. Heating and air conditioning systems release greenhouse gases from offices and factories into the atmosphere, which leads to further global warming. |
| Land pollution | Waste that cannot be recycled finds its way into landfills. Harmful and possibly nuclear waste from factories can end up in landfills too. Some of this does not decompose (break down) and is toxic and unpleasant to the senses. |
| Light pollution | Electronic billboards used by businesses for advertising and over-illumination (lighting) can interfere with ecosystems and astronomical observations. |
| Water pollution | Caused by improper waste disposal and contamination by toxic, chemical waste from factories. This can seriously damage the plant and animal life in the water and can be life-threatening if consumed by humans. |
| Visual pollution | Unattractive views such as power lines (needed by a manufacturing plant) and overcrowding can be unpleasant and prevent people from enjoying the natural environment. |
| Noise pollution | Caused by manufacturing plants and cars and aeroplanes. Can be an irritant (annoyance) and affect people's quality of life. |

To reduce the amount of pollution, governments of most countries place controls on pollution. For example, they may do this by charging a fee on the release of pollutants or introducing laws to ban the release of dangerous chemicals. In some countries, however, laws are not as strict. Controlling pollution has to be a combined effort of governments, scientists, businesses and individuals.

## Waste

**Figure 28.3:** Waste often ends up in a landfill site

The types of waste produced by businesses are shown in Figure 28.4. Factories, offices and farming and mining activities, in particular, produce large amounts of waste.

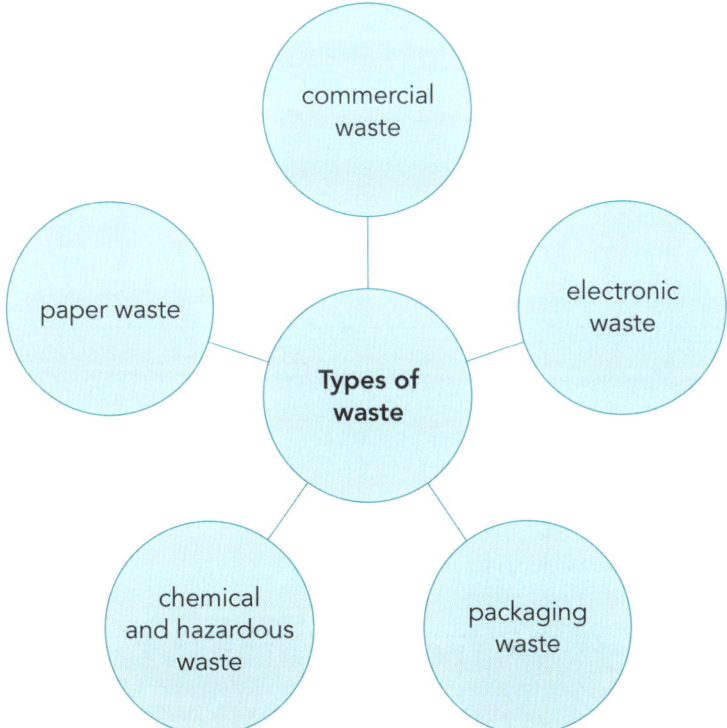

**Figure 28.4:** Types of waste produced by business activities

> **TIP**
>
> Remember, all these examples are simply different types of pollution. If a question asks about different ways a business might affect the environment, include other points such as waste or use of energy instead of two types of pollution.

> **TIP**
>
> Do not worry about learning specific laws – you only need to understand why protection is important. Also, think about how laws affect businesses. Do they have to change what they do? Is it expensive? What could happen if they do nothing?

Globally, many governments are trying to deal with the issue of waste by introducing initiatives (steps) based on the 3Rs – reduce, reuse and recycle. Businesses are also trying to be more environmentally friendly by reducing the amount of natural resources they use and recycling their waste. Waste is not just a problem caused by primary and secondary sector businesses.

Not all types of waste can be recycled. For example, electrical waste such as computers and packaging waste often ends up in landfills where toxic chemicals and harmful gases then flow into the ground and air.

Another example is packaging and plastic bags. Although packaging is a very important part of the marketing mix, packaging waste can have a serious impact on the environment. Many businesses are trying to reduce the quantity of packaging materials that they use or are finding other ways to minimise its impact.

> **LINK**
>
> For more information on packaging, see Chapter 12.

### CASE STUDY 28.1

**How Samsung has implemented the 3Rs**

**Figure 28.5:** Eco-packaging can be upcycled

Samsung's sustainability initiatives include using recycled materials in its interior packaging and replacing packaging materials with sustainable materials such as paper instead of plastic and other disposable materials. It also packages its products with its eco-packaging boxes, which can be upcycled/reused into small furniture and other useful items. Even though the packaging is recyclable, using it for another purpose avoids the long and expensive process.

**Discuss in pairs or groups:**

1. How has Samsung implemented the 3Rs (Reduce, Reuse and Recycle) in its packaging?
2. What sustainability steps have been taken in your country to minimise waste created from packaging?
3. Do some research on a company of your choice which you know has taken steps for being sustainable. Present your findings to the class. What more do you think they could do?

## Use of energy

Office equipment, lighting, heating and air conditioning and machinery use large amounts of a country's energy sources, such as coal, gas, oil and electricity. Coal, gas and oil are natural resources that cannot be replaced once they have been used. By turning off lights and equipment when not working, businesses reduce the amount of energy they use. Many countries are developing renewable sources of energy, such as wind and solar power. These do not produce greenhouse gases and can easily be replaced.

## Depletion of natural resources

Many manufacturing businesses use non-renewable raw materials which may lead to scarcity. Overfishing and deforestation (cutting down large numbers of trees) can affect the plants and animals in those areas, destroying their natural food source or habitat. Deforestation contributes to global warming. Trees absorb and store carbon dioxide. If forests are cleared, they release carbon dioxide and other greenhouse gases which contribute to global warming.

### BUSINESS IN ACTION

**COP28**

**Figure 28.6:** COP28 was held in Dubai in 2023

What measures are being taken internationally to tackle climate change?

1. Carry out some research to find out about specific organisations and agreements created for this.
2. The 2023 United Nations Climate Change Conference or Conference of the Parties, more commonly referred to as COP28, was the 28th United Nations Climate Change conference held in Dubai. What were the main outcomes of the COP28 conference?
3. When and where is the next COP conference? What are the main topics due to be discussed?

### ACTIVITY 28.1

Working with a partner, think about what a business can do to minimize the environmental impact in the following areas:

- packaging
- energy sources
- minimising pollution
- waste management.

1. Which factor do you think is the most significant?
2. For the factor that you think is the most significant, make a poster with your response and present it to the class.

### LINKS

For more information on external stakeholders, see Chapter 5, and sustainable production of goods and services see Chapter 17.

## 28.2 Why businesses need to respond to environmental issues

If a business shows consideration for the environmental impact of its business activities and has environmentally friendly practices then it gets it good publicity. On the other hand, if a business fails to respond to environmental issues then it may face threats. Environmental issues pose both opportunities and threats to a business and that is why businesses need to respond to them. Table 28.3 shows the opportunities and threats faced by businesses due to environmental issues.

Table 28.3: Opportunities and threats faced by businesses due to environmental issues

| Opportunities | Threats |
| --- | --- |
| • Recycling and using energy-efficient machines may lead to cost savings.<br>• Governments may provide financial incentives (motives) to encourage firms to use environmentally friendly methods of production.<br>• Publicity gained from greener methods can attract new customers, employees and investors and keep existing ones.<br>• Telecommuting (working from home) benefits the environment and is a great motivator for employees.<br>• The green revolution has led to the growth of new businesses dealing with environmental management.<br>• Following government regulations and standards can give a firm a competitive advantage over other businesses. | • The business's reputation may be damaged. It may lose customers, employees and investors.<br>• The business may be closed down if government regulations to use greener methods of production are not followed.<br>• Inability to meet government regulations may create legal problems for businesses.<br>• Pressure groups may oppose the business, produce negative publicity and prevent the company's growth. |

## How businesses respond to environmental issues

Businesses respond to environmental issues by following sustainable business practices as outlined below:

- using green manufacturing methods, which produce less waste and pollution
- reducing their use of energy or using renewable sources of energy such as solar power
- replanting trees where land had been cleared for use
- using recycled materials when possible
- minimising water use
- obeying government regulations and standards.

## 28.3 Effect of legal controls over business activity

Governments can use legal controls/laws to discourage the negative effects of business activity on the environment. Table 28.4 shows the role of legal controls in discouraging negative effects on the environment.

## 28 Environmental and ethical issues

Table 28.4: Role of legal controls in discouraging negative effects on the environment

| Legal controls to discourage negative effects on the environment |
| --- |
| Setting targets for the amount of waste or pollutant that can be produced. |
| Governments may impose penalties in the form of fines, closure of facilities and imprisonment on businesses that ignore pollution targets or waste disposal regulations. |
| They may charge a tax on the commercial use of natural resources for energy or disposal of waste to be more energy efficient and reduce waste. |
| They may set standards that businesses have to meet when using natural resources such as wood or energy; for example, a certain percentage of this must come from renewable sources. |
| Businesses may not be permitted to set up in some areas, for example, in conservation areas. |

### CASE STUDY 28.2

**Topiku**

Topiku, which means 'My hat' in Indonesian, creates eco-friendly, sustainable hats that are responsibly crafted from upcycled and recycled waste materials. It maintains close relationships with the artisans (skilled workers) and suppliers to ensure ethical and fair conditions of their supply chain (all the stages from buying raw materials to production). The various methods it uses for sustainable development are as follows.

Figure 28.7: Recycled materials can be used to create garments

**Responsible production methods**

Hats are created from responsibly sourced alternative materials, such as brims made from buckets rescued from landfill and fabric and leather scraps sourced from the leftovers of garment manufacturers. Due to reusing and recycling materials, Topiku has managed to reduce its carbon footprint from production significantly. As the company continue to grow, they aim to utilise more sea transportation for distributing their products so that they can reduce their emissions from distribution.

This creative use of the waste from other industries in producing another product has not only been economically beneficial but environmentally friendly too. This prevents material from ending up in landfills and significantly reducing the production of new fabric, saving huge amounts of water and energy required to produce new fabric.

**Enabling and empowering local skilled people**

Since it began operations in 2015, Topiku has allowed its employees to produce the hats from the comfort of their own homes in Cigondewah, West Java, Indonesia. The company has enabled and empowered the local craftsmen and provided them a platform to share their crafts. Both men

> **CONTINUED**
>
> and women are given living wages and equal work opportunities.
>
> **Social and environmental protection**
>
> Topiku is a socially responsible business that makes decisions to benefit society at large. It leads by example by using business practices that benefit the community they work with and supporting both social and environmental non profit organisations in Indonesia and beyond. In 2022, they donated a value of 11% of their annual revenue to invest in reforestation and renewable energy projects. They also collaborate with, sponsor, and support various non-profit organisations fighting against plastic pollution across the globe.
>
> **Discuss in pairs or groups:**
>
> 1. Why is it important for Topiku to consider the environmental impact of its activities?
> 2. Working in pairs, make a mind map of all the steps Topiku is taking to reduce the environmental impact of its operations.
> 3. Identify one positive environmental impact caused by Topiku's operations.
> 4. What do you think Topiku could do to be socially responsible to its customers?
> 5. Why do you think it is important for Topiku to take steps to support social and environmental organisations beyond its operations?

## ACTIVITY 28.2

ABC Tyres, a tyre manufacturing company, wants to open a new plant to make green or eco-friendly tyres. Although the site is located on the outskirts of a big city, it is close to a residential area. The government has formed a committee to consider the environmental impact of this plant before allowing the company to go ahead.

The tyres will be made from materials that are more sustainable and have a lower environmental impact. However, the government's analysis shows that manufacturing of tyres involves the use of toxic chemicals and generates large amounts of waste. The plant will also require huge amounts of water and power. The government does recognise that the plant will generate employment in the local area. To benefit from increased employment and support a more environmentally friendly product, the government is also looking at ways in which the environmental impact can be reduced or controlled.

Imagine you are part of the committee formed by the government to determine the environmental impact of this plant. Working in groups, consider the following factors and create a report of your analysis:

1. Analyse the impact this new plant may have on the environment.
   (**Tip**: Consider the use of toxic chemicals, the production of a large amount of waste and the requirement of huge amounts of water.)
2. How will it affect the residents living in the area?
   (**Tip**: Consider that it is close to a residential area and that it will generate employment.)
3. How can the government control the environmental impact of the plant?
4. Identify and explain two opportunities and threats faced by ABC Tyres because of its environmental impact.

## 28.4 Ethical issues faced by businesses

Businesses must make sure that they satisfy the interests of all stakeholders, whether they are individuals, organisations or the community. We usually expect businesses to behave responsibly when carrying out their activities irrespective of the impact it has on business profits. This is known as business ethics. Although not always enforced by law, business ethics have a vital role to play in decision-making and many businesses set ethical objectives. Figure 28.8 shows ways in which businesses can be ethical.

Most businesses now aim to make their operations sustainable. There are also companies such as Fairtrade, a global organisation working with businesses, consumers and campaigners trying to ensure better prices for producers, fairer working conditions and promoting sustainability for producers.

Some businesses, however, do not behave in an ethical way. Some examples of unethical business practices are shown in Table 28.5.

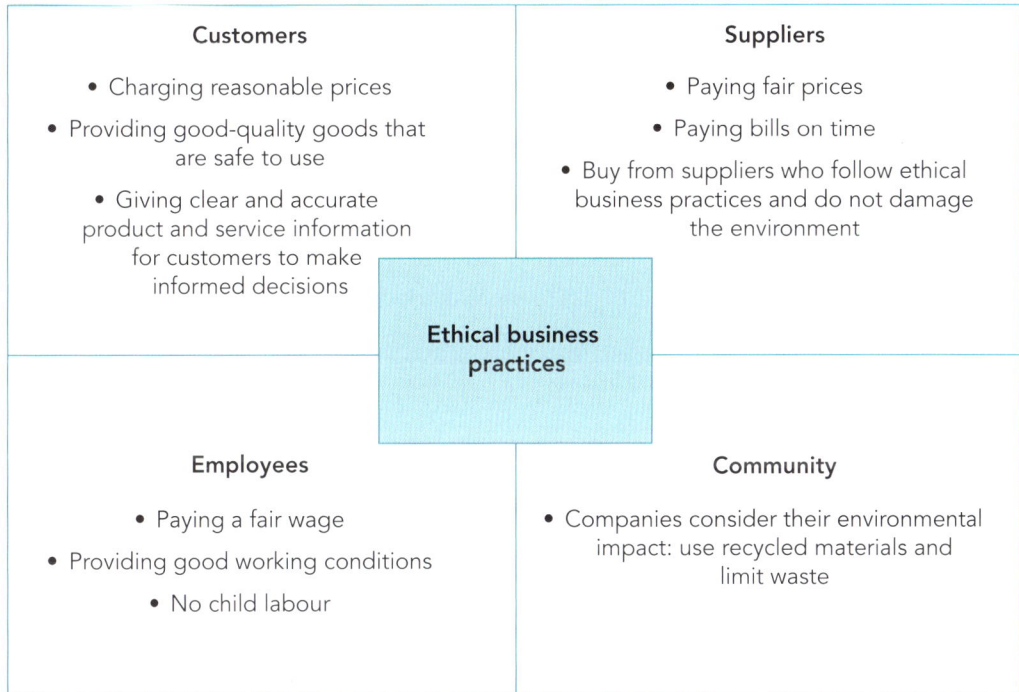

Figure 28.8: Different ethical practices that can be followed by businesses

Table 28.5: Unethical business practices

| Stakeholder | Examples of unethical practice |
|---|---|
| Customers | • Try to sell extra products that are unnecessary. |
| Employees | • Unfair payment to employees, for example, unequal pay for the same work done by different groups of people. |
| | • Use of child labour. |
| Suppliers | • Not paying fair prices for inventory. |
| | • Using suppliers that damage the environment. |

Primark Stores Limited is an Irish multinational fast fashion retailer with headquarters in Dublin, Ireland, with outlets across Europe and in the United States. It is a company that has been in the news for several ethical issues, including environmental reporting, pollution and toxics, workers' rights, animal rights, animal testing, use of controversial technologies and likely use of tax avoidance strategies.

## CASE STUDY 28.3

### Is the use of AI ethical?

**Figure 28.9:** Most big companies use AI systems

Artificial intelligence refers to human-made technology that teaches machines to think, analyse and learn from data and make intelligent decisions. Most big companies now have AI systems. AI algorithms can analyse vast amounts of data to customise products, services and experiences to users. So, it is important to ensure that data privacy is protected and that data is used in an ethical way. Data privacy allows individuals to maintain control over their personal information – think about how you set privacy settings on the various online platforms you are on. It allows users to decide how their data is collected, used and shared.

AI is becoming increasingly important to us. For example, facial recognition software on most smartphones and digital assistants such as Amazon's Alexa and Apple's Siri use AI.

Entertainment and social media platforms also use AI to give users a personalised experience. For example, Facebook, Instagram, X and other platforms suggest or show a list of people we might know or those who are on our contact list. These apps analyse user usage patterns and recognise user friends from photos and news feeds. Similarly, entertainment platforms such as Netflix, Prime Video and others give viewers many suggestions on what to watch next.

**Discuss in pairs or groups:**

1. Are there any other digital assistants, entertainment and social media platforms available in your country that you have used? Do you think they use AI?

2. In a group, discuss the advantages of the use of AI as mentioned in the examples above.

3. Why is the privacy of data an ethical consideration? (Relate this to how you are in control of your privacy settings on various online platforms you are on and why this is important.)

Alibaba, the world's largest ecommerce platform uses AI in its daily operations to predict what customers might want to buy and offers them tailored product suggestions. While AI allows customers' needs to be matched with products in a cost-efficient way, it also raises an ethical concern by favouring top sellers creating an unfair market for smaller merchants.

In its drive to be ethical in its use of AI, Alibaba has developed technologies to enhance the diversity of search results and promote stores from new merchants. It has also increased its investment in related technologies to protect users' privacy and enhance data security.

# 28.5 How businesses might respond to ethical issues

When faced with an ethical issue, a business has to consider the interests of all stakeholders. When stakeholders have conflicting interests, decision-making may not be easy. Both the advantages and the disadvantages of ethical behaviour need to be considered. These are shown in Table 28.6.

Table 28.6: Advantages and disadvantages of ethical behaviour

| Advantages | Disadvantages |
| --- | --- |
| • Good brand image/reputation, which may allow them to charge higher prices.<br>• Potential for increased sales as some customers want products that have been made fairly, which increases revenue.<br>• Better supplier relations (as they pay fair price).<br>• May help in attracting new investors, which can help fund business growth.<br>• Can help attract new employees or be a motivating factor for existing employees, which will help retain them. | • High costs may be involved when choosing raw materials ethically (such as using recycled materials), leading to higher prices.<br>• Limited/fewer sources of materials which could reduce output.<br>• Improving pay for employees or not using child labour may increase labour costs. All this leads to lower profit margin. |

> **TIP**
>
> Questions on social or environmental issues will usually require you to give an opinion on a given statement. Try to look for both the positive and negative points and make a decision. Make sure the points are relevant to the type of business identified (this is what is meant by the word 'context').

Overall, it is in the long-term interests of a business to act ethically. Although there is a cost involved initially, it pays off over time and society as a whole is likely to benefit. Greater costs may lead to lower profits. For example, an increase in production levels may lead to economies of scale and possibly more sales, but it also causes an increase in pollution.

Paying employees higher salaries rather than earning higher profits is another example of an ethical decision.

For some businesses, their failure to follow ethical policies may bring unwelcome publicity, which can damage their reputation.

### CASE STUDY 28.4

**Fast fashion**

**Figure 28.10:** Fast fashion creates huge amounts of waste

Fast fashion describes cheap, mass-produced clothing that moves quickly from design to retail stores with new lines constantly released. This includes clothing, footwear and accessories designs that are mass produced to sell current trends in cheap retail stores across the world. Zara, GAP, UNIQLO and H&M are some of the popular retailers in the fast fashion field.

Countries such as India, Bangladesh, Vietnam and others account for almost all textiles made for fast fashion retailers in the western world. The aim of fast fashion businesses is to produce designs from the catwalk to a retail store as quickly as possible. While such businesses help customers afford current styles at a low cost, fast fashion is detrimental to the environment. Its negative impact on the environment includes:

- mass production of clothing contributes to significant worldwide greenhouse gas emissions
- production requires a large quantities of water
- use of dangerous chemicals for dyeing
- exploitation of natural resources in economies where these products are often produced
- huge amounts of waste as latest trends go out of fashion very quickly and are discarded very quickly too
- some of the synthetic material used in fast fashion, when thrown away, take hundreds of years to decompose.

The countries producing fast fashion garments have low labour costs and often less stringent (strict) labour laws. Women are the dominant work force in the garment industry. Labour practices in fast fashion are known to be exploitative. It faces criticism for hiring garments workers from other countries for their low wages, providing poor working conditions and some even use child labour.

**Discuss in pairs or groups:**

1. Which environmental impact of the fashion industry do you think is the most detrimental? Order the factors mentioned in the extract above from the least to the most detrimental.
2. Discuss whether retailers in high-income countries are being ethical in buying fast fashion garments.
3. What ethical considerations should Western retailers ensure that their suppliers are making?
4. What are the advantages of fast fashion businesses being set up in countries such as India, Bangladesh and Vietnam?
5. What legal controls can countries use to make the fast fashion business practices more ethical?

## 28.6 Pressure groups

A **pressure group** is a group of people who join together for a common cause (ethical or environmental). It aims to change the way businesses function. It often does this by trying to influence government policy. For example, the pressure group Greenpeace campaigns on environmental issues. Another example is the Environmental Justice Foundation (EJF), a non-profit organisation working globally to protect the environment and human rights. One of its campaigns is against the negative effects of shrimp farming in Brazil, which is destroying the lives of coastal communities and damaging the environment.

> **KEY TERM**
>
> **pressure group:** a group of people who join together for a common cause (ethical or environmental).

### How pressure groups can influence business decisions

Pressure groups use different methods to make their point and influence business decisions.

Figure 28.11 shows the methods used by pressure groups to influence business decisions.

- **Demonstrations** - a group of people protesting a business's actions or policy, either at a rally or outside the company's offices
- **Boycotting** - refusing to buy a business's products or services and trying to influence other consumers to do the same
- **Increasing awareness of the issue** - through the pressure group's website and possibly causing negative publicity with the help of the media
- **Petitioning** - making an oral or written official complaint to the government or concerned authority on an issue.
- **Lobbying** - attempting to influence the policymaking of the government

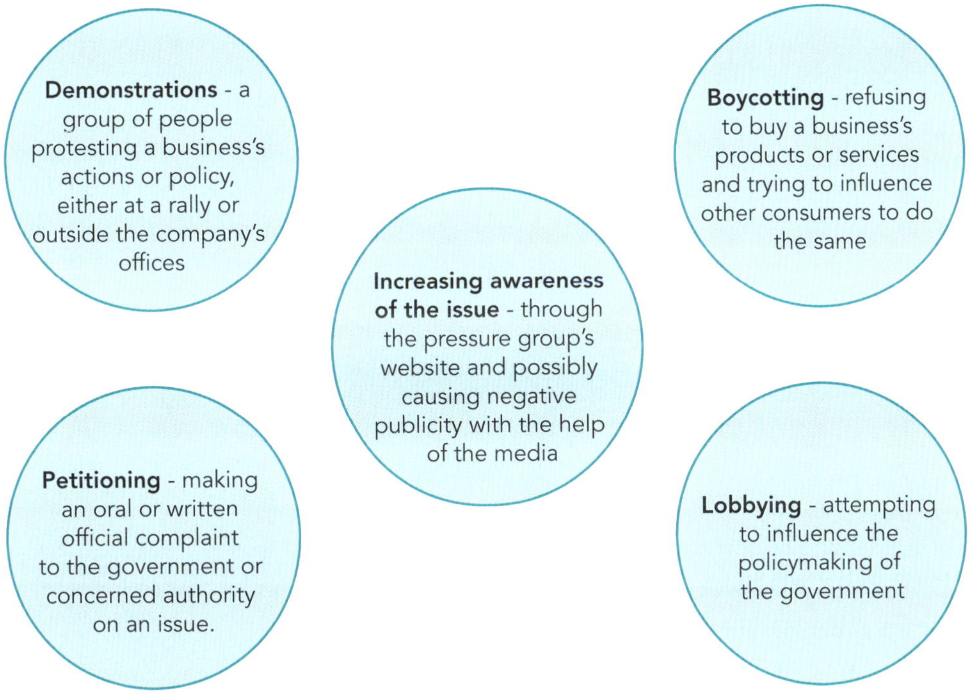

Figure 28.11: Methods used by pressure groups

> **TIP**
>
> Remember, pressure groups do not have the power to make laws, so companies are not legally bound to comply with their demands. They only try to influence consumers, businesses or the government. When evaluating the impact of pressure groups on business activity, consider the threats as well as the opportunities businesses face.

## Impact of pressure groups

Businesses can defend their business decisions to improve their image, which may have been damaged by pressure groups and can also take legal action against pressure groups. However, pressure groups may oppose the business, produce negative publicity and prevent a company's growth. The business's reputation may be damaged. It may lose customers, employees and investors. Therefore, businesses have to respond to the threat they face from pressure groups.

Pressure groups may also have a positive impact. They may approve businesses that have environmentally friendly practices, which gives these businesses good publicity. Pressure groups have also encouraged new businesses to arise. For example, CECEP Environmental Consulting Group Limited (CECEPEC) is a company that has benefited from the environmental pressures faced by businesses. It is a professional sustainability consulting company that provides professional advisory services to various international organisations and enterprises in China.

### ACTIVITY 28.3

Country X has one international airport in its capital city. The existing airport is unable to handle the increased air traffic. The company that owns the airport wants to open a second runway. The proposed location is near a residential area. The government thinks this will be good for the economy (which is in recession) and wants to give its approval. However, there has been a lot of opposition from an environmental pressure group and the community in the area of the proposed location who say the levels of noise and air pollution would be unacceptable and unethical. Members of the community say that the demolition of homes in order to free up space for the second airport is also unethical. They claim that the long-term ill effects on health and well-being outweigh the short-term financial advantages. Some people in the government also feel that the huge investment that opening a second airport will involve could be spent on more important areas.

1. Working in groups of 3–4 students, identify the stakeholders involved in this business decision.

2. Each person in the group should choose the role of one of the stakeholders mentioned below:

    - As a spokesperson for the community, identify and analyse the environmental impact that the community would have to experience because of a new airport near them. Present these points to the rest of the group.

    - Imagine you are a government official placed in a decision-making committee of this project. Explain the economic benefits of this decision and how they will help the economy grow. Present these benefits to the rest of the group.

    - From the point of view of an environmentalist, identify and present the impact that this business decision would have on the environment.

3. Identify and explain how opening another runway might be unethical?

4. Why do you think it is important for the airport company to consider the points being raised by the pressure group?

5. Make a list/mind map of the above arguments of at least **three** of the stakeholders and analyse and evaluate as a group whether this project is worth considering.

6. Present your findings to the rest of the class.

> **REFLECTION**
>
> - In evaluating whether the proposal should be approved, did you consider just one cost and benefit or several? Which factor did you think was the most significant? How did you evaluate the factors that led you to your conclusion?
>
> - Compare your conclusion to that of another group's. Did you reach the same conclusion? How would you defend your own conclusion? Could you make your analysis and evaluation stronger?

**SUMMARY**

You should now know:

- Businesses have a positive and negative impact on the environment and the community.
- Governments place legal controls to minimise the impact of business activity on the environment.
- Businesses should have environmentally friendly and ethical business practices in order to avoid opposition by pressure groups.
- The different methods used by pressure groups to influence business decisions.

# Chapter 28 practice questions

1. Bakary runs a small rubber plantation in Ivory Coast where latex is tapped from rubber trees and then processed into rubber. The rubber industry has come under a lot of international pressure from environmentalists about the effect of this industry on environmental degradation and destruction of natural forest cover to establish new rubber plantations, biodiversity loss and pollution. It has also been linked to human rights abuses, such as child labour and unfair payments and working conditions. The government has been trying to minimise the harmful effects of deforestation and promote sustainable development to meet the ever-increasing global demand for rubber.

    a  Identify **two** negative effects of Bakary's rubber plantation on the environment. [2]

    b  Outline **two** reasons why Bakary needs to consider environmental issues. [4]

    c  Explain **two** effects Bakary's business may have on the environment. [6]

    d  Explain how the government can use legal controls and incentives to minimise the effect of businesses such as Bakary's on the environment. Which way is likely to be the most effective? Justify your answer. [8]

**2** Omar Tanneries is a small company that tans animal raw hides to make leather. It buys its inventory of raw hides from local slaughterhouses and meat and dairy farms at low cost. However, one of Omar's main suppliers has had bad publicity about the treatment of cattle on its farms. The larger and more established suppliers can afford the cost of meeting the appropriate animal welfare and hygiene requirements but charge more for the raw hides. The cheap production costs enable Omar Tanneries to have a high profit margin which Omar wants to use to improve the tanning machinery. Although Omar Tanneries pays competitive wages to its own employees, Omar is aware that his suppliers may not be following ethical business practices. With increasing awareness of ethical issues and the presence of pressure groups, Omar is thinking about changing his suppliers.

    **a** Define a 'pressure group'. [2]

    **b** Outline **two** advantages to Omar of running his business ethically. [4]

    **c** Explain **two** problems pressure groups could cause for Omar Tanneries. [6]

    **d** Omar is aware of the unethical business practices followed by his suppliers, but if he sources his products from different suppliers, then his costs may go up. Should he change his suppliers? Justify your answer. [8]

**Total available marks: 40**

## CHECK YOUR PROGRESS

How well do you think you have achieved the learning intentions for this chapter? Give yourself a score from 1 (still need a lot of practice) to 5 (feeling very confident) for each learning intention. Provide an example to support your score.

| Now I can … | Score | Example |
|---|---|---|
| explain how business activity can impact the environment | | |
| understand how and why businesses might respond to environmental issues | | |
| outline the effects of legal controls over business activity affecting the environment | | |
| understand the ethical issues that might affect businesses | | |
| understand how businesses respond to ethical issues and the advantages and disadvantages of being ethical | | |
| understand what a pressure group is and how they can influence business decisions. | | |

# Section 6 case study

**CASE STUDY**

**Sports and More Limited**

Sports and More Limited (SAM) is a retail company that manufactures Sports goods and is based in Country X, which is in Europe. The company has become hugely popular as a discount store providing quality sports goods. It sources its goods from various local and international manufacturers and suppliers. Despite the economy going through a recession, SAM has experienced tremendous growth in the last ten years and is thinking of expansion into international markets as a growth strategy, either by exporting its goods or by setting up operations in the host countries. The company wants to find out which is the best country to focus on. It has gathered relevant information on Countries Y and Z (see Appendices).

# Appendix 1

**Fact file for Countries Y and Z**

|  | Country Y | Country Z |
|---|---|---|
| Location | Southern Asia | Southern Africa |
| Population | 50 million | 10 million |
| Language | English – the preferred language for communication – and eight other official languages. | English and three other regional languages. |
| Proximity to a port | The country has two ports that are used for international trade. | The country is landlocked (entirely enclosed by land). Transportation by air is the main means of international trade. |
| Infrastructure | • Reliable supply of power but mainly form nonrenewable sources of energy<br>• Road network is quite poor, but rail networks are quite good<br>• It has invested in upgrading its digital infrastructure. | • The country suffers from a shortage of reliable power supply.<br>• The road and rail networks are very good.<br>• Current technological infrastructure is quite old. |

# Appendix 2

**Economic and political profiles of Countries Y and Z**

|  | Country Y | Country Z |
|---|---|---|
| Economic growth as measured by the GDP growth rate | 2% | 5% |
| Average change in inflation in the last year | +2.5 % | +1.5% |

|  | Country Y | Country Z |
|---|---|---|
| Average interest rates in the last year | 4% | 1.5% |
| Unemployment rate | 10% | 6% |
| Barriers to entry | Tariffs and quotas exist for many sectors of trade. | Very few tariffs and quotas exist. |
| Health of economy (stage of business cycle) | Growth | Boom |
| Political stability | The country is peaceful and has been politically stable | Country Z has had two elections in the last four years. |

# Appendix 3

**Below is an extract from a recent article in a local newspaper in Country X.**

**Protests by pressure group**

An international pressure group has been lobbying and recently held a protest outside the headquarters of SAM in country X. The company is facing criticism over the unfair business practices followed by its suppliers and manufacturers as well as its own. The pressure group claims that some of SAM's manufacturers are sourcing their products unethically (especially leather goods) and also causing huge external costs by damaging the environment in their production process.

1 a Explain **two** benefits that the host country, Country Z, will have because of SAM's setting up operations there as a multinational.

   Benefit 1:

   Explanation:

   Benefit 2:

   Explanation: [8]

  b Explain the advantages and disadvantages of the following **two** countries for SAM when choosing a new location. Which country do you think SAM should choose? Justify your answer.

   Country Y:

   Country Z:

   Recommendation: [12]

2 a Pressure groups are currently posing a threat to SAM. Explain why SAM should consider pressure groups as both an opportunity and a threat.

   Opportunity:

   Explanation:

   Threat:

   Explanation: [8]

**b** The exchange rate of Country X's currency with respect to Country Y's currency has been fluctuating in the past year. Explain how each of the following might affect SAM if it decides to export to Country Y.

Which of these do you think is the most beneficial for SAM? Justify your answer.

Appreciation of Country X's currency:

Depreciation of Country X's currency:

Conclusion: [12]

**3 a** Use Appendix 2 to compare **two** economic features of Country Y and Country Z and explain their impact on business activity.

Feature 1:

Impact on business activity:

Feature 2:

Impact on business activity: [8]

**b** Explain how SAM's activities might have an economic and environmental impact. Do you think the government of Country Y or Z should approve the proposal? Justify your answer.

Positive impact:

Negative impact:

Conclusion: [12]

**4 a** What are tariffs and quotas? Explain how they may impact the business activity of SAM if it decides to export to or set up operations in Country Y.

Tariffs:

Impact on SAM:

Quotas:

Impact on SAM: [8]

**b** Should SAM respond to the threats posed by the pressure group? Justify your answer. [12]

Total available marks: 80

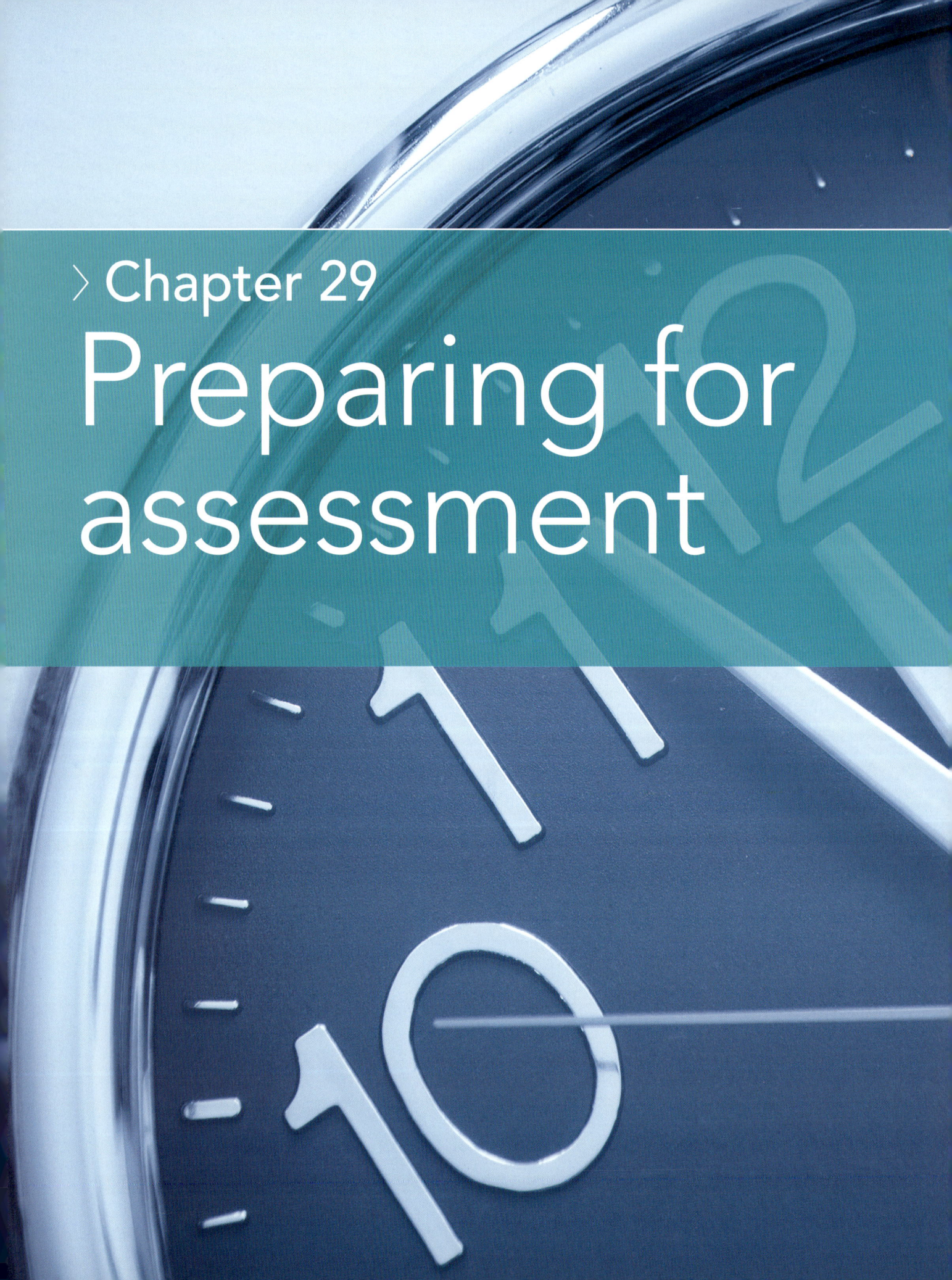

# Chapter 29
# Preparing for assessment

# 29 Preparing for assessment

Now that you have studied the content of this coursebook, the next step is to help you feel confident about applying that knowledge in your examinations in an assessment setting. This chapter will help you prepare for assessment. It will consider the different types of questions and include some sample answers (written by the authors) to help you understand what you might encounter in your exam.

## The layout of the exam

Cambridge IGCSE and Cambridge O Level Business have the same assessment structure. For the assessment of these syllabuses there are two exam papers - short answer/data response and a case study. Both papers are equally important, so allow enough time to revise everything you have learnt throughout your course.

## Short answer and data response paper

This paper consists of short answer and data response questions that are used to check your knowledge and understanding of the concepts. The paper is split into four compulsory questions and each question has four parts to it.

*Note: Any example answers to questions taken from past question papers, practice questions, accompanying marks and mark schemes included in this resource have been written by the authors and are for guidance only. They do not replicate examination papers. In examinations the way marks are awarded may be different.*

## Case study paper

In this paper, all questions are based on a single business scenario. The paper is split into four compulsory questions and each question has two parts to it.

## The assessment objectives

Assessment objectives are the skills that are being assessed in your examinations in an assessment setting. The four skills being assessed are:

- Knowledge and understanding
- Application
- Analysis
- Evaluation.

Understanding which questions are assessing each skill is important. Most questions will include a word which shows which skill is being assessed in each question. For example, 'define', 'calculate', 'explain' or 'justify'. These words are known as 'command words'. Different questions will assess different skills. For example, if the command word is 'explain', the answer cannot simply list knowledge points because the command word requires analysis skills to be shown as well.

**What is Knowledge and understanding?**

This involves showing knowledge and understanding of terms, concepts and theories, and using business terminology.

Questions assessing this skill usually start with:

- Define

Definition questions require you to show clear understanding about what a term like 'market research' means. Be precise when defining terms. The wording does not have to be identical to the key terms in the coursebook if it has the same meaning.

- Identify or state

This type of question can ask for factors, advantages or reasons. For example, 'Identify two methods of primary market research a business might use'. These are general questions, so the answers do not have to be linked to a specific business.

**What is Application?**

This means using your knowledge and understanding of terms, concepts, theories and techniques, and applying them to a given situation.

Questions that require application refer to the specific business by name in the question. Use the information given there to help you link the answer to the questions. For example, what the business makes or sells, the number of employees or any other relevant information from the scenario.

Questions assessing this skill usually start with:

- Outline

You can be asked to use your knowledge in relation to a given situation.
To show application, it is important to select options/points that are appropriate for a given situation. For example, imagine Dewei owns a small business selling books and the question is: 'Outline **two** possible reasons why Dewei might want to grow his business.'

Mentioning that Dewei's business sells books or that it is a small business are simple ways to gain application. To fully answer the question, the answer must include an appropriate reference to Dewer's business.

- Calculate

Application can also be assessed in calculation questions. For example, 'Calculate the value of working capital.' Alternatively, interpret data from a chart or diagram, for example, calculating values for break-even output or margin of safety from a break-even chart. Remember to include the units in the answer. For example, profit margin is expressed as a percentage, so the % sign should be included.

## What is Analysis?

This involves selecting, organising and interpreting business data and information in written, numerical and graphical forms, and analysing business information.

Questions assessing this skill usually start with:

- Explain or consider

These questions ask for points to be developed to show how or why the factor or point identified is important. A question may involve interpreting some data or a chart and explain what this might mean for a given business situation.

For example, imagine the question is based on a private limited company (Company A) that is planning to grow by building a new factory. The question might be, 'Explain **two** possible sources of finance that Company A might use to grow its business.'

Not all sources of finance might be relevant, so choose two suitable sources and then, for each one, explain how or why that source of finance might be appropriate for company A.

## What is Evaluation?

This involves being able to make justified (supported) decisions, reach conclusions and make recommendations based on evidence.

Evaluation is a difficult skill. It requires a clear decision to be made, a supporting reason and then explain why it is better than the alternative discussed. The evaluation should follow on from points discussed. This type of questions will assess all four skills: knowledge, application, analysis as well as and evaluation.

Questions assessing this skill usually include the phrase:

- Justify your answer/choice

This wording tends to appear at the end of questions that assess this skill. For example, 'Using the information in Appendix 2, and other information, do you think ABC was right to choose option A? Justify your answer.'

It is important to make a decision. It does not matter whether the decision is 'yes' or 'no', or X or Y, as there is no single right answer. A decision on its own is not evaluation. It is the reason behind the decision which is important. In the justification/recommendation, do not simply repeat points already made in the analysis part. The focus should be on explaining relevant points that support the decision made. Try to include why the chosen option/view is better that the alternative(s) discussed.

**Skills in a sample answer**

The example below shows a question and then an annotated sample answer (written by the authors) to highlight how each skill could be shown in a given answer:

Anika is an entrepreneur. She plans to open a new café in the city centre, selling hot drinks and cakes. Anika is considering different methods of promotion to help attract customers.

Explain **two** methods of promotion Anika might use to promote her business. Which is likely to be the best method for Anika to use? Justify your answer. [6]

**Knowledge** for identifying methods

**Analysis** for relevant development of points

Anika could use **free samples** which allows people to try her products and if they like it, and more likely to buy. She could also use **social media** which is a low-cost method for a *new business*. Social media is the best way because being low cost can reduce cash outflows, which is especially important for a new business which is likely to have limited funds. Whereas there is no guarantee that they will buy any *cakes* which could result in no revenue to cover the cost of providing the free samples for *customers*.

*Application* for linking points to the context.

Evaluation for justified decision and for explaining why chosen method is better than the alternative

> **REFLECTION**
>
> When answering Practice questions, do you review them to indicate skills shown?
>
> Annotating Practice questions is a good way to highlight which skills you have shown in an answer – this could help you work out which skills you may need to improve.
>
> Remember that the more you practice these skills, the more confident you will become at using them.

29 Preparing for assessment

# How to prepare for your assessment

The assessment includes AOs that cover the four skills in your examinations: knowledge and understanding, application, analysis and evaluation skills.

The next part of this chapter includes example questions, answers and mark schemes that have been written by the authors.

## How to approach short answer and data response questions

Here are some simple points to remember when answering short answer and data response questions:

- Always start by reading the question stem. This gives information on a particular business situation, upon which the questions are based. Make a note of key details that could be useful when answering the questions.

- There are four short scenarios or stems – one for each question. Do not use the information from one question to answer another question.

- All questions (except those starting with 'define', 'identify' and 'state') are applied, it is important that answers are linked to the scenario. The information in the stem should be used ....

You should now read the following sample stem (written by the authors):

Omar is a sole trader. He owns a small taxi business in Main City called Call4Cab. Omar has three full-time employees who each complete 1 000 journeys every week. He uses many methods to promote his taxi business. Omar wants to expand his business and plans to offer a chauffeur service for events, including weddings and celebrations. The new vehicle will cost $5 000. Omar will need to choose a suitable source of finance for this new vehicle.

| | | |
|---|---|---|
| a | Define 'fixed costs'. | [2] |
| b | Outline **two** ways the size of Omar's business can be measured. | [4] |
| c | Explain **two** methods of promotion Omar could use to promote his business. | [6] |
| d | Explain **two** sources of finance Omar could use for the new vehicle. Which is likely to be the best source of finance for Omar to choose? Justify your answer. | [8] |

> **REFLECTION**
>
> When you answer these questions yourself, what points would you make?
>
> After you have written down your answers, ask someone else to mark them for you. Asking someone else to look at any sample questions you have answered can be helpful, as the other person can check that what you have written is easy to understand and clearly written. If you read someone else's answers, it can be a good opportunity to learn different approaches to answering questions.

# BUSINESS FOR CAMBRIDGE IGCSE™ AND O LEVEL: COURSEBOOK

## ACTIVITY 29.1

Read the following sample answers (written by the authors). How many marks would you give each of the following responses to the sample questions? Extracts of a mark scheme are included to help you decide. Afterwards, compare the marks you would give with the comments provided.

a   Define 'fixed costs'. [2]

Mark scheme: Two marks for an answer such as 'Costs that do not vary with the number of items sold or produced in the short term'.

Sample answer:

*These are costs which are fixed. This means they do not change.*

Comments for part (a):

The first part of the answer is wrong because the words have simply been reordered which shows no understanding of fixed costs. The second part of the answer shows some understanding of the term, but it is missing the link to level of output or sales.

b   Outline **two** ways the size of Omar's business can be measured. [4]

Mark scheme: One mark for identifying each way, plus one additional mark is available for an appropriate reference to the context.

Points might include:

- number of employees
- capital employed
- level of revenue
- number of sales.

For example:

Number of employees [knowledge and understanding] as Omar only has three employees working for him [application].

Examples of application might include: sole trader, taxi business, successful, small, cars, drivers, 1000 journeys (each week), three employees.

Sample answer (written by the authors):

*Way 1: the number of employees as Omar only has three employees.*

*Way 2: profit as Omar's business has been successful, which is why he is looking to expand.*

Comments for part (b):

Way 1 has identified employees as a measure of size and by mentioning that the business has three employees, the answer is clearly applied.

### CONTINUED

Way 2 is incorrect because profit is not recognised as a measure of size. While the reference to success is true, application needs to be based on relevant knowledge.

c  Explain **two** methods of promotion Omar could use to promote his business. [6]

Mark scheme: One mark for identifying each method – plus one additional mark available for relevant development and one mark for linking the answers to the context.

| Appropriate methods might include: | Relevant development (analysis) could include: |
|---|---|
| Leaflets | • which customers could refer to<br>• can include images |
| Specialist magazines | • can target people who are likely to want to use this new service |
| Social media | • as able to reach a wide range of people<br>• low cost |
| Buy One Get One Free (BOGOF) | • as this could make the products more affordable |
| Gifts | • as customers will use his business more often to gain the extra items |

Examples of application might include: sole trader, taxi business, successful, small, cars, drivers, 1 000 journeys (each week), three employees.

Sample answer (written by the authors):

Way 1: Local newspapers
Explanation: So, the potential customer will read it and can call Call4Cab if they want to use the new service.

Way 2: Social media
Explanation: As it is able to reach a wide range of people which could help the business raise awareness of its new wedding service.

Comments for part (c):

Way 1 is a relevant method and advantage is explained (customers can read it). However, there is no link to the context as using the business name is not application. The reference to 'new service' is taken from the question so this cannot be used as application. For this answer to be applied, it could have added that this method might be suitable for this small business.

## CONTINUED

Way 2 is valid, and the reference to weddings shows application. However, the analysis is a similar point to the one written in Way 1 so this is repetition. It is important to include different development for each point made. For example, social media might be a good idea as it is a low-cost way to promote this new wedding service.

d   Explain **two** sources of finance Omar could use for the new vehicle. Which is likely to be the best source of finance for Omar to choose? Justify your answer. [8]

Mark scheme: One mark for identifying each source of finance, plus up to two additional marks for relevant development and a further two marks available for linking the answers to the context.

Up to two marks for making a justified decision, explaining why the chosen source of finance is better than the alternative.

| Appropriate methods might include: | Relevant development (analysis) could include: |
|---|---|
| Profit | • there is no interest to pay<br>• may not be sufficient funds |
| Government grant | • no need to repay<br>• may be restrictions on what the funds can be used for |
| Crowdfunding | • could also allow for the public reaction to be tested<br>• no guarantee that it will raise the full amount |
| Bank loan | • gain the funds all at once<br>• need to pay interest |
| Leasing | • as could pay month by month for the use of equipment/vehicle<br>• never own the asset |

Examples of application might include: sole trader, taxi business, successful, small, cars, drivers, 1000 journeys (each week), three employees.

Sample answer (written by the authors):

A bank loan is good because Omar can get all the money at once for the new taxi. He could use profit, which he will not need to repay this money. Omar should use a bank loan as he gets all the money at once.

> **CONTINUED**
>
> Comments for part (d):
>
> The answer identifies two sources of finance – bank loan and profit. Both points have been developed to explain an advantage of each source. The references to 'taxi' and $5 000 shows good application.
>
> A decision is made, but this is not supported as it simply repeats the earlier point.
> The answer needs to explain why profit might be the better source of finance compared to using a bank loan. For example, a bank loan may be better because being a small business Omar may not have $5 000 in profit and the loan will allow him to buy the vehicle straightaway, and the revenue gained could allow him to repay the loan.

# How to approach case study questions

Case study questions require more detailed analysis than short answer or data response questions. Think about what each point means and how this could affect this particular business. For example, because of X, this means Y will happen and this will therefore lead to Z. This is a good way to show more developed analysis.

The answer does not need to discuss lots of different points. Two or three well-developed points are likely to be sufficient (depending on the question).

Here are some simple points to remember when answering case study questions:

- Read through the case study information first and make a note of important details, including the type of business and the number of employees. All the questions are based on the case study, so the information offers valuable information to help write answers that show application skills.

- Not all case study information will be relevant for every question. Learn to select appropriate information to support the points you are making.

- All case study questions are applied, so always look to link points to the scenario. Use the information from the case study as the basis for application.

- Take your time and plan out the points to discuss in the 12-mark questions. This can help to ensure your answer remains focused on the question being asked.

Read the following case study extract (in the assessment, the case study may have appendices as well.)

# BUSINESS FOR CAMBRIDGE IGCSE™ AND O LEVEL: COURSEBOOK

> **CASE STUDY**
>
> **Early Riders (ER)**
>
> ER is a private limited company based in Country X. The business manufactures children's bicycles, using batch production. The bicycles are sold to large retail shops in 80 countries.
>
> ER is located on the edge of the capital city in Country X near to a small airport. Most of the components to make the bicycles are purchased from local suppliers, but some components, such as tyres, are imported. ER's Managing Director is considering locating its current factory in another country, due to increasing costs and new legal controls. She said, 'Legal controls mean extra costs, and I am determined to keep ER's profit margin high.'
>
> ER has 75 production employees and 15 office employees. All production employees are unskilled and are paid by time rate. The Production Manager has an autocratic leadership style. Some of the production employees do not like doing the same tasks every day. ER's Human Resources Director is worried about the high level of labour turnover and is considering ways to increase the motivation of the production employees. The three methods are – job rotation, increase wages and fringe benefits.

**a** Explain **one** advantage and **one** disadvantage to ER of using batch production.

Advantage:

Disadvantage: [8]

**b** Consider the following **three** methods ER could use to increase the motivation of production employees. Which method should ER use? Justify your answer.

Job rotation:

Increase wages:

Fringe benefits:

Recommendation: [12]

## ACTIVITY 29.2

Read the following sample answers (written by the authors). How many marks would you give each of the following responses to the questions above? Extracts of the mark scheme are included to help you decide. Afterwards, compare the marks you would give with the comments provided.

**1** Explain **one** advantage and **one** disadvantage to ER of using batch production. [8]

Mark scheme: One mark for each advantage/disadvantage – with up to three marks for relevant development, including one mark for linking the answer to the context.

Relevant advantages might include:

- Flexibility–so easy to adapt to any sudden change in demand for different bicycles–sales are likely to increase–leading to a possible increase in market share.

- Some variety of jobs–so this could make the work more interesting in the factory–increasing motivation–leading to less absenteeism.

- Less effect if one machine breaks down–so some output produced–able to meet demand from large retailers–protecting its reputation.

> **CONTINUED**
>
> Relevant disadvantages might include:
>
> - Warehouse space is needed for components and finished bikes–increasing costs–which could increase cash outflows.
>
> - Time to switching between batches–might mean that at busy times there may not be enough finished products ready for delivery–this might damage its reputation–less customer loyalty.
>
> - Added cost of moving semi-/finished goods–around the factory–lower efficiency–increasing average costs.
>
> Application could include:
>
> Children's bicycles, components, local suppliers, tyres, imported materials, factory located near an airport, 75 production employees, unskilled labour, autocratic leadership style, 15 office employees, sold to large retail shops, 80 countries.
>
> Sample answer (written by the authors):
>
> *Advantage: It is a flexible way of working because it is easy to change production from one type of bicycle to another to meet demand. This means that if there is an increase in the number of orders for a particular size or style of bicycle, ER can easily change what they make. This means the large stores have the bikes they want, which can increase its sales leading to higher revenue.*
>
> *Disadvantage: Part-finished goods need to be moved around a lot. This will increase transporting and storage costs, and it will take time, which reduces employees' efficiency. Inefficient employees need to be trained. Efficiency is important for a business as this can help lower costs and increase profits.*
>
> Comments:
>
> Advantage: Flexibility is a valid point. There is some development explaining how flexibility can benefit ER's business in terms of being able to meet demand which could increase sales and revenue. There is clear application for recognising that ER makes bicycles.
>
> Disadvantage: The disadvantage is a valid point, and there is some development of why it is a disadvantage (time and lower efficiency). However, there is no attempt to link the answer to ER's particular business. Application could have been gained for an appropriate reference to the factory or mentioning that the employees were unskilled.

> **CONTINUED**
>
> 2   Consider the following **three** methods ER could use to increase the motivation of production employees. Which method should ER use? Justify your answer.
>
> **Job rotation:**
>
> **Increase wages:**
>
> **Fringe benefits:**
>
> **Recommendation:** [12]
>
> Extract from sample mark scheme (written by the authors):
>
> | Level | Skills you need to show | Possible marks |
> |---|---|---|
> | 3 | Detailed discussion of **two** or more methods in context of this business. Well justified decision including why the alternative methods were rejected. Comprehensive/excellent answers discuss three methods in detail, in context, with well-justified recommendation. | 9–12 |
> | 2 | Detailed discussion of at least **one** method of motivation. Simple judgement with some justification/some evaluation of choice made. | 5–8 |
> | 1 | Limited ability to discuss the methods with little to no explanation. Limited application shown to the case study. | 1–4 |
> | 0 | No relevant knowledge. | 0 |
>
> Sample answer (written by the authors):
>
> Job rotation: This can make the work more interesting for employees because they are currently making the same thing in each batch, so it can be boring. Job rotation could allow them to swap from putting wheels on to adding the tyres. Giving some variety is likely to make employees less bored and this can help reduce the number of employees leaving each year. However, ER will have to train employees, which could increase its costs, which could lower the profit margin. But if they end up spending less money having to keep recruiting new employees, it might be worth it.

> **CONTINUED**
>
> Increase wages: As the employees are unskilled, the only way to motivate them is to give them more money. Taylor's theory said that everyone wants more money, so they have a clear incentive to work harder as this means they can earn more money. The only problem is that not everyone is motivated by money. People have other needs such as social and esteem, so just paying them more might not satisfy the 75 production employees. ER might end up with higher costs for wages and people could still leave.
>
> Fringe benefits: many employees might have children, so getting discounts on bicycles might interest them as it saves them money. The business also benefits with extra sales. With birthdays and festivals every year, buying bikes as children grow is expensive. If employees have access to low-cost bikes this might motivate them and make up for the low wages paid. However, this will only work for people who have, or know, children so it may not work for everyone.
>
> Recommendation: The best option is job rotation. The employees do not like doing the same job every day so this method directly helps solve this problem. Higher wage rates might work for a short while, but then they might just want more pay which will simply increase costs and lower the profit margin, which is the opposite of ER's objective. However, discounts may only work if they want to buy a bicycle, so it is unlikely to work for everyone.
>
> Comments:
>
> Relevant knowledge is included for each of the three methods including job rotation which provides variety, understanding that increased wages could act as an incentive and fringe benefits could help the employees save money. There are plenty of references throughout the answer that link the points to ER's business. Examples such as tyres, batch production and 75 employees show good application.
>
> There is clear development showing how each method could help increase motivation, as well as problems with each method.
>
> For the evaluation, a choice has been made, namely job rotation, which is supported by the points made. As part of the evaluation, the answer has tried to explain why job rotation is better than the other two methods.

# Revision

There is no one way to revise. Everyone is different and methods that work for one person might not suit someone else. You need to try out ideas and find out which approach is likely to work best for you.

Here are some simple points to bear in mind:

- **Check what you need to learn** – you only need to learn about concepts that are included in the syllabus. Business is a huge topic and covers more concepts than the ones you will need to understand for this course. Ask your teacher about what you need to revise.

- **Make a revision timetable** – plan your time. Set aside time every week for study. You are likely to be sitting exams for more than one subject so allow yourself time to revise for everything. Give yourself time to relax as well.

- **Revise effectively** – do not spend hours just looking at your coursebook or workbook. Split up your time into smaller revision periods, such as 30–40 minutes. This can help you focus on what you need to do. Give yourself a break. Rest is important and it gives you time to reflect on what you have learnt.

- **Revise actively** – do not simply read your coursebook. Think about different ways to remember ideas. The following suggestions can help you to remember key points or associations: make notes, create flash cards, construct summary charts, draw mind maps (see Figure 29.1) or create your own mnemonics.

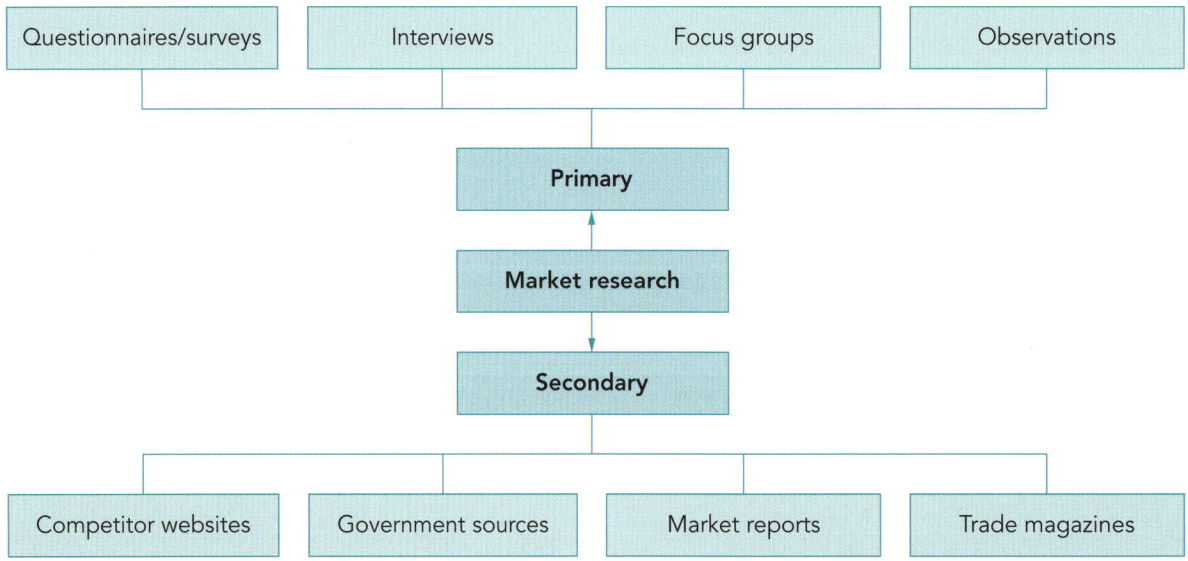

**Figure 29.1:** Example mind map showing methods of market research

A mnemonic can take the form of an acronym, tune or anything that helps you remember important information. The following example is one idea for remembering ways to improve cash flow:

> **C**ustomers asked to pay quicker
> **A**ssets not being used can be sold
> **S**uppliers asked for longer to pay
> *h*
> *f*
> **L**oan
> **O**verdraft
> **W**orking Capital managed better

- **Use past papers or practice questions** – these help you to check your progress. They can help you to understand the style and demands of different questions, and learn to answer them in the time allowed.
- **Ask for help** – if there are topics or concepts you do not understand, re-read your notes or ask your teacher for help.

## Revision checklist

Use the following checklist to help make sure you are ready to do your best in your exam.

- **Get a good night's sleep** – it seems obvious, but sleep is important, especially the night before an exam. This can help you to stay alert during the exam.
- **Keep calm** – you have done your revision, so there is nothing to worry about. Exam questions are simply designed to find out what you know and can do.
- **Read and follow the instructions** – these are on the front of the paper and tell you what needs to be done.
- **Attempt every question** – no marks can be gained if nothing is written down.
- **Manage your time** – do not spend too long on any questions with only 2 or 4 marks. Allow enough time to answer the longer ones. If you do not know the answer to a question, move quickly on to the next one. You can go back to any unanswered questions later.
- **Quality not quantity** – the lines provided in the answer book can act as a guide to show you how much you might be expected to write for each question. It is not how much you write, but what you write, that matters.
- **Read each question carefully** – you need to be clear about what the question requires you to do. You must answer the question that has been set; not the one you wanted to be set.

- **Check the command word** the command word in the question will let you know which skills are being assessed. For example, 'identify' will be assessing knowledge, while 'explain' will be assessing analysis.

- **Understand which skills are being assessed in each question** – one way to help work out which skills are being assessed is to look at the number of marks available for each question. Questions worth 6, 8 or 12 marks will be assessing a wider range of skills.

- **Write all answers in the answer booklet** – do not write on the insert of the case study as this is not marked. If you need more space, ask for additional paper.

- **Show your working for calculation questions** – it is easy to make a mistake copying out the answer. If you show your working, you may gain some credit for the method.

- **Apply** – link the answers to the scenario. For example, think about what the business makes or sells. Use the information provided in the question and/or case study as a guide.

- **Make a clear decision** – questions assessing evaluation require a supported decision to be made. There is no right or wrong answers to evaluation questions. What matters, is that a clear reason is given to support the choice made.

- **Check** – leave time at the end of the exam to check what you have written. You should have attempted every question.

As you approach your exam, it can become easy to worry about what you need to do. Stay positive and trust yourself – you have learnt the content and have prepared for your assessment, so all that is left to do is go out there and do your best!

Wishing you all the best for your exams and for a successful future.

Medi Houghton

Leanne Burslem-Curl

Veenu Jain

# Accounting formulae and ratios

**Marketing**

Market share (%) = $\dfrac{\text{sales revenue of a business}}{\text{total sales revenue for the whole market}} \times 100$

**Production**

Labour productivity = $\dfrac{\text{output per period (units)}}{\text{number of employees}}$ = units per employee

Total variable costs = variable cost per unit × number of units

Total cost = fixed costs + total variable costs

Variable cost per unit = $\dfrac{\text{total variable cost}}{\text{number of units}}$

Average cost = $\dfrac{\text{total cost}}{\text{number of units}}$

Break-even output = $\dfrac{\text{fixed costs}}{\text{contribution per unit}}$

Contribution per unit = selling price per unit − variable cost per unit

Margin of safety = actual output − break-even output     OR     actual number of sales − break-even number of sales

**Business finance**

Working capital = current assets − current liabilities

**Profit or loss/Profitability**

Revenue = selling price per unit × number of units sold

Gross profit = revenue − cost of sales

Profit = total revenue − total costs     OR     gross profit − expenses

Profit margin (%) = $\dfrac{\text{profit}}{\text{revenue}} \times 100$

Gross profit margin (%) = $\dfrac{\text{gross profit}}{\text{revenue}} \times 100$

Return on capital employed (%) = $\dfrac{\text{profit}}{\text{captial employed}} \times 100$

**Liquidity**

Current ratio = $\dfrac{\text{current assets}}{\text{current liabilities}}$

Acid test ratio = $\dfrac{\text{current assets} - \text{inventory}}{\text{current liabilities}}$

# Glossary

| | | | |
|---|---|---|---|
| **added value** | the difference between the selling price and the cost of bought-in materials. | **cash flow forecast** | an estimate of the future cash inflows and outflows of a business. |
| **advertising** | the methods used by a business to inform customers about its products or persuade customers to buy its products. | **cash inflow** | the money coming into the business. |
| | | **cash outflow** | the money going out of the business. |
| **appreciation** | a rise in the value of a currency against another currency. | **chain of command** | the way in which authority and instructions are passed down through an organisation. |
| **assets** | resources that are owned by a business. | **channels of distribution** | the ways used to get a product from the producer to the final consumer. |
| **autocratic leadership** | a leadership style where the leader makes all the decisions without any input from employees. | **closing balance** | how much cash the business expects to have at the end of a specific period, e.g., a month. |
| **average total cost** | the total cost of producing a single unit of output. | **commission** | a payment to sales employees based on the value of the items they sell. |
| **bank loan** | provision of finance by a bank that the business will repay with interest over an agreed period of time. | **communication barrier** | something that stops a message from being sent, received or understood clearly. |
| **batch production** | where groups of identical products are made; each group passes through one stage of production before moving on to the next stage. | **competitive pricing** | setting a the price similar to that of competitors' products in the market. |
| | | **cost of sales** | the cost of purchasing the raw materials/goods and packaging for producing or selling of products and services. |
| **bonus** | an additional reward paid to employees for achieving targets set by managers. | | |
| **brand image** | the name, logo or identity of a product that distinguishes it from competitors. | **cost-plus pricing** | setting the price by adding a fixed percentage mark-up to the cost of making or buying the product in order to make a profit. |
| **break-even** | the level of output where revenue equals total costs; the business is making neither profit nor loss. | **crowdfunding** | financing a business idea by obtaining small amounts of capital from a large number of people, most often using the internet and social media networks. |
| **business plan** | a detailed written document outlining the aims and objectives of a business and what it intends to do to achieve them. | | |
| **capital employed** | the total amount of capital invested in a business for the purpose of generating profits. | **current assets** | resources that the business owns, which it will have for less than one year. |
| | | **current liabilities** | short-term debts of the business that need to be paid within one year. |

# Glossary

**curriculum vitae (CV)** — a document that outlines the details of the education, qualifications and work experience of a potential employee which can be sent to an employer when applying for a job.

**delegation** — when a manager gives authority to a subordinate to carry out specific tasks and make decisions.

**democratic leadership** — a leadership style where employees are involved in the decision-making process.

**depreciation** — a fall in the value of a currency against another currency.

**direct to consumers** — where the product is sold by the producer directly to the final consumer without the need for any intermediaries.

**diseconomies of scale** — an increase in average costs as the scale of output increases.

**dynamic pricing** — where different prices are paid for the same product at different times.

**ecommerce** — the marketing, buying and selling of goods over the internet.

**economic growth** — an increase in the value of goods and services produced by an economy over time.

**economies of scale** — the reduction in average costs as the scale of output increases.

**employee of the month** — a scheme designed to recognise high-performing individuals within an organisation over a certain period of time.

**entrepreneur** — an individual who has an idea for a new business and takes the financial risk of starting it.

**exchange rate** — the price of one currency in terms of another.

**expenses** — the costs that are not directly linked to the production or the selling of products and services.

**extension strategies** — actions taken by a business to keep a product in the maturity stage of the product life cycle to help maintain sales.

**external benefit** — where a business decision has a positive impact on a third party.

**external cost** — where a business decision has a negative impact on a third party.

**external recruitment** — filling a vacant post with somebody not already employed in the business.

**factors of production** — the resources needed by a business to produce goods and services – land, labour, capital and enterprise.

**fixed cost** — costs that do not change with output.

**flexible hours** — this allows employees to adjust when, where and for how long they work each day to suit their needs or personal situations.

**flexible working** — an agreement between employer and employee that allows the employee to change when, where and for how long they work to suit them.

**flow production** — the continuous production of large quantities of identical goods.

**franchise** — a business agreement where one person or business buys the right to use the name, logo and product of an existing business.

**fringe benefits** — non-monetary rewards which are offered to employees in addition to their wages or salary.

**globalisation** — the process by which countries are connected with each other because of the trade of goods and services.

**gross profit** — the difference between revenue and cost of sales.

**hierarchy** — the number of levels of responsibility in an organisational structure.

| | | | |
|---|---|---|---|
| **hire purchase** | the purchase of an asset by paying a fixed repayment amount per time period over an agreed period of time. The asset is owned by the purchasing company on completion of the final repayment. | **job production** | production of one-off items specific to customer requirements. |
| | | **job rotation** | increasing variety in the workplace by allowing employees to switch from one task to another. |
| **homeworking** | the business allows employees to work from home instead of working at the business office. | **joint venture** | two or more businesses agree to work together on a project and set up a separate business for this purpose. |
| **horizontal integration** | when two businesses at the same stage of production join to become a single, larger business. | **labour productivity** | the number of units of output produced for every unit of labour input in a given time period. |
| **hygiene factors** | one of the factors that must be present in the workplace to prevent job dissatisfaction. | **labour turnover** | the rate at which employees leave a business in a given period of time. |
| **import quota** | physical limit on the quantity of goods that can be imported into a country. | **laissez-faire leadership** | a leadership style where most of the decisions are left to the employees to make with limited or no input from managers. |
| **import tariff** | a tax applied to the value of imported goods into a country. | | |
| **induction training** | a training programme to help new employees become familiar with their workplace, the people they work with and the procedures they need to follow. | **lean production** | the production of goods and services whilst aiming to minimise the waste of resources. |
| | | **leasing** | obtaining the use of a non-current asset by paying a fixed amount per time period for a fixed period of time. Ownership remains with the leasing company. |
| **inflation** | an increase in the average price level of goods and services over time. | | |
| **interest rate** | the cost to a person or business of borrowing money from a lender such as a bank. | **level of unemployment** | the percentage of the population that are willing and able to work, but are unable to find a job. |
| **internal recruitment** | filling a vacant post with someone already employed in the business. | **liabilities** | debts of the business that will have to be paid sometime in the future. |
| **inventory** | the stored raw materials, work-in-progress and finished goods held by a business. | **limited liability** | owners of a company are only responsible for the debts of the business up to the amount they have invested in the company. |
| **job description** | a document that includes the job title and a list of the key points about job, key duties, responsibilities and accountability. | **liquidity** | the ability of a business to pay its short-term debts. |
| **job enrichment** | employees are given tasks that involve more responsibility or more challenging work. | **long-term finance** | used to finance the purchase of non-current assets or finance expansion plans. Long-term finance is borrowing a business does not expect to repay in less than five years. |

# Glossary

| | | | |
|---|---|---|---|
| **margin of safety** | the difference between the current level of output of a business and the break-even level of output. | **non-current liabilities** | debts of the business which will be payable after more than one year. |
| **market research** | the process of collecting, recording and analysing data about the customers, competitors or market for a product. | **objective** | a statement of a specific target to be achieved by a business. |
| | | **off-the-job training** | training that takes place away from the workplace and the day-to-day duties of the job that the employee does. |
| **market segmentation** | dividing the whole market into segments based on consumer characteristics and targeting different products to each segment. | **on-the-job training** | training at the place of work; watching or following an experienced employee. |
| | | **opening balance** | the projected bank balance at the start of a specific period. |
| **market share** | the value of one firm's sales as a percentage of total sales in the market. | **opportunity cost** | the next best alternative given up by choosing a different option. |
| **marketing** | the process of identifying, anticipating and satisfying customer needs. | **organisational structure** | the formal, internal framework of a business that shows how it is managed and organised. |
| **marketing mix** | the four key marketing decisions that a business makes in order to market products effectively and help attract customers. | **overdraft** | an agreement with the bank that allows a business to spend more money than it has in its account up to an agreed limit. The loan has to be repaid within 12 months. |
| **marketing strategy** | a plan to achieve the marketing objectives of a business using a given level of resources. | **owner's equity** | the amount invested in the business by the owners. |
| **mass market** | selling the same product to the whole market. | **partnership** | a business owned and controlled by two or more people. |
| **merger** | when two business agree to join to become a single, larger business. | **penetration pricing** | setting a low price for a new product in order to attract customers to buy the product. |
| **mortgage** | a long-term loan used for the purchase of land or buildings. | **person specification** | a list of the qualifications, skills, experience and personal qualities looked for in a successful applicant. |
| **motivators** | the factors that influence a person to increase their efforts at work. | | |
| **multinational company (MNC)** | an organisation that has operations in more than one country. | **piece-rate** | a payment system where employees are paid based on the number of units they produce. |
| **net cash flow** | cash inflow minus cash outflow. | **pressure group** | a group of people who join together for a common cause (ethical or environmental). |
| **niche market** | a small part of the total market where consumers have specific needs and wants. | **(price) skimming** | setting a high price for a new product that is unique or very different from any other product on the market. |
| **non-current assets** | resources owned by a business and expects to use for more than one year. | | |

| | | | |
|---|---|---|---|
| **primary research** | the collection of first-hand data for the specific needs of the business. | **reference** | a trusted person who agrees to comment on an applicant's previous work, skills or abilities. |
| **primary sector** | business activity which involves the extraction or harvesting of natural resources. | **retailer** | a business that sell goods and services to the final consumer. |
| **private limited company** | business that is owned by shareholders that can only sell its shares to family and friends. | **retained profit** | profit remaining after all expenses, tax and dividends have been paid and which is ploughed back into the business. |
| **private sector** | the part of the economy that is owned and controlled by individuals and companies for profit. | **revenue** | the amount earned from the sale of products or services. |
| | | **salary** | employees are paid a fixed amount per year, which is usually paid monthly. |
| **product life cycle** | the stages a product goes through over time, determined by the volume of sales made in each stage. | **sales promotion** | incentives used to encourage short-term increases in sales or repeat purchases. |
| **production** | the process of combining inputs together to turn them into product outputs. | **sampling** | involves conducting market research on a small portion of the total market, which is representative of the entire market. |
| **profit** | the difference between revenue and total costs. | | |
| **profit sharing** | an additional payment to employees based on the profits of the business. | **secondary research** | the collection of data that already exists and that has been collected for another purpose. |
| **promotion** | a range of methods designed to encourage interest or raise awareness of products that a business is trying to sell. | **secondary sector** | businesses that turn raw materials into manufactured goods. |
| **public limited company** | businesses that is owned by shareholders that can sell its shares to the general public. | **share issue** | a source of permanent capital available to limited liability companies. |
| **public sector** | the part of the economy that is owned and controlled by the state or central government. | **shareholder** | a person or organisation who buys shares in a limited company, which means they own part of the business. |
| **quality assurance** | where employees check the quality of products at each stage of the production process. | **shareholders' equity** | alternative term for owner's equity, but can only be used by limited liability companies. |
| **quality control** | checking the quality of goods through inspection at the end of the production process. | **short-term finance** | loans or debt that a business expects to pay back within one year. |
| **quota** | physical limit on the quantity of goods that can be imported and exported. | **social enterprise** | a business with social objectives that reinvests most of its profits back into the business or into benefiting society at large. |
| **redundancy** | ending of employment by the employer because the job is no longer needed. | | |

# Glossary

| | | | |
|---|---|---|---|
| **sole trader** | a business that is owned and controlled by just one person. | **total fixed costs** | all of the fixed costs of producing the total output. |
| **span of control** | the number of subordinates that a manager is responsible for. | **total variable cost** | all of the variable costs of producing the total output. |
| **stakeholder** | an individual or group that has an interest in a business because they are affected by its activities and decisions. | **trade payables** | the amount a business owes to its suppliers for goods bought on credit. |
| | | **trade receivables** | the amount of money owed to the business by customers who have been sold goods on credit. |
| **statement of financial position** | an accounting statement that records the assets, liabilities and owners' equity of a business at a particular date. | **trade union** | a group of employees who join together to protect the interests of its members. |
| **statement of profit or loss** | a financial statement that records the revenue, costs and profits of a business for a given period of time. | **variable cost** | costs that change in direct proportion to output. variable cost per unit the variable cost of producing one single unit of output. |
| **takeover** | when one business buys a controlling interest in another. | **venture capital** | a source of finance provided by individuals or companies to start-up companies that have huge growth potential and are likely to give high returns. |
| **tariff** | a tax applied to the value of imported and exported goods. | | |
| **tax** | a charge/fee paid to the government on individual's income, business profit of its goods and services. | **vertical integration** | when two businesses at different stages of production within the same industry join to become a single, larger business. |
| **tertiary sector** | involves providing services to consumers and other businesses. | **wholesaler** | a business that buys products in bulk from producers and then sells them in smaller amounts. |
| **time-based** | a payment to employees based on a fixed amount for each hour worked. | **working capital** | the capital needed to finance the day-to-day running costs and pay the short-term debts of a business. |
| **total cost** | all the variable and fixed costs of producing the total output. | | |

# > INDEX

3D printing, 286
    case study, 287
3Rs, 466
4Sight, 200

absenteeism, 151
accounts
    limitations, 414
    use of, 412–13, **413–14**
    *see also* statements of financial position; statements of profit or loss
acid test ratio, 410–11, 499
added value, 17–18, *17*
    case studies, 19
    ways to increase it, **17**
    *see also* profit
advertising, 179, **182**, 248–9
age, market segmentation by, 187
Agrid South Africa, 330–1
aha moments, 36
AI (Artificial Intelligence), 472
    effects on stakeholder groups, 82, *83*
Air Asia, 309
air pollution, 462, **463**, 464
Airbnb, dynamic pricing, 230
Alibaba, 384–5, 472
analysis, exam assessment, 485
application, exam assessment, 484
application forms, 99
appreciation of exchange rates, 457
assessing job applicants, 101
assets, 391, 392
autocratic leaders, 125, **126**, *127*
automation, 275, *276*
average total cost, 294, 296, 499
awareness campaigns, **475**

backward vertical integration, 49
bank loans, 349–50
bankruptcy, 368
banks, 79
    use of accounts and ratio analysis, **414**
bar charts, *208*, *418*
Barra, Mary, 128
Bata shoes, 175

batch production, 282, *283*
    advantages and disadvantages, **284**
billboards, 248
Body Shop, The, 376
Bogawantalawa Tea Estates, 411–12
bonus schemes, 159–60
Boogertman + Partners, 273
boom, *426*
    possible effects on business, **427**
Botswana, interest rates, 438
boycotting, **475**
BRAC Bank Limited, 30
brand image, 215
branding, **17**
break-even analysis, 303–4, *304*
    calculations, 304–5
    case study, 306
    margin of safety, 307
    uses and limitations, **309**
break-even charts, 305, *306*
break-even output, 305, 499
BUA cement, 384
Buffet, Warren, 128
Build Your Dreams (BYD), 93
bulk buying, 293
business activity, 12–13
business culture, 167
business cycle, 426, *426*
    possible effects on business, **427**
business ethics, 471–2
business growth, 74
    advantages and disadvantages, 47, **51**
    external, 48–9, **50**
    internal, 47, **50**
    possible problems, 51
    reasons for remaining small, **52**
business ideas, 370
business in action
    Air Asia, 309
    Alibaba, 384–5
    business ideas, 370
    BYJU'S, 131
    communication methods, 146
    COP28, 467
    expansion into Southeast Asia, 439

# Index

Grow Green Tea Company, 233
Hello Chef, 167
The Hive, 190
HS2, 21
Hypnos, 320
Jumia, 252
JYSK, 209
LG Electronics India, 454
Lojas Renner (LR), 111
Lux Island Resorts (LIR), 397
New Balance, 331
Ørsted, 32
Patagonia, 84
Ryobi Limited, 289
Schweppes tonic water, 264
Shamsi, investment decision, 415
Shark Tank India, 355, 370
Starbucks, 53–4
Tivoli Gardens, 221
Tony's Chocolonely, 68–9
Trafigura, 242
business in context
    aha moments, 36
    air pollution, 462
    Bata shoes, 175
    Body Shop, The, 376
    Boogertman + Partners, 273
    Build Your Dreams (BYD), 93
    BYJU's, 403
    Coconut Bowls, 245
    construction industry, 72
    Dyson in Singapore, 324
    Fairsew, 313
    globalisation, 444
    Grab Holdings, 257
    Handmade Heroes, 57
    Infosys, 194–5
    Jameela Tutoring, 339
    job satisfaction, 150
    Mark Wang, 390
    Natura & Co, 135
    Rattan by Abbie, 360
    Reliance Jio, 225
    retailers, 236
    SA Metals, 115
    Shoprite Holdings, 293
    Sustenir, 24
    unemployment in South Africa, 425
    water desalination, 12
business objectives, 73–4, *73*
    importance of, 75

business organisations, *58*
    choosing the best option, 67
    franchises, 64, *65*
    joint ventures, 66
    limited companies, 61–4
    partnerships, 60
    social enterprises, 68–9
    sole traders, 58–9, **59**
business performance measurement, 403–4
    liquidity, 409–11
    profitability, 404–8
business plans, 36
    importance of, 40–1
    key elements, **40**
business profit tax (corporation tax), 435
    effects of rate increases, *436*
business size measurement, 44–6, *46*
businesses
    factors affecting success or failure, 52–3, **52**
    functional areas, 116
BYJU'S, 131, 403

CAM (computer-aided manufacturing), 285
Canva, 383
capital employed, 393
capital expenditure, 340
capital investment, 45, *46*
capital resources, 14
case studies
    4Sight, 200
    Agrid, 330–1
    AI, 472
    Airbnb, dynamic pricing, 230
    Bogawantalawa Tea Estates, 411–12
    BRAC Bank Limited, 30
    BUA cement, 384
    Canva, 383
    Chow Tai Fook Jewellery Group, 396
    communication methods, 140–1, *142*
    Debswana, 161
    Eco Hustle, 39
    ecommerce in Mexico, 252
    Egis, 101–2
    fast fashion, 474
    flexible working, 123
    GE HealthCare, 265
    Glass2sand, 43–4
    Hasbro, 320
    Hotel Properties Limited (HPL), 81
    Indian Railways, 31
    interest rate in Botswana, 438

Jardine Schindler Group, 66–7
Jet Airways, 365
Karma Drinks, 62
leadership styles, 128
Lockheed Martin Kaizen events, 280–1
Malaysian economy, 431, *431*, *432*
Malón Bambú Bikes (MB), 25–6
Marriott Hotels, 109
Mauritius, multinational companies, 450–1
Melia Hotels, 142
Michelin, 220
MTN, 177
Myntra, 238
N.Bar, 327
Neeman's shoes, 19
Ocean Bottle, 75–6
online streaming, 184
Peloton, 306
PetSnowy, 353
Pottery Town (PT), 169–70
R4R, 318
S-Mart Group, 420–1
Samsung, implementation of 3Rs, 466
Shonaquip, 342
Siemens AG, 102–3
Sky Mavis, 204
Smart Logistics Solutions, Kenya, 15 16
Sports and More Limited (SAM), 479–80
Spotify, 258
Sunshine Foods, 334
Tabansi's Drinks and Smoothies, 87–8
Tao Kae Noi, 63
Team UnLimbited, 287
Teen Fashions, 268–9
Telsa, globalisation, 448
The1, 247
Topiku, 469–70
Toys"R"Us, 368
Twiga Foods, 350
unemployment rates in the Philippines, 429
Virgin Group, 300
Walt Disney Company, 165
Wilko, 408–9
Yao Secret, 48
case study questions, 490–5
cash
    difference from profit, **377**
    importance of, 361
cash flow, 360
    positive and negative, *362*

cash flow forecasts, 361, **364**, **369**
    completion and amendment, 363
    interpretation, 364–5, 366
    main features, 362–3
cash flow management, 361
cash flow problems, 369–70
cash inflow, 361, 362
cash outflow, 361, 362
chain of command, 118–19
channels of distribution, 236–7, *237*
    advantages and disadvantages, **238–9**
    choosing the best option, 240
Chow Tai Fook Jewellery Group, 396
climate change, 467
clocking in, *158*
closing balance, 363, 365, 366
Coca-Cola, 444
Coconut Bowls, 245
commission, 159
communication, 135–6
    diseconomies of scale, 302
    importance of, 136–7, *145*
    internal and external, 136
    and relocation to another country, 329
communication barriers, *145*
    causes, **143**
    reduction or removal of, 144–5
    resulting problems, 144
communication methods, 137–8, *145*
    advantages and disadvantages, **139–40**
    case studies, 140–1, 142
    choosing the best option, 141
    effect of technology, 146
competition, 53
    influencing factors, 180–1
    market research, 196
    responses to, 181, **182**
competitions, sales promotion value, 247
competitive pricing, 228–9, **232**
competitor websites, 202, *203*
computer-aided manufacturing (CAM), 285
construction industry, 72
consumer income changes, 179, 180
consumer spending patterns
    changes, responses to, **182**
    influencing factors, 179
contracts of employment, 105
contribution per unit, 304, 499
convenience, **17**
coordination, **127**, *127*, 137
    diseconomies of scale, 302

# Index

COP28, 467
corporation tax, 435
   effects of rate increases, *436*
cost of sales, 379
cost-based decisions, 296–7
cost-plus pricing, 230, **232**
costs
   classification, 293–4
   examples, 295–7
   relationship to scale of operation, *303*
creativity, **38**
crowdfunding, 353
cultural differences, 263, 329
currency fluctuations, **447**, 457
current assets, 341, 392
current liabilities, 341, 393
current ratio, 410, 499
curriculum vitae (CVs, resumes), 99–100, *100*
customer base, 176
customer demand, influence of price, 225–6
customer feedback, 204
customer loyalty, 176
customer needs, 176, 196
   changes in, 177
customer relationships, 177
customers, 78, **80**
customers versus consumers, 13

data privacy, 472
Debswana, 161
decisiveness, **38**
deforestation, **463**, 467
delegation, 124
   advantages and disadvantages, **124**
democratic leaders, 126, **126**, *127*
demonstrations, **475**
depreciation of exchange rates, 457
design features, **17**
determination, **38**
direct to consumer sales, 237
   advantages and disadvantages, **238**
   case study, 238
discrimination, 105, *106*
diseconomies of scale, 301–3, *301*
   relationship to average costs, *303*
distribution methods *see* channels of distribution
diversity, 111
downsizing, 129
dynamic pricing, 229, **232**
   case study, 230
Dyson, location in Singapore, 324

Eco Hustle, 39
ecommerce, 181
   advantages and disadvantages, 251–2, **252**
   case studies, 175, 252–3
   new markets in other countries, 262
   types of, 250–1, *251*
economic growth, *426*
   effects of government spending, 436
   effects on business activity, 430
   possible effects on business, **427**
economies of scale, 298–300, *299*, **447**, *452*
   relationship to average costs, *303*
economy, changes in, 53
efficiency, **182**, 275
Egis, 101–2
emails, 137, **139**
   use in advertising, 248
employee of the month schemes, 164
employees, 77, **78**
   diseconomies of scale, 302
   number of, 44, *46*
   recruitment and selection *see* recruitment and selection
   skill levels, 275
   training, 106–9, *111*
   use of accounts and ratio analysis, **413**
   ways of working, 121–3
employment, legal controls, 104–6
employment agencies, 96, **98**
energy use, 466
enterprise, 14, 37
entrepreneurs, 12, 36, 37–9
   case studies, 39, 43–4, 342
   characteristics, **38**, *38*
   TV platforms, 355, 370
environmental benefits, 455
environmental impact, 462–4, **463**
   business responses, 84, 468
   energy use, 466
   fast fashion, 474
   opportunities and threats faced by business, 467–8, **468**
   pollution, 464–5
   resource depletion, 466–7
   role of legal controls, 468, **469**
   waste, 465–6
esteem, **153**
ethical issues, 471–2
   case studies, 472, 474
   relocation to another country, 329

ethical practices, *471*
   advantages and disadvantages, **473**
   social enterprises, 68–9
evaluation, exam assessment, 485
exams
   assessment objectives, 483–6
   case study questions, 490–5
   layout, 483
   short answer and data response questions, 487–90
exchange rates, 457, 458
expenses (overheads), 379, *380*
extension strategies, 219–21, *220*
   case study, 220
external benefits, 454, 455
external costs, 454–5
external growth, 48–9
   advantages and disadvantages, **50**
external recruitment, 102, 103–4, **103**
external sources of finance, 347–52, **347**
   crowdfunding, 353
external stakeholders, 78–80, **80**

factors of production, 14–16, *15*
Fairsew, 313
fashion, 179
fashion clothing, product life cycle, *217, 218*
fast fashion, 474
feedback
   case study, 204
   *see also* questionnaires; surveys
finance, 52, 116, 339
   case study, 342
   for cash flow problems, 369–70
   crowdfunding, 353
   external sources, 347–52
   factors influencing choice of, **354–5**
   internal sources, 343–6, *343*
   short- and long-term, 340
   why it is needed, 340
   working capital, 341
financial economies, economies of scale, 299
financial methods of motivation, 157–60, *157*
financial statements
   limitations, 414
   use of, 412–13, **413–14**
   *see also* statements of financial position; statements of profit or loss
fixed costs, 294
flat organisational structure, *118*
flexible hours, 121
flexible working, 121
   case study, 123

flow production (mass production), 283, *283*
   advantages and disadvantages, **284**
focus groups, 198
forward vertical integration, 49
franchises, 64
   advantages and disadvantages, *65*
free trade agreements, 180, 446
fringe benefits, 160
full-time employees, 122, **122**
functional areas, 116

GE HealthCare, 265
gender, market segmentation by, 188
Glass2Sand, 43–4
global warming, 467
globalisation, 444–5
   advantages and disadvantages, **447**
   case study, 448
   characteristics of, *445*
   multinational companies, 450–4
   reasons for, 446
goods, 213
   *see also* products
government grants, 352
government incentives, role in location decisions, 328
government policies, 432–3, *433*
government spending, effect on business activity, 436
governments, 79, **80**
   benefits of high employment levels, 428
   intervention in markets, 180
   legal control on environmental issues, 468, **469**
   as source of data, 202
   sources of income, 432
   support for business start-ups, 42–3
   use of accounts and ratio analysis, **414**
Grab Holdings, 257
gross domestic product (GDP), 180
gross profit, 376, 379, 382, 499
gross profit margin, 405–7, 499
Grow Green Tea Company, 233
growth, *426*
   case studies, 48, 53–4, 57
   effects on business activity, 430
   possible effects on business, **427**

habitat loss, 455, **463**
Handmade Heroes, 57
Hasbro, 320
health and safety, 106
Hello Chef, 167
Herzberg's two-factor theory, 154–5, **154**, *156*

# Index

hierarchical structures
    chain of command, 118–19
    levels of hierarchy, 117–18, *117*, *118*
    span of control, 119–20, *119*, **120**
hierarchy, 117
Hierarchy of Needs, Maslow, 153–4, **153–4**, *153*, *156*
hire purchase, 351
Hive, The, 190
homeworking, 121
horizontal integration, 48, *49*
Hotel Properties Limited (HPL), 81
HS2, 21
human resources, 116
    *see also* employees; recruitment and selection
Hydro Wind Energy (HWE), 12
hygiene factors, 154–5, **154**
Hypnos, 320

import quotas, 449
import tariffs, 449
    role in location decisions, 328
income, market segmentation by, 187
income tax, 434
    effects of rate increases, *434*
Indian Railways, 31
induction training, 107
industrial action, 131
inflation
    effects on business activity, 428
    Malaysia, *431*
informative advertising, 249
Infosys, 194–5
infrastructure investments, 455
initiative, **38**
interest rates, 433, 436–7
    in Botswana, case study, 438
    effects of rate increases, *437*, 438
intermediaries ('middlemen'), 237
    *see also* retailers; wholesalers
internal growth, 47
    advantages and disadvantages, **50**
internal recruitment, 102–3, **103**
internal sources of finance, 343–6, *343*
internal stakeholders, 77, **78**
interviews
    market research, 200–1
    recruitment and selection, 100, 102
inventories, 277–8, 410
    just-in-time control, 279, **280**
    reasons for, **278**
Islamic banking principles, 437

Jameela Tutoring, 339
Jardine Schindler Group (JSG), 66–7
Jet Airways, 365
job advertisements, 96–8, **98**
job analysis, 95
job creation, 455
job descriptions, 95
job enrichment, 162, *162*
job production, 273, 282
    advantages and disadvantages, **284**
job rotation, 161, *162*
job satisfaction, 150
joint ventures, 66
just-in-time (JIT) inventory control, 279
    advantages and disadvantages, **280**
JYSK, 209

Kaizen, 280–1
Karma Drinks, 62

labour productivity, 274–5, 499
labour resources, 14
labour turnover, effect of motivation, 144, 152, 302
laissez-faire leadership, 126, **127**, *127*
land pollution, **464**
land resources, 14
leadership styles, 125–6, *127*
    case study, 128
    choosing the best option, 128
leaflets, 248, *249*
lean production, 279–81
leasing, 351
legislation
    controls related to marketing, 260
    differences between countries, 263
    effect on marketing strategy, **261**
    employment issues, 104–6
lenders, 79, **80**
letters, 138, **140**
level of unemployment
    effects on business activity, 429
    low, benefits for governments, 428
    in the Philippines, 429
    in South Africa, 425
LG Electronics India, 454
liabilities, 391, 392–3
lifestyle, market segmentation by, 188
light pollution, **464**
limited companies, 61–2
limited liability, 61

liquidity, 341, 404, 409, **412**
   acid test ratio, 410–11
   current ratio, 410
lobbying, **475**
local community, 79, **80**
location, market segmentation by, 187–8
location decisions, 324
   case studies, 327, 330–1
   choosing the best option, 329
   influencing factors, 324–5, **326**
   relocation to another country, 324, 327–9
Lockheed Martin, Kaizen events, 280–1
Lojas Renner (LR), 111
long-term finance, 340, 349–52
loss, *304*
   statements of profit or loss, 378–84, **379**, **381**
loyalty cards, *176*
Lux Island Resorts (LIR), 397

MADE acronym (exchange rates), 457
Malaysian economy, 431, *431*, *432*
Malón Bambú Bikes (MB), 25–6
management
   delegation, 124
   diseconomies of scale, 303
   functions of, 123–4
   leadership styles, 125–6, *127*
   *see also* organisational structure
management skills, 52
managerial economies, economies of scale, 299
managers, 77, **78**
   use of accounts and ratio analysis, **413**
manufacturing businesses, 25
   impact of technology, 285–6, 300
   impact on the environment, **463**, **464**, 466–7
   location decisions, 325, **326**, 328
margin of safety, 307, 499
market changes, 178–81
market knowledge, 264
market research, 53, 194–5
   accuracy of data, 206–7
   advantages and disadvantages, **203–4**
   analysis of results, 207–8
   case studies, 200, 204
   methods of primary research, 197–201, *197*
   methods of secondary research, 201–2, *201*, *203*
   primary and secondary, 197
   role of, 195–6
   sampling, 205
   uses of information obtained, 196
market research reports, 202
market segmentation, 186, *186*
   advantages and disadvantages, **188**
   choosing the best method, 189
   ways of, 187–8
market share, 47, 74, 182–3, *183*, 499
   case study, 184
market size, 196
marketing, 116, 175, 196
   influence of product life cycle, 219
   legal controls, 260
   roles of, 175–7
marketing budget, 250
marketing economies, 299
marketing mix, 213
   and marketing strategies, 258
   place, 236–43
   price, 225–33
   product, 213–21
   promotion, 245–53
marketing strategies, 258–9
   effect of legal controls, **261**
markets, *178*
Marriott Hotels, 109
Maslow's Hierarchy of Needs, 153–4, **153–4**, *153*, 156
mass markets, 185
   advantages and disadvantages, **186**
mass production (flow production), 283
   advantages and disadvantages, **284**
Mauritius, multinational companies, 450–1
meetings, 137, **139**
Melia Hotels, 142
mergers, 48
Michelin, 220
minimum wage laws, 106
mixed economy, 30
motivation
   benefits of, 151–2, *152*
   diseconomies of scale, 302
   importance of, 150–1
   job satisfaction, 150
motivation methods, *157*
   case studies, 161, 165
   choosing the best option, 165–6
   financial, 157–60
   non-financial, 161–4
motivational theories, *156*
   Herzberg's two-factor theory, 154–5, **154**
   Maslow's Hierarchy of Needs, 153–4, **153–4**, *153*
   Taylor's scientific management theory, 154
motivators, **154**, 155
MTN, 177
multinational companies (MNCs), 445, 449, 450
   advantages to businesses, *452*
   advantages to host countries, **453**
   case study, 450–1

disadvantages to host countries, **453–4**
*see also* globalisation
Musk, Elon, 128
Myntra, 238

N.Bar, 327
Natura & Co, 135
needs, 13, 176
Neeman's shoes, 19
negative cash flow, *362*, 364
net cash flow, 362, 363, 364
New Balance, 331
new markets in other countries, 439
    advantages, 262
    case study, 265
    disadvantages, 262–4, *263*
new product development, 214
    advantages and disadvantages, **214**
niche markets, 184–5
    advantages and disadvantages, **185**
    case study, 190
noise pollution, **464**
non-current assets, 340, 392
    hire purchase, 351
    leasing, 351
    sale of, 344
non-current liabilities, 393
noticeboards, 138, **140**
number of employees, 44, *46*

objectives, 72
    short-term and long-term, 74
    *see also* business objectives; stakeholder objectives
observations, 199
Ocean Bottle (OB), 75–6
off-the-job training, 108
    advantages and disadvantages, **109**
online recruitment, 96, **98**
online streaming, case study, 184
on-the-job training, 107, *108*
    advantages and disadvantages, **108**
opening balance, 363
operations, 116
operations management, 274
opportunity cost, 20
organisation charts, 116–17
    *see also* organisational structure
organisational structure, 115, 116
    chain of command, 118–19
    levels of hierarchy, 117–18, *117*, *118*
    span of control, 119–20, *119*, **120**

Ørsted, 32
overdrafts, 348, 366
overheads *see* expenses
owners, 77, **78**
owner's equity, 393

packaging, 215–16
    3Rs, 466
partnerships, 60
    advantages and disadvantages, **60**
part-time employees, 122, **122**
Patagonia, 84
payment methods
    bonus schemes, 159–60
    commission, 159
    fringe benefits, 160
    piece-rate, 158
    profit sharing, 160
    salaries, 158
    time-based, 157
Peloton, 306
penetration pricing, 225, 228, **231**
person specifications, 95, *96*
persuasive advertising, 249
petitioning, **475**
PetSnowy, 353
Philippines, unemployment rates, 429
phone calls, 137, **139**
physiological needs, **154**
pie charts, *183*, *207*
piece-rate payment, 154, 158
pollution, 455, 462, **463**, 464–5
    types of, **464**
population changes, 179
positive cash flow, *362*, 364
posters, 138, **140**
Pottery Town (PT) case study, 169–70
praise, 163
pressure groups, 475
    impact of, 476
    methods used by, **475**
price, 225
    influence on customer demand, 225–6
price changes, 179
price skimming, 227, **231**, 233
pricing methods, 227–30, *227*
    advantages and disadvantages, **231–2**
    choosing the best option, 232–3
primary research (field research), 197
    advantages and disadvantages, **203**
    case study, 204
    methods, 197–201, *197*

sampling, 205
*see also* market research
primary sector, 25, **27**, *29*
    environmental impact, **463**
private limited companies, 62
private sector, 30–1
    importance of profit, 377–8
product life cycle, 217–18, *217*, *218*
    extension strategies, 219–21, *220*
    influence on marketing decisions, 219
product suitability, 52
production, 273
    difference from productivity, 274
    lean, 279–81
    sustainability, 288–9
production costs, 328
    case studies, 376, 411–12
    effects of inflation, 428
    effects of technology, 285
    multinational companies, *452*
production methods, 281–3
    advantages and disadvantages, **284**
    choosing the best option, 284
    effect of technology, 285–6
production process, 274
productivity, 274–5
    effect of motivation, 151
    effects of technology in the service sector, 286
    relationship to costs, 277
products, 213
    brand image, 215
    new product development, 214, **214**
    packaging, 215–16
profit, 45, 74, 297, *304*, 376–7
    difference from cash, **377**
    effect of business growth, 47
    importance of, 377–8
    retained, 344, 377
    statements of profit or loss, 378–84, **379**, **381**
    tax on *see* corporation tax
    *see also* added value
profit formula, 379, 382, 499
profit margin, 406–7, 499
profit sharing, 160
profitability, 404, **412**
    gross profit margin, 405–7
    profit margin, 406–7
    return on capital employed, 407–8
promotion, 163, 179, **182**, 246
    aims, 246
    marketing budget, 250

promotion methods, *246*
    advertising, 248–9
    sales promotion, 247
public limited companies, 63–4
public sector, 30–1
purchasing economies, economies of scale, 300

quality, **17**, 313–14
    importance of, *315*, **316**
    and relocation to another country, 329
quality assurance, 319
    advantages and disadvantages, **319**
    case studies, 320
quality control, 317
    advantages and disadvantages, **318**
    case study, 318
questionnaires, 200
quotas, 449

R4R, 318
ratio analysis
    limitations, 414
    liquidity ratios, 410–11, **412**
    profitability ratios, 404–8, **412**
    use of, 412–13, **413–14**
Rattan by Abbie, 360
recession, *426*
    possible effects on business, **427**
recruitment and selection, 94
    case studies, 101–2, 103–4
    identification stage, 95
    internal and external recruitment, 102–3, **103**
    job advertisements, 96–8, **98**
    selection process, 99–102
    stages, *94*
recycling, 466
    case studies, 19, 43–4, 75–6, 84, 469–70
redundancy, 129–31
references, 100
Reliance Jio, 225
renewable energy, 12, 32, 455
resource depletion, 455, **463**, 466–7
resumes (CVs), 99–100, *100*
retailers, 236, 237, **239**
retained profit, 344, 377
return on capital employed (ROCE), 407–8, 499
revenue, 376, 379, 381, 499
revision tips, 496–8
reward schemes, 247
risk spreading, 47, **447**, *452*
risk taking, **38**
Ryobi Limited, 289

# Index

S-Mart Group case study, 420–1
SA Metals, 115
safety needs, **154**
salaries, 158
sales promotion, 247
sales revenue, 45, *46*
sales volume, 45, *46*
sampling, 205
Samsung, implementation of 3Rs, 466
savings, as source of finance, 343
Schweppes tonic water, 264
secondary research (desk research), 197
    advantages and disadvantages, **204**
    methods, 201–2, *201*, *203*
    *see also* market research
secondary sector, 25, **27**, *29*
    environmental impact, **463**
sectors
    primary, secondary and tertiary, 25–6, **27**, 28–9, *29*
    private and public, 30–1
selecting candidates for jobs, 99–102
self-actualisation, **153**
self-confidence, **38**
service sector
    effects of technology, 286
    location decisions, 325, **326**
services, 213
    *see also* products
share issues, 352
shareholders, 61
    private limited companies, 62
    public limited companies, 63
    use of accounts and ratio analysis, **413**
shareholder's equity, 393
Shark Tank India, 355, 370
Shonaquip, 342
Shoprite Holdings, 293
short-term finance, 340, 348–9
    for cash flow problems, 369–70
Siemens AG, 102–3
skimming, 227, **231**, 233
Sky Mavis, 204
slump, *426*
    possible effects on business, **427**
Smart Logistics Solutions, Kenya, 15–16
social enterprises, 68–9
social media, 138, **139**, 181
    advertising, 248
social needs, **154**
social responsibility, 74
    case study, 469–70
soil erosion, **463**

sole traders, 58–9
    advantages and disadvantages, **59**
span of control, 119–20, *119*, **120**
special offers, 247
Sports and More Limited (SAM) case study, 479–80
Spotify, 258
Stagecoach, 140
stakeholder objectives, 77–80
    conflicts, 82, *83*
stakeholders, 76, *76*
    external, 78–80, **80**
    internal, 77, **78**
Starbucks, 53–4
start-ups
    advantages to the economy, 42
    government support, 42–3
statements of financial position, 390–1, **391**, **394**, **395**, **396**, **397**, **398**
    assets, 392
    calculations based on, 394
    liabilities, 392–3
    limitations, 414
    main elements, *391*
    use in decision-making, 394–5
statements of profit or loss, 378–80, **379**, **381**, **386**
    calculations based on, 381–2
    limitations, 414
    use in decision-making, 383–4
Sunshine Foods case study, 334
suppliers, 79, **80**
    use of accounts and ratio analysis, **413**
surveys, *195*, 200
sustainability, 24, 288–9, *288*, 313
    3Rs, 466
    advantages and disadvantages, **289**
    case studies, 25, 30, 48, 72, 81, 101, 111, 289, 313, 320, 466, 469
Sustenir, 24

takeovers, 48
tall hierarchical structures, *117*
Tao Kae Noi, 63
tariffs, 449
    role in location decisions, 328
taxes, 432
    effects of rate increases, *434*, *436*, 438
    types of, 434–6
Taylor's scientific management theory, 154, *156*
Team UnLimbited, 287
technical economies, economies of scale, 300
technological advancement, 455

technology, 275
   advantages and disadvantages, **287**, 288
   effect on efficiency, 275
   effect on production methods, 285–6
   effects on productivity in the service sector, 286
   role in globalisation, 446
TED, 141
Teen Fashions case study, 268–9
telecommuting, **468**
tertiary sector, 26, **27**, *29*
   environmental impact, **463**
Tesla, 448
testing job applicants, 101
text messages (SMS), 137, **139**
The1, 247
time-based payment, 157
Tivoli Gardens, 221
Tony's Chocolonely, 68–9
Topiku, 469–70
total cost, 294, 295, 376, 379, 499
total fixed costs, 294
total variable costs, 294, 295, 499
Toys"R"Us, 368
trade credit, 348, **349**
trade magazines, 202
trade payables, 393
trade receivables, 341, 392
trade unions, 130–1
traffic congestion, 455
Trafigura, 242
training
   advantages, 106–7
   case study, 109
   effect on motivation, 163
   methods, 107–9, *111*
transport infrastructure, 181
Truckistan, 37
Twiga Foods, 350
two-factor theory, Herzberg, 154–5, **154**, *156*

unemployment
   effects on business activity, 429
   low levels, benefits for governments, 428
   Malaysia, *432*
   in the Philippines, 429
   in South Africa, 425
unethical practices, **471**
unfair dismissal, 105
unique selling points (USPs), 196
upcycling, 39

variable cost per unit, 294, 499
variable costs, 294
venture capital, 349
vertical integration, 49, *49*
Virgin Group, 300
visual pollution, **464**
vouchers, 247

Walt Disney Company, 165
   focus groups, 198
Wang, Mark, 390
wants, 13
warehousing, 278
waste, **464**, 465–6
   fast fashion, 474
   sources of, *279*
   types of, **465**
   upcycling, 39
water desalination, 12
water pollution, **463**, **464**
water scarcity, **463**
ways of working, 121–3
websites, 138, **139**, 250
   of competitors, 202, *203*
   *see also* ecommerce
wholesalers, 237, **239**, 240
   Trafigura, 242
Wilko, 408–9
workforce size reduction, 129–31
working capital, 340, 341, 499
   use as a source of finance, 345, **346**

Yao Secret, 48

Zappos, 140
zero-waste stores, *190*

# > Acknowledgements

*The authors and publishers acknowledge the following sources of copyright material and are grateful for the permissions granted. While every effort has been made, it has not always been possible to identify the sources of all the material used, or to trace all copyright holders. If any omissions are brought to our notice, we will be happy to include the appropriate acknowledgements on reprinting.*

*Thanks to the following for permission to reproduce images:*

*Cover* Akinbostanci/GI; *Inside*

**Chapter 1** Baona/GI; Andrea DiCenzo/GI; Ascent Xmedia/GI; Peter Cade/GI; Mint Images/GI; Rodger Shagam/GI; Roy Morsch/GI; Westend61/GI; Image Source/GI; Pixelonestocker/GI; Luis Alvarez/GI; billnoll/GI; PM Images/GI; Ron Levine/GI; Wendy Stone/GI; Xavier Lorenzo/GI; Richard Newstead/GI; Thana Prasongsin/GI; Peter Dazeley/GI; Klaus Vedfelt/GI; Yuji Sakai/GI; CR Shelare/GI; Michael Dunning/GI; **Chapter 2** Peter Schiazza/GI; Sergey Mironov/GI; Anton Petrus/GI; Fotoholica Press/GI; Alistair Berg/GI; Kelli Merrick/GI; Monty Rakusen/GI; Indeed/GI; Neil Thomas/GI; Dinodia Photo/GI; Pareto/GI; **Chapter 3** Eugene Mymrin/GI; Maskot/GI; Amir Mukhtar/GI; JW LTD/GI; 10'000 Hours/GI; Shapecharge/GI; Saulgranda/GI; Jetta Productions Inc/GI; Xpacifica/GI; Jordi Salas/GI; Maskot/GI; Karl Tapales/GI; Onurdongel/GI; Michael H/GI; Jose Luis Raota/GI; Zhang Peng/GI; **Chapter 4** Abstract Aerial Art/GI; Ljubaphoto/GI; Boonchai Wedmakawand/GI; BSIP/GI; Kampee Patisena/GI; Andrea Pistolesi/GI; Jose Javier Ballester Legua/GI; **Chapter 5** 3dts/GI; Firemanyu/GI; Richard Drury/GI; Catherine Falls Commercial/GI; Tara Moore/GI; Alvarez/GI; Levente Bodo/GI; Ascentxmedia/GI; **Chapter 6** Cocoon/GI; Fanpro/GI; Kate_Sept2004/GI; Ariel Skelley/GI; Lordhenrivoton/GI; Claire Plumridge/GI; Monty Rakusen/GI; Jasmin Merdan/GI; Sturti/GI; 10'000 Hours/GI; Blue Sky In My Pocket/GI; **Chapter 7** Nicoelnino/GI; Arctic-Images/GI; Ippei Naoi/GI; Westend61/GI; Stephen Olker/GI; Bloomberg Creative Photos/GI; Ryan McVay/GI; Jonathan Kirn/GI; **Chapter 8** Imaginima/GI; Geostock/GI; John Lamb/GI; Image Source/GI; Skynesher/GI; Jordi Salas/GI; We Are/GI; Morsa Images/GI; **Chapter 9** PM Images/GI; Portra/GI; Roberto Westbrook/GI; Izusek/GI; Halbergman/GI; Bluecinema/GI; Per-Anders Pettersson/GI; Bgblue/GI; Sesame/GI; Jon Feingersh Photography Inc/GI; AaronP/Bauer-Griffin/GI; Plan Shooting 2/Imazins/GI; Ma-K/GI; **Chapter 10** J Studios/GI; Georgijevic/GI; Photographer, Basak Gurbuz Derman/GI; Stuart Fox/GI; Emad Aljumah/GI; Dmytro Aksonov/GI; Insung Jeon/GI; Abstract Aerial Art/GI; Smith Collection/Gado/GI; Oscar Wong/GI; **Chapter 11** Bussarin Rinchumrus/GI; 10'000 Hours/GI; Thana Prasongsin/GI; Hispanolistic/GI; Smith Collection/Gado/GI; Azmanjaka/GI; Pixelseffect/GI; Fabio Formaggio/GI; Luca Sage/GI; Damircudic/GI; Solstock/GI; **Chapter 12** Daniel Grizelj/GI; Thomas Barwick/GI; Renelyn Cunanan-Dinh/GI; Monty Rakusen/GI; SOPA Images/GI; Walter Bibikow/GI; **Chapter 13** Sakchai Vongsasiripat/GI; Nurphoto/GI; Walter Zerla/GI; Tara Moore/GI; Frank Rothe/GI; Georgie Wileman/GI; Atelier Knox/GI; **Chapter 14** Alice-Photo/GI; Natalia Lebedinskaia/GI; Nurphoto/GI; Bloomberg Creative/GI; SOPA Images/GI; **Chapter 15** J Studios/GI; Apomares/GI; D3sign/GI; Images By Tang Ming Tung/GI; Mstudioimages/GI; Brianajackson/GI; **Chapter 16** Yuichiro Chino/GI; Leopatrizi/GI; Delmaine Donson/GI; Nora Carol Photography/GI; James Leynse/GI; Pallava Bagla/GI; **Chapter 17** Srinophan69/GI; Gallo Images/GI; Monty Rakusen/GI; Alvarez/GI; Jack Guez/GI; Eclipse Images/GI; Monty Rakusen/GI; Maciej Frolow/GI; Anadolu/GI; Simonkr/GI; **Chapter 18** Monty Rakusen/GI; Bloomberg/GI; SOPA Images/GI; Jacobs Stock Photography/GI; Justin Paget/GI; Mohd Rasfan/GI; **Chapter 19** Eoneren/GI; Pete Starman/GI; Hispanolistic/GI; Me 3645 Studio/GI; Gillian Vann/GI; Bloomberg/GI; Kinga Krzeminska/GI; **Chapter 20** DKart/GI; Bloomberg/GI; Isayildiz/GI; Peter Cade/GI; Cecilie Arcurs/GI; Mat Hayward/GI; **Chapter 21** Andriy Onufriyenko/GI; Afriandi/GI; Wavebreakmedia/GI; Bloomberg/GI; ssi77/Shutterstock.com; **Chapter 22** Yulia Reznikov/GI; Guillermo Spelucin/GI; SOPA Images/GI; AaronP/Bauer-Griffin/GI; Stuart Fox/GI; **Chapter 23** Microstockhub/GI; Iryna Veklich/GI; FatCamera/GI; Sean Justice/GI; SOPA Images/GI; **Chapter 24** Boonchai Wedmakawand/GI; Krisanapong Detraphiphat/GI;

Bloomberg/GI; Tuul & Bruno Morandi/GI; **Chapter 25** Jorg Greuel/GI; Deepak Sethi/GI; Matthew Horwood/GI; Tunart/GI; D3sign/GI; **Chapter 26** Baona/GI; Westend61/DMP/GI; Paul Russell/GI; Davidf/GI; Tdub303/GI; **Chapter 27** Sean Gladwell/GI; Imaginima/GI; 3alexd/GI; Pavel Tochinsky/GI; Bloomberg/GI; **Chapter 28** Kevin Schafer/GI; Lapandr/GI; Elena Popova/GI; Ugurhan/GI; Patrick T. Fallon/GI; World Pieces/Shutterstock; Monty Rakusen/GI; SOPA Images/GI; Ondacaracola Photography/GI; **Chapter 29** Franckreporter/GI

GI = Getty Images

Video content is compiled using clips from Getty Images.